Also by Jim Curran

Trango The Nameless Tower

K2, Triumph and Tragedy

Suspended Sentences

K2 The Story of the Savage Mountain

High Achiever The Life and Climbs of Chris Bonington

The Middle-Aged Mountaineer

here, there and everywhere

the autobiography of Jim Curran

edgebrook

PUBLISHING

an imprint of Vertebrate Graphics Ltd.

Here, there and everywhere
the autobiography of Jim Curran

EDGEBROOK PUBLISHING
of Sheffield
an imprint of Vertebrate Graphics Ltd.

First published in 2012 by Edgebrook Publishing

This book is the work of non-fiction based on the life, experiences and recollections of Jim Curran. The author has stated to the publishers that, except in such minor respects not affecting the substantial accuracy of the work, the contents of the book are true.

A CIP catalogue record of this book is available from the British Library

ISBN: 978-1-906148-36-2

Photograph scanning by Ian Smith
Paintings and drawings photographed and scanned by Ian Smith, Tony Riley and Jim Curran
Typeset by Ian Smith from a design by Bob Burn
Printed and bound in China on behalf of Latitude Press

'To climb a mountain is to
tread not only the heights of Earth
it is to adventure to the very boundaries
of Heaven'.
Frank S Smythe

*To the memory of my childhood
friend and oldest climbing partner
Steve (Buzzard) Durkin*

*Also for my grandchildren
Patrick, Sophie and Theo*

Jim Curran climbing April Arête *(HVS 4c) at Millstone Edge, belayed by Tony Iveson.*

Acknowledgments

This book was squeezed out of me by Jim and Marcia Fotheringham, Sarah Cullen and Chris Gibson who must all share the blame.

My erstwhile editor Maggie Body, as usual, converted my literary equivalent of semi-skimmed milk, into full-Bodyed double cream, Ed Douglas wrote the Foreword and Terry Gifford the words of praise (or fantasy) on the rear cover, while Julie Summers wrote the appraisal, critique, essay or whatever one would call it, of the paintings. The production of this book is a testament to the meticulous work of Ian Smith who scanned all the photographs and designed the layout. My special thanks to all of the above.

Thanks also to the following (in no particular order) without whose support and friendship there would have been nothing to write about: Phil and Heather Curran, Geoff and Jackie Birtles, Pam Beech, Pam Gleadall, Sue Coonan, Mac and Loreto McNaught Davis, Steve Dean, Allen and Sarah Jewhurst, Joe and Val Brown, Dr Stephen and Marcia Oliver, Adrian Mallet, Dr Nikki Hall, Sue Evans, Gemma and Stuart Driver, Becky and Bob Hetherington, John Porter, Brian Hall, Alison Price, Annie Holdsworth, Hugo Clarke, Chris and Wendy Bonington, Carole Innocent, Neil and Sheila Murison, Caroline White, Laraine Richardson, Pip Hopkinson, Frances Hegarty, Trish Mohan, Tony and Tina Iveson, Ken Wilson, Liz Sharples, Dr Charlie Clarke, Martin and Maggie Boysen, Tony Riley, Barry Reynolds, Liz Vizzard, Julian and Linda Cooper, Michael Richardson, Hilary Nunn, Viv Smith, Derek Walker, Kay Dowling, Robin and Maureen Devenish, Bob and Pat Burn, Mike Watkins, Paul, Kate and Ella Hodgkin, Gill Round, Chris Rawson-Tetley, Jim Smith, Bruce and Andrea French, Catherine Destivelle and all those who I have forgotten and who will doubtless take great delight in reminding me.

Thank you all.
JC 2011

Contents

Foreword   *10*

Here

Chapter one   Childhood *13*

Chapter two   School Years and Relatives *21*

Chapter three   Young Love *34*

Chapter four   Schooldays Cut Short *38*

Chapter five   Art School *49*

Chapter six   Art School Part Two *61*

Chapter seven   A Few Ladders and a Big Snake *68*

Chapter eight   The Alps *78*

Chapter nine   Not So Grim Up North *84*

Chapter ten   Another Unexpected Blow *92*

Midword   *97*

Chapter eleven   A Job I Loved *99*

Chapter twelve   Calmer Waters *105*

Chapter thirteen   Self-Destruct Button, Please Press *110*

Chapter fourteen   Coronation Street – A Fiasco, a Fulfilment and a Future *117*

Chapter fifteen   A Great Effort *127*

there

Chapter sixteen   An Opportunity of a Lifetime *135*

Chapter seventeen   If at first you don't succeed, try, try and fail again *142*

Chapter eighteen   Putting the Art Before the Course *155*

Chapter nineteen   The Bat and The Wedding *161*

Chapter twenty   Pilgrimages to Pembroke and the Death of My Mother *167*

Chapter twenty one   "Aye-aye-aye Kon-Gur!" *173*

Chapter twenty two   "Down, Down, Deeper and Down" *181*

Chapter twenty three   Old Friends *187*

Chapter twenty four   A Gringo Not a Sahib *193*

Chapter twenty five   K2 Tragedies and Traumas *198*

Chapter twenty six   More Old Friends *210*

Chapter twenty seven   Disillusioned with Work, but the Beginning of
Four New Friendships *215*

Chapter twenty eight   Curran Versus Perrin *225*

Chapter twenty nine   Two Little Trips (And the End of the Road in Bristol) *231*

and everywhere

Chapter thirty   Fifty Not Out – Celebrating Freedom *235*

Chapter thirty one   Bombay Mix *249*

Chapter thirty two   African Double Top *259*

Chapter thirty three   I Chose to Trek *266*

Chapter thirty four   Africa Again *272*

Chapter thirty five   Patagonia, Yosemite and visits to Pebble Mill *278*

Chapter thirty six   Sepu Kangri – One *289*

Chapter thirty seven   Hoy *295*

Chapter thirty eight   Tibet for The Last Time *300*

Chapter thirty nine   Floundering Around *306*

Chapter forty   Millennium *310*

Chapter forty one   Why Me? Why Not? *316*

Chapter forty two   A Broken Heart and a New Knee *324*

Chapter forty three   The Loss of an Old Friend *329*

Chapter forty four   Two Old Loves Revisited: A Woman and a Country *332*

Afterword   Putting All My Egos in One Basket (Typo from Sue Evans) *337*

The Paintings   An Appraisal by Julie Summers *342*

Photo Credits   *384*

Index   *385*

Foreword

In retrospect, the late 1980s was the last flowering of a quixotic literary tradition, 'extreme marginalia' if you like, that had tied mountaineering to wider British culture since the late Victorian era. It wasn't that British culture was ever much interested in climbing, more that climbers felt themselves to be absorbed in the wider world, and that climbing gave them an original perspective on the biggest themes — politics, art and so on. A mountain was an unusual laboratory for the latest thinking.

A brief glance at the list of those contending for and judging the Boardman Tasker Award for Mountain Literature at this time makes my point. Winners included M John Harrison, Alison Fell and Jim Perrin, who were all born in the 1940s, and were all absorbed in the political and cultural radicalism of the late 1960s and early 1970s. Judges included Janet Adam Smith, literary editor of the *New Statesman*, the publisher Livia Gollancz, the writer Al Alvarez and the poet Ronnie Wathen, among the brightest and most progressive voices of earlier generations.

Jim Curran published one of his best books in this period, *K2: Triumph & Tragedy*, but found himself matched against Joe Simpson's *Touching the Void* that year and didn't win. (He has been short-listed more than anyone else without winning.) Simpson's book was just the kind of compelling narrative non-fiction that saw a surge in popularity in the 1990s, and is pretty much the only kind of climbing book mainstream houses still publish today.

Curran's book told the fraught and agonising story of the tragic summer of 1986 on K2, when his friend Alan Rouse perished having made the first British ascent. But while that book prefigured the current publishing obsession with death in the mountains, he comes very much from the other tradition, which sees climbing as a rich fragment in a broader mosaic of life.

At the time, I knew him as a writer and filmmaker, and more the latter given that as a schoolboy I had organised a lecture for him at Uppingham School where he showed his Kongur film. Joe Tasker had shot the high-altitude footage, before disappearing on Everest the following year, and the small gang of climbers I knew were reading his book *Savage Arena*. It was thrilling — as these things are to adolescent boys — to meet someone who had known one of my heroes. I had no idea at the time that Curran had been born in the town. I don't think either of us found Rutland to be our natural habitat.

When I started writing about climbing, a little while after his experiences on K2, Curran brought a libel action against Jim Perrin who was, and remains, a good friend of mine. Consequently, Curran and I talked neither often nor long. These things happen. Yet looking back now to this confrontation, I'm struck by what

Curran and Perrin had in common, at least in terms of how richly they connected the different facets of their lives with their love of mountains. Set these two figures against the sterile landscape of commerce that climbing has become and you might agree with me.

Coincidentally, it was through Curran's own landscapes that I came to know him better. Like many writers who lack a creative visual imagination, I find art and artists compelling subjects. As a journalist I've worked with several outstanding photographers and learned a great deal from them.

I've also become intrigued with the role visual imagination plays in how mountaineers are motivated to choose their objectives. It's one of the things that separates mountain climbing at its best from mainstream sport. We have the narrative compulsion and athletic performance of sport, but there's also a richer creative aspect that sets climbing apart, the act of imagination that redraws psychological boundaries and leaves a line drawn on a mountain to prove it.

Jim Curran has used prose, filmmaking and art to explore the strange complexity of climbing, its obsessions and its grandeur. He wonders in these memoirs whether he became simply a jack-of-all-trades and might have done better to focus on just one of these disciplines. I'm glad he didn't. The insistent restlessness of the climbing life might preclude concentrated effort as an artist, but the scope and ambition Curran shows is admirable, even when things don't go right. Despite periods of crushing depression, he has dragged himself back into the light and had another go.

Above all, these memoirs show him to be a fearless observer of his own self, especially in the account of his childhood and the origins of his ambitions as an artist and a climber. Like a Proust of West Ealing, he recreates a 1950s childhood with almost unbearable clarity, the smell of mown grass in suburban gardens, reading *The Beano* and the taste of orange squash. Life, as it will, became much more complicated, but you sense that through it all, the false starts, the missed opportunities as well as the successes, mountains have offered Curran both a refuge and a wellspring for the next chapter.

Ed Douglas
Sheffield, August 2011

here,

Chapter one: Childhood

Hilaire Belloc *Cautionary Tales*

There was a boy whose name was Jim
whose friends were very good to him.
They gave him tea and cakes and jam
and slices of delicious ham
and chocolates with pink inside
and little tricycles to ride.

Family legend has it that I was born in a snowstorm. Not actually *in* one obviously, but during one at my parents' house, Fives Cottage, Orange Street, Uppingham, Rutland, an address I have always felt proud of, though it has nothing to do with me. Fives Cottage got its name because it was next to a fives court. Fives is, as far as I know, an exclusively public school activity and is basically squash without racquets. Played with a gloved hand, it is one of those strange, elitist activities that presumably make sado-masochism acceptable.

The only family evidence of the weather at the time is a porcelain polar bear given to my mother by her doctor. Apparently I was known as the Polar Bear for a year or two. The bear still exists. It was given to Alison, my ex-wife, who was a much better bet with regards to its safety than I was. Somehow my eldest daughter Gemma acquired it and it is still in one piece. If it had been entrusted to me, it would long since have been lost or broken.

Naturally my earliest memories are few and far between and not terribly reliable. The Japanese performance artist, Yoko Ono, claims to remember 'slipping out of my mother's thighs… Many people do remember their births but they deny it'. Well, it is only of academic interest to me whether or not I ever remembered it. Like most people, I'm afraid that, if I had, I would have tried to forget it as soon as possible, along with most other facts of babyhood: breast feeding, nappy-changing, teething, being sick, strangers going "ahh" in your face and generally being treated as a particularly useless pet. The only other vaguely interesting fact relating to my birth was the date: January 8th. Unknown to me at the time, and to him always, was that on the same day in East Tupelo, Tennessee, Elvis Aron Presley was celebrating his eighth birthday. The year, by the way, was 1943; I was, therefore, a war baby. My father didn't put in an appearance until I was nearly three, apart from presumably a brief encounter nine months earlier, (an event, of which, even with Ms Ono's memory, I could have no recollection). He was occupied in trailing around North Africa, then Italy. He was a radar operator in the RAF and, like most fathers, hardly ever talked about the war. This was not false modesty; he claimed to have only ever seen one German plane on his radar screen and followed the action at a comparatively safe distance, arriving at many of the famous battle scenes about six months too late.

Before the war Dad had taught music at Uppingham School. He had been something of a child prodigy coming from a working-class family in Gateshead and, in 1924, at the age of 14, gaining a place at the Royal College of Music, where he met my mother, a pianist. Dad would have loved to have been a soloist or a member of a string quartet, but that was not to be. The war certainly

Mum and Dad before the war. >

robbed him of his best years and much of his ambition. When he returned another generation of violinists was on the scene.

Once on the European mainland, Dad was seconded to ENSA (Entertainments National Service Association), a motley collection of musicians, comedians and all-round performers who entertained the mass of increasingly bored servicemen and women waiting to be demobbed at the end of the war. A couple of photos show Dad playing his violin solo in front of a huge audience. He never really talked of those days and, as far as I know, never mentioned any of his fellow performers. Subsequent household names like Spike Milligan, Humphrey Lyttleton and Peter Sellers also performed for the troops and I have often wondered who his fellow entertainers were, for surely some of them would go on to make a name for themselves in Civvy Street.

Meanwhile I, like thousands of others, was being brought up as a single child of a one-parent family. My mother was a complex woman. Converted with the rest of her family to Roman Catholicism as a child, she was a devout worshipper all her life (as opposed to Dad, who, rather unusually, was a self-proclaimed atheist). Uppingham, a small town in Rutland, revolved around its school with its strong upper-middle-class Church of England

14

culture. Mum was driven every Sunday to Oakham, which had the nearest Catholic Church. As the wife of a lowly (and absent) music teacher she always seemed to oscillate between being a shy woman, unsure of her place in a closed and quite rigid society, and one with a steely determination coupled with a complex awareness of social mores. She could be quite a snob, without, I often felt, much to be snobbish about. Her favourite hobbyhorse was her definition of 'common'. From the earliest days and ever since, I found some of her criteria baffling.

She must have found the problems of raising me alone quite daunting both practically and financially. Her parents lived in Stevenage in Hertfordshire. Some of my earliest memories were of seemingly interminable train journeys to visit them. Gran was a typical grandmother — forever fussing and worried — from whom I imagine my mother must have inherited a lot of her insecurity.

My grandad worked in a London bank and was the epitome of the grim Victorian patriarch, enquiring soon after I was born when I could do my National Service. I was always frightened of him. I recently discovered a letter from him in 1947 to one of my uncles, which said: 'Jimmy [a name I have always detested] is a headstrong child and greeted me by spitting in my face. I shall avoid him as much as possible in future'. Indeed he did, by dying suddenly in 1948. I never knew, or think I ever met, Dad's side of the family with the exception of his sister, my Auntie Truda. The male members of Dad's family all apparently died young.

^ *A non-spitting author with his grandad and an anxious maternal hand.*

When Dad returned from his minor role in beating Hitler, I remember a figure in RAF blue uniform standing at the top of the stairs. Apparently my first words of greeting were: "Is that man going to sleep in your bed?" Many years later I read that this pertinent question was one of the most frequently asked by a generation of shocked children whose short reign as the centre of attention for their mothers had come to an abrupt end.

Unlike many families, Dad was neither traumatised by the war nor was Mum shocked by his reappearance. If there had been any difficulties I was blissfully unaware of them. The major problem was that Dad, who hated teaching, had returned to a job, kept open for him by the school, which he didn't want. Probably aware that a solo career was not a realistic possibility Dad applied for, and got, a position with the London Philharmonic Orchestra and in 1948 we moved south. The only reason I can be certain of this is that I can remember the severe winter of 1947 very clearly. The Great Freeze meant the boys from the school had to dig a trench through deep snow from Fives Cottage down to the road. This was only about seven metres, but to me it was a long corridor of towering snow walls that seemed to be about two metres high. I must make it clear that snowstorms and the Great Freeze were not, as far as I am aware, any pointers to my future obsession with climbing mountains. Doubtless had I been French, German or Italian I would be making the case, 'From the earliest days, my future was defined by my relentless battles with the elements…' I think not.

We moved to Alperton, a dreary suburb in north-west London, to a small house on an estate which my mother loathed (COMMON writ large!). We were only there for a few months before another move. For me this short stay was marked by two events. Playing with a neighbour's child, I was riding a tricycle when the thought entered my head that I should run him over to see what happened. This I did, with a satisfying thud of wheels on flesh and the subsequent scream of pain. This juvenile assassination attempt clearly hadn't been completely successful. I was rewarded with a thrashing and confined to my bedroom, which even I could see was quite justified. The second formative event was when Mum turned off a single-bar electric fire. Warned that it was still hot, in the spirit of discovery I immediately touched it and found my mother's assertion to be quite correct. I hadn't bargained for:

   a) the pain,

   b) the sizzling noise and

   c) the smell of frying bacon that accompanied the experiment. My mum's outraged reaction was: "How could you have been so stupid?" It goes without saying that I taught myself a lesson I've never forgotten. Fire is hot. So maybe the move Mum wished for might curb my destructive tendencies as well.

West Ealing, only a few miles away was then, as now, the epitome of London suburbia. Number 27 Rathgar Avenue was about a 10-minute walk to two parks and 15 minutes to Ealing Broadway station. The house was a good old turn-of-the-century semi. For me the huge attraction was an attic which became a source for many childhood adventures. It even had a 'secret' panel that led to close-up views of sooty rafters, roof tiles and beams. In its dark confines we played games that frequently involved lighting matches or destroying asbestos sheets that someone had thoughtfully left lying around. Amazingly, the house never caught fire and I didn't develop premature lung cancer.

Childhood, I thought, was a breeze, all fun and games. As far as I could see it would last forever. So it came as a frightful shock one day when I was taken by my mother to St Ann's Convent, about a mile away and abandoned there for all eternity (9am to 3pm). Outraged at this unprovoked act of cruelty, I stood by the gates all day, bellowing furiously, until Mum collected me. She did the same the next day and the next and it slowly dawned on me that this

^ *Mum, unaware that she was training a*
young would-be assasin.

was a sentence with no obvious end, and no remission for good behaviour. My memories of St Ann's were almost all of subdued misery. The nuns, apart from one Sister Philomena, were all sadists and I quickly developed a huge inferiority complex, as it was then called. I was, and still am, completely left-handed and my attempts to write were typical; letters facing the wrong way, back to front and whole lines of writing going from right to left. At least they didn't force me to use my right hand. The nuns thought I was just thick. I thought so myself. On one memorable occasion Mum was asked to come to the school for me to demonstrate just how dim I was. Unfortunately for the nuns, but not for Mum and me, they made me read a passage from quite an advanced book. What they didn't realise was that I had been able to read well from an early age and I stood up and nonchalantly read out loud a paragraph or two. If the same had been performed in 2009 rather than 1950 it would have involved high fives, a bit of whooping and some air punching. As it was, I can remember Mum allowing herself a thin little smile, and the nuns looking decidedly pissed off, as well they might.

Curran 1 Nuns 0.

It didn't seem to change much, and the next memorable event was when two or three boys, including me, thought it a good idea to show each other our willies. For some reason we did this at lunchtime in the crowded refectory. I remember the guilty excitement producing an embryonic erection. I can also remember even more clearly, a nun, (of course it *had* to be Sister Philomena) passing by and doing a classic double take as she glimpsed what to her mind must have been as horrifying as a personal appearance by Satan himself. I was carted off for a bout of solitary confinement, and another visit to the school from Mum, which, needless to say, was less successful than the first.

Curran 0 Nuns 1.

Maybe because of this, and maybe because I had by now developed an impressive stammer, I was sent to what were then called 'child guidance clinics'. This one was on the Uxbridge Road near the Old Fire Station. Presumably to start the assertiveness process, I was left to walk on my own down the path to the front door and ring the bell, which I did in a hideous paroxysm of embarrassment. Once inside all I can remember is playing with plasticine while being asked loads of what, even then, I thought were damn fool questions. Whether or not this cured me, or for how long I had to attend, I have no recollection, but the stammering gradually got better, if not the feelings of inadequacy. Neither of these has ever completely disappeared. Curiously, when speaking to a large audience, I occasionally do still stammer, which is easily cured by pausing for a moment and starting again. This

18

invariably has the effect of making the audience pay attention and even start to feel sorry for me, both of which I welcome. As for the inferiority complex, as most of my friends think that I possess a colossal ego and rampant self- regard, all I can say is that either they or I must be wrong. Maybe these pages will help you decide.

By the time I was seven or eight I had developed another trait, which my parents must have felt worrying. Not just simple childish crazes, but quite a serious obsession with a variety of subjects including octopuses, sharks, volcanoes, trains (with the inevitable desire to be an engine driver), bagpipes, *Treasure Island* and pirates. Common to all these was drawing and painting. I filled dozens of exercise books with attempts to recreate the subject as accurately as I knew how. Had I been born 50 or so years later I might well have been diagnosed with obsessive-compulsive disorder. In retrospect, drawing was always the way to make these obsessions real, and I can't remember a time when I didn't want to become an artist. Sadly, most if not all these childish works have been lost, but I remember my frustration at trying to draw a steam engine in perspective at a time when most children rely on simple schematic symbols to identify their subject.

The Natural History and Science Museums in South Kensington were places of total wonder and going there frequently was a real treat. I do remember that on one occasion in the Natural History Museum, which had been badly bombed in the war, I wandered off from my parents, under a barrier and marched up a closed gallery with floorboards either damaged or missing until frantic cries from attendants and parents stopped me from plunging to my death. But mainly I wanted to see the huge stuffed shark and a rather moth-eaten giant squid, plus, of course, the whale room, with the gigantic plaster blue whale without which no visit would have been complete.

Mentioning *Treasure Island* reminds me of the single most frightening image of my childhood. In a beautifully illustrated edition of Robert Louis Stevenson's pirate epic one picture reduced me to abject terror — Long John Silver at the stockade with a hideous grin/snarl on his face and the caption "Them that dies will be the lucky ones." I still have the book, and can quite understand why the pictures frightened me so badly, though nobody else understood. This leads me to believe that things that really frighten children are often completely unpredictable and unintelligible to adults and banning or censoring violent or unsuitable material may not do much good. My other big phobia was octopuses in my bed — an unlikely event in retrospect and a fear that my parents could do little to alleviate.

19

At quite a young age, my mum took me to see a performance of *Treasure Island* at a London theatre. All went well until the moment in the book when a pirate, Israel Hands, is shot from the rigging of the *Hispaniola* and falls dying into the sea. It was my favourite single scene from the book, but it was (probably understandably) cut from the play. My howls of disappointment caused Mum to gather me up and leave the theatre with me still blubbing noisily. It was the first example I witnessed of tampering with a good story and one that many years later as a film-maker, I was determined to avoid. Even now my most common reaction to any film based on a book is, why do they have to bugger about with a perfectly good story?

The only other thing of interest during this time at St Ann's was a very pre-teenage crush on a beautiful little blonde girl two years older than me who lived in the next road. In fact, I can't even remember ever having the courage to talk to her. She was called Mary O'Brien (good Catholic name). Years later she grew up to be Dusty Springfield.

Chapter two: School Years and Relatives

A t last I had served my sentence and left St Ann's to go to St Benedict's, a large Catholic fee-paying public school, though it took no boarders. It was run by the Benedictine monks of Ealing Abbey and had close links with Ampleforth, a much better known monastic public school in Yorkshire.

The school was divided, physically as well as theoretically, into Junior, Middle and Senior Schools, each with its own house system. I have to say I enjoyed most of my schooldays immensely. This was due to a seemingly complete acceptance by both the monks and lay teachers of my lack of interest in most subjects except art in exchange for my growing enthusiasm for rugby and cricket, which became my new obsessions, proved by still more drawings of cricketers. At that time huge numbers of schoolboys all over Britain were fans of Denis Compton, the pin-up star of English cricket. For some strange reason I never shared the enthusiasm for the 'Brylcreem Boy' (perhaps he was too common) and became a devout disciple of Len Hutton, a Yorkshireman who combined classical grace with a stubborn self-discipline and possessed an underlying aura of almost tragic vulnerability. He was the first professional captain of England and famously regained

Brothers. ^
With Phil and Dad. >

the Ashes in 1953. He had sustained a serious injury and as one arm was shorter and weaker than the other, he played with a light schoolboy's bat. I followed his career with devout attention and remember when, unexpectedly, in the winter of 1955, he retired. There was a thin covering of snow that night as I walked tearfully round the streets of Ealing concealing my heartbreak from my parents.

In the summer of 1950 I was woken by Dad who told me I had a baby brother. Philip was seven years younger than I, and

21

born with what I felt was a vile and completely unjustified temper that lasted (at home anyway) until well into primary school days. Needless to say, his teachers told my mother he was an angelic child at school, which I found almost impossible to believe.

Schooldays meandered on with only unfortunate breaks from cricket and rugby for periods of academic study providing minor flies in the otherwise pleasant ointment. I slipped inexorably to the lowest 'C' stream, whilst childhood classmates like Robin Devenish and Steve Durkin (both later to be my first climbing partners) rose to 'A' stream glory. Curiously I never seemed to register what was a fairly severe assessment of my ability. My parents, who must have been worried, never put much pressure on me to pull my finger out. As Dad, the atheist, was paying my school fees, I can only imagine how he must have felt, particularly as I later failed my 11-plus (no surprise there) and he carried on forking out his hard earned salary for me to be indoctrinated into Popeish ways. Dad had by this time got a better paid job at the Royal Opera House, Covent Garden, a job he held until his death in 1967.

During those formative years Mum's concern for me not to be 'common' seemed to be at its strongest. For instance I was allowed two comics: *The Eagle*, obviously safe and unutterably middle-class, and *The Beano*, a slightly risky downmarket publication. Its sister rival, *The Dandy*, was, in my view, virtually identical but considered by my mother to be beyond the pale. Amongst other objects that were banned for their inability to rise above their common status were roller skates, candy floss, toffee apples, chewing gum, cigarette cards and Saturday morning pictures. Various adjacent streets were condemned in their entirety. They seemed to me to be indistinguishable from our own, while whole suburbs of London suffered the same fate: Acton, Hanwell, Southall, Ruislip. Pronunciation was another bone of contention: "You used to speak so beautifully," was a common refrain. Apparently I now had a common London accent, which, listening to a surviving fragment of tape recording, is quite embarrassingly and self-consciously 'posh' which, strangely enough, was another 'common' word. Talking of pronunciation, it now intrigues me how Dad had managed to kick over any trace of the Geordie accent of his youth and always spoke in the BBC approved English. His sister, Auntie Truda, who came to stay every year, still retained her broad accent. Now, having lived most of my adult life in Sheffield and Bristol, my own accent is, I think, a strange combination of north and south. In Sheffield I seem to have a London voice, but in London, as my brother once remarked, my Yorkshire accent in almost unintelligible. A girlfriend in Bristol once described me as her 'bit of Northern rough'. Fair enough, but I know I also put it on a bit, depending on my audience.

Back to school. I think that my ability in sport must have done a lot to help me heal my lack of self-confidence. Which is strange as I was always crippled with nerves before (and sometimes during) cricket matches. Waiting to go into bat was as scary as sitting in the dentist's waiting room, yet I often surprised myself by being quite cool when I was actually batting. I was always at my best in a crisis, mainly because others had failed, and there was nothing left to lose.

One foggy afternoon towards the end of the autumn term the school held some sort of talent-spotting contest. I can't remember the competing acts but my contribution was to recite the poem 'You are old, Father William' with a cushion stuffed up my jumper. At rehearsal I was so nervous I could barely speak. In front of the whole Middle School, however, it was as though someone had flicked a switch and I instantly became supercharged with adrenaline. I overacted disgracefully, turned somersaults and belted out the verses, easily winning whatever prize it was. I loved controlling an audience and though, even now I still suffer appalling pre-match nerves, I know I am good at it.

Since our move from Uppingham my two uncles, Wilfred and Harold, started to figure more prominently in family life. Both were Catholic priests working in west London parishes. Wilfred was a devout man who had an unfailing and often ribald sense of humour. He used to visit Mum, arriving on an ancient bicycle. He would sit in the kitchen, cycle clips still on his ankles, smoking tiny roll-up cigarettes and telling outrageous stories of parish life. On at least one occasion I wet myself laughing. His parish priest, Father Matthew, was a keen but incompetent golfer and Wilfred's re-enactments of temper tantrums, on one occasion, chucking his clubs in a pond, were told in a haze of tobacco smoke amid bellows of laughter.

Only one story remains in my memory. While hearing confessions, Wilfred was concerned at a series of long sighs from the other side of the confessional. Fearing he was about to be told of at least a rape, or even a murder, he couldn't get a word out of his penitent. At last he got up and went round to the other side of the confessional where he found a large Alsatian dog sitting with his nose pressed up to the grille. No one else was in the church at the time and eventually the dog wandered off. Whether or not his canine misdemeanours were forgiven was open to question. Wilfred had huge charisma and, over the years, many of his female parishioners were infatuated with him, a situation that he did little to discourage, though I am quite sure that relations were never carried further than rather gauche flirtations.

It is difficult to talk about Uncle Harold without admitting that he was gay. Not that Mum, nor Phil or I realised that for many years. He was incredibly knowledgeable with a wide-ranging enthusiasm for the arts. From quite an early age he took me to many of London's museums and art galleries, and further afield to the Ashmolean and Fitzwilliam Museums, giving me a grounding in European art that has never left me. Unfortunately, he was prone to explosive and quite childish temper tantrums. Any visit to 27 Rathgar Avenue was quite likely to end in a hysterical eruption. The sound of a violent slamming of the front door and the sight of his bald head receding up the road was all too frequent. I know now that he was a deeply unhappy man who should never have been a priest. Nobody had the courage to stand up to his appalling behaviour, but on his next visit he would arrive as if nothing had happened. Even when he took me out I was always on edge, fearing that I would get an unjustified bollocking, such as the time he introduced me to someone and I (horror of horrors) said: "Pleased to meet you," instead of "How do you do?" It might have been the same occasion that I said "Pardon," instead of "What did you say?" In which case I scored a double whammy. Like Mum, his antennae for commonness were acute, whereas Uncle Wilfred couldn't have cared less.

Wilfred had a hugely resonant bass voice. It had apparently frightened me to death when I first heard it on an early visit to Uppingham. In the 50s, 60s and 70s he was an eminent conductor of church music. His choir performed all over Europe, including Cologne Cathedral. Wilfred never rose above the rank of Monsignor, only one stage up from parish priest, which he remained until his death in 1987.

My brother, who retained much closer contact with him when I moved away from London, still wonders whether the reason for his never becoming a bishop could have been bound up with Harold, whose reputation may well have been a source of embarrassment within the church.

The only other relatives we knew of were three Scottish cousins Chris, Sheila and Jean, and the aforementioned Auntie Truda. Truda suffered badly from asthma and always seemed to be at death's door, but lived to be about 150. Her only interest was Esperanto, the language designed to become a universal panacea for world peace and mutual understanding. I think it was a great disappointment to her that I never learnt a single word in aid of what seemed to be an eccentric, almost barmy hope — a view shared, alas, by most of the world.

Of the three cousins, Chris was my favourite by a long way. She lodged with us and had some sort of secretarial job. Rumour had it that she had a boyfriend who was killed in the war. She had a dry, rather hesitant sense of humour and made up wonderful stories about a horse, unimaginatively called 'Horse'. Horse stories were, I now recognise, as delightful to me as they were tedious for her, and delivered in a cloud of cigarette smoke. Chris, seeing a possible escape route, taught me to read at an early age. However, I remember Horse stories being much in demand long after I could read perfectly well. Of her two sisters, Sheila became a headmistress at a 'progressive' school and she taught, among others, Peter Sellers's son, meeting his father on several occasions. As I became an addict to the iconic *Goon Show*, I was impressed.

Jean, the third sister, was a mystery to me. She suffered from some sort of mental illness which was never discussed and possibly never treated. She lived with her father, who I called Uncle Angus, a dour, white-haired man who was a commercial artist. Jean produced vast swathes of colourful watercolours but my interest was with Uncle Angus who let me see his studio on visits to their dark, rather forbidding house near Ealing Common. Here, at the back of the house, was an Aladdin's cave of paints and photographs and, to my intense curiosity, a spray gun. Uncle Angus derived most of his income from tinting black and white photographs to make them appear as full colour prints. It must have involved immense skill and patience, a good example being the photo of me holding a Kodak box camera reproduced on the rear cover. As I had already decided I wanted to be an artist, my fascination for his work was genuine, and this reinforced my childish ambition.

The obsession with art was, as I have already mentioned, nurtured by visits to art galleries with Uncle Harold. However, when I was 10 my other major passion exploded into my life like a bolt from the blue. Once again, Dad woke me up, this time on Coronation Day, June 3rd 1953: "Everest's been climbed." This news excited me far more than the Coronation and my burgeoning fascination was fed for the next six years by the mountaineering section in Ealing Public Library. Both my parents were avid readers and weekly visits to the library were a source of endless pleasure. Dad had already converted me to the humorous delights of P G Wodehouse, Jerome K Jerome and Stephen Leacock. As in thousands of other homes, John Hunt's *The Ascent of Everest* soon came to be a family possession on our bookshelves, but it was Wilfrid Noyce's *South Col* that gripped me. I devoured every climbing book I could get and both uncles chipped in with *The Untrodden Andes* by Eggeler and DeBooy, and *The Ascent of K2* and *Nanga Parbat*, written by Ardito Desio and Karl Herrligkoffer respectively. I was completely unaware of how these last two had generated so much controversy, libel cases and ill-feeling that would last to the present day. But the story that really fired me was the haunting mystery of Mallory and Irvine who had disappeared on Everest in 1924.

That, together with an outing with the school to see *The Ascent of Everest* at a local cinema, saw me hooked, though my passion was of much the same nature as that provoked by reading *Treasure Island*. It seemed to me to be an activity only to be undertaken by a race of supermen whose courage, strength and bravery were beyond my comprehension. At the time, cricket and rugby were my outlets for physical activity. I loathed PT, as it was then called. As a fat child I hated my lack of ability to climb ropes or vault over a great brown thing called a 'horse', though there was no obvious resemblance. As for running, I was truly pathetic and never tried. Oddly enough I did come third in the Middle School High Jump and the following morning I was rushed into hospital with acute appendicitis that was on the verge of bursting to cause peritonitis, in those days a serious complication.

When I awoke after the operation, I found my mother in a nightie and dressing gown sitting next to me. She was a patient in the same hospital after developing breast cancer and she had had a mastectomy. This was followed by a huge dose of radiotherapy which caused dreadful scarring and a permanent oedema of her left arm and hand — so bad that she could never play the piano again. I was oblivious to all this, and more concerned with an incredibly sore stomach. I was told later that the young surgeon who had operated on me had performed his first appendectomy. I could well believe it. The good news was that I missed the last weeks of term. And what's more, a holiday worthy of the Famous Five books by Enid Blyton was in the offing.

Mum and Dad had retained close ties with Uppingham. Friendship with a housemaster and his family, Dennis and Dorothy Oswald, and their four children, Richard, Mick, Claire and Derek, meant annual visits to Meadhurst. Meadhurst, particularly when empty of pupils, was a magical place with tennis courts, a small wood and a boys' common room with a billiard table. Every year Dad took a busman's holiday, leading the school orchestra in their annual Gilbert and Sullivan production.

But, this year, aware of Mum's illness, the Oswalds invited me to Cornwall. This was the most exciting holiday I had ever had. We stayed in an old farmhouse near Carbis Bay and, in what I remember as fairly typical Cornish weather, did everything that you should do on a seaside holiday in Cornwall. One thing you should not do is get drowned, which I nearly did, swimming out of my depth to recover a beach ball. I have always been a good swimmer, but I remember the feeling of helplessness as I tried to swim back

^ Kynance Cove.
Pencil drawing aged 10.

against the tide, without the beach getting any nearer. Being polite and well brought up, it never occurred to me to shout for help and when I finally struggled ashore and flopped exhausted on the sand I was embarrassed by the fuss I was causing. As I was in their care, Dennis and Dorothy were mortified by what they saw as their lack of attention, particularly as I was supposed to be recovering from an operation. But I knew it was all my fault, and couldn't understand why my apologies seemed to upset Dorothy even more.

The other memory was of the savage Cornish coastline: the cliffs of Kynance Cove and Gurnard's Head being the highlights. I tried to paint Kynance Cove several times with limited success and remember the horror of looking straight down to the sea at Gurnard's Head. Many years later I climbed the easy classic route, *Right Angle*. I emerged at the top at the precise spot I had peered down on that wonderful holiday. The romance of the place has never left me.

If the Oswald family were the treasured holiday friends, at home the Oliver family and their sons, Stephen and Max, were my day-to-day companions. Their father, Dr Oliver, was our GP and they lived almost opposite in a large corner house. Stephen, about two years older than I, was my best friend and we shared all sorts of enthusiasms, the most enduring being a love of model aircraft.

27

Joe Simpson seconding Right Angle. ^
With Stephen Oliver, my best friend. >

Over the years we graduated from simple balsa wood kits to large-scale models powered by temperamental little diesel engines. Or rather Stephen did — my preference was for ever larger gliders. In those days radio controlled models were large, heavy and expensive, and almost out of the question. Our models were tested in our local park, and at weekends we would be taken by the long-suffering Dr Oliver to Richmond Park, where we normally crashed one or the other of our latest creations, or occasionally, and more memorably, lost one as it caught a thermal and disappeared over the horizon.

But the most enjoyable part was in their construction in the Olivers' large and well-lit attic. There we cut out wing ribs and fuselage formers, gluing them together with balsa cement, covering them with tissue and shrinking tight with aircraft dope — great memories of hours of concentration and patience. The Olivers'

28

Stephen with his piece de resistance, the Tiger Moth. >

attic later played a far more important part in my life, but I have no doubt that the discipline of making model aircraft was a lesson which helped me a lot in later years.

When Stephen went to Epsom College as a boarder, and I started at St Benedict's Senior School, it felt like the end of an era. Even if constructing model aircraft continued in the holidays, our paths would slowly diverge, though the friendship has continued to the present day.

Entry to the Senior School meant three things. Sport, in the form of cricket and rugby, played an ever-increasing part in my life. Art, under the influence of a great teacher, John Innes, was by far and away the subject that engrossed me most. And joining the CCF (Combined Cadet Force) was almost as hateful as maths.

Taking the last first, I could never understand (though I now have my suspicions) why Catholic monks should enjoy dressing up as soldiers one day a week and indoctrinating young teenagers in techniques of warfare, even though most of them dated from before the war, as did much of the equipment. From the word go, I hated all the palaver at home on Thursday evenings ironing box creases into my battledress and trousers, rubbing soap into the inside to keep them intact for Friday afternoon parade, endless polishing buckles and hat badges, blancoing belt and gaiters and, worst of all, polishing boots to a lustrous shine. This was achieved (or should have been) by running a hot spoon over the corrugated leather surface and then hours of spit and polish. In fact, I discovered a simpler way, by simply painting the boots with black Valspar lacquer, which gave an instant mirror finish until a fateful parade when I dropped my ancient Lee Enfield 303 rifle onto my foot, shattering the surface like a broken mirror. For that, I spent several hours cleaning rifles in the old Nissen hut masquerading as

29

^ *A gormless teenager with Mum and Phil.*

the 'Armoury'.

But, oh God, the boring futility of drill, and of lectures by pimply 'sergeants' of 17 years old on how to kill people. All this seemed to occur on dreary Friday afternoons in November in fading light and dire discomfort as my soapy creases gave me a form of teenage nappy rash. The only vaguely useful knowledge was map reading which, though I never mastered the intricacies of grid references, did prove useful in later life. I have always found my way around mountains reasonably easily. I have, I like to think, a fairly good sense of direction – much better than one or two famous mountaineers who shall remain nameless (oh, go on then — Chris Bonington).

The only enjoyable parts of CCF were field trips when we were bundled into the back of army lorries and taken down to the pleasant wooded countryside near Aldershot to play cowboys and Indians. Instead of cap guns we actually had blank ammunition in our rifles, which made a satisfying bang when shot. Here in bracken-strewn countryside we learned to smoke cheap cigarettes and, on the way back, the words to filthy songs such as 'Four and Twenty Virgins'.

While nearly all my classmates passed various tests and gained 'promotions' to corporal, sergeant or even under officer, the most exalted position in the CCF, I eventually passed something called

Phil persecuted in the back garden. >

'Cert A part 1' which qualified me for absolutely nothing except to carry on endless parades and drills, and listen to the same boring lectures. Strangely enough, despite being told so often, I can't for the life of me remember any other way to kill an enemy apart from shooting at point blank range. This, with only blanks in our rifle would result in, at worst, temporary deafness and a light deposit of burnt gunpowder and charred paper on the presumably immaculately soap-creased battledress of the enemy.

Sport on the other hand was all consuming. Since the middle school I had kept a regular place in rugby, playing at number eight at the back of the scrum. Which was a satisfying, even creative position that had none of the brutal powerhouse drudgery of a second row, nor the evil mysteries of the front row, which, even at the tender age of 11 or 12, could produce cauliflower ears and the occasional broken nose.

My first love, however, was still cricket. I developed into an erratic left-arm spin bowler and a reasonably stylish batsman. I never had the power or courage to drill sixes back over the bowler's head. I preferred cuts, glances and the odd cover drive in the style of my hero, Len Hutton. All these were executed with tremendous grace and élan, particularly in front of a mirror where there was no ball involved. But the joy of a well-placed square cut is as fresh in my memory now as though it had only happened yesterday.

There is no doubt that my cricket was improved by the help of my housemaster, Steve Walker, who, out of sheer kindness, paid for me to go to an indoor cricket school in the winter months. Here, in a dingy Chiswick side street. I found myself pitched into a man's world. The changing rooms smelt of embrocation oil, sweat and jockstraps, as hairy old Middlesex county professionals went through their paces. I suffered a recurrence of nerves and, despite Mr Walker's generosity, came to dread those Wednesday evenings, coming in from the dark street into the unforgiving fluorescent lights. I have a horrible feeling that Steve Walker felt a bit let down when I left school at 16 and never reached the dizzy heights of the First 11, though later on brother Phil more than made up for this.

As far as art was concerned I had never previously got much satisfaction from school, which in Junior and Middle, meant powder paint, rough paper and ancient, worn out brushes. Instead I did the majority of my painting at home, most of which was over-ambitious and unsatisfactory as I wrestled with thick oil paint on Daler boards. I relied heavily on the 'How to Draw' series — trains, birds, the figure, flowers, etc., but progress was limited. Once in Senior School, we had a proper art room and the aforementioned Mr Innes, who had been to the Slade School of Art and was a terrific draughtsman. Under his patient encouragement my work improved by leaps and bounds. I think it is fair to say that his academic rigour was only appreciated by those few boys who were really interested. The vast majority just fooled around and I can understand why. For instance, Mr Innes once set us to draw an egg on a saucer, a daunting prospect for even the most gifted of us. But it was the discipline I needed and I spent every available minute in the art room including lunchtime breaks. True, the dreaded powder paints still featured, which had the unhappy knack when mixed, however briefly, of going a flat turgid grey-brown. But as a promising student I was allowed oil paints and pastels, both of which I revelled in. Though I had never thought seriously about any other career, going to art school now seemed a realistic possibility, though I had little idea of what 'going to art school' entailed.

Apart from regularly coming top in art, my other subjects languished. Occasionally a good teacher could revive some interest. English was okay, and once or twice I had a brief burst of enthusiasm for History, but sadly the 'C' stream tended to be taught by the worst teachers whose main task was to keep us quiet. Although I normally came around eighth in overall performance, it was done with minimum effort, and not much more encouragement. I suspect, had I been allowed, I would have stayed at school indefinitely so long as I performed well on the sports field. ('Twenty-five year old schoolboy dies of nappy rash.')

So far I have not mentioned my Catholic upbringing and education. I had dutifully made my first Communion, been confirmed, went to Mass on Sunday, ate fish on Friday and went to Confession every two weeks. Occasionally I felt slightly devout (not enough to worry about), but most of the time I accepted the orthodox party line unquestioningly. The monks did not encourage debate, and it never seriously occurred to me that there was any reason to. The Pope was infallible and that was that. Mum kept me on the straight and narrow. In many respects I was a very naïve teenager. Outside school, however, all kinds of changes were afoot that would, before long, make teenage life so exciting that religion gradually became a matter of lip service. But it would be many years before I ditched it, once and for all, with a huge sense of relief.

Little did I know it at the time, but it was an innocent school fête on a summer Saturday afternoon in 1957 that was the precursor to a lifetime's 'Trouble with Women'.

Chapter three: Young Love

Apart from a very youthful crush on Mary O'Brien and a few lewd thoughts centred round a bubble bath occupied by Jane Russell in the Bob Hope/Bing Crosby film *Son of Paleface*, I don't think I had any great interest in the opposite sex until I was about 14. All that changed in five seconds. Amongst a gaggle of schoolgirls milling around one of the stalls at a St Benedict's fête, one stood out a mile. Raven-haired and obviously the centre of attraction amongst her friends, she was the prettiest girl I had ever seen. Her name, I later found out, was Penny Davis and she was a pupil at St Augustine's Convent just up the road from St Benedict's.

This teenage romance was so one-sided I doubt that she was even aware of my presence. But for weeks she dominated my waking hours and a few of my sleeping ones as well. I took to riding my bike slowly past the school gates in an agony of embarrassment that she would think I was stalking her, which of course I was, albeit unsuccessfully. It was a complete waste of time and energy, but my hormones/testosterone, or whatever it is that triggers this exquisite form of insanity, had exploded with the shock of a starting gun.

I read recently that the first experiences of romance affects every subsequent one throughout life. A fulfilling, settled relationship is likely to be repeated; an unhappy one will tend to be the blueprint for others. This episode with (not even with) Penny Davis didn't really count, but the next one only a few months later certainly did.

Before that occurred, other events conspired to heighten teenage lust and angst. 'Heartbreak Hotel' by Elvis had struck the youth of Britain, particularly the young males at first, though hysterical girls soon followed once his astonishing good looks became known. His combination of black rock and roll, white country and western and a deep feeling for the blues had the force of a medium-sized earthquake.

In Ealing Broadway a coffee bar called 'The Caprice' had opened. In the eyes of the monks, this was the equivalent of Babylon on a particularly wanton night. Pupils were promptly banned from entering it which, of course, made it doubly attractive. The only way round the ban was to adopt a cunning disguise. This was achieved by removing our school caps. In a fever of guilty excitement we could sip frothy coffee and listen to the sound of Elvis or, heaven help us, Tommy Steele, while surreptitiously eyeing up what Mum would think of as particularly common girls (mostly from St Augustine's) with whom any meaningful contact was as rare as rocking horse shit. Decadence didn't come any lower than this, though if it did, I wondered just how wonderful it could possibly be. Ah, innocence! In fact, apart from a lurid explanation of the Facts of Life on the school playing field, and an exquisitely embarrassing half hour chat with Dad on a park bench, I was woefully ignorant.

For almost as long as I can remember Mum had taken in lodgers to supplement Dad's income at Covent Garden. A succession of mainly middle-aged ladies had come and gone without incident. More recently she had started taking in overseas students — French, Swiss and German — who came to London on various crash courses in English. Again they were unmemorable. Then one autumn day Mum announced that we would be taking in an Italian student. Late that evening a taxi arrived and the doorbell rang. I glimpsed a pale oval face behind the frosted glass. I swear to this day that my heart turned over before the door opened. When it did, Luciana Vezzulli stood in the hall smiling nervously, while I actually thought I was going to faint. If Sophia Loren had arrived, I couldn't have been more affected. Penny Davis was instantly relegated to a distant memory. The next six months were an intoxicating mixture of ecstasy and misery.

Luciana was, by any standards, beautiful, with dark straight hair and large brown eyes. But quite apart from her looks she had a personality and intelligence to match. She was 18, four whole years older than me. As I got to know her she told me her parents had sent her to England because she was having an affair with an older married man. Whether or not this affair had been consummated I never found out (this was, don't forget, 1957). While emotionally loathing this anonymous man for his very existence, common sense told me that if he had not done whatever it was that had so enraged her parents, Luciana wouldn't be here at all.

She had arrived with another student, Gigliola, a large bespectacled girl who was lodged in the house across the road. The two were inseparable and a great deal of my life consisted of inventing ever more ingenious ways to get Luciana to myself. The best argument was that if they spent time together, they wouldn't be learning English. In fact, I actually became quite good at understanding Italian, so desperate was I to spend any available minute with the beloved.

Luciana was, I think, loved by both Mum and Dad. (Phil, aged seven didn't, so far as I was concerned, have feelings and certainly didn't understand mine until after she left.) She was absorbed easily into the family and we often took her to see various London sights as well as picnics in lesser-known local spots like Osterley and Gunnersbury Parks.

My adolescent devotion/passion needs little explaining. More interesting was her attitude to me which over the months, if not totally reciprocated, was certainly far from non-existent. Was she flattered by a young boy's love? Undoubtedly, but as time passed, though we never actually went to bed, we got pretty close — a lot closer than Mum and Dad seemed to realise. At night we did a lot of fairly intense kissing and cuddling (her in bed, me lying on the bedclothes next to her). Was she a tease? I don't think so. Perhaps she needed an innocent love that had escaped her in Italy. Did she realise the effect she had on me? Probably, but she was also lonely and in some strange way our feelings were not quite so one-sided as they might have appeared. Was it doomed? Of course, and I knew it. She would go back to Italy, get married, have children and I would never see her again. The thought, like an impending execution, hung over me as the months, weeks, then days, ticked inexorably down to the moment of departure.

She left from Victoria Station on the long train journey to Milan. I went with her to see her off. I can't remember the actual moment we said 'goodbye'. I was blinded by tears and I remember the humiliation of crying on the Underground as I returned to Ealing Broadway. Was it possible to feel so incredibly sad? Well yes, it was, and it wasn't to be the only time, or even the worst, but having nothing to compare it with, it felt as though my world had ended. Even brother Phil realised how badly I had been affected.

We wrote frequently. She described her life as though she was imprisoned like a princess in a tower, forever restricted in her movements by her parents in case she strayed again. I wrote long letters of undying love of which, thankfully, I can remember no relevant details. Naturally, as time passed, they petered out on both sides and other events eventually took over. But I never forgot the intensity of that first love and, surprisingly, neither did she.

How do I know this? Well, there was an unexpected postscript some 20 years later in 1978. I had made my first film, *A Great Effort*, and it was to be shown at the Trento Mountain Film Festival. Mum had kept in contact with Luciana with Christmas cards and the odd letter. She still lived in Milan and Mum wrote and told her I would be in Trento. She and her husband arranged to drive over and booked into the hotel I was staying in. I had driven out with Joe Tasker and Pete Boardman who were the blue-eyed boys of the British mountaineering scene. Joe, with Dick Renshaw, had made a brilliant ascent of Dunagiri in the Garhwal Himalaya and Pete had shot to fame in 1975 when with Pertemba Sherpa he climbed the South West Face of Everest. Pete and Joe had then teamed up in 1976 to make an astonishing two-man ascent of the West Face of Changabang. This ascent had been fêted worldwide. Their presence in Trento was political as well as recreational, for there was a very good chance that they could win the coveted 'Piolet d'Or' for the most outstanding ascent of the year, a prospect that Pete viewed with some trepidation. They were intrigued by my impending reunion, and lost no time in concocting various far-fetched scenarios that are best not repeated.

Halfway through the festival they arrived, husband, wife and teenage daughter. Luciana hadn't changed, except that her hair was absolutely white, not a trace even of grey. But facially and physically she was just as I remembered her.

Astonishingly, despite 20 years and some rusty English, neither had our friendship changed. Husband and child, neither of whom spoke a word of English, looked pretty bored. They were not helped by the screening of *A Great Effort* in the Trento Opera House which mysteriously lacked the Italian translation I had supplied that would have made some sense to a puzzled audience. Back at the hotel father and daughter went to bed, to my relief. Luciana and I stayed up talking for hours. She found it hard to believe I was now 35, divorced with two children. She knew I had been to art college and now taught in one, but the climbing side of my life obviously bewildered her. I suppose I naively thought that most Italians were far more aware of the mountains than the British, but Luciana seemed horrified that I was consumed by climbing them. She seemed to think I would almost certainly be killed sooner or later.

However, the old affection was still there and gazing into those brown smiling eyes, my heart melted as it had done years ago. In the morning they left for the long drive home. This time, I realised with a shock, it was Luciana whose cheeks were streaked with tears as the car drove away. She must have realised, as I know now, that this time would be the last. I have never seen or heard from her since. If she were still alive she would be 72. Our reunion confirmed to me that it was not just a teenage crush. Love — what can you say?

Chapter four: Schooldays Cut Short

It goes without saying that six months of unrequited love had produced nothing except a serious crop of spots. My schoolwork went from bad to worse. Only cricket, rugby and art could still galvanise me and in the latter I had good reason for my enthusiasm. In common with many art schools at the time, Ealing Art School ran Saturday morning classes for anyone who wanted to go. Suffering as usual from embarrassment and nerves, I turned up and was accepted without question. Although the work set was academic — still life, plant drawing, a bit of landscape painting — it was done in a real art college environment. We were a fairly motley crew and not many went on to art education. This was probably no bad thing as it was the first stage of sorting out potential, however unformed.

The Saturday mornings were memorable for seeing full-time students' work. Most were big, dark, ominous oil paintings on hardboard, using vast quantities of cheap decorator's paint. I realised later that Auerbach was teaching part-time at Ealing and his influence was all too apparent. Frank Auerbach, born in Germany in 1931, was the son of Jewish parents who sent him to England in 1939. They were never to see him again, both killed in the Nazi death camps during the war. Auerbach established himself with Francis Bacon and Lucian Freud as one of the three leading British figurative artists, but in 1959 he was still teaching part-time in London art schools. His technique of vastly thick impasto paintings based around the female form and landscapes of London still ravaged by war damage were finding both recognition and imitation by his protégés. Most of the student paintings were pretty ghastly, but seemed to me to be the real thing, even if I hadn't the faintest idea what they were about.

At school too, Mr Innes was a model of quiet, patient encouragement. At that time I had a natural facility for paint and colour but my drawing always let me down. It would be the weakest part of my work until well into college education. Mr Innes did all he could to improve it, but with little or no competition around me it never seemed to get much better. Like the rest of my schoolwork, I found it almost impossible to motivate myself if I wasn't really interested — a state of affairs that continues to the present day. The only solution is to stick with things I do want to do.

Beneath all this another problem was lurking. I was determined to go full-time to art school when I reached 16 after my O-Levels. Sixth Form and A-Levels were never a remote possibility and I was convinced that even O-Levels were irrelevant in what I assumed would be my star-studded career as a painter. Dad, on the other hand, was more practical. Five GCEs seemed to be the minimum requirements for any sort of future and St Benedict's was unlikely to make this possible. The thought of paying school fees forever had finally got to him, and he and Mum decided I would leave at Christmas 1958 and go to a crammer where six months' intensive study should (might) get me the required passes.

The institution chosen was Davies, Laing and Dick, in a rabbit warren of a Georgian building in Holland Park. It mainly catered for public school failures. Many of the pupils had been expelled from much better known schools than mine, often for a surprising variety of sexual misdemeanours. Most were older than me and exuded a worldliness that I found intimidating.

All I can say about the next six months of education is that time passed. But outside of the crammer my life was anything but boring. The musical revolution of rock and roll had, in Britain anyway, evolved into Skiffle, essentially a homemade product popularised by Lonnie Donegan who was formerly a banjo player in Chris Barber's Jazz Band. Skiffle needed only a guitar or two, a metal washboard (played with thimbles on each finger to provide rhythm) and a tea chest, a broom handle and a piece of string. The handle was wedged into the corner of the chest, the string attached to the opposite corner and to the top of the handle. By plucking the string and varying the tension on the broom handle, various unmusical thudding noises were produced that bore a vague resemblance to a double bass. But the guitar was, of course, the sexy instrument. My first was a cheap steel-stringed model that quickly developed a warped fret board, which meant that the higher notes were horribly out of tune. Not that it mattered, for I was spending hours with sore fingertips trying to master basic chords. Literally thousands of teenage boys all over the country were doing exactly the same thing and later four of them in Liverpool became quite well-known.

I had a sort of friend at St Benedict's, a boy of Polish extraction called Kaspczyk, pronounced by us as Kaspercheck. I don't think I ever knew his first name, everyone just called him Kaz. He lived up the road from me in a sinister Hammer Horror Victorian house with an exotic family who seemed to know no English. Kaz was the hero, or villain, of the school. He was so handsome that 'beautiful' was the only way to describe him, with long, fair, Teddy boy hair brushed back in a classic DA (duck's arse) style at the neck. He had the tightest drainpipe trousers in the world and winkle-picker shoes that tapered to stiletto points about a foot long. He spelled Trouble with a capital 'T' and was always in it. He also had a fabulous cutaway cello guitar, the sexiest object in West Ealing. Not, you would think, the sort of person that would endear himself to Mum, and you would be right. But Kaz had a brilliant

39

trick up his sleeve. Every time they met he would greet her with a sort of mid-European formal bow and kiss her hand. To my utter amazement she melted and put up with him, against her better judgement.

We formed a sort of group. Both our guitars had electric pick ups but we couldn't afford amplifiers. So we connected the leads of the pick-ups to the wires from the stylus on our gramophone. As neither of us was electrocuted it probably wasn't as dangerous as it seemed and with the volume on full it sounded like the real thing. Kaz knew some simple riffs and taught me a few new chords. His impersonation of Elvis was beyond admiration and he had a great singing voice.

He was nothing if not self-confident and somehow arranged for us to play at a dance at a youth club in Shepherd's Bush. Dressed in white shirts, black ties and black jeans we arrived at the venue in dry-mouthed anticipation. I had an appalling attack of nerves. When we rigged the guitars into the PA system I was appalled as the first deafening E major chord thundered round the hall. It took a few seconds to realise it had come from my own guitar. I nearly wet myself. By the time our spot was announced I wanted to do a runner, but it was too late. We limped through 'Be-Bop-a-Lula' and Elvis's 'One Night With You' to a smattering of applause and fled. It was one of my only two live performances (the other was on my 60th birthday) and I am reluctantly beginning to accept that my chances of being a rock and roll star are now just about non-existent.

I always felt that Kaz was destined for fame and glory, if not fortune. By the time I started art school we had drifted apart and he completely vanished out of my life. Did he change his name and become a rock musician, an actor, a writer? I don't think so, for I would surely have recognised him. Did he end up in jail? No, he was not a bad person, though he sailed close to the wind. I'll probably never find out, a pity, for I'm certain that his life has been nothing if not exciting. He was that kind of boy.

My other friends at the time couldn't have been more different. Robin Devenish, Steve Durkin and Mike Watkins were all at St Benedict's. Robin, the son of a surgeon, was destined for academic brilliance. Both he and Steve were definitely not into sport. Mike was a year or two younger, and a very good cricketer, which probably explains our friendship. On face value, Robin and Steve had little in common with me, except that we had grown up together from Junior School. Steve and Robin fitted into the role of mad scientists and Robin in particular was addicted to making large and dangerous explosions, one of which blew all the glass out of his parents' greenhouse. He and Steve concocted ever more ambitious experiments which these days would have the anti-terrorist squad down on them like a ton of bricks. I can only remember witnessing one such event in Richmond Park when they fired a cigar tube hundreds of feet into the air with an ear-splitting crack that sent all the birds out of the trees with squawks of alarm.

Robin and I were keen cyclists and when his bomb-making craze came to an end, thankfully without any prosecutions, we started cycling every weekend, at first round the hills and lanes of Surrey and the North Downs, later farther afield to the south coast. On one occasion, we managed 150 miles in a day.

A youth hostelling fortnight to Land's End and back was the highlight of my cycling career until 2000. After our return we cycled out with Steve to a disused sand quarry on the side of St Ann's Hill, near Chertsey. We had noticed this on an earlier ride and wondered what it would be like to climb the steep, unstable slope. Armed only with a length of rope (probably a legendary mother's clothes line similar to the one that had helped Joe Brown on his journey to become the greatest rock-climber in Britain) we just about had the sense not to kill ourselves, and with one end tied to a tree at the top, we somehow arranged a primitive belay. We took it in turns to scrabble up the steepening slope until I decided to find out what it felt like to fall off (shades of the electric fire experiment many years before). I deliberately climbed diagonally up and, when a decent distance away from the vertical line, I threw myself off. Amazingly, the rope didn't snap as I described a huge pendulum, stopping in a flurry of sand and the rope tight around my chest. It was a remarkably unpleasant experience and, chastened, I rode home unimpressed. But somehow a seed had been sown.

In fact, it had been sown earlier, but not in me. Our old Latin master, Mr Williamson (who once told me that if I didn't give up learning Latin he would give up teaching it) had, unbeknown to me, been a member of both The Climbers' Club and The Alpine Club. Steve Durkin had let it be known that he was interested in climbing and Mr Williamson had kindly written to Alan Blackshaw suggesting he took Steve to Harrison's Rocks, near Tunbridge Wells, to introduce him to the rudiments of rock-climbing. Alan Blackshaw was responsible for writing the definitive mountaineering instruction book a few years later, and Steve could hardly have had a better mentor. He struggled up a few of the easiest routes and learned the basics of rope work. All this passed me by — maybe Steve didn't think it worth mentioning, or letting on that Mr Williamson had presented him with his old ice-axe. This was almost indistinguishable from Andrew Irvine's axe found on Everest in 1933, a sad reminder of the disappearance of Mallory

^ Me, on the left, and Mike preparing to bivouac at Harrison's (now strictly forbidden).

and Irvine nine years earlier. Steve still has it — a venerable old relic that seems to have come from Victorian England, as indeed did Mr Williamson.

So in March 1959, stuffed full of quadratic equations, quotes from *Henry V* and chunks of incomprehensible French, I was easily persuaded to go climbing with Steve one Saturday. Steve was the proud possessor of the current sandstone guidebook, a slender tome with a brown cover. Inside large sections were soon learnt verbatim, a pleasurable task that sadly was quite impossible for me to transfer to Shakespeare or French grammar. In a state of some embarrassment at our novice status, we chose to visit a strictly private outcrop instead of the obvious Harrison's Rocks. It was one of two days that fundamentally changed my life. Chiddingly Wood guards the finest outcrop in south-east England, surpassing even Harrison's Rocks. The crags, the guidebook pointed out, featured in R Thurston Hopkin's *Ghosts over England*, which reports an interview with a local poacher. 'There's one thing I dare not do. I'd be afeared to walk through that girt valley below Big on Little [a famous boulder] after dark. It's a terrible ellynge place and a girt black ghost hound walks there o' nights ... they call the hound Gytrack'.

Early days at Harrison's, note the steam engine in the background. >

42

I only retain a few impressions of that day in March 1959, but they are vivid ones. The wonderful heady smell of sandstone, leaf mould, hemp rope and sweat; a grim struggle, plimsolls flapping, up one of the two or three easy climbs we managed on a tight top rope (i.e. using a rope running through a sling attached to a tree at the top of the crag); furtive skulkings down rhododendron-lined paths with the bulging rounded buttresses like big beer guts poking through the undergrowth; a hermit's cave with ancient lettering carved on the walls and a long, dark walk to East Grinstead station to catch the last train back to Victoria. There, sitting looking out into the dark night and the lights of suburban Surrey as London drew closer, nursing aching arms and fingers, I felt the stirrings of a strange elation that 30 years on is as addictive as ever. Much later on we returned and bivouacked in the hermit's cave in the hope or dread of seeing the legendary Gytrack, which we didn't.

Robin Devenish was soon hooked, as was Michael Watkins, and trips to Groombridge station and Harrison's Rocks were frequent. We travelled via Victoria on an ancient steam train we called the Spook Special. Later, when Robin had passed his driving test, he occasionally persuaded his father to lend us his Rover. This was a sedate green monster with lots of wooden interior design. We travelled in style, rolling ponderously down the leafy Sussex lanes. The return, with clapped-out fingers, often needed the help of the passengers to operate the handbrake.

We were, I think, quite imaginative in choices of venue and visited many private crags, including another visit to Chiddingly Wood when, under the protective camouflage of the eminently respectable Rover, we drove straight past the lodge guarding the road into the estate. On these youthful outings Robin and Steve were probably the better performers, but none of us was particularly good.

In March 1989, I celebrated my 30th 'birthday' as a climber. With Steve Durkin I drove down to Sussex and on a wretched, misty, rainy day returned to Chiddingly Wood Rocks. In the new guidebook to south-east England it is now referred to as Chiddinglye Wood, which I found strangely disturbing. We took great delight in being 46-year-old trespassers. In pouring rain we soloed the first route we ever climbed and failed to top rope the one next to it. We walked down the valley to 'Great upon Little', the strange boulder perched on a tiny plinth. In the valley the rhododendrons had been cleared and a primitive show jumping course with huge ugly petrol drums and crude fences had been laid out. There was still no sign of the ghostly canine apparition

Harrison's; top roping. >

Gytrack, but I imagine he must have given up in disgust for there is now nothing much left to haunt. However, the hermit's cave was still the same, and the strange tree roots embedded in the dark recesses that a 16-year-old Mike Watkins had been convinced was a snake. We returned to the car and I was suddenly once more aware of the evocative smell of sandstone and leaf mould. A pity we didn't bring a hemp rope for the day.

We left and drove over to High Rocks Hotel for a nostalgic pint. Then, late in the afternoon, the rain stopped and we went to a dark and sodden Harrison's Rocks. There was just time to top rope a few old classics. Despite the evil, slimy sandstone and at least a 20-year absence, I remembered how to do *Hell Wall* and *Moonlight Arête*. In the dusk, walking back to the car, the years compressed and memories flooded back. "I think we definitely ought to come back for our 50th anniversary, Steve, even if we need wheelchairs and nurses to get us here!"

Well yes, we did go back to Chiddinglye to celebrate our 50th anniversary. Sadly, with a knee replacement, old age and infirmity, but without wheelchairs (but with a climbing friend of ours, Sarah Cullen, who stood in for the nurse), I failed to get up our first route. But to my delight it had proved to be a first ascent and is written up in the new guidebook as 'First Visit 4a 1959 S Durkin, J Curran'.

Back in the spring of 1959 our enthusiasm for climbing took off and visits to Harrison's became increasingly important, particularly as, since leaving St Benedict's I had also left behind cricket and rugby, and life at Davies Laing & Dick was driving me quietly mad.

Over this period I had a new girlfriend, Vivien Harris. She was a cousin of the Olivers and lived in Wallington, near Croydon. We used to meet in the West End, go to see films, kiss in St James' Park and visit each other's homes. She had long dark hair and I fell for her without any of the traumas of Luciana. It was a shock when she dumped me after about six months. I was hurt and bewildered for I hadn't seen it coming (I never do). At least this time there were enough new experiences to keep me occupied.

1959, as ageing climbers will tell you, was fine, sunny and hot. Crags that were normally running with water became snuff dry. In North Wales, the invincibility of Joe Brown and Don Whillans was being challenged for the first time, with several early repeats of their hardest routes. All this was wasted on me for I was sitting O-Levels with the worst attack of hay fever I had ever experienced. In fact, it had been a problem for several years. Although I was told, endlessly, that I would soon grow out of it, June and July were always a misery to be endured with dozens of remedies tried, most of which sort of worked for a year or two before the immunity

< Mike Watkins on Long Layback.

< Mike on Moonlight Arête.

wore off and I was back to square one. Eventually, the attacks did stop, in 2005, when I exchanged hay fever for prostate cancer. It seemed a cruel swap, and needless to say, if given the choice, I would still be sneezing for England for two months every year.

It would be dishonest to say hay fever totally buggered up my O-Levels but I only scraped through French, English Language and Literature and failed Maths by a couple of marks. I re-sat Maths the following autumn and this time failed by a colossal margin, only managing single figures in one paper. I could hardly blame the hay fever for that, but it was a disappointment for Dad, who, like many musicians, had a keen interest in maths. He did give me two bits of advice when solving mathematical problems, which have stuck to the present day: "Is it a sensible answer?" and "Keep your eye on the ball." Both are simple, sound and worth remembering in dealing with most, if not all, of life's little problems.

Now with dreaded Davis Laing & Dick behind me, I was free to do what I had always wanted — to be a world famous painter and start life again at Ealing Art School.

Chapter five: Art School

Here is a good, if trivial, example of false memory syndrome. I was just about to start this chapter by describing how, far from fulfilling all my fantasies of becoming a latter day Van Gogh, I spent the first day at art school drawing a daffodil in the morning and a Roman Letter 'A' in the afternoon. This is a story I have told countless times and how, suitably deflated, I walked home disillusioned after a long and frankly boring day. The lettering bit is, I'm sure, correct, but a daffodil? On September 20th or thereabouts? No. Nevertheless it was a plant of some sort and my group, First Year General A, drew it all morning in complete silence on pieces of quarto imperial cartridge paper with HB pencils.

The afternoon brought my first confrontation with Miss Ockendon, a lady of about 120 with a pronounced moustache. By now I had just about mastered writing, though to this day it slopes the wrong way and is frankly horrible to look at. But western letter forms were created by right-handers and the thicks and thins of Roman lettering arose naturally from pen and ink, hammer and chisel. Left-handers automatically do it the wrong way round. I could see that Miss Ockendon and I would never see eye to eye, particularly when, on that first afternoon, she told us, with evident relish, that though we might have dreams of being successful painters or sculptors, the only guaranteed living was from being a professional letterer. I was delighted to find that she couldn't have been more wrong, as the subsequent inventions of Letraset and then the computer proved. However, despite the reality check, that first day, like the visit to Chiddinglye Wood, changed my life forever. The rest of that week improved with lessons in still life, figure composition, cast drawing, costume (i.e. clothed) life drawing — nude being saved for the second year — architectural drawing, perspective, clay modelling and probably one or two other classes which I have forgotten.

By the late 1950s art schools across the country had evolved, almost by accident, into rather quirky add-ons to further education. Neither fish nor fowl, they were based on some sort of Victorian craft-based ideal and a lot of subject matter, like lettering, reflected this. Following a general first year, there were two exams, Intermediate and the National Diploma in Design (NDD), both taking two years. Fine Art — painting and sculpture and Art History — were lumped into this mix. Many art schools, like Ealing, were part of technical colleges, though some were independent and the odd one, like the Ruskin School at Oxford, were part of a university.

It was normal to attend a local art school or college, and not unusual, as in my case, to start at 16. So, most, if not all, art

49

students lived at home. Post-Diploma studies were largely confined to the Royal College of Art, The Slade, and Royal Academy Schools. Entry to them meant another three years, plus possibly another year doing teacher training. You could spin the whole process out for nine years — longer than it took to be a qualified surgeon! With grants in those days easy to come by, and quite generous unless your parents were filthy rich, 'going to art school' was just about the nearest thing to heaven.

In 1959, it didn't take much to look like an art student, mainly because most other students conformed strictly to the grey flannel trousers, sports jacket and ties, the image epitomised by the film *Lucky Jim*. Art students could, and did, look outrageously Bohemian by simply wearing corduroy jackets, jeans and duffle coats, though winkle-picker shoes à la Kaz were a useful addition. Bohs — short for Bohemians — were the fashion for the first year or two, then Beatniks took over, though the difference between the two was minimal. I'm not even sure that I could tell the difference.

Social behaviour was fairly well-defined: 'in' were modern jazz, French films, pubs, cider, thin ties, black clothes and polo necked sweaters; 'out' were organised sport, organised religion and most, if not all, classical music. As a recently enthusiastic cricketer and rugby player, a practising Catholic and with a father who played the violin at Covent Garden, I had to keep quiet if I wanted to be a fully paid-up Beatnik. Strangely enough when I look back, the most non-conformist thing I did was rock-climbing. This never seemed to figure in either camp as acceptable behaviour or otherwise. Maybe it was because its participants were spread fairly evenly across the student world. In those days it was viewed as quite incomprehensible by most students and almost all adults, unless they did it themselves.

Back to those first weeks. Despite the earlier Saturday morning classes I found it disconcerting to find myself amongst dozens of other students, many of whom were as accomplished as I was. Some seemed to be far better. In particular my drawing, still the bane of my life, remained depressingly average, whereas several girls in my group were, to my eye, far more talented. It wasn't until I started teaching in foundation courses years later, that I realised that many 16 to 18-year-old girls are far more sophisticated than boys of the same age. But it was still a shock and a blow to my pride to find I had a lot of catching up to do.

All this might make it appear that art school was a let down. Far from it. For the first time in my life, education had a purpose, and even though some of the disciplines like architectural drawing were highly technical, I could see the point of doing it, unlike maths. Suddenly my life made sense. Every day was another adventure, and at the end of the first year exams, I came top in my group's assessments in every subject except lettering where I came bottom. Hey, not bad, I thought, but was dismayed to be carted off to the principal's office where an odd little man with a bow tie called Mr Drew bollocked me for my lack of effort. Bloody hell, I thought, what do you have to do to get a bit of praise?

Almost as an afterthought, we all took A-Level Art at the end of the year. Despite arriving halfway through one of the papers, I got a Grade A which, with my meagre O-Levels, would just give me the basic qualifications to do a teaching course. A few years later O-Level Maths was added to the list. So, in all my art college teaching career, I was actually less qualified than most of the students I taught. A fact I never considered worth mentioning.

At the start of the second year we were allowed to do proper life drawing, and also museum studies. The life drawing was invariably a let-down as most of the female models were far from sylphlike. This is not a criticism, by the way — look at Rubens whose models were particularly well-endowed. But to be told by a long suffering tutor where the rib cage or pelvis was, when all that was visible was a generous coating of flesh, made the whole analytical process more like a party game. Our inexperienced eyes had to guess the whereabouts of a bone structure that was completely invisible. Male models were more satisfactory, though much rarer. On occasion, Quentin Crisp modelled for us. His overtly gay appearance was unique in London at the time, but rather lost on me. I was still very naïve.

Most of our tutors in those first two years were well-meaning but dull, and coming to the end of their careers. But for museum studies we had a young artist who positively sparkled with enthusiasm and motivation. His name was Ken Howard. Ken went on to fame and fortune as an eminent Royal Academician and his work is still very popular. During the time we knew him at Ealing he was just a part-time lecturer, but he lit up my life as no teacher ever had done before.

Every Tuesday our group would wend its way up to South Kensington or Holborn and spend the day drawing and painting in one or other of the London museums. My personal favourite was always the Victoria and Albert. With literally thousands of potential objects to choose from I tended to gravitate towards sculptures. The V&A has a huge Cast Room where Greek, Roman and Renaissance masterpieces were faithfully reproduced, even if most of them were decidedly dusty. A life-size plaster cast of Michelangelo's 'David' dominated the room. Once the embarrassment of working in public had been overcome it was a wonderful place to concentrate, in almost complete silence, waiting for the moment when Ken Howard would dart up and give criticism and encouragement.

At the time the V&A cafeteria was shared by the Royal College of Art, and every week David Hockney and friends would sit drinking and smoking and looking famous even if, at the time, they weren't. But we were quite impressed and soon it became my ultimate dream to get into the Royal College.

One morning I approached the museum, half asleep with folder and drawing board under my arm. I was dimly aware that instead of the normal revolving doors, the main entrance was open with a red carpet running up the steps. I walked in and past a group of be-suited officials. Glancing back, I saw I was being followed only a few steps behind by the Queen Mother smiling and waving. Nobody paid me the slightest attention and, suppressing a giggle, I went on my way. Nowadays this little scenario would be news headlines: I would be arrested, security would be reviewed and questions asked in the House. Maybe in those days we all had a rather better sense of proportion.

Ken Howard stretched the term 'museum study' to include painting on London Bridge (I still have the results) and the back streets of Camden Town. Ken was a devout disciple of Walter Sickert and even though the Camden Town school of drab, subdued colours was quite unfashionable, Ken would set us up in the same sort of situation from which his hero painted.

Another place Ken loved was the old railway yards in Neasden. By this time I had become very friendly with a tall, serious boy called Adrian Mallett. Adrian, I thought, could draw miles better than I, and he lived in Neasden. At weekends I would cycle over to his home and we would trespass on the railway sidings (nobody seemed to care) and revelled in the stark geometry of coal hoppers and cooling towers, often half concealed in London fog, with steam and smoke from the old steam engines clanking to and fro.

During the first couple of years at Ealing, my own hero was Paul Cézanne. His lonely struggle to represent his 'sensations' was a story I could easily identify with. Thinking about it now, I wonder whether there were similarities with sporting heroes like Len Hutton or climbers like Menlove Edwards. The idea of a kind of tragic genius wrestling against the odds was far more attractive than the more obvious talents of Impressionists like Claude Monet, whose prolific talents were easy to admire.

Like Cézanne (well, not really) I seemed to paint far more failures than successes, though one still life is still hanging in my bedroom. It features a Chianti bottle (ugh), onions and apples and a carriage clock à la Cézanne, and, rather incongruously, a primus stove, an odd choice of subject matter. It certainly shows off my strengths and weaknesses — good colour, some nice 'painterly' marks, and some frankly dubious drawing skills. Not, I think, a bad effort for a 17-year-old. The fact that it survives at all is more a reflection of how poor most of my other paintings were, though I still have a couple of museum studies that aren't too bad.

Ken Howard continued to impress and cajole me. On one occasion he took me to his parents' house just off the North Circular Road and showed me dozens and dozens of his own paintings, unframed and piled up around his bedroom. If nothing else, he led by example. Hard, obsessive work paid off. However frustrating and discouraging it may seem, you have to put in the hours to become any good at anything, something that students today seem to find hard to accept (here speaks the voice of an intolerant Old Fart).

But, I hear you say, what about climbing? Well, it occupied a sort of parallel universe. Whenever possible we went to Harrison's or one of the outcrops. At that time, before climbing walls and cheap car transport, the sandstone cliffs around Tunbridge Wells, particularly Harrison's, were the main outlet for London-based

^ *Mono verson of early still life.*

^ *Me with my bike under Tryfan on my first visit with Mick Oswald.*

climbers. Because of its nature — short steep and highly technical — top roping was, and still is, the accepted way of climbing. The advantages were that you could climb up to, and beyond, your limits and it was virtually 100 per cent safe. The disadvantages were that it wasn't a good preparation for leading on mountain crags and also that unless you went at least every week it was hard to improve your grade. Nowadays it is accepted that to climb really well you need to do it almost every day, along with additional workouts in the gym. Consequently our improvement was a slow business, and if we didn't go frequently we lost ground, which was depressing. Despite the setting, I was only interested in the climbs, and the thought never crossed my mind that the sandstone landscapes were interesting subject matter for painting. This did happen almost 50

^ Arête and Slab, *Bochlwyd Buttress; my first lead on Welsh rock.*

^ *Robin Devenish on* Dives, *Dinas Cromlech.*

54

^ *Mike and me at the top of Bochlwyd Buttress.*

^ *On Belle Vue Terrace, Tryfan.*

years later, when the penny finally dropped. Quite early on, Steve and I made our first visit to North Wales to climb, though I had been on a cycling holiday years before with Mick Oswald during which time we had failed to climb both Tryfan and Snowdon in driving rain. In order to train for this first visit we decided to walk home after a day at Harrison's — a distance of about 50 miles. I had bought a new pair of heavy leather climbing boots with Vibram soles. We managed about 25 miles in the middle of the night until, in a state of exhaustion and agony of blisters, some angel of mercy took pity on us and gave us an almost miraculous lift home.

In those far off days, hitching was *de rigueur* for nearly everyone, and though neither of us had any experience, we stood, thumbs raised, at the bottom of the M1, which was about 80 miles long and stopped more or less where Watford Gap services now stands. Somehow, many hours later, and in the middle of the night we ended up in Liverpool. As dawn broke, we caught the first ferry across the Mersey to Birkenhead. (Good song title possibly?) Eventually, completely knackered, we ended up in the Ogwen Valley where we climbed my first route in Wales — *Arête and Slab*, a tiny Diff on the equally miniscule Bochlwyd Buttress, high above Llyn Ogwen. Coming from the steep fingery sandstone climbs, I found that climbing in boots on huge holds demanded a very different technique. This, combined with the psychological problem of leading for the first time, made those early routes very frightening.

In retrospect, doing all our early climbing by ourselves made us over-cautious. What might have happened if we had had an older, more experienced mentor is open to question. In those days unless you were a member of a university climbing club, or came from one of the northern cities where local clubs were long established, the chances were that you started like we did, on your own. Indeed, the only local club we had heard of at the time was the Sandstone Club, an elitist group of very high performing climbers that none of us had any chance of joining.

However enthusiastic I was, and

^ *The author on* Scrambler's Gate, *Clogwyn y Grochan.*

55

however fulfilling the weekend, it was back to college on Monday morning. This was sometimes harder than it seemed. When we hitched back from North Wales we frequently had Sunday night epics, arriving home in the small hours or even later. On one winter trip to Ben Nevis I managed to get a lift in the middle of the night from Scotch Corner to the North Circular on the back of a lorry. It was bitterly cold and I was dropped off in time to catch the first 112 bus to Ealing Broadway. I got home at about 7.30 am and, despite a hot bath, I spent most of the day shivering under the bedclothes, quite unable to warm up. Nowadays it would be called hypothermia. Then we just thought it was bloody cold.

Towards the end of the first year I had started going out with a fellow student, Liz Hawkins. In many ways it was the most fulfilling relationship of my teenage years. We were both incredibly serious about the course, and about each other. There was only one enormous problem (apart from sex). She was brought up in a strict Baptist family and I was Catholic. Her father ran a chemist shop and the local Boys' Brigade. As a Catholic, I represented, in his eyes, just about the worst choice Liz could have possibly made, though he was unfailingly polite and friendly towards me. I was, initially, quite bewildered at the sudden manifestation of religious prejudice, particularly as Liz could, and did, quote the Bible chapter and verse, whereas my own faith, or lack of it, had never been seriously questioned, and now I was having to defend it when I was far more interested in having sex.

It certainly put a strain on our relationship and arguments about Catholic dogma were frequent. At the time, I wasn't just acting out my role as a reincarnation of Cézanne. I also fancied myself as a latter day Michelangelo, and for months the Hawkins garage was knee deep in stone carving debris. Liz's mother was far more understanding, and often fed me, sitting at their table, white with stone dust, and waxing eloquent about Rodin's sculpture and Michelangelo's Slaves. I am sure I was a pompous little prig in those days and I blush to remember how dogmatic and ill-founded many of my opinions were. (I can hear a massed chorus of "no change there, then" as I write these words apart, of course, from 'little'.)

The highlight of our relationship was when we managed to persuade our respective parents that we should go for a three-week camping holiday in France, together with Adrian and Liz's friend Anne. Eventually they relented and we had two idyllic weeks in Brittany and then caught a train to Paris where we stayed in a run-down hostel on the Rue de Vaugirard next to the Luxembourg Gardens. I shared a room with a gaunt, hollow-cheeked young man who I thought must have been seriously ill, for he frequently injected himself with some sort of medicine that rendered him comatose. As I say, I was still incredibly naïve.

We spent most of our time in the Louvre, or the Jeu de Pommes, revelling in the Impressionists, and in my case, being blown away by Monet's colossal 'Waterlilies' which completely surrounded the spectator in the specially built oval-shaped galleries. We returned to England without fulfilling our parents' worst fears (or my fervent hopes) and things returned to normal. But the combination of religious tension and sexual frustration continued to the inevitable point where we split up and, apart from a couple of minor encounters, I spent the rest of my time at college irritatingly single. Liz, I'm pleased to say, got married but has stayed in touch to the present day.

Towards the end of the intermediate course it became obvious that change was afoot in and out of college. New staff were being appointed and quite suddenly the old order was changing. Rhythm 'n' blues was the new rock and roll and I was aware of a tall, serious looking lad in the year below us, with an extraordinary long nose, strumming his guitar in the common room. His name was Pete Townshend. We started going to Eel Pie Island at the weekends when trad jazz was giving way to the new sounds. Eel Pie Island in the Thames was a wonderful place. Originally, a Victorian hotel and ballroom had been built on this tiny island linked by a footbridge to Twickenham, more famous then, as now, for its rugby stadium than avant-garde music. The near-derelict building featured a sprung dance floor, now so ancient that standing in the middle of a crowd you bounced up and down without any effort, creating the illusion of helpless drunkenness or severe seasickness. Not that you needed an illusion, for everyone seemed to get paralytic every weekend, if not on alcohol then possibly something worse, though serious drug-taking was still a few years away.

Great evenings those, and we 'went down the Island' most weekends until we left college. I recall standing below the stage watching a group with a skinny lead singer and harmonica player. The group was called The Rolling Stones. A few weeks later, crossing the road outside the art school, I was nearly run over by a speeding, aged van and had a fleeting glimpse of the driver laughing as he swerved to avoid me. It was the nearest I ever got to an introduction to Mick Jagger.

When I was much younger Dad had built me a crystal set, the simplest form of radio that, before the invention of the transistor. I listened with old-fashioned army headphones, to the The Goon Show, Take it From Here and latterly to Radio Luxembourg, the only station devoted entirely to pop music. My set was mounted above my bed — now in the attic. One night in the autumn of

57

1962 I listened, amidst the fades and atmospheric interference that plagued the station, to a song that I assumed was a new one by the Everley Brothers, with its jangly guitar and close harmony. But it also had a plaintive harmonica refrain, which did not sound quite like the Everleys. When it finished the DJ said it was called 'Love Me Do' by a new British group called The Beatles.

Once we had all more or less strolled through the hurdle of the intermediate exams we could at last specialise. It was hard to tell whether opting for Fine Art was more gratifying than the relief of ditching many of the other subjects to which I still had to pay lip service. Moving into the large painting studios, and realising that another option, printmaking, was available was exciting, as well as the prospect of being taught by first-rate teachers. Bill Brooker was Head of Painting. He was a short stocky man with receding hair. He smoked Gauloises and drank Glenfiddich malt whisky. He was very much part of the London art scene at the time and exhibited at Tooth's Gallery. His paintings of spare, refined still lives owed a lot to the Italian artist Morandi and to William Coldstream, who still represented the old academic tradition with carefully measured life paintings. We thought that Coldstream's work was old-fashioned and rather sterile, yet his influence, particularly in life drawing, was considerable.

Brooker was a genuine educator and assembled a set of part-time tutors around him that now read like pages of artists' Who's Who. Names like Bernard and Harold Cohen, Ron Kitaj, Peter Startup, Derek Hirst, Brian Wall and Brian Perrin (Head of Printmaking). We also had visits from established artists like Terry Frost, and William Scott whose one enigmatic comment to me I have never forgotten. I was engrossed in a large painting and he stood behind me for ages. By this time traditional kidney-shaped wooden palettes were seen as the mark of the amateur painter and I, like everyone else in the studio, used a large piece of glass, painted white on the underside, on top of a table with the rest of my brushes and paints. At last he broke the silence: "It's hard to know what to do with your other hand when you don't use a palette." Thanks, William.

Without doubt the man who most influenced me at art college and beyond was Bernard Cohen. Bernard was a short, tubby man with dark curly hair. Like Ken, he radiated enthusiasm and an almost missionary zeal for his philosophy of creativity. In the first three years virtually all our work had been skill-based. True, subjects like architectural drawing and perspective demanded intellectual appreciation, but it was all directed at acquiring knowledge that already existed. Bernard, in his very first life class, sent all those preconceptions out of the window. He made

^ Steve and Adrian on the top of The Cioch, Skye.

us question everything. What is a line? Why are you trying to create an illusion of space on a two-dimensional surface? How do you use colour to enhance form? Can you make an illusion of movement? I can honestly say he made my brain ache, and I was not alone. Liz found Bernard an inspiration, both then and later in her teaching career. Recently she likened much of his teaching to a cross between a drama workshop and a psychology seminar: "We spent a day acting out one word self-descriptions, and then exchanged with another in the group and took on their persona. We shared paintings, passing our incomplete work to a partner and in turn continuing theirs. Bernard had the knack of disturbing and questioning all our previously learned and complacent habits which was both exciting and invaluable."

In 2011 this doesn't sound quite as earth-shattering as it did in 1962. But that was just the beginning. Next September would bring more change.

In the summer holidays between the Intermediate exam and the start of the National Diploma in Design course Robin, Mike, Adrian, Steve and I hired a car and drove to Skye. For some reason it still remains my only visit and we were frankly disappointed. The weather was poor and we only managed a few of the classics, and suffered an ignominious defeat on the *Crack of Doom*. The Tolkeinesque name appealed to us, but somehow we lacked the commitment to climb it. Sadly, when the weather did change, we and the other climbers at Glen Brittle spent most of it searching for a hill-walker who had disappeared somewhere on the southern end of the Cuillin Ridge. We never found him and his body was discovered weeks later in Coire Ghrunnda which we had, we thought, searched thoroughly soon after his disappearance. It was the second time I had to face death in the mountains, however distant, and it brought home to me just how dangerous they could be. The first had been headline news earlier that summer when a young climber, Barry Brewster, was killed on the North Face of the Eiger. The rescue of his partner, Brian Nally, by Chris Bonington and Don Whillans received huge media attention and generated some controversy at the time, but the death of Barry hit home. He had been an exceptional performer at Harrison's — Steve had got to know him quite well — before he had gone to Bangor University where he had started to make a name for himself by leading hard routes in nailed boots as training for the Alps. Though I scarcely knew him, the death of someone I had met, who was only a year or two older than I, upset me more than I cared to admit at the time. I returned from Skye chastened.

Life at home around this time was notable for two things. Almost since he could walk, I had taken it upon myself to indoctrinate Phil into the skills of cricket. Hours of practice in the back garden using a stump and golf ball (I had read somewhere that the great Don Bradman had used these to refine his technique) made Phil a far better player than I ever was. At St Benedict's he later got into the First Eleven at only 16 and I think still holds the record for the number of wickets taken. Phil and I took our cricket seriously and to this day it remains the main topic of conversation between us.

The other perennial subject, and one that caused a huge rift between Mum and me, was one that was repeated in almost every middle-class family in the land. Long Hair. For any male reader who, like me, is in his mid to late 60s, the following paragraph will be familiar territory.

Ever since the rise of Elvis, long hair in men had, above all else, become the symbol of youthful rebellion, if not downright decadence. Until my third year at art school I had dutifully had my hair cut 'short back and sides'. Now that I could shave and grow sideburns, I wanted, quite reasonably I thought, longer hair. Words cannot begin to explain how much Mum detested it. Arguments were frequent and futile. Even now I can get quite irritated by the memory of her intransigence. I thought she was wrong then, and I think she was unwise now. By making such an issue over something I saw as a matter of principle, she nearly undermined our relationship completely. Neither of us ever won the battle until I left home, though there was one funny postscript. Years later, when about to act in my own film *A Great Effort*, I forced myself to have what by then were almost shoulder-length locks cut back to the dreaded short back and sides. When I first saw Mum after the deed was done she said: "You know I think I prefer you with your hair a bit longer." I could hardly believe my (exposed) ears and dug out a photo of me at the time of most controversy. "Do you realise, Mum, that my hair is still longer now than it was when you said it was too long?" Mothers. You can never win.

Chapter six: Art School Part Two

In an interview in *The Times* in 2009 Pete Townshend opined that it was the lecturers at Ealing that were directly influential in the creation and philosophy of The Who, one of the three or four greatest rock bands of the 1960s and beyond. His words were quoted verbatim in the Pseud's Corner column of *Private Eye*. Pete's words didn't seem to me anymore than the truth, and were not particularly funny. But they do require more explanation.

When I started the NDD course in September 1962, the changes that had already started above us became even more radical below. The Intermediate exam was being swept away and replaced by something called the Groundcourse. This was created by a young lecturer called Roy Ascott, who seemed determined to kick over all the traces of the past. Buzzwords like 'cybernetics' and 'auto-destructive art' became current parlance, and Ealing quickly (and, sadly, briefly) established itself as the most exciting and dynamic college in the country.

Our year escaped the full onslaught of the revolution, but we saw it at first-hand. I think that in a way we got the best of both worlds. Ascott and his fellow lecturer, Gustav Metzer, were brilliant at questioning pre-conceived ideas, but I always thought that they never thought through what they wanted to put in their place. It was, I think, the beginning of a crisis of confidence in art education that has never been resolved.

Before I get back to my own time at Ealing there is no doubt at all that with or without cybernetics, the college was a breeding ground for more than its fair share of musicians, of which Pete Townshend wasn't even the most famous. Freddie Mercury has to take that honour. Ealing also produced Ronnie Wood, of The Faces, and later of Rolling Stones fame, and Roger Ruskin Spear of Bonzo Dog Doo Dah Band. If there are more I apologise for not knowing them. Not far removed, though, was the pop poster guru Michael English, who later achieved fame with his psychedelic images which were almost as well-known as the musicians he promoted, notably Pink Floyd, Cream and Jimi Hendrix. Michael died in 2009. Like Pete Townshend I never knew him well, but when their names were in the news I gleaned vicarious pleasure at their fame and fortune (as well as the odd pang of jealousy).

By the time we started the NDD course, I had become firm friends with Adrian and Dave Price. Dave was easily the most talented in the year, a natural draughtsman and a painter with a fluid grace and finesse. His problem was that he was moody and insecure, often abandoning what seemed to be perfectly good paintings. When he was on form he seemed to work on a different plane from the rest of us, but he was prone to self-doubt.

Adrian and I both suffered as well, Adrian far more than I recognised at the time. His father, an ex-RAF pilot, had little sympathy for his chosen career and undermined Adrian's confidence in a way that now seems quite shocking. And I seemed to suffer irrational mood swings that much later developed into major bouts of depression, though I was unaware of the warning signs.

Which is not to say that for most of the time we were anything other than enthusiastic, competitive and very committed. I hardly ever left the studio until chucking out time at nine and then it was straight over to The Castle or New Inn to discuss and argue about art. Is this the hindsight and failing memory of old age, or did we really spend so much time talking about art? I think we did and the same was still true 10 years later for students at Bristol. But since then students became progressively more inward looking and by the time I left Bristol in 1993 the college was invariably deserted by six in the evening. I'm not saying there weren't good students, or that we were better, but the overt enthusiasm we displayed seems to have evaporated.

It was one of those late evenings in November. I was kneeling on the studio floor, stretching a new canvas when one of the porters burst in: "President Kennedy is dead!" I walked home in a state of shock and disbelief. Mum had heard the news and Dad, when he got back from Covent Garden, said that it had been announced to the audience. I went to bed early to hide my tears and cried myself to sleep. Never had I been so affected by the death of a public figure.

Apart from the intellectual battles with Bernard Cohen (I once resorted to writing to him and later received a note from his wife saying she knew how I felt!), the other major revelation of the year was the etching studio. Under the guidance of Brian Perrin, and the technical assistance of Maurice Payne (who later became David Hockney's assistant) I took to etching in a big way.

Unlike silkscreen and lithography, which essentially use flat planes of colour, etching is a form of low-relief sculpture and the plate itself is an object in its own right. I became so absorbed in printmaking that, apart from a few life paintings, I produced little else in that year. Etching, with the richness of textures, lends itself to landscape imagery and my subject matter reflected that. One large print was based on gnarled tree roots at Harrison's Rocks, another on wrecked tanks on a firing range near Aldershot, and a third was taken from a drawing I made of Dinas y Gromlech in North Wales. These last two were as near as I got to using any sort of mountain imagery in my work, and I am still pondering why.

Weekends carried on much as before with trips to Harrison's

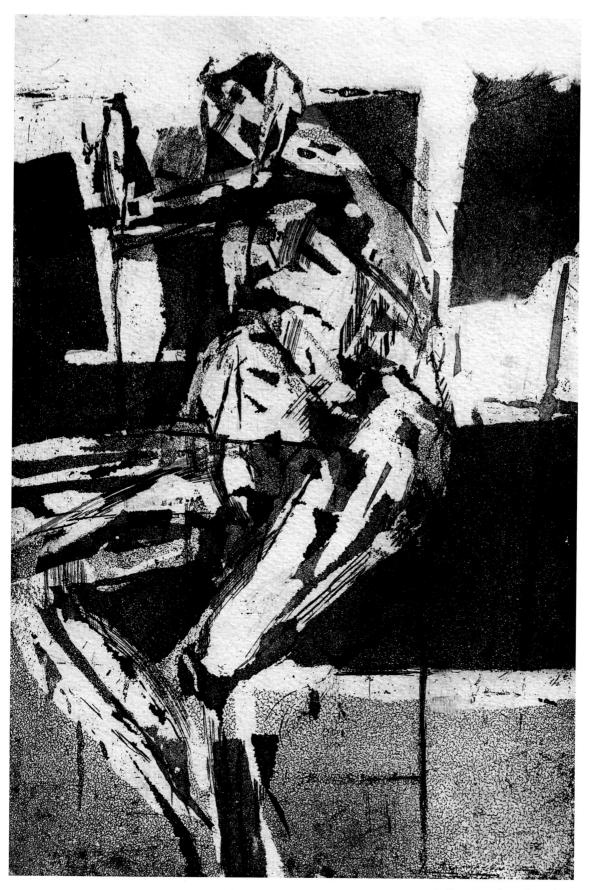

^ *Seated male nude, etching.*

^ *Tree roots at Harrison's, etching.*

alternating with hitching up to North Wales. By this time we had risen to the not very great heights of leading Very Severes, and now camped in the Llanberis Pass by the Gromlech Boulders, where the local farmer would collect his nominal fee for providing no more than a few square feet of boggy ground to camp on.

The winter of 1962-3 was a really cold one and during the Easter holiday I made my first trip to Ben Nevis with Mike Watkins. Hitching up the M1 we saw real cornices overhanging the deep drifts on the verges, but by the time we got to Fort William there was no snow at all. The locals said there had hardly been any in the town but that the Ben itself was plastered and potentially very dangerous. We only managed to climb one easy gully and Castle Ridge, the easiest of the great Nevis ridges. When we got to the summit plateau we had a wonderful walk around the ridge to the Carn Mor Dearg Arête, culminating in a glorious sitting glissade all the way back to the CIC Hut, where we were illegally based. It was on that occasion that I had the very grim lift from Scotch Corner. Overall we had enjoyed our first real experience of snow and ice, and planned a more ambitious summer.

The cold winter had also given me a very odd experience. Every evening I used to take our dog Nick for a walk. Late on one bitterly cold January night I was walking the dog around the edge

^ *Wrecked tanks near Aldershot, etching.*

of Walpole Park. Nick, as usual, was off the lead. As I walked past a terrace of big Victorian houses I heard a baby crying. For some reason I stopped and listened. The crying seemed to come from the open air. Surely nobody would be outside with a baby at this hour of the night? More out of curiosity than anything else, I walked up the path through a rundown garden and there, in the shadows of the porch was a tiny baby, wrapped in a piece of cloth. Horrified, I started banging on the door. Eventually lights came on and a young lady in a nightie opened the door. Unable to think of what to say I eventually stammered: "Should this be here?" Other girls, similarly clad emerged and I realised that it was a nurse's hostel. The hospital (where I had my appendix out) was just around the corner. Gently they carried the baby in. It was quite blue with cold. Naturally, they were panic-stricken and dialled 999. I seemed to be getting in the way, so I left my name and address and walked off to find the dog looking puzzled at my absence. I can't honestly remember telling my parents when I got home, and by the time I got to college the next morning I had almost forgotten it. When I got home that evening I found a reporter from *The Evening Standard* waiting. I told my story and they took my photo looking embarrassed with the dog sitting at my side. Next evening I found that we made the bottom of the front page — or rather Nick had,

65

below the headline 'Dog Finds Baby'. No sign of me at all.

Back at college, two people I haven't mentioned so far were Derek Hirst and Juliet Yardley Mills — JYM to all who knew her. JYM was our more or less permanent model throughout NDD. She had modelled for Frank Auerbach since the 1950s and was far and away the best model we ever had, so much so that I could make a reasonably accurate memory drawing of her even now. She had strong features — a rather beaky nose, and deep-set eyes and a strong jaw. She must have been very beautiful when she was young. She looked slightly top heavy, with big breasts, slim hips, thin legs and tiny ankles. She took her work very seriously and was totally involved in our own development. On one occasion she invited Adrian, Dave and me for tea in her flat in South London. Here amongst her clutter of possessions — postcards, catalogues, books and drawings — we began to realise her utter devotion to Auerbach who was clearly the most important man in her life.

Derek Hirst was originally from Doncaster with the swarthy good looks that are quite common in Yorkshire but which gave him a Mediterranean aura, enhanced by his love of Spain and all things Spanish. He and Bill Brooker were both obsessed with bullfighting and his work at the time was based around Spanish doorways: dark, low relief and rather oppressive. They were quite puzzling and I was never sure if they were any good or not. Derek was a good teacher (though it was always easy to get him to talk about himself — probably where I get it from) and, like Bill Brooker and Bernard Cohen, he was prepared to break boundaries and became a friend. Both he, Bill and Bernard had one-man shows in prime galleries in the West End. Bernard was with the Kasmin Gallery. At the time the number one trendy venue in Bond Street, Kasmin showed David Hockney, Howard Hodgkin, Richard Smith and Gillian Ayres, as well as important American artists like Kenneth Noland, Frank Stella, Morris Louis and Helen Frankenthaler. Almost every month there was something new and important to see there and it was during this time that I found out something about myself that I really didn't like.

Without actually being a plagiarist, I was very easily influenced by anything new, and I had the painterly knack of picking up mannerisms very quickly. I vividly recall Bill Brooker, arm around my shoulders, walking me up and down the corridor outside the studio, suggesting in all seriousness that I should stop going round the galleries. I took his advice with a pinch of salt, and a little bit of me was amused that Bill, who was almost a walking amalgam of Morandi and Coldstream, could talk to me like that without embarrassment. Later, of course, I realised that the easiest things to spot in a student are your own weaknesses. I think I actually carried

66

out his advice for a month or two, but temptation was always there. One thing that has stuck from Ealing is in condemning work as 'slick'. I think that then our antennae were quite highly tuned to spot easy evasions. Ever since, I still react to any work that I find superficial with the old comment — "bit slick, isn't it?"

Amongst the upheavals surrounding us at Ealing was the introduction of Liberal Studies. As some of the options were both mandatory and sometimes far from studious (trampolining, archery?) it always seemed a curious title. It evolved over the years to Related Studies which suffered the same anomalies. But one option stands out. We had seminars with a genuine Austrian psychiatrist called Anton Ehrenzweig. His probing questions about the nature of both our work and us was quite uncomfortable at times. I'm afraid a lot of it went over my head and I regret not taking him as seriously as I should have. Many years later I noticed inside my copy of *Nanga Parbat Pilgrimage* that one of its co-translators from the German had been one Anton Ehrenzweig. The book deals with the controversial solo first ascent of the mountain by the legendary Hermann Buhl. Ever since, there have been bitter controversies surrounding the ascent. I would have been intrigued by Ehrenzweig's take on the subject and I wondered whether he did the translation just as a job, or whether he did have a real interest in mountaineering.

The other interesting visitor was a young historian from the Courtauld Institute whose name I have completely forgotten. He bombarded us with facts and figures from the Renaissance onwards. At this time I think most of us found his erudition a bit of a pain, but years later, when I taught A-Level Art History, I was surprised at how much of his knowledge had stuck somewhere in the recesses of my brain, along with Uncle Harold's cultured excursions years before. I am truly grateful for having an, admittedly sketchy, appreciation of art history.

As the summer term drew to a close thoughts turned towards an ambitious climbing holiday (good). To pay for it I would need a holiday job (bad). The previous year Adrian and I had spent a month at the Showerings depot in Greenford. This involved unloading cider lorries up from Somerset and was gruelling manual labour, though quite well paid and we were also able to drink vast quantities of cider — a drink I have loathed ever since. There were no vacancies this year and the only work I could find was in the local Parks Department, actually quite an enjoyable job but not so much cash in hand. It was basically simple gardening, though doing the same job the following year I graduated to a motor mower, which was even easier and a lot more fun. Even so, time passed slowly and only the thought of the climbing to come kept me going.

Chapter seven: A Few Ladders and a Big Snake

Robin Devenish was now at Cambridge studying Pure Maths and it was he who planned our summer holidays. Mike Watkins was at Oxford reading Spanish which, as we planned to go to the Pyrenees, could be rather more useful than either Robin's equations or my knowledge of aquatint.

Why the Pyrenees? Like my first visit to Chiddinglye rather than Harrison's, it was born out of caution. We thought that the Pyrenees were lower, with hardly any glaciers, and had a lot of medium grade rock-climbing. Robin was going on a mountaineering course in Austria first. He would meet up with us in Tarbes, a town just north of the Central Pyrenees. He would presumably be armed with an array of new techniques and be outrageously fit. I can't remember much of the former, but the latter was horribly in evidence from the very first day as he easily outpaced us on every uphill plod, which were many.

Our first objective was the Vignemale, at 3298 metres the highest French peak in the Pyrenees. For reasons that seemed a good idea at the time, we decided to camp high, just below the jagged ridge that culminates in the summit of the Vignemale. This we wanted to climb by the Arête de Gaubes. It involved a long descent to the valley at the foot of the imposing North Face, then an interminable

^ *Vignemale, climbed by the right-hand skyline. The North Face of the Petite Vignemale is out of sight.*

68

^ *Looking down on Mike on the first pitch of the North Face of the Petit Vignemale.*

slog up to the ridge leading eventually to the summit pyramid. The ridge was simple scrambling, but on a clear hot day I was too tired to take it in properly. We roped up for the last few pitches and I stood on my first real summit with fabulous views in every direction. The only advantage of our high camp meant that the descent around the edge of the Vignemale Glacier was mercifully short.

We later found out the story of an Irish eccentric, Count Henry Russell, who in the late 19th century became obsessed with the Vignemale. He climbed it no less than 33 times, and even dynamited a cave just below the summit so that he could spend more time on his precious mountain.

When we recovered we set our sights on the North Face of the Petit Vignemale. This was a shorter but harder proposition. At 3032 metres the summit was within a stone's throw of our tents, but we still had to make the same long descent to the foot of the climb. The crux was the first pitch — a steep limestone wall. In those days we knew nothing of nut runners and we carried only a few slings to drape over spikes to give some protection. I wanted to atone for my miserable performance earlier and led off.

It seemed to me to be long, steep and terrifyingly without any protection at all. Doubtless today with an array of modern gear it would seem easy, but then, with the rope trailing uselessly behind, I felt more scared than I had ever been before. At last, dry-mouthed with fright, I reached a stance and with huge relief banged in a piton. Mike and Robin, with the security of a top rope, found the pitch easy, which depressed me.

After that the rest of the climb seemed quite straightforward and I even managed to enjoy myself. It still took most of the day to climb, but with the knowledge that food and drink were only minutes from the top I felt a lot less stress. This time the wisdom of our high camp had paid off.

Next day, following Robin's master plan, we packed up and walked to Gavarnie, some 10 miles away and mostly downhill. Gavarnie is the most popular resort on the French side of the Pyrenees, set below the magnificent Cirque de Gavarnie, a natural amphitheatre of tiered limestone walls bedecked with spectacular waterfalls. In winter they now provide high standard ice climbs — some of the best in Europe. In the summer they are a famous beauty spot and the main reason for Gavarnie's popularity. Of the village I remember two things above all else — donkeys, and their excrement. Every day trains of the animals would carry tourists to the base of the waterfalls and the whole place smelled of donkey shit. Treading in it was inevitable.

We managed to stay in an old barn on the edge of town and it was there I suffered a James Bond moment. Awaking in the middle of the night in a hot sleeping bag I felt, then saw, by moonlight streaming through the open barn door, a truly enormous spider crawling up my chest. With a yell of terror I brushed it off and dived into the bag, only to shoot out a minute later, fearing I had swept it into, not out of, the bag. Robin and Mike, rudely awoken, were unsympathetic.

Our next venture was to trek over and out of the Cirque, into Spain and do a couple of routes on the southern side of the range. To get there meant walking through the famous Brèche de Roland, an imposing gap like a pulled tooth in the highest terrace. It is named after Count Roland, who with his sword Durendal, smote a mighty blow to create the gap. A likely story and one that is also told about the gap on the Puig Campana, the great landmark peak near Benidorm. Obviously Roland was either a bit handy with Durendal, or had some good PR working for him. As we walked through the gap, 100-metre walls reared up like the bows of two battleships about to collide. Our first steps into Spain provided an amazing contrast. The French landscape is very similar to any Alpine valley, green, wooded with lush grass and vegetation. The Spanish side is dry, bleak and imposing with the Ordesa Gorge far below looking like a miniature version of the Grand Canyon. Not far from the Brèche is a cave entrance. The floor of it was solid ice, the size of a ballroom and at the rear it disappeared down into the darkness. Definitely cavers' territory.

^ *Robin wiping his perenially runny nose near the summit of Mont Perdu.*

We stayed in a small hut on the Spanish side, where Mike was disgusted to find that nobody understood his Spanish. Not that it mattered — English climbers in those days were a rarity and we were made very welcome. I remember a bottle of Spanish red wine that I thought was the most wonderful I had ever tasted. Recent experiences with similar vin ordinaires around Alicante where it is bought by the bucket load are equally delicious — but only in Spain. Bring a bottle home and it is almost undrinkable.

We spent two days there, first climbing Mount Perdu (or Monte Perdido), at 3355 metres the third highest mountain in the Pyrenees. This was basically a long plod up scree to a cold, cloud-enshrouded summit to earn a tick for effort, but no view. The

^ *Robin on a new route on the Spanish side.*

following day we climbed what was almost certainly a new route on a limestone tor, with curious weather-worn flutings giving most of the interest. Satisfied, we returned to Gavarnie for our last and most ambitious climb.

After a day's rest (and conscientiously trooping off to Mass in the village church on Sunday), we set off at dawn to attempt to climb all three tiers of the Cirque, which would bring us out on the Spanish side again, and a long walk back to the Brèche de Roland.

The climbing on the first tier was more notable for dodging the waterfalls than for the climbing. Between the tiers were the inevitable ghastly scree slopes. Next came a huge corner rather like a large version of *Cenotaph Corner* in Wales, but very much easier. By the time we climbed it, followed by yet another long scree plod, I was knackered and trailing behind. On the third tier Robin persisted in knocking stones down on me and I cursed him as eloquently as I knew how. At the top the light was fading fast and we still had to traverse around and through the Brèche before the descent to Gavarnie.

Possibly because we were brought up on black and white war films, often featuring the French Resistance, we had half-convinced ourselves that at night the Brèche would be protected by border guards and we had no passports with us. We crept up and slipped through the great gap for the last time, imagining bullets through our backs, but of course it was deserted. An hour later with no head torches and in pitch darkness we lost the path and were stumbling around tripping over boulders. I was on my last legs and eventually even Robin was persuaded that we could kill ourselves if we pressed on. So, only about an hour above Gavarnie, we sat down for our first experience of an Alpine bivouac. It was not enjoyable. The night lasted forever. It was cold and we were

^ *Gavarnie, Robin stares at the wall.*

Robin and me between the second and third tiers. >

71

^ *Looking down at Mike on the second tier of the Cirque du Gavarnie.*

desperately thirsty. A few minutes of fitful dozing were all we could manage. The rest of the time we moaned at each other about anything we could think of. When, eventually the grey light of dawn seeped, oh so slowly, into our befuddled consciousness, we found we were only a few metres from the path. An hour later we were frying eggs and drinking tea as fast as we could brew it.

I made a futile attempt, with Mike, to hitch home across France. This petered out at a crossroads outside Montpellier and necessitated a long, expensive train ride. That was the end of our first foreign climbing holiday. In retrospect I am glad we chose the Pyrenees, for it forced us to be self-reliant and increase our mountain judgement. Had we known that it was quite such a remote and sparsely populated area (I can't remember ever seeing

Robin Devenish high on the Cirque du Gavarnie. >

another climber), we might have settled for a more popular venue. But nearly all the memories were happy ones and, despite being constantly irritated by the ever-present drips on the end of Robin's nose, and the sight of his calves and ankles receding into the distance, our friendship remained intact. All too soon it was back to college for my final year. Hanging over us was the realisation that, whatever else happened, this time next year we would be Somewhere Else. For Dave Price, Adrian Mallett and me, we fervently hoped that Somewhere Else would be the Royal College of Art, and most of our work now began to be directed at what we hoped would be a winning application to South Kensington Paradise.

The Christmas term had hardly got underway when rumours abounded of a Very Important Visitor. I was amazed one morning, when Bill Brooker briefly metamorphosed into my mum, and told me to go and get my hair cut. Baffled, I did so, and on my return Bill told me that Anthony Armstrong-Jones, Lord Snowdon, was coming to take photos. At the time Snowdon was married to Princess Margaret and had already made a name for himself as a still photographer. Why us we wondered? When he arrived, accompanied by two large wary-looking blokes, who were obviously bodyguards or detectives, Bill introduced me and asked me to show him around and explain what we were doing. This was actually another of Bernard's projects. My faltering explanation of a rambling assemblage on the floor, built almost entirely by Adrian, was met with blank incomprehension. (That makes two of us, I thought.) I was surprised and rather reluctantly impressed by Snowdon who quickly bashed off a couple of rolls of film and, given his lameness caused by childhood polio, showed surprising agility by climbing onto the high window sills to get unusual viewpoints. His minders looked worried. By the time we had registered his presence he had gone.

The photos were for a lavish art book called *Private View*, an all-embracing look at the British art scene of the 1960s. We were included as a small monochrome photo showing Liz, Dave and me peering at the construction, but not Adrian who was justifiably miffed. Shades of Nick in the Abandoned Baby story.

The book itself is now a collector's item. Today it looks very dated, and not a little pretentious. The most interesting part is the contrast between those young 60s artists who have stayed the course, and not a few who have vanished without trace. David Hockney, Howard Hodgkin, Richard Smith, Peter Blake and the Cohen brothers all went on to fame and fortune but others, who it would be unfair to mention, did not. Looking at some of their work, it isn't hard to see why.

73

By now, in the autumn of 1963, Pop Art was in full swing, as were The Beatles and The Rolling Stones. My daughters, Gemma and Becky, have both expressed amazement and some envy that I was around at what is now known as the 'Swinging Sixties'. Yes, it was exciting but it was also, to us, quite normal. We were not really a part of the London scene, except for the fact of being there, and, in any case, what is now labelled the 'Swinging Sixties' really refers to the last three or four years of the decade and the first few years of the 70s when the full impact of Flower Power, Psychedelia, Pop and Op Art percolated down to the mass of British youth. Anyone who doubts this should look at the photos in Snowdon's book. Most of the students look to our eyes like throwbacks to the 1930s. Even a photo of Roy Ascott's revolutionary 'groundcourse' shows a group of male students wearing collars and ties, and the girls looking as though they were on a secretarial course.

During the last year at Ealing a new visitor burst into our lives. Larry Rivers was a New York painter and sometime modern jazz virtuoso with quite extraordinary talent. It wasn't easy to fit him into any category, though he influenced Pop Art both here and in the States. He had prodigious drawing skills and the ability to bring together all kinds of disparate images with effortless virtuosity. He spent a couple of weeks with us. He was not just a breath, more a gale, of fresh air. As a finale, he addressed the whole of the art school. His opening remarks went something like: "So you want to be an artist? Get yourself an attic – you do have an attic? Take a large canvas, and paint it. Paint it green if you like – do you like it? If you do, then the painting is finished."

It was all too much for Miss Ockendon, who in an embarrassed silence, stood up and denounced him for his decadence. She stalked out of the lecture theatre amongst some sniggering and booing. For the first time I did feel a bit sorry for her, she simply couldn't recognise Rivers's ability, which actually included the use of letter forms in his paintings. Larry Rivers had a one-man show at the Gimpel Fils Gallery before he went home. I was hugely impressed at the ease and fluidity of his work, and doubtless was influenced by him in precisely the way that Bill Brooker had warned me against.

Rivers's whole career was nothing if not eclectic, and because of this he was hard to pin down, which meant he probably didn't get the recognition he deserved. He died in 2002 aged 89, still producing his complex, vibrant pictures.

A tiny taste of fame came with the 1963 Young Contemporaries exhibition. This was seen as a big deal in the early 60s: an open exhibition entirely for students. The previous year or two had been dominated by Hockney, Blake and the Pop Artists from the Royal

74

College. This year they were all ineligible, and there were no big names to compete with. I was delighted to have a large painting of JYM accepted. It was a stark black and white image that, in the studio, was quite striking. In the YC Gallery off Piccadilly, it had shrunk to the size of a postage stamp. At the opening I bumped into Bernard Cohen who said: "Looks good there, doesn't it?" I was astonished at his comment. In the last resort all his intellectual theorising went out of the window and the painting was just a bit of good taste. At least he didn't think it was slick.

Art school and climbing were totally separate activities. At Ealing they did come together once on what must rank as the most stupid, irresponsible and dangerous escapade of my youth — if not my whole life. The art school took up the top two floors of the typical 50s building that was Ealing Technical College. (Now, incredibly it has managed to be promoted to a University, but that's another matter.) The two sides of the building had two right-angled inset corners. In a desperate attempt to add a bit of architectural interest, the brickwork was recessed about half an inch on alternate courses. At the time, frequent weekends at Harrison's had given me as much finger strength as I was ever likely to possess. I also weighed about half as much as I do today. In the era before climbing walls, I sometimes climbed up and down the first few feet of the brickwork, probably more to show off than get any stronger. A fellow student, Keith Pearson, bet me I couldn't climb the whole thing — about 60 feet to the flat roof of the building. I accepted the bet, which was only a couple of pints of beer, and made sure I could do it by calculating the number of identical moves I needed to make and doing a bit of training to be certain that I was strong enough. One quiet evening, watched by Keith and Adrian, I set off, heart in mouth.

The first 20 feet went easily but, as I gained height, I could feel the drop snapping at my ankles. About halfway I was not just frightened but horribly aware that descending would be harder than going on. Above, the top looked tantalisingly close but I hadn't bargained on either my own panic and worse, the fact that the higher I climbed, the more brittle the weather-worn brickwork became. Edges for both hands and feet were crumbling and there was no way of deciding what was and wasn't sound. Almost at the end of my tether, I reached the top parapet, which overhung slightly. I had assumed that it would just be a matter of putting both hands over and a quick heave. To my horror the parapet was much wider than I had imagined, it also sloped slightly to let rainwater drain off. But at the junction of the corner the parapet had a thin crack, into which my sweaty fingers just fitted. In a flurry of flapping feet and snapping brickwork I heaved over

^ *The scene of my greatest stupidity.*

the top and rolled to safety. Huge relief. After a while I looked down the corner, a horrifying sight. If I had taken the trouble to reconnoitre it, I would never have embarked on such a hair-brained act of lunacy. Far below Adrian looked up ashen-faced. Keith had been unable to watch and had retired to The Castle to drink double whiskies.

All that remained was to find my way back to the studio window, which I had left wide open. The top of the building was more interesting and complex than I had imagined. To my surprise I found myself peering down a skylight into a male staff lavatory. Someone glanced up and did a classic double take as I dropped out of sight. Five minutes later I had regained the studio, changed out of my rock boots and, all innocence, sauntered over to The Castle to drink my winnings. No one had seemed to have noticed my ascent. I had got away with it in more ways than one.

I don't think I ever told Mum and Dad, and even today I get sweaty palms just thinking about it. There is no doubt that had I fallen off near the top I would have been killed, presumably making a small paragraph in *The Evening Standard*, 'Student dies in tragic prank — coroner's verdict'. Or, even worse, 'Student whose dog found baby dies'. A last word on the subject came from Steve Durkin who, several years later, studied accountancy at Ealing. "It doesn't seem to have had a second ascent yet — it's held out longer than *Woubits Left-Hand*." (A reference to one of Joe Brown's hardest routes in Wales which waited for years before anyone dared repeat it.)

During the last two years, the Olivers had very kindly allowed me to use their attic as a studio. It was a superb room, airy and spacious, and I did most of my painting there, including one of Dinas y Gromlech which Stephen bought and still has, beautifully framed, at his home in Bury St Edmunds. It was here that I prepared my submission to the Royal College of Art. Adrian and Dave applied as well and now all we had to do was wait.

One morning in January an envelope slipped through the letterbox. It was ominously slim and even before I opened it my heart was sinking. It was a rejection. I felt numb with shock and disappointment. Everything I had wished for disappeared in a couple of short sentences. I forced myself into college, where Dave and Adrian had both been asked to an interview. It was, I suppose, the first real rejection I had experienced and my world seemed to have come crashing down. What on earth was I going to do?

In fact, many of us had already applied to do a year's teacher training course. In my case it was a back-up position not to be taken seriously. I had already had one interview at Leeds, which had gone well until a comment was made on my very thin folio: "Have you applied to the Royal College?" Yes I had.

"If we and they offer you a place which would you accept?"

1) Correct answer: "You, of course."

2) Incorrect answer: ""Don't be fucking ridiculous – The Royal College obviously."

Without the expletive 2) was my answer and I was duly rejected. Moral: honesty is not always the best policy.

Now I had only one shot left, which was teacher training at Manchester. For the first time I made myself think about a teaching career. Above all else I wanted to carry on painting, and already a little idea was forming, which was that teaching in an art college would be quite acceptable. (I had no idea of just how unlikely this was.) So I went to Manchester in a slightly more positive frame of mind than Leeds, waffled my way through a tough interview, and was offered a place.

So life would go on, though not in the way I had expected. Adrian, by the way, was rejected by The Royal College and Dave was offered a place. To rub salt into the wounds, Brian Perrin told me casually that if I had applied to Printmaking instead of Painting, I would probably have got in. Why the fuck didn't you say that three months ago? I thought, but fortunately didn't say. So anticlimactically, I went through the NDD exam which seemed to go okay but nothing more, and soon afterwards my time at Ealing came to an end with the inevitable piss-up in the New Inn.

The next morning I carried out a resolution. I went over to the Olivers, and started a new painting in the attic. This was a symbolic gesture because from that day, Bill Brooker, Bernard Cohen and the rest of them (and my fellow students) wouldn't care whether or not I did any of my own work ever again. That Saturday was important for me, as I realised that self-motivation is 95 per cent of being any sort of creative person. At least, I thought, nobody else would be working so I've got one day's advantage over the rest of the field. It was a tiny crumb of consolation.

Chapter eight: The Alps

^ *The Vajolet Towers L to R Delago, Stabeler and Winkler.*

I spent the next month behind the motor mower, brooding darkly on my fate, but still looking forward to my first trip to the Dolomites, then the French Alps. Unfortunately the work in the Parks Department wasn't a good way of getting fit, and weekends at Harrison's gave only strong arms and fingers which were not the best preparation for Alpine hut flogs. In any case, this year we were the proud owners of an ancient Austin A35 van, and it would probably take the best part of three days to trundle down to Northern Italy, by which time, crammed in the van with all our gear, we would have lost a lot of our fitness.

At last, after transforming my bit of park into a lawn worthy of Wimbledon, I had saved enough money for what we hoped would be an even better adventure than last year. I imagined it would be my swan song, for next year I would be grown up and a responsible teacher. Fat chance.

It did take three long days to get to Bolzano in Northern Italy but one of them had been spent by the roadside in Germany outside Ulm where the van mysteriously refused to go any further, until it had had a long rest. Then, equally mysteriously, it started again — an affliction to which it succumbed on several occasions in the following weeks.

Our first objective was to climb the famous Vajolet Towers. The three spires, the Delago, the Stabeler and the Winkler, are only around 150 metres high and gave us our first taste of Dolomite exposure, particularly on the first pitch of the Delago, which traversed easily out to a stance on the edge of a steep arête. As we gained the edge we were suddenly aware of a truly colossal drop on the left that caused me nearly to faint with horror. The climbing, on steep limestone, felt harder than its grade. At the summit we abseiled a long rope length to a huge jammed chockstone and climbed to the summit of the Stabeler. By then, having taken far too long, and this combined with nervous tension, we gave Winkler a miss and abseiled off. Two things were apparent:

1) we were too slow and
2) unprepared for the psychological effects of extreme exposure. Also none of us had much experience of limestone climbing, apart from

< *Decending the Stabeler Tower.*

the Pyrenees the year before. Our preconceptions of Dolomite limestone as rough and covered in huge holds received a knock when we found it polished and unprotected. Nowadays there are probably *in situ* bolts every two metres, making it relatively safe.

After our first baptism of fire the weather deteriorated and we settled for a via ferrata. In those days they were seen as a combination of walking and scrambling, with various ancient chains and ladders at the difficult bits. Today vie ferrate have become almost a separate sport, participants wearing harnesses and carrying slings and karabiners to protect themselves. The one we did had its moments, but my main recollections were of a party of young Italian schoolboys and girls, in the charge of two nuns in full regalia, being shepherded over dizzying drops and up and down rickety ladders, with no safety equipment whatsoever. Presumably with God on their side they would come to no harm, but I could hardly bear to watch as the long crocodile of children swarmed gaily over the sort of ground where a slip would be all too easy, and obviously fatal.

With no sign of the weather clearing we decided to drive over to Chamonix in the hope that by the time we got there it would have cleared up. Approaching Mont Blanc for the first time from the south we were rewarded with the best long-distance view of the mountain. The colossal South Face, with the Peuterey Ridge, and the great snow and ice routes of the Brenva Face, looked huge beyond my comprehension. As we entered the Mont Blanc Tunnel, I felt stabs of fear. Was I cut out for this Alpine climbing business?

Chamonix, the Promised Land, gave mixed impressions. It was a town of contradictions and I quickly developed a love/hate relationship with it. At its worst it looked like a cheap seaside resort with gift shops, clubs and, later on, discos proliferating. But the town centre was better, with the statue of de Saussure pointing to the distant summit of Mont Blanc. Some of the buildings still had a faded elegance and gave the place a bit more gravitas. The place with no gravitas whatever was the Brasserie Nationale, known to every British climber as the Bar Nash. This attracted the Brits like no other bar, and it was the nearest thing in Cham to a British pub/café. For many years it was run under the proprietorship of Maurice Simmond. Maurice, to all who knew him, seemed to have a special affinity with the penniless Brits.

The best view in Cham was of the gothic cathedral-like architecture of the Aiguille Verte, the Dru and the Flammes de Pierrre. Mont Blanc itself didn't look anywhere near as impressive as it had from the south. And peeping tantalisingly above the forested valley was the foreshortened view of the Chamonix Aiguilles from the Blatière round to the Midi with it téléphérique cabins endlessly crawling spider-like up and down the steel cables.

We camped on the Biolay camp site where the impecunious English stayed, trying to avoid paying the few francs charged by the owner. It was only a stone's throw from the town centre and an easy stagger from the Nash.

Robin had joined a Cambridge University meet and Mike and I were climbing together. Our first climb was just about the most obvious. The North West Ridge of the Aguille de l'M was a route beloved by inexperienced Brits. The climbing was similar to North Wales and the climb only about as long as a route on the East Face of Tryfan. What was different, and intimidating, were the surroundings. In the Alpine setting of snowfields, glaciers and soaring granite spires it all felt serious. We were, in those days, climbing in boots. It never occurred to us to use PAs. These were the original French light rock boots designed by the Parisian climber Pierre Allain for use on the sandstone crags of Fontainebleau. Now their descendants are used in the Alps and even the Himalaya for extreme rock-climbing and were by now popular in the UK. The climbing frequently used jamming cracks and chimneys and in boots everything seemed far more strenuous. With a bit of altitude thrown in and a modicum of nervous tension the routes almost always felt much harder than their grade suggested.

After the M and a day or two enjoying the fleshpots (I could easily understand how so many British climbers never seemed to actually do anything else) we decided on a more ambitious route — the Mayer-Dibona line on the Requin. This involved a proper hut walk via the Mer de Glace to the Requin Hut. Here, deep in the heart of the mountains, was the incomparable scenery that surpassed every photograph I'd seen of any mountains anywhere. However often I had seen photos of the Grandes Jorasses, the Rochefort Ridge, and the Aiguille du Géant, the reality was beyond my wildest expectations. It wasn't until 1976 that the peaks of the Baltoro Glacier eclipsed Chamonix, and another 20 years before FitzRoy, Cerro Torre and the Towers of Paine in Patagonia edged into the top spot.

Why none of the experienced climbers at the hut didn't warn us off the Mayer-Dibona I don't know — maybe we didn't tell anyone. While most of the mountain was dry and in condition, the first couloir at the foot of our route was not, as we found out early the following morning. Icicles dripped from every overhang and rotten snow was plastered all over the gully walls. Every pitch became a fight, and the higher we got the worse conditions became. We felt horribly vulnerable; everything seemed loose and ready to slide off. When we reached the top of the hideous gully

80

and emerged into warm sunlight, we were hours behind schedule and mentally drained. By traversing into the middle of the sunlit face we found plenty of evidence of abseil retreats in the form of old sun-bleached slings and did so ourselves, arriving back at the hut in mid-afternoon, shattered and depressed.

Unsure of what to do next, we stayed in the hut for a second night. Next morning, sitting outside in the sun, we were telling our miserable tale to another couple of English climbers, when there was a sudden loud crash and, looking across, we watched our couloir of yesterday avalanche in a cloud of snow, ice and rocks, spewing out onto the glacier below. Had we been in it we would have almost certainly been killed. We slunk back to Chamonix, overwhelmed by the danger of these beautiful mountains. In retrospect I can think of dozens of better climbs we could have chosen. Experience, as the matchbox motto said, is what you get when you are looking for something else.

The debacle certainly didn't do my mental state much good and probably caused a semi-permanent anxiety about Alpine climbing. The objective dangers were one thing and the constant need to move quickly and efficiently were lessons that took a lot of getting used to. In fact, it wasn't until my last trip to the Alps with Ian McNaught Davis in 1993 that Mac said something that made a lot of sense. Had I been told it 30 years earlier it might have made a difference. Mac's point was that it is almost impossible to climb faster than you are able — obviously you speed up a bit on easy ground, but are correspondingly slower on harder pitches. What makes the difference is speed in belaying and setting up stances. The French guides may seem to the Brits to be cavalier and potentially dangerous in their belaying techniques, but they save valuable time on every pitch. British climbers can take 10 minutes or more setting up a stance and then the second man unbelays and then the rope is taken in and then the leader puts the rope on a Sticht plate and then lights a cigarette and then… and then. Quite often more time is actually spent not climbing. But in 1964 we were a long way from learning these valuable lessons.

Our next climb was going to be on good rock and, as far as possible, free from objective danger. We chose the Chamonix Face of the Aiguille du Peigne, a choice influenced by the fact that in order to save money we had decided to camp for a few days high on the Plan des Aiguillles, quite near the halfway téléphérique station leading to the summit of the Aiguille du Midi. From here, the foot of the Peigne was only an hour away and the route seemed to be fairly straightforward, apart from the top few pitches.

To our delight it was, and even the dreaded Lépiney Crack near the summit didn't feel particularly hard. At last we seemed to be

81

getting the hang of things, and sitting on the tiny summit in the sunshine, with plenty of time to get down, we felt almost happy.

Needless to say we made a pig's ear of the descent and ended up abseiling all the way down a hideous gully, following ancient abseil slings. A few years later, Paul Beney, a talented young Derbyshire climber was killed in the gully when a sling broke and he fell the whole way down to the glacier.

We returned to our tents as the rain started. The weather we thought was particularly foul. In fact, given my experience in later years, it wasn't bad at all. Even so the weather forecast posted at the Meteo office seemed to warn of *orages* (storms) most afternoons, a message I secretly welcomed as it meant another day of festering.

Camping quite near us was the all-star team of Joe Brown, Dr Tom Patey and Chris Bonington. Mike Watkins had teamed up with Chris Oakley, a friend of ours, and they climbed the Aiguille des Pélerins, a similar route to the Peigne. On the descent Mike had somehow tripped on a ledge and smashed his face. In agony he called out: "Chris, Chris!" He was surprised when Bonington appeared and helped shepherd him down to the téléphérique.

Next day his nose was swollen and bloody so I took him to see our local GP, Tom Patey. Joe Brown looked on curiously as Patey, after the briefest examination, told him his nose was broken and his best bet was to go home and get it fixed. Sadly Mike left.

With Robin now teamed up with Brian Chase, one of the best young climbers in the Cambridge Club, I joined Chris Oakley to try the Mer de Glace Face of the Grépon, one of the great classic Chamonix rock-climbs. As we left the camp site a track from A Hard Day's Night, the Beatles new LP was playing on someone's transistor — it was called 'If I Fell'.

In the spirit of romantic nostalgia, we decided not to use the big Envers des Aiguilles Hut and instead climbed to the ruins of the Tour Rouge Hut, a semi-derelict wooden structure perched precariously about 100 metres up the Grépon. It had no water supply but there was an ancient tin bucket hanging on a rusty hook. I abseiled down a nearby gully and filled it, only to find it had a huge hole and by the time I regained the hut it was empty and I was soaked.

We spent a cold, hungry and thirsty night and at first light climbed to a tiny snow patch for a brew and a bite to eat. It was a glorious day and we had the route to ourselves. Across the glacier was the sombre North Face of the Grandes Jorasses and the horizon was cluttered with stunning peaks culminating in Mont Blanc itself. I felt for the first time a real joy in being in such a landscape. Despite all the effort and stress incurred, it was emphatically worth it.

It took most of the day to climb the 700 metre face and at the top we failed miserably to climb the Knubel Crack to the summit. But that was just a detail, and after an abseil descent to the Nantillon Glacier, and a frustrating bivouac (like the one in the Pyrenees) when we couldn't find the path to the Plan des Aiguilles, we caught the first cable car down to Cham. Here instead of a long and glorious fester, we were bundled into the van by Robin and Brian Chase and set off to Switzerland to attempt the North Face of the Badile, one of the seven great Alpine North Faces.

I thought it was a ridiculously over-ambitious project to attempt in my first Alpine season and was mighty relieved when the weather broke down completely. So much so that when we returned to Chamonix there was nothing else to do except go home, which we did.

I felt that, although it had been a wonderful holiday, we hadn't done as much as we should have, though on subsequent visits I never achieved more than a couple of climbs, and on two occasions none at all. Now, with the summer holidays drawing to a close, my thoughts turned again to Manchester. Before that though, I had one last glorious visit to Harrison's Rocks. Here the combination of fitness and weight loss in the Alps paid off, and after five years of trying I finally succeeded in climbing some of the 5c classics. Routes like *West Wall*, *Unclimbed Wall*, and *The Niblick* (both these last two were later downgraded to 5b to my irritation) seemed quite reasonable and in a long weekend I seemed to get up everything I tried.

There was an irony in all this. Having supposed that the Alpine trip would be my last, I thought that in the future I would just have to be satisfied with weekends in Wales, and odd visits to Harrison's. In fact, I never climbed seriously at Harrison's again, and big mountains eventually took over my life.

So on the 19th September 1964 I boarded a bus at Victoria Coach Station and set off in steady drizzle to Manchester. I was not over-excited at the prospect.

Chapter nine: Not So Grim Up North

Number 30 Clothorn Road, West Didsbury, was a standard Victorian semi, not designed to hold 16 male students. It was run by Mr and Mrs Dunderdale. They could have been the models for Mr and Mrs Jack Spratt of nursery rhyme legend. Mr Dunderdale was a thin wispy man with a cadaverous face who always wore a grubby white waiter's jacket. His wife, a vast, greasy apparition, was more or less confined to the kitchen.

Every morning we inmates were greeted by Mr D with the same two questions delivered in a slow, nasal whine: "Would you like porridge or eggs for your breakfast?" If the answer was the latter there would be a pause before the next querulous enquiry, "Boiled ... or fried?" The gap between the alternatives grew so long that there was a temptation to interrupt and settle for porridge. This substance may have contained some of the ingredients of Araldite or Super Glue and there always seemed to be a chance that the eater would simply set in mid-mouthful.

The Art Teachers' Diploma building was only a few minutes walk away and on the first morning we gathered to be welcomed. The very first thing we were told was to forget all our fine art pretensions: "Don't think oil paint; think powder paint. Don't think silkscreen, litho or etching; think potato prints." For the tutors engaged in training us to be teachers it was a psychologically dumb thing to say — an instant belittling of our past, and a lowering of our expectations. We were, apparently, to be known as 'peds', short for pedagogical students — a pathetic appellation and one that nowadays would be subject to misunderstandings too horrible to contemplate. All in all, that first morning succeeded in nothing more than filling me with seething resentment. Much better was the news that we were to be given an induction course, staying at Lyme Park on the edge of the Peak District.

There is no getting away from the fact that the first person I noticed was a dark-haired girl called Cherry Bishop. Once again it was love at first sight for me and, to my amazement, it seemed to be reciprocated. Cherry came from Sunderland and was far more worldly wise than I. (Oh come on, spit it out — by that I mean sexually experienced.) I found her presence exciting but also intimidating, and felt that I couldn't compete with her maturity. Despite my feelings, after a few weeks I told her I couldn't go out with her any more, a blindingly stupid decision and one I regretted almost as soon as the words left my mouth. I think I must have been frightened that she was about to ditch me. Cherry was understandably very upset and a promising relationship was over before it had begun.

The first half of the term was given over to lectures on

Education, Psychology and English, as well as one day a week 'observing' in a local primary school. However, I was pleasantly surprised to find the academic work interesting and two tutors in particular must take the credit. Mr Saunders (I don't think we ever knew his Christian name) was a highly intelligent, erudite man, and took a real interest in my experiences at Ealing, particularly in the so-called 'Groundcourse' which, though I didn't attend it, had begun to influence my thoughts about teaching art. The other tutor was a rather po-faced lady called Mrs Casey, for whom I wrote a short essay about a journey. This was a description of hitchhiking back to Manchester after a weekend in London. I enjoyed describing the sight of lorries at night in streaming rain, water coursing down their flapping canvas sheets that secured their loads, and the back of a Guinness tanker, black with gold lettering, almost completely covered in mud and spray. For some reason, Mrs Casey really liked this and not only did I get an A- for it but she held it up as a good example. Of what? Creative writing I suppose, though the term has never appealed to me. (What is uncreative writing?) Anyway, the result was a growing confidence and fluency and Mrs Casey must take a big slice of the credit for this.

The second half of the term was given over to teaching practice: four days a week at whatever school was chosen for you. Mine was North Manchester Grammar School which involved two long bus journeys across the city. I quickly found that I possessed one quality needed to be a reasonable teacher — the ability to stand up and sound as though I knew what I was talking about. Nearly all teaching involves acting and, remembering reciting 'You are Old Father William' all those years ago, I could almost always rely on an adrenaline rush to see me through most classroom situations. I say almost always as I also experienced the gut-wrenching horror when a lesson went tits up. Thankfully this didn't happen often.

Four days a week involved a lot of preparation and evenings at Clothorn Road were hardly fun times as 16 tired and sometimes fraught young men tried to keep ahead of the game. The Dunderdales' front room had gloomy sepia wallpaper with a repeat pattern of a mare and her foal standing by a tree. To provide relief we slowly transformed them into zebras, which seemingly went unnoticed by Mr and Mrs D.

At last the six weeks drew to an end. My school had a lot of building work in progress and for those staff without cars this meant a dodgy shuffle along duckboards and planks crossing the muddy drive, avoiding the worst of the puddles to gain the main buildings.

I had, apparently, done well and the reports to the college from the resident art teacher had been, I thought, remarkably

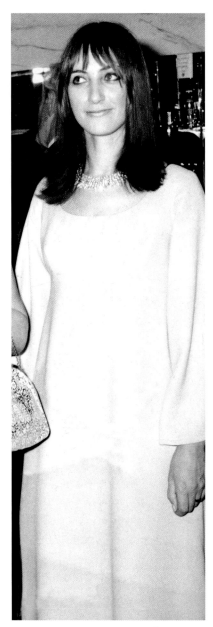

^ *Alison.*

complimentary. On the last morning I was called to see the headmaster, a little bald-headed man with a bristling white military moustache. He congratulated me and wished me well. As I turned to go he added, "Just one thing — Mr Wilson [the prime minister] cleans his own shoes every morning and so do I." Nonplussed, I stopped in my tracks and stared at him. What the...? Then the penny dropped. He, of course, swept up the drive in his car. What did he expect me to do — fly? Stupid prat. I left even more determined not to be a schoolteacher, though even less confident about how to escape my fate. Whatever it was, I doubted that I would be spending every morning with the Cherry Blossom and stiff little brushes until I retired. I also hoped Harold Wilson had better things to do with his time at Number Ten.

Before I went home for Christmas I went to a student party in Didsbury armed, I cringe to admit, with my guitar. Amongst the crowd of half-drunk students, I saw an apparition of sheer beauty (here we go again). Honestly, she really was — slightly aloof, with perfect features, long hair, and very reminiscent of the French pop singer Françoise Hardy, on whose song 'Tous les garçons et les filles' I had wasted precious francs in the Bar Nash. (It was played on a telejuke machine that played prehistoric film strips as well as the record, thus predating pop videos by about 20 years.) Alison, I quickly found out, was only just 18 and was a pupil at Withington Girls High School, the female equivalent of Manchester Grammar School. She came from Wilmslow, then, as now, a Cheshire suburb renowned for wealthy *arrivistes,* though her mother's family had always lived there. But almost before I could ask her out, the term ended, and with huge relief and anticipation of food that wasn't boiled eggs, cabbage and potatoes. I returned to Ealing — almost for the last time to call it home.

The holidays came and went, and on my return to Manchester I teamed up with a fellow inmate, John Cann, and staged a breakout from Clothorn Road to a truly gruesome flat in Lloyd Street North behind the university. This was a slum dwelling by any standards, complete with rats and a crooked landlord, but compared with Dunderland it was Wonderland.

Early in the term came the break I was looking for. Volunteers were needed to help out running the Art College Saturday morning class in the Foundation Courses premises in Openshaw. I had my hand up before the announcement had finished and found the Saturday mornings, working with the sixth formers, pure joy. So much so that I carried on for the rest of the year, and then was appointed to do the job the following September. It was hardly a foot in the door, but it was at least a toehold.

Meanwhile I had fallen for Alison in a big way. She would turn

86

^ First taste of freedom in the grim Lloyd Street flat.

up in her mother's blue and white Anglia. Think Harry Potter — though it didn't fly. She had passed her driving test long before I did. Alison was equally smitten. At last, at 22, I was about to lose my virginity. Not before time. But to do this John and I moved from our hovel to a rather better flat in Riga Road, Fallowfield — not solely for sexual fulfilment but because even our acceptance of dirty student flats was being put under strain in Lloyd Street as the rats got bigger and bolder. It is strange how some memories linger. My last recollection of Lloyd Street was of watching Winston Churchill's funeral on John's little black and white TV. I had never been particularly patriotic and watched more out of curiosity than anything until the time when his coffin was taken by barge down the Thames. As it passed the long rows of tall cranes lining the river, each one dipped in tribute. For some reason I found the image incredibly moving and even now the memory brings tears to my eyes.

Life at number 4 Riga Road was good. I was enjoying the course and Ali and I were getting along brilliantly. Not to put too fine a point on it, the end of 22 years of celibacy was well worth celebrating. My next teaching practice was at a boys' school called Openshaw Technical High School. I enjoyed it far more than North Manchester and got a huge kick when my lessons went well. The boys were rough and tough but, it seemed to me, far more receptive than those at the grammar school. I was also finding a bit of time for my own work and even managed to get out climbing on Stanage Edge once or twice. At last the disappointment of the Royal College was receding and I could even imagine a life away from London.

Which was a good thing, because one Friday evening Ali broke the news with the dreaded 'P' word that turned my blood to ice. How could I have been so stupid? Why hadn't we talked about it before? In short, how could I cope with fatherhood and she with becoming a teenage mum? In one act of stupidity I had deprived Ali of her youth and her university education. How were we to tell our parents? Though we were obviously not the first or last to grapple with the problem, there were no leaflets available to help you break the news, or make it anything less than cataclysmic, particularly as Ali's parents were away and we had to wait the whole weekend for their return. It was not my finest hour, and neither was the next day when I hitchhiked down to London to tell Mum and Dad. At least I had the foresight to write to them first, so that my arrival wasn't quite such a bombshell. After I had dodged the first salvo of parental rants, they both became surprisingly sympathetic.

There was no question but that we would get married. This was

^ Alison and me on our wedding day.

despite Alison's father Stan, who I grew to like and admire enormously, asking me privately if it wouldn't be easier if I just disappeared. I can't imagine how disappointed he must have felt that his beautiful, intelligent daughter was going to marry a rock-climbing art teacher. These were the words he used in his speech at the wedding reception, except that he said how pleased he was. It might have fooled some of the guests, but not me. We were married, incidentally, by my Uncle Wilfred in a Catholic church that had just had a PA system installed, a piece of technology that Wilfred wasn't used to. I fumbled with the ring, his voice boomed out across the church: "Wrong finger — stupid bugger."

After the reception we drove to the Farmer's Arms in Lowick, near Newby Bridge in the southern Lake District, for a few days alone before I had to go back to Manchester to finish the course. Ali had a violent 24-hour bug, but we returned to Manchester, happy with each other, and full of cautious optimism for our future.

Before the final exams I had been offered a job at St Ignatius Catholic Secondary Modern School on the fringe of Moss Side. The problem of supporting a wife and child meant that beggars couldn't be choosers and I accepted the post with the unspoken vow that it wouldn't be for one moment longer than necessary. I would move heaven and earth to get a job in an art school, even though I only had the Saturday morning class to start with.

At the end of the course it was announced that Cherry Bishop and, I think, two others, had been awarded Distinctions and several more, including me, were given Commendations, which I honestly thought I didn't deserve because, as usual, I had only worked hard at the bits of the course that interested me. Still, never mind, it wouldn't do me any harm and might even do a bit of good in future applications. (In fact, I never, ever, had to produce any academic evidence whatsoever in all the jobs I applied for.)

In the summer, Ali and I moved into a large ground-floor flat in Palatine Road, West Didsbury. It was a better class of student doss. (It probably still is.) I thought it was great, and Ali thought it was okay, but her parents must have been horrified that their daughter had come to this. She had been expelled from Withington Girls School but allowed back to sit her A-Levels, which she passed easily. I managed to do a bit of painting that summer but all too soon it was time to start work at St Ignatius.

The art department was run by a tiny sparrow-like woman called Jill. She was incredibly conscientious and announced to my thinly disguised horror we would sometimes have to work over the weekends. But it was the headmaster, Mr Cunningham, that I really loathed, and with good reason. He would stand at the school gates from about 8.15 am, not, as you might think, to check the pupils' timekeeping, but the staff's. He treated all of us like simpletons. What was worse, most of the staff seemed to love it. One morning he announced to the whole school at assembly that he had stopped at a road works. One of the labourers had exceptionally long hair: "I thought for a moment that Mr Curran had left us." Oh, ha ha. Hilarious, not least as my hair was not particularly long at the time.

In addition to art, I taught games on two afternoons a week. I had volunteered for this to get away from the school premises, and tried, unsuccessfully, to introduce rugby to a football-mad school. But this was quite enjoyable, certainly more so than having to teach RE for the first period every morning to a class of 11 year olds. My faith by this time was so rickety I hated every minute of this and can only remember reading one line of an essay I had set, which was, 'Moses was born in a basket and found by a lady who was floating down a river'. This seemed to me to be as good, or better, than the Old Testament story.

By now Ali's pregnancy was quite advanced, and her parents were understandably keen on us moving back to their Wilmslow home. The problem was that their well-meaning intentions had the effect of undermining my own role as a husband, but it was hard not to agree with their case, which was that if we lived rent-free in Wilmslow we would save enough for a deposit on a home of our own. So we did.

In those days (1965) there was no question of husbands being present at the birth (not in Manchester anyway) and when Ali's contractions started I delivered her to a maternity home in Bowdon and retired gracefully to let her get on with it. After a fairly short and trouble-free labour, she gave birth to a baby girl on 8th

89

December. We called her Zoë Marie. The middle name was chosen in memory of Ali's younger sister Marice, who had been a spina bifida baby and had only lived for a few months.

The following day I went to visit her after school. She greeted me red-eyed with crying. The nurses had become concerned about Zoë's colour and she had been taken to Manchester Children's Hospital. She had a hole in her heart and was very poorly. The cause of it, as surmised by Zoë's specialist, was probably the bug that Ali had suffered on our honeymoon when she was less than three months gone. He explained that it was well-known that German Measles could cause birth defects, but so apparently could any severe viral infection.

We visited her every day hoping that she would survive and become strong enough for an operation. One day, after five weeks, we arrived at her side ward to any empty oxygen tent. The sister on duty said she had deteriorated. Everything was being done to save her. The best thing we could do was to go home and ring the hospital. Bemused and fearing the worst we did what we were told. I rang the hospital to be told that Zoë had died. It was January 15th 1966. And that was that. We never saw her to say goodbye and it was never suggested that we should. Unbelievably I had only one day off from school for the funeral, which was a rainy Thursday. The short drive to the cemetery in the hearse with the tiny white coffin was beyond description. The service in the chapel confirmed to me that there was no God, or if there was, he wasn't worth worshipping.

Ali was so grief-stricken that I never felt I was helping her as much as I should. I just didn't know how to. Her mother probably did more, but Stan shut himself off completely.

The next day I was back at St Ignatius. A class in the morning pushed their luck too far and I decided to keep them in for half an hour after school. Bad move. Mr Cunningham gave me a bollocking about making decisions without consulting him. I could have happily smashed his self-satisfied face into a pulp.

There is no doubt that had Zoë's death happened today we would be inundated with social workers, grief therapists and help from all sides. In 1965 we had nothing except each other. Would outside help have made it any less difficult to face? Hard to say. Maybe the loss of a child is so great that nothing is going to make much difference.

A couple of weeks after the funeral Ali and I went for a long walk round the bleak Cheshire countryside. She actually suggested that with the death of Zoë the main reason for our marriage had disappeared and asked if I wanted to carry on with it. Of course I did, though I occasionally wondered whether she had a lot more foresight than I. As it was, we clung together and tried to pick up the pieces.

During the year at St Ignatius I had carried on with the Saturday morning class at the Art College and made two good friends in lecturers Ruth Hopwell and Neville King. Ruth was a wonderful draughtsman/woman/person and had gathered a huge collection of natural and manmade forms — bones, dried plants, musical instruments, clockwork toys, etc. She had unlimited patience with the students who appreciated her total commitment to drawing and I learned a lot from her example. Nev King could hardly have been more different: a practicing painter, emotional, passionate and, as our friendship developed, all too obviously manic-depressive. We must now call his condition bi-polar, but the old appellation summed him up much more accurately. Both Ruth and Nev were hugely supportive and both tried unsuccessfully to get me more part-time hours on the Foundation Course. During the summer term we had saved enough for a maisonette in nearby Handforth on a new estate. The day after I had signed up for a mortgage I handed in my notice. After the trauma of the year, and with no job to go to, I am still quite impressed that I took what I am sure everyone except Ali must have thought was a wildly irresponsible decision. I posted the fateful letter with the same feeling of diving off the top board in a swimming pool — fear but real elation.

At the end of term I left St Ignatius for the last time without a backward glance. I have never set eyes on the place since, and doubt if I could even find it again. Presumably it is now part of a comprehensive or maybe it is something completely different. Who knows? Who cares? Not I.

Chapter ten: Another Unexpected Blow

All too soon the summer of 1966 was over. England had won the World Cup — an event I watched through the window of a TV rental shop in Carmarthen on a wet camping holiday in Pembrokeshire. At the end of August my full-time salary stopped, and I only had three hours' work a week confirmed. I should have been panic-stricken. Instead Ali got a job in a newsagent in Handforth, which just about kept the wolf from the door and I slowly built up my part-time hours at schools and colleges around Manchester. Even so, it was odd to begin with, to have that Monday morning feeling at 9.30 on Saturday morning, and that Friday afternoon feeling at half past 12. I felt bad about Ali's job, but somehow with a misplaced confidence of youth I knew it wouldn't be for long and that I would soon fall on my feet. (Hope, hope, cross fingers, cross everything.)

In my own potted version of my life story, I came to think that, almost from the moment I got off the coach at Manchester bus station, I was instantly converted to all things northern and would spend my life up here. But looking through the letters I wrote at the time to Mum and Dad, there are plenty of references to applications for jobs in Devon (Dartington), Guildford, Epsom and Falmouth. None of these came to anything, but I clearly wasn't quite as committed to staying around Manchester as I liked to think.

At the end of the Christmas term I decided to hitch home for a few days to see Mum and Dad. I arrived as Dad left for work, dark green scarf tucked into his overcoat covering a dinner jacket and bow tie (the real thing, not the stick on sort which I've always worn, being quite incapable of tying the knot). "Not too late tonight — I'll see you later."

Mum and Phil were willing listeners to my egocentric account of whatever recent events had happened and the evening passed quickly until the noise of the key in the lock and the frantic barking of Nick, who always greeted Dad as if he had just returned from a round the world voyage. Dad was more talkative than usual and for some reason we got round to climbing. Dad, to my surprise, confessed that he had always fancied climbing the Matterhorn but he was now much too old. At 57 he probably was, though he was always quite fit and walked everywhere. I suggested that one year we would walk the Haute Route from Chamonix to Zermatt, which he could do easily.

In the morning I had arranged to meet Robin Devenish in town and we would go round the Bond Street galleries — something I hadn't done for two years. Dad was taking Nick for a walk and on a bright December morning we strolled to Ealing Broadway station, chatting about this and that, before I descended the steps to the ticket office.

That evening, after a day I have no memory of at all, I returned to Rathgar Avenue. The door was instantly opened by cousin Chris, and Mum rushed up the hallway and almost pushed me into the sitting room. "It's your father. [An appellation she never normally used.] He's collapsed and… he's dead." I was quite numb and unable to speak. She said that shortly after we had parted he had suddenly collapsed in the middle of Ealing Broadway. She had arranged to meet him later and by chance spotted Nick tied to a railing looking at the people gathered round Dad as an ambulance arrived. As so often happens in extreme shock, she repeatedly told me how lucky it was that she had found the dog.

I can remember the tears and hopeless misery of the next few days. Because Dad's death had occurred so close to Christmas the funeral would have to be afterwards. I met Ali off the train and cried in her arms, thinking quite ridiculously, as I did so, that this was the second London terminus I had wept in. Would I ever get the full set? A kind of lachrymatory game of Monopoly.

I remember Mum being worried about Phil. At 16 he had been hit very hard, but seemed not to be able to express his grief. I can't remember seeing him cry. Instead he seemed to spend long hours staring out of the window. Waiting? Hoping? We never knew.

On the day of the funeral I remember the curtains being kept closed, and someone muttering: "The hearse is here." In the hall were flowers to take to the car, and an enormous wreath with the inscription 'With deepest sympathy' under the insignia of the Royal Opera House, Covent Garden, and the Royal Coat of Arms. Below was the handwritten message, 'Farewell Sam from all your friends at The Garden'. It was that simple juxtaposition that moved me, and the memory has done so ever since.

Despite Dad's atheism, Wilfred conducted the service, and both Mum and I got the giggles as the coffin slipped away. After the funeral Mum found one of Dad's Christmas presents to Phil — 'Good Vibrations' by The Beach Boys. I still find it hard to listen to.

Nobody copes well with a sudden death, and I was no exception. Mum and Phil somehow began to deal with their grief in Ealing, but up in Manchester I could do little to help Mum, whose life had been so brutally altered. As with the death of Zoë only a year ago, I didn't know how to behave. I was plagued by a recurring dream that Dad had somehow survived. He had actually died of a cerebral aneurysm, a death that was almost instantaneous and painless. In my dreams he was alive but fragile and about to die. The dream, and variations of it, continued with diminishing frequency over the years, but started to happen again when I was diagnosed with prostate cancer. Now they are quite matter of fact. Dad is here watching television, or doing DIY in the kitchen. But I still wake up with that thud of disappointment.

Dad's death when he was still comparatively young and full of energy had a curious effect on me. Dad, I felt, had sacrificed some of his own ability and potential for the sake of his family. He was the very model of the unselfish parent and loving husband whose loyalty to his wife and children came first. I thought that if I could fulfil every bit of my own ambition, I would live out that bit of Dad's life that he had forfeited. It was, I now know, a dangerous notion, because it could easily give me carte blanche to do whatever I wanted, shunning my own responsibilities as a husband or father. Some would say that's exactly what I did, and I would find it hard to disagree.

Back in Handforth after Dad's funeral, Ali and I clung together sharing our sorrows, but probably as close to each other as we ever could be. My life revolved almost entirely around teaching and interminable bus journeys across Manchester.

Climbing was in danger of disappearing completely. Lack of time was an obvious reason, but an initial aversion to Derbyshire was not far behind. North Wales was, for many years, my spiritual home. To my eyes the harsh moors and short, steep gritstone edges of the Peak District were strangely alien. My conversion obviously took longer than I have since chosen to remember. I was also lacking a regular climbing partner. Robin was back in London (with a First) and on the verge of marriage. Mike had taken off to Brazil, where he has stayed more or less ever since and Steve, after only a year at Manchester University, had also returned to London. It is hard to imagine now, but in those days I simply didn't know any other climbers.

Steve did come up occasionally. One visit turned into an epic February day in North Wales. This involved a bad mountaineering decision and a long, cold ascent of Lliwedd, the highest cliff in Wales. We both pushed ourselves almost to the limit and were lucky not to have been rescued, or worse. For many years it remained a yardstick when things went wrong, 'At least it's not as bad as Lliwedd'. Despite the errors of judgement, that day showed me that I hadn't completely lost touch with the mountains.

By Easter I was working all the hours I could manage at Stockport, Manchester and Salford Art Colleges, evening classes at an institute in Whitefield, North Manchester, and supply work at Burnage Grammar School. In fact, on a weekly basis I was earning more than I would have done full-time. But it wasn't what I wanted which was still full-time in a college. On the basis of designing and painting a coat of arms for a school play, I was offered Head of Art at Burnage, which I turned down without a second thought. Then the job I really wanted came up on the Foundation Course at Stockport. I was definitely the favourite, but somehow blew the interview and the job went to a part-time lecturer from Rotherham. I was deeply disappointed, and applied for a job at Rotherham without much hope. After a long interview, and what seemed an even longer wait, I was offered the job. Ironically, my nemesis from Stockport was a favourite, and so two of us, both married with houses to sell, were effectively swapping jobs. But, oh the elation! And the relief! I was a college lecturer and could finally wave goodbye to secondary education. Let joy be unconfined! The sadness of the last 18 months could be, to some extent, put in the past.

That summer, as if to remind me that life wasn't all a bed of roses, I had my worst ever attack of hay fever. Our little maisonette backed onto an unkempt field, and you could see clouds of pollen drifting on the breeze. The hay fever developed into an acute asthma attack. Worried, Ali called the doctor out. Remember that old-fashioned phrase? Concerned at my state, he gave me an injection of aminophylline, which he probably administered far too quickly. My world went black, and far away, I heard Ali say: "Will he be all right?" The reply wasn't reassuring: "Christ — I hope so. Dial 999." Somehow this penetrated my brain enough to fight the compulsion to sleep (or whatever it was that might follow). Eventually I forced my eyes open to see the doctor slumped at the end of the bed: "Thank God," he said, which I took to be a little-used medical term. An ambulance arrived and, equipped with a huge oxygen cylinder and mask, I was put in a wheelchair. To the curiosity of the neighbours, I was driven off to the local hospital in Stockport where I spent several days before being diagnosed with chronic hay fever and an acute allergic asthma attack, which I knew already.

All this took it out of me more than I realised, and I spent a couple of weeks recovering, during which time Ali bought me the best possible present: the new Beatles LP, Sergeant Pepper's Lonely Hearts Club Band. It's hard to write anything about the Beatles that hasn't been written before. From their earliest days I had been an enthusiastic fan, not just because of their huge charisma, but because I found their music compelling with an indefinable quality — magic? genius? — that could move me as much or more than any book, film, painting or indeed other music. There were endless juxtapositions between happy/sad, sweet/sour, simple/complex that were apparently produced quite effortlessly, though of course they weren't. Their lyrics too were not just clever or amusing, but as their work developed, showed an insight into so many of life's great themes, all written by John Lennon and Paul McCartney (and to a lesser extent George Harrison) during their 20s. Perhaps above all, I found a quality of quite piercing insight into mundane subject matter: parking meter attendants, bankers, tax men, fire engines, funerals, Vera, Chuck and Dave. All their songs seemed to have been based on everyday personal experiences, which resonated across every social stratum.

So in the sunny summer days of 1967, our old Dansette Major gramophone was rarely silent with 'Lucy in the Sky with Diamonds', 'She's Leaving Home', and of course 'A Day in the Life', all threatening to blow the speaker (no stereo yet, and not for years to come).

Despite the rabbit hutch dimensions of 140 Caldy Road, I did use the spare room as a studio and was part of a staff exhibition at Stockport Museum and Art Gallery. I also shared a two-man show with Nev King at the Moyen Gallery at Brown Street in the middle of Manchester. Neither shows resulted in a single sale, but the important thing was that I was painting with my ambitions still very much alive. Now I was away from Bernard Cohen I was unashamedly influenced by him. Bernard's painting was constantly evolving and had recently become incredibly complex: linear motifs; meticulously painted-over diffused spray gun arabesques; little boxes containing their own abstract 'stories'; hints and illusions to all kinds of modern painting. I always found Bernard's painting intriguing and occasionally frustrating. There was an elusive meaning to them that seemed tantalisingly just out of my reach.

Now, in my little bedroom studio in Handforth, I could pay homage to an absent teacher. That my paintings were almost wholly derivative, some embarrassingly so, wasn't quite the point: by acknowledging my debt to Bernard I learnt a huge amount about the language of painting. Indeed, for the next four or five years my paintings were all abstract, but were a constant learning process that bore fruit many years later.

So as the new job at Rotherham loomed nearer Ali and I prepared to move across the Peak to the place that more than any other has defined my life: Steel City, Sheffield.

Midword

You might wonder why my story breaks off at this point. It was not intended. So far I have dealt, in a reasonably chronological way, with the first 21 years of my life. It has taken longer and is more complicated than I expected, but until last week I found it interesting, time consuming and, I thought, a not too bad account. Then I received a parcel from my brother. In it were early photographs, the odd postcard and some letters. One card was from my Grandad, when I was five and the year before he died in which he wrote, 'Thank you for the post card, I am sure you will be an artist… Thank you for your clever drawing'. Great, I thought, my very earliest ambition has been unexpectedly confirmed. Then I read the letters. They were all from me to my parents when I first moved to Manchester. The contents were no problem, though I had completely forgotten writing any of them. But hang on — I don't recognise me at all. Who is this young impostor?

I suppose I have been writing as though the 'me' I think I am now is the same me, only a smaller and younger me that wept outside St Anne's Convent, a slightly larger me that built model aircraft with Stephen, and virtually the present me that showed Lord Snowdon round the painting studio. But the letters are a subtly different me — and not one I easily recognise. It is as though I am reading letters from a young nephew or a grandchild — not just naïve or comic or altruistic, though they are all those things, but elusively and indefinably different.

One of the friends who urged me to write this book is the author Julie Summers, who threatened (not seriously I'm sure) that if I didn't, she would do it herself. At the time I thought, but didn't say, that she would be hard put to paint a convincing portrait with so little evidence. Now I am not so sure. I am, of course, only revealing those bits of me that I want to, or think interesting enough. Maybe a biographer, by virtue of detachment, might get closer to some sort of objective reality than I can ever hope to.

So, more than ever, I am fretting over writing what will be the bulk of this book. If I can scarcely recognise myself as a boy, how am I going to deal with what will be infinitely more complex situations — marriage, infidelity, bereavement, to name but three? Does it matter so long as I tell an entertaining story? Obviously not, in the greater scheme of things. But I only started writing on the promise to myself that I would pull no punches. 'Tell it like it is (was)' and risk the consequences. Now, after only the briefest of skirmishes with, for example, early romances, I have found it impossible to avoid omissions and compromise, to be wise after the event, and make each story nicely rounded and complete. The other much greater problem is that if I find it hard to recognise myself, how do I deal with others — friends, wives, daughters, lovers? Will my assessment of them be one they recognise? How truthful is my side of the stories I tell when they can't tell theirs? (Not in this book anyway.)

So, this 'Midword' is a warning. I must buck my ideas up, weigh my words more carefully and question my own version of events. You, dear reader, may find you have to take it all with a few pinches of salt as you turn these pages, and be prepared to forgive both omissions and inclusions. Between us we will somehow muddle through. Together, I hope.

Chapter eleven: A Job I Loved

When I went to Rotherham, for the interview and for the first couple of visits to the college afterwards, I went by train and bus. The first time we drove over (still in Ali's Mum's Anglia) was to have a look at houses. I made an astonishing discovery. I had climbed, perhaps 10 or 15 times on Stanage Edge and, coming from Manchester, had assumed it was more or less in the middle of the Peak District. Certainly from the top of the Edge there was no indication that the bleak moorland didn't roll away eastwards for ever. But driving up the A625 from Hathersage and past the Fox House Inn I was quite taken aback at the sight of Sheffield, suddenly revealed at the bottom of the long winding road. In the days before power steering and brakes, I confess that on more than one occasion this had to be freewheeled almost into the middle of the city with the petrol tank showing completely empty. I didn't realise for many years that Stanage itself marks the westward boundary of the city, and that there are literally thousands of climbs within 20 miles of the centre. It still gives me huge pleasure to live in a built-up area that stops so abruptly as you drive towards the Peak District. Drive up Ringinglow Road and you go from suburbia to farmland in the space of 100 metres, and into moorland within a mile. No other city in the UK has quite such a sudden transition.

I'm afraid that Ali and I never considered living in Rotherham, despite house prices being generally lower than in Sheffield. What we wanted was somewhere in the west side of Sheffield that would give me an easy escape to the Peak, or across to Wilmslow for Ali, and a reasonable journey to college. It remains a source of some bewilderment that in those days mortgages were only given to the value of three times your annual salary (fair enough) and whereas they would give them easily to any old jerrybuilt house on a modern estate, it was almost impossible to raise a mortgage on a solid Victorian semi, which was what we wanted. Eventually, we succumbed to an anonymous modern semi on an estate in north Sheffield, Burncross, which was one bus ride into Rotherham.

My first impressions of the college were mixed. An old 1930s building on Howard Street housed the Art School on the top floor. Access was either by stairs or by one of those frightening old lifts with two doors concertina-ering to give access. There was a lot of wrought iron and art deco around, through which the contraption climbed and groaned up the building, each journey threatening to be the last.

The Principal, Richard Ford, had his office next to the lift. He was 'Mr Ford' to all who spoke to him, 'Dickie' when they didn't. He was an interesting man and I always got on well with him. Balding, with a high domed forehead, I always wondered whether he hadn't exacerbated this condition by his habit of brow-smiting when stressed — which was often. Staff meetings could be rowdy affairs, for he would prepare for any confrontations by half-opening all the drawers on his desk, so that he could slam them shut when things got heated and a mere brow-smite was insufficient. I remember once he called all the staff to his office: "I was down in the town centre yesterday and looked in the window of the second hand bookshop. (Smite) There was a big volume of Renaissance painting on display. (Smite) I bought it. (Slam) When I got back I opened it to see the inscription inside — (Smite and slam) — Rotherham School of Art and Crafts. I'd bought one of my own bloody books!" Silence, broken only by suppressed snorts of laughter from us, and a final slamming of the desk. If Mr Ford had invented the word 'Doh!' and turned himself into a cartoon character, he would have become a multi-millionaire.

But there was no question in my mind that he was an excellent leader. He could, and did, delegate, not a common quality in the teaching profession. He told me that I was responsible for all drawing and painting in the college. Other tutors each had responsibility for sculpture, ceramics, fashion and textiles. Graphic Design was actually a separate department, physically as well as philosophically. The only minor snags were that I would be teaching A-Level Art History, and also the Saturday morning class. But a fabulous perk (for me) was that I could do my own work in a large studio shared with the full-time courses.

While we waited for all the interminable house buying/selling to sort itself out, I stayed with one of Ali's school friends, now at Sheffield University. She and her boyfriend lived in Crookes in the highest, windiest and coldest terraced house this side of Moscow. Every morning I caught the bus down to a lower altitude, then another one to Rotherham. This went via Attercliffe and passed close to some of the biggest steelworks in the country. One mill, Steel, Peech and Tozer, was so close to the road that when molten steel was being poured into the moulds, the radiated heat would lightly toast the bus passengers over 100 metres away. Hard to believe that its days were numbered; it quickly became British Steel and eventually — oblivion, along with almost all the great old Sheffield steel mills.

Looking back, I think my best teaching days were at Rotherham. I was young and enthusiastic, and with the misplaced confidence of youth I got terrific results from the students, though I am sure that I was often dogmatic and intolerant. The worst part of the week was Tuesday mornings when I regurgitated hastily memorised facts from the night before, about Mannerism, Post-Impressionism, or Futurism to a group of bored students. There was a notable exception when, one morning, they listened with rapt attention to my pearls of wisdom. After about 20 minutes they burst into wild applause: I had beaten my own record for saying "you know" 50 times in under half and hour. Despite my inadequacies, most of them passed A-Level Art, an achievement that I happily lay at the feet of the young art historian at Ealing. Even if I still can't remember his name, I must have digested far more of what he said than I realised.

After Ali and I finally moved to Burncross, I began to explore the Peak District which was almost completely unknown to me, apart from Stanage. When I had come over from Manchester to Sheffield by train one route went through the Woodhead Tunnel (long closed) and into Sheffield from the north along the Don Valley, passing under a melancholy, soot-stained outcrop called Wharncliffe Edge. The name derives from 'Quern cliffe', a quern being an ancient name for a millstone. They were quarried from almost all the outcrops on the eastern side of the Peak District. I found, to my delight, that Wharncliffe was only a three- or four-mile walk from our house. For me, who had spent my previous climbing career relying on the car or the thumb, this had huge symbolic meaning. At last I lived so close to one of my beloved crags that I could actually walk to it. Still having no one to climb with, I often soloed easy routes on Wharncliffe and in doing so, leant the mysteries of hand jamming which had been an anathema to me (and many other sandstone-raised softies). And then I could walk home. Total expenditure: £0.00.

A bit further away was Agden Rocher, a big sprawling crag above the pretty village of Bradfield. It had been developed in the 1950s and, despite being vegetated and loose, it gave some of the longest easy routes on gritstone. I loved climbing at Agden; very few climbers frequented it and it was in a beautiful, peaceful setting. In recent years it has almost completely fallen out of favour, becoming horribly overgrown. It is now probably more popular with the twitching fraternity, for it is the home of some quite interesting birds. So I won't publicise the crags any more (though I suppose I just have).

As 1967 and my first term at Rotherham ended, we seemed to have shaken off a lot of the sadness of the last two years. Ironically, though Ali had almost instantly become pregnant with Zoë, we had now been trying for over a year for another child, without success. Ali's older sister Carole had married a year after us and already had a baby girl. While Ali was not seriously worried, it can't have been easy for her to become an aunt before she became a mother. To both our delight and relief, she found at the end of March that she was pregnant again.

Life at Rotherham continued to be stimulating and enjoyable. Within two years of leaving Ealing everything in the art college world had changed. NDD was scrapped and in its place was the Diploma in Art and Design (Dip AD). This was a three-year specialist course awarded to selected colleges on quite rigorous criteria. Ealing, like innumerable others, was too small and outgunned by Hornsey College of Art. But most colleges in the big cities in England were awarded Dip AD status which could be in Fine Art, Graphic Design, Industrial Design, Fashion, Textiles and Ceramics, plus any number of less subscribed specialisms: Theatre Design, Stained Glass, Furniture Design, Jewellery and Silversmithing to name a few. In order to gain admission to these courses, it was normal to undertake a Foundation Course. These were scattered in small colleges like Rotherham, all over the country, and also within big colleges that had the new Diploma.

The whole idea of Foundation Courses was to give a broad introduction to the basic principles of art and design and, depending on the student's strengths and weaknesses, attempt to guide them towards the most appropriate diploma course. Much of their philosophy was based on the Bauhaus, that iconic college in pre-war Germany which rigorously applied maths, geometry and biology amongst other disciplines, to attempt to form a kind of universal visual language. The British colleges were a diluted version. Perhaps the famous Ealing Groundcourse was the most authentic. Over the years many concentrated on specialising from day one and became artistic crammers, which rather missed the point of their existence.

It was inevitable that many more students did a Foundation Course than could possibly get onto a Dip AD, and the competition for some courses, particularly in the London colleges, was horrendous. Some of the bigger colleges blatantly favoured their own Foundation Course students which made the competition even worse for places like Rotherham.

Academically the minimum requirement for Dip AD was five O-Levels, or three Os and one A-Level. But there was also a clause exempting those with outstanding natural ability. One of the hardest decisions that Foundation Courses had to make was in allowing very talented students without the minimum qualifications to come on the Foundation Course. The diploma courses could, and often did, decide that the student wasn't exceptional enough and their year could be seen to be a waste of time. To try and alleviate this Rotherham, and many other small courses, ran two-year Foundation Courses in the hope that those students who needed to could take or re-sit O-Levels to bring them up to a bare minimum. Which those with long memories will recall, was exactly what I had just about managed to scrape together. So I was probably rather more sympathetic than most to the plight of those students. I agree wholeheartedly with David Hockney who has often opined that entry to art school should be based primarily on ability. I also have to say that, over the years, the degree courses have frequently shown bizarre judgement in their selection procedure. When I worked on the Graphic Design course after I'd moved to Bristol I often sat on the selection panel and was frankly horrified at how poor their panel judgements were. But more of that later.

The Dip AD, soon became a BA, and art colleges were absorbed into polytechnics which themselves became universities (sort of). All this meant that the one year Foundation Courses tended to divide naturally into three terms: the first to give as wide an experience as possible, the second to concentrate on a chosen specialisation, and the third dealing mainly with applications and interviews. The bulk of the course was, therefore, concentrated into two terms.

At Rotherham there was a strong work ethic. Not to put too fine a point on it, most students saw entry onto a Dip AD course as a real way out of what could easily be a bleak future. One had told me that if he didn't get in, the steelworks were the only alternative, and they were themselves doomed. For girls it would be working in Woolies. Probably both of these prospects were exaggerated, but three years later when I was at Bristol I asked a not very talented female student what she would do if, as seemed all too likely, she didn't get a place. Her reply was: "I thought maybe I'll go to Paris for a year." This, it need scarcely be said, was not a realistic option for any students, male or female, at Rotherham.

By the beginning of my second year I felt that the work we were doing should at least be brought to the attention of Sheffield College of Art, and I invited a young lecturer, Bill Beech, to come and spend a day with us. He came and in the afternoon gave quite an extraordinary illustrated lecture to our students. It was a combination of student work, his own painting, fragments of pop images, slides of outer space from NASA and, curiously, a few climbing slides. What Bill actually said was exciting but incredibly confusing, so much so that one student asked me, in all seriousness, if Bill had actually been into space.

^ *Bill Beech on* Medusa, *Ravensdale.*

^ *Drawing of Bill Beech belaying Paul Beney on the first pitch of* The Girdle *of Kinder Great Buttress.*

^ Twenty Foot Crack, *Burbage. I must have sooled this well over 100 times.*

Afterwards Bill told me he was a climber, and this was the beginning of a long and, at times, volatile friendship. It was also to be a turning point in my life and one where the first inklings of thinking that art, teaching and climbing were part of a greater whole.

Ali and I invited Bill and his wife Pam to dinner. They had met and married in Birmingham, for exactly the same reason that Ali and I had. They had two small children and rented a wonderful old farmhouse, Lee House, in Edale. Pam and Ali hit it off from the beginning, and over 40 years later, Pam is one of my closest friends. I can't remember if on this occasion we arranged to go climbing, but fairly soon afterwards I went out with Bill to Burbage North for the first of a few million visits.

Burbage is a great soloing area and Bill showed me around his circuit of favourite problems. He was clearly a natural climber, strong and technically competent, but I could never quite work out how good he was, for he was remarkably hard to pin down. You could easily get the impression that he was Birmingham's answer to Joe Brown, and he certainly seemed to be on Christian name terms with most of the top climbers at the time, as well as many big names in the art world. Much of this was undoubtedly true, but Bill, never a shrinking violet, did tend to lay it on a bit thick, and although I felt he was a far better climber than I, he was always very reluctant to make on-sight leads of routes he hadn't done before, which is, of course, the best way of finding out how good you actually are.

All this was easily overlooked. I enjoyed Bill's company, had found someone else to climb with, and was impressed with his considerable artistic talent. Even though I took his stories with a pinch of salt, he did offer me an entreé into both the climbing and art worlds based around Sheffield. Now I felt it was up to me to take advantage of my good fortune.

Chapter twelve: Calmer Waters

On January 5th 1969 Ali gave birth to another daughter, Gemma Abigail. She was born in a maternity hospital in Chapeltown, only a mile down the road. At the risk of her never reading another page of this missive, being born in Yorkshire enabled her to qualify to play cricket for the county, a hoary old cliché she has heard many times before and never found remotely funny. Now I have written it down, I think she's probably right. Anyway it would also require both a sex change operation, and an outstanding talent for the sport, neither of which has ever been a remote possibility.

This time Ali and the baby were both fine and once they were safely home I could indulge in being a proud father. I have to admit that I have never been one of those dads who become emotionally involved from the first moment of pregnancy. But once Gemma was born my love and pride was quite overwhelming and unconditional. It goes without saying that Ali's parents and my mum were equally delighted. Life seemed to be working out after all.

It didn't last long. After about two months Gemma developed a chest infection that seemed to get progressively worse until, in the middle of the night, she was rushed by ambulance to the Sheffield Children's Hospital and the terrible world of oxygen tents and guarded comments from doctors and nurses started again. Surely not this time…? For a couple of days Gemma, who had contracted bronchiolitis, hovered between life and death before she came round and very slowly recovered. It was the beginning of a long series of childhood problems, bronchitis and asthma being the worst. The Sheffield Children's Hospital became an all too familiar destination. We had nothing but praise for the staff, who undoubtedly saved Gemma's life on this, and several other occasions.

Back at college and remembering the staff exhibition at Stockport, I organised a similar one at Rotherham Museum and Art Gallery. Four of us were involved: Derek Allport, whose zany clockwork sculptures had echoes of Heath Robinson; John Dyer who was the Head of Foundation showed his ceramics and Jill Gabbani displayed her textiles. My own work was now embarrassingly large. During the late 60s shaped canvasses (i.e. other than rectangular or square) had become very fashionable. I was hugely impressed by a large piece by Richard Smith, which is often on display at Tate Britain. Called 'Riverfall', it is a beautiful luminous green three-piece canvas that splays out at the bottom as if the paint is about to pour over the floor. Quite independently I remembered my model aircraft days and started building up the edges of my canvas with shaped hardboard, then stretching canvas

over them. When they were primed, the canvas automatically tensioned into undulating surfaces, that gave a curious sensation of floating. On the surface I played various illusionistic devices, painting discs of pure colour, with trompe-l'oeil shadows. The result, I thought at the time, was, if not breaking new ground, at least getting away from the shadow of Bernard Cohen. Now, they all seem to me to be pretentious and derivative, but, and it is quite a big 'but', I did learn a lot about the nature of paint and painting, and the fascination with illusion has stayed with me to the present. To my surprise, and four decades later, a Rotherham ex-student, Chris Rawson-Tetley, told me recently that he recognised my new paintings immediately. I didn't know whether to be to be pleased or annoyed.

Anyway, the exhibition at Rotherham got under way with the most lavish and extraordinary opening I have ever attended. As well as unlimited quantities of booze, the nibbles included bits of tripe on little sticks and black pudding! Bill and Pam Beech came over and they brought with them Geoff and Jackie Birtles. At the time Geoff was a young Derbyshire hot shot putting up hard new routes, many at his spiritual home of Stoney Middleton with his climbing partner, Tom Proctor. It is a sobering thought that our first meeting was over 40 years ago, yet we have remained good friends through thick and thin.

It was around this time that rumours began to abound that Foundation Courses outside the degree colleges would close. Subsequent history showed that these were only rumours, but at the time they seemed real enough. Many, if not most, art schools running Dip AD courses were being absorbed into the newly formed polytechnics and I felt that a job in one would be my best option. Ideally a job at Sheffield would be the perfect solution, but it never materialised. One on the Foundation Course at Bristol did and I applied, remembering a few odd trips to the Avon Gorge which is the biggest crag in the country set completely inside the city limits. Slightly to my surprise I got an interview. By now, under Ali's excellent tutelage, I had easily passed my driving test, bought the ubiquitous grey Mini-van that seemed obligatory for young lecturers and rock-climbers and again, almost obligatorily, written it off. We inherited Ali's Mum's car, the dreaded Hillman Imp, the worst car I have ever owned. It was in this, with a large painting tied precariously to a roof rack, that I drove down to Bristol and to the Faculty of Art and Design at Bower Ashton. The college is set in parkland, on the Somerset side of the Avon Gorge about a mile from the Suspension Bridge. It is possibly the most attractive location of any art school in the country. This, I quickly realised, proved to be a double-edged sword in that it attracted thousands

< Drawing of Clifton Suspension Bridge, looking towards the Somerset side.

of student candidates whose main concern seemed to be the view rather than the quality of the courses they were applying for.

At the interview, I met Dennis Curry, Head of Foundation Studies, and Dr Bolland, the recently appointed Director of the whole Polytechnic, who, by a stroke of good fortune, wanted to see for himself how the faculty made its appointments. There was also a silent, grey-faced, bearded man who looked to be on the verge of death. The interview was easily the toughest I had experienced, but I was glad I had brought a folio of student work from Rotherham, as well as my own, which seemed to interest them. After the usual interminable wait in the library I was offered the job. I found out later that bringing the student folio down had swung it, and that Dr Bolland had told the others that I had made the most effort. I also found out later that the ashen-faced man who was to become a great friend, was the normally ruddy -faced Neil Murison who had, the previous evening, attended a private view of a Peter Blake exhibition, sponsored by Harvey's, the famous old Bristol sherry importers. Neil, like many of the other guests, had availed himself of their over-generous hospitality, which explained his ghostly pallor.

I had been offered the job in the Easter term of 1970 and was able to hand in my notice in time to start the new job in the summer term. I was genuinely sad to be leaving Rotherham. In only two and a half years I had matured as a teacher and the team I had worked with had made the Foundation Course a dynamic and successful one. I have occasionally wondered since what my life would have been like if I had stayed, but, of course, there is absolutely no point in 'what-iffing'. Curiously, I vividly remember after the Bristol interview, on my return to Sheffield, Bill Beech saying he hoped I had made the right decision and that I wouldn't come to regret it.

And so, after a short Easter break, I found myself starting my new job. It was very strange. As I have said before, the summer term on Foundation is mainly concerned with applications and interviews. My presence was hardly necessary and most of the students were already certain of their destination. But one thing became quickly apparent, Dennis, the course leader, wanted us all to sing from the same hymn sheet — 'us' being Dennis, Neil Murison, Nev Aston, Rob Swain and myself. I found this very hard to understand. Why, with five opinions available, did we all have to toe the party line? And if that were the case, why were five lecturers deemed essential to run the course when one, with a megaphone, would have done as well?

My first impressions of Bristol were mixed. It had been awarded Dip AD in Fine Art, Painting and Sculpture, Graphic Design,

Ceramics, Fashion and Textiles, and something called Construction. It took some time before I actually understood what that was all about. In fact, I don't think I ever did as will soon become obvious.

Frankly, I found the Fine Art Department very disappointing. The prevailing ethos was harking back to the Cornish school of painting. Artists like Peter Lanyon and Roger Hilton were still revered, both of whom I thought were old hat. The Fine Art staff, under Paul Feiler and Ernest Pascoe, were incredibly élitist and Foundation Course staff were made to feel small to the point of non-existence. There were exceptions, particularly Alf Stockam, and Bristol blue-eyed boy Dave Inshaw who was already a very successful and sought-after painter. As for the other areas, Graphic Design was by far the largest, but seemed to be embedded in the past, with the exception of a good illustration course. Ceramics was a small course, highly sought after and, allowing for my complete aversion to the medium, seemed to be pretty good. Fashion and Textiles was almost a separate entity set on the third and fourth floors of the college. There seemed to be virtually no contact with Foundation, or indeed any other courses. And then there was the Construction course, a pretentious name for Furniture Design which, due to an obtuse philosophical history, was never referred to as such. The Construction Department, like the question of how many angels could balance on a pinhead, seemed to spend an inordinate amount of time questioning whether it should exist or not. A few years later it actually declared itself non-existent due to the aforesaid philosophical difficulties. To my sniggering delight, the Polytechnic promptly declared the lecturers' salaries equally non-existent, which seemed to do the trick and the course existed once more (the next day, in fact).

So as Ali and I spent the summer of 1970 preparing to move down to Bristol, I was going with slightly mixed feelings; pleased that job-wise, I was sailing into calm waters, but already mildly concerned at my role on the course. Ali, who had given me total support throughout the difficult years, continued to do so, yet she would be moving, with a young baby, quite a long way from her parents and all the friendships we had made in Sheffield. Strangely, I don't think that I had even begun to realise just how much Sheffield had already got under my skin.

Chapter thirteen: Self-Destruct Button, Please Press

During my first full year at Bristol, Ali and I moved from a fairly grotty flat just off the Gloucester Road, to a truly palatial apartment in Leigh Woods on the Somerset side of the Gorge and only about a quarter of a mile from the Suspension Bridge. It was a first-floor flat, with two bathrooms, several balconies, a hallway big enough for games of indoor cricket and football, and a superb view over Bristol. I could walk down the hill through Ashton Park to college — Bower Ashton. It could hardly have been better. Ali was pregnant again and at last we felt that we had every good reason to be happy.

Why then did I harbour the first terrible doubts about the future? If I am honest, a lot of it was due to my own immature feelings that I had missed out sexually. Alison had been my only partner and I felt, however wrongly, that I hadn't had my share. Still not yet 30, I was working in the permissive art college environment where everyone seemed to be having a lot more fun than me. Maybe this hankering for a freedom I felt I never had was a delayed reaction to all the trouble we had experienced in the first years of marriage.

I think that on top of this I was possibly showing the first symptoms of depression which has affected me periodically ever since. I had actually had the first intimations of this back at Ealing when I seemed to have inexplicable bouts of sadness for no apparent reason. I know now that this horrible condition can strike at almost any time, often regardless of events, good or bad. It has taken most of my adult life to deal with what is now recognised as a real illness, but apart from identifying the early symptoms and seeking medical help a bit quicker, not much has changed. At worst, bouts of depression are almost impossible to describe — Churchill's 'Black Dog' comes nowhere near explaining the depths of misery that sufferers experience. The condition seems to have a life of its own and lasts for as long as it wants to, often only lifting after months rather than weeks. Anti-depression drugs help a bit, but they are not a cure.

However, compared with what was to come in later years, this episode was almost trivial, and there were still plenty of good things to enjoy. Gemma was obviously going to be highly intelligent and was, even at under two years old, a delightful and funny child. (Of course, I would say that, wouldn't I?) And she was about to be joined by a baby sister. Ali was to give birth in the maternity hospital at the top of Whiteladies Road overlooking the Clifton Downs. Once again there was no question of me attending the birth. Ali, when asked if I was going to be there, replied tersely: "Christ, I hope not. It was bad enough having him there at the conception." I have always thought her remark hilarious and have told the story against myself for almost 40 years. It has only just occurred to me that maybe it wasn't a joke…

Without my presence, on May 28th 1971 Ali gave birth to Rebecca Lucy who quickly became just 'Becky', and has remained so ever since. I have always maintained that, whereas Gemma was generally a good baby, who slept through the night from quite early days, Becky always seemed to be awake and crying. I know Ali doesn't remember this in the same way at all, but I do recall feeling quite bewildered that two children of the same parents could be so different almost from birth. Of course, they have now changed again. Gemma is emotional, strong-willed and quite highly strung, whereas Becky is calm, focused and wise. (Oh God, I am in danger of creating a small civil war if I am not careful — Gemma, of course, is wise, but bases a lot of her arguments on instant reactions. Becky is more cautious. Please, both of you, don't fight.)

At college I was slowly finding a role, and it was not one that came naturally, not at first anyway. Neil, Nev and Rob were all supportive kind and understanding. Coming as I did from Sheffield, though I'd only been there for a few short years, I was probably more abrasive than the others, and I gradually started to play the Devil's Advocate, arguing sometimes for the sake of it, but trying to give an alternative point of view. Sadly, Dennis Curry didn't appear to understand this at all and seemed to think I was undermining his authority. I don't want to get on a high horse and start banging on about free speech, but I must admit that whenever I hear those dreaded words, 'I know we all agree', my heart sinks. I know you will all agree with me on this one.

The move to Bristol had brought about a big change in my work. The big, shaped, abstract canvases didn't seem to lead anywhere, neither intellectually nor financially, and I felt it was time for a new start. I had the luxury of a good-sized studio in our flat, but what to do? I decided that I would go back to basics, and make a series of single observational drawings and see where they led. In the first summer holiday I spent weeks drawing large cardboard boxes arranged in geometric patterns. Each drawing could take anything up to three or four days to complete, and I tried to be as rigorous as possible in measuring proportion and assessing light and shade. I progressed to drawing the moulded window frames and curtains in the sitting room, and eventually produced about a dozen pieces of work that I felt reasonably happy with.

The only problem was Ali, who until now had been long suffering in her acceptance and encouragement of what I was doing. I felt that she only ever saw my art as a time-consuming hobby — certainly there had never been any financial gain. It was hard to convince her that I wouldn't be lecturing in Bristol without

111

^ Drawing of photos in an alcove.

> ^ Twelve cardboard boxes.

> Television and table.

producing my own work. I fear that her feelings about climbing were even stronger. At the time it certainly was only a hobby, but one that she couldn't share and didn't much like. I was, I thought, quite restrained in taking as little time as possible to go down to the Gorge, but basically I always thought that Ali would be much happier if I gave up both painting and climbing. She was certainly not the last woman to have these feelings. I couldn't help thinking that, as these two activities were such a big part of what had attracted her to me in the first place, it was counter-productive to try and stop them.

Re-reading this I am sure Ali would vehemently disagree, but my main memories of our time together in Bristol were of devising ever more ingenious ways of stealing time to paint, and almost

112

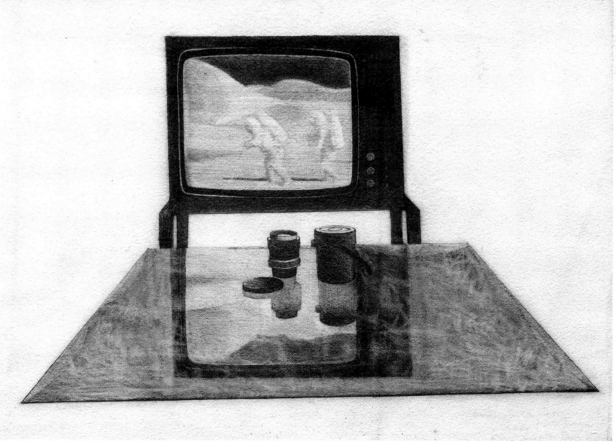

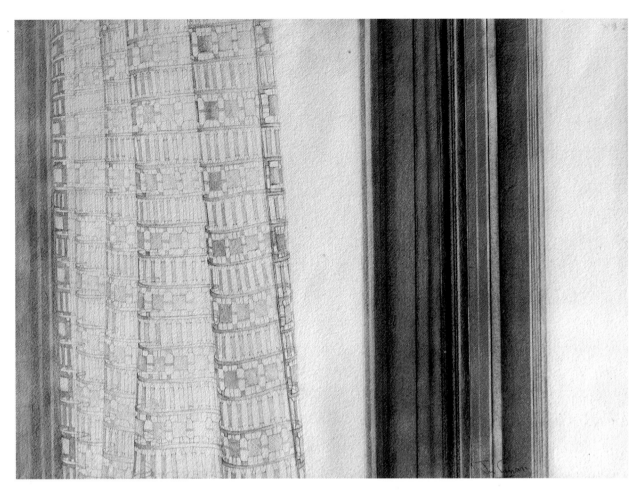

^ *Window frame and curtain.*

giving up climbing completely. Then, one day in the middle of the autumn term, Ali turned up in college with the two children, for reasons long forgotten. I was teaching in one of the studios and on the way out Ali mentioned a student wearing a torn top and paint-stained jeans. "She's very attractive, don't you think?" Why had she noticed her? I had barely registered her until now. Was it just coincidence, or an acute awareness of trouble ahead?

Jane Cavinder was indeed a stunning looking girl and almost from that day I fell hopelessly for her. She shared a tiny terraced house with two other girls, one of whom, Helen Chadwick, would become famous as a conceptual artist of the 80s and 90s before a tragic early death of a heart attack in 1996. The house in Hotwells Road was built almost into the side of the Avon Gorge and faced the docks. The girls, away from home for the first time, revelled in their freedom and Hotwells Road was open all hours to drop in, listen to music, and if one was so inclined, smoke a joint.

In those days staff and students were far closer than they are today. Staff went on field trips with students in hire vans without ever thinking of insurance, or health and safety issues. Bower Ashton was famous for its Thursday night college bops and it was quite natural for college staff to attend. The early 70s were just

114

^ *Table top with child's shoes.*

about the height of the permissive society as the flower power pop scene of the late 60s filtered down to every college and university in the country. Sexual relationships between staff and students may have been unprofessional, but were not uncommon.

So I blundered into a situation that eventually led to the break-up of my marriage. It was really rather pathetic. Ali found out and was justifiably incandescent, though I had never technically been unfaithful. Jane was still a virgin and once she realised my feelings she very sensibly got herself a real boyfriend. I was distraught and racked with guilt about Ali and the children. I also made the classic mistake of confusing depression with heartbreak. Always good for the spectacular look-at-me gesture, I took to camping in the depths of Ashton Park in thick woods in an old mountain tent and sleeping bag that disgorged feathers all over me. I could wash, shower and shave in the toilets at college, where students probably assumed I had gone quite mad.

It was a situation that couldn't continue and eventually Ali took the children back up north, not to her parents, but to Sheffield where she lived in the same house as Bill Beech whose marriage was also drifting onto the rocks.

Returning to Bristol from a trip to London in the middle of a

115

hot, claustrophobic July night, I walked past the house on Hotwells Road. The door was open and inside was dark and empty, apart from a sad little bunch of dead flowers which, in an agony of self-pity, I dropped into the mucky waters of the Avon. I sat on the dockside. My life had collapsed around my ears. I was nearly 30 and had not much to show for it.

In a desperate attempt to retrieve something from the wreckage, I remember thinking, 'Well, there's only two things I'm any good at, art and climbing. If I'm going to make anything of my life I'd better try and combine my talents, such as they are'. A tiny crumb of consolation, but, as I walked back up to Clifton and over the Suspension Bridge in the first grey light of dawn, I really didn't have the faintest clue as to how to go about it.

< Gemma aged three.

Chapter fourteen: Coronation Street – A Fiasco, a Fulfilment and a Future

I nevitably, after I had allowed my marriage to implode I had to give up the baronial splendour of the flat in Leigh Woods and moved into a tiny basement bedsit in St Paul's Road in Clifton. Even so, I was virtually penniless as I paid over half my salary to Ali, and after the rent for the flat was taken I had almost nothing to live on, no car, of course, and not much prospect of life getting any easier in the foreseeable future. As the situation was entirely my fault I couldn't really complain. Even so Ali found it even harder to look after the children and was poorer than I.

My only luxury was to join a gym, the Empire Sports Club in St Paul's, an institution far removed from the trendy gyms of today. It catered mainly for boxing and weight lifting, but also offered circuit training for football and rugby players, and oddballs like me. Its clientele was largely drawn from the West Indian population of St Paul's who provided a constant background commentary of patois humour, encouragement and piss-taking in equal measure.

I did circuit training two or three times a week, and also went on a really severe diet. It had a dramatic and beneficial effect on my climbing as well as my weight, and for the next year I climbed whenever I could in the Avon Gorge, and occasionally in North Wales, Derbyshire and the Cheddar Gorge. This last was becoming a bit of a fixation.

When Ali and I were still together, Bill Beech and Pam had come down for the weekend, bringing with them Paul Nunn, already a major figure in British climbing. Paul and Bill climbed what was, at the time, an aid route at Cheddar called *Paradise Lost* on the overhanging Sunset Buttress. I took a roll of black and white photographs of Paul leading the big second pitch,

< Painting in my flat in St Paul's Road.

117

and later made an assemblage of some of them, using Sellotape, cow gum and brown sticky paper. I mention this because it was 10 years before David Hockney started producing what he called his 'joiners' which eventually used a huge quantity of images placed together to give an absorbing, almost cubist view of his subjects. Mine were not like that and they were never intended to be an end in themselves. I was aware that photographers had used the same sort of ideas many years before. I was particularly struck by the Italian mountain photographer Vittorio Sella who made stunning composite images of the Karakoram and Caucasus ranges. My humble set of glued together images of Paul became the subject of a painting in which I treated the photos as a trompe l'oeil still life, faithfully painting the strips of Sellotape and brown sticky paper holding them together. So at last I had managed to combine climbing and painting, albeit in a simple way. From a climbing point of view the call of the Cheddar Gorge was becoming an obsession, and I was determined to become competent enough to climb Chris Bonington's great classic of the Gorge — *Coronation Street*.

Despite my climbing growing in importance, lack of money was the perennial problem. One way of alleviating this happened almost by accident. Ali and I had made friends with Bob Burn and his wife Pat. Bob was a young lecturer in Graphic Design and we had somehow both become the *enfants terrible* of our respective departments. Together with their two young children, Lucy and Becky, they were living in a modern semi on an estate in Clevedon, but Bob had just bought an old cottage, or rather the wreck of two cottages, in the little Somerset village of Banwell. It needed some renovation work and Bob asked me if I fancied 'a couple of weekends' labouring to sort it out. 'Sorting it out' eventually took Bob several years, but the initial rebuilding took almost a year of weekends and evenings of hard labour.

I always enjoyed simple labouring jobs, whether as a student stacking cider crates at Showerings, or mixing sand and cement in Banwell. Anything that required brute force, but no thinking, and I was happy. I could never in a month of Sundays (which is roughly what we did that year) undertake the jobs that Bob thrived on. Just the thought of how many plans, calculations, measurements, setbacks, material decisions, orders, modifications and, above all, responsibilities were involved could make me feel quite faint. All I wanted was to be told 'do this', 'lift that', 'dig there', 'stack them there'. But I did take pride in the kitchen we built from scratch, with a pitched roof and rafters that were almost sculptures in their own right, cut, even carved, to fit the irregular wall that they were bedded in to. With old buildings like Banwell, right angles were non-existent and, despite my reluctance to make any decisions at

Paul Nunn surveying an unclimbed sea cliff near Cape Wrath, November 1969. >

all, the whole building work was made of a million guesses and compromises from which, to my surprise, I got a great deal of satisfaction.

We actually managed to get the roof on in the middle of winter. Bob had built up scaffolding, but as the length of the kitchen was much longer than the width, he was reluctant to cut the plank we walked on. It protruded almost three metres into space on the short side and, always slightly cowardly about falling off, I frequently reminded Bob not to walk too far on the unsupported end, before absent-mindedly doing just that myself. The plank tipped up and I ran down it and hurtled into the frozen garden. I completed two back flips, a somersault and several cartwheels before coming to rest with all the poise of Olga Korbett (that's how I remember it). I had travelled a surprisingly long way from my point of departure and was completely uninjured, apart from my pride, while Bob collapsed in hysterical laughter and relief that I hadn't broken my neck.

Although a lot of the work was pretty grim and undertaken on dark winter evenings, I still have vivid memories — of listening to an old Miles Davis LP 'Sketches of Spain' encrusted with cement dust and played on an equally cruddy record player; of pints and last orders in The Bell, thawing out our chilled bodies in the warmth of the pub; of Bob dropping a full wheelbarrow of cement on my head as it fell off the plank he was wheeling it along: and of 'liberating' stone from a half-demolished wall in the garden of the police station at Congressbury, and being caught by the local plod who, instead of arresting us, told us we could help ourselves.

Another friend from the Foundation Course, Nev Aston, was also heavily into home building. It seemed to be more than a hobby, for no sooner had he transformed one house than he sold it and started again. This one was in another village, Pensford, and probably had as much work to be done as Banwell, though a lot of it was more to do with exterior design rather than structural necessity. Nev was fastidious to the point of complete obsessivness and work at Pensford was slower but more demanding.

The work took a big chunk out of the summer before I had earned enough to escape and go the Alps with Paul Nunn. It marked the beginning of a long friendship with Paul, one of the two or three closest male friends of my adult life.

Back at Bower Ashton, in the autumn of 1973 a significant event happened. I had done a lot of climbing in the Avon Gorge with a sculpture student, Pete O'Sullivan, who had started climbing in his first year and had made rapid progress. Pete was tall, very strong and very pushy. He had rapidly surpassed me but I was still just about hanging on to his coat tails. It was time for a visit to Cheddar and an appointment with fear.

Coronation Street, Chris Bonington's masterpiece, takes a great and nearly direct line up High Rock. At over 400 feet it is more like a Dolomite route — serious and incredibly exposed. I had climbed on High Rock before with Steve Durkin. We had climbed *Sceptre*, an undistinguished, vegetated Very Severe, except for a great last pitch which gives a hint of what the situation on *Coronation Street* would be like, looking straight down to the road and car park. It was one of the few climbs I did with Steve at Avon and Cheddar. He always found steep limestone quite daunting, but I was pleased that we did *Sceptre* together. It provided me with two or three of my better climbing photographs, including Steve, with a smile or grimace, jamming up the final pitch with safety only a few feet away.

For *Coronation Street* Pete and I caught the bus to Cheddar and bivouacked in a bed of wild garlic in the shadow of Castle Rocks. Up early and, in my case, quaking with nerves, we set off up the first two long pitches of *Sceptre*, which were just as overgrown and unpleasant as I remembered. But then, when *Sceptre* branches rightward, the first pitch of *Coronation Street* goes straight up a steep wall that gives a taste of things to come. I led this and hauled out onto a flat-topped pedestal — the last comfortable stance before the serious bit. Above was the famous Shield. This is (or was) a bulging flake at the end of a strenuous traverse. It looked as though it could part company with the parent rock at any moment and, in fact, some of it now has. I followed Pete and found him tied to several pegs and standing on a small foothold. As I had no intention of leading the next pitch, the crux, we spent ages carefully changing over, aware of almost 300 feet of fresh air snapping at our ankles.

The weather, which had been grey and gloomy all day, threatened to rain and as Pete confidently climbed the slim elegant groove it started spitting. By the time he had finished the pitch it was drizzling and soon it turned into a relentless downpour. Reluctantly I untied from the belay and, with plenty of help from above, started the groove, which was already slippery. I have to say that I then lost it completely. Wet, frightened and with feet skidding off every hold, I fought my way up to an overhang, beyond which the crack widened to give proper jamming, which I should have revelled in. But now, tired and almost beyond rational thought, I fought and groaned up the last 20 feet, where Pete was belayed on a tiny ledge looking decidedly unimpressed.

Once again we performed the slow motion choreography of swapping belays and then Pete set off up the last pitch. Then an amazing thing happened. With a heart-stopping roar, a helicopter appeared, and clattered slowly past the crag at almost the same

^ *High Rock Cheddar.*

^ *Steve on* Sceptre, *High Rock,*
Cheddar.

Chapter fourteen: Coronation Street – A Fiasco, a Fulfilment and a Future

^ *Steve Durkin, me and Pete O'Sullivan in Cornwall.*

height as us. It turned and came back hovering closer now and I could see someone taking photos. It made several more passes before disappearing up the Gorge, the thwack-thwack of the rotor blades echoing off the cliffs. Both of us had tried to ignore this intrusion, conscious that any acknowledgement might be seen as a sign for help. To this day I have no idea what it was doing, and back in college I tried unsuccessfully to trace it, in the hope of getting hold of what would have been some unique photographs.

Meanwhile Pete had finished the climb and, wet and almost weeping tears of relief, I followed him. We coiled ropes and descended in silence down the tiny paths that led to the bliss of flat, safe ground. In the pouring rain Pete took off his helmet, and savagely drop-kicked it at the bottom of the crag. I was relieved at being alive; he was furious that such a brilliant route had been spoilt by the weather and my performance. We caught the bus back to Bristol and ate fish and chips. Pete slept at my flat — both of us talking in our sleep — me yelling "Tight!" and Pete, quite reasonably, telling me to fuck off.

So it was done. A flawed ambition realised. Ten years later I did *Coronation Street* again — this time with Joe Brown and the irrepressible Mo Anthoine. I probably only climbed it marginally better this time, but in fits of giggles at Mo's running commentary. It was the best and last climb I did with Mo before he developed the brain tumour that led to his death in 1989, aged just 50.

Soon after *Coronation Street* I became mobile again. Having spent the last year or so reverting to hitch-hiking (and becoming very good at it), I was delighted to be given temporary custody of Bob's VW minibus. Bob and family had done a year's swap with an American tutor in New York State who couldn't cope with driving an ancient VW round the tiny lanes of Somerset. I offered

> *About to climb* Coronation Street *with Joe Brown and Mo Anthoine.*

to look after it. Ages ago the ignition key had snapped inside the steering column and it could only be started by inserting a sawn-off fork into the barrel. It drank petrol and I tried not to use it for long journeys, but it was really useful for visiting Mum. She had moved from Ealing to a flat in Malvern, a move that she and Dad had planned for his retirement. As Malvern was full of ancient old ladies, and not much else, I questioned the wisdom of her move, but she did it anyway.

In November we took the Foundation students on a coach trip to London. We did this every term and gave them a wide choice of what to see — the National Gallery, Tate and V&A etc. There was a girl on the course called Trish Mohan. She was a good all-round student who quickly showed a real talent for theatre design. With long dark hair and a lovely face, she had a passing resemblance to the Leonardo drawing of St Ann, although she had Irish, not Italian ancestry. She was extrovert, intelligent, funny, self-deprecating, independent and, well, I was going to say, wise beyond her years, but in the light of what happened next, obviously not.

To cut a short story even shorter, after a liquid lunch we found ourselves with our arms round each other gazing, somewhat bewildered, into each other's eyes. It was the beginning of one of the better relationships of my life. Despite her youth, she had a rare empathy and tolerance of the many contradictory chunks of my life. She accepted without question the break up of my marriage, my two girls now living with Ali in Altrincham, my painting and my climbing. She even did a route with me in the Avon Gorge and came down to Cheddar where I tried to impress her by pointing out the line of *Coronation Street*. We went to Wales in her beloved mini and she sunbathed in the Llanberis Pass while I climbed *Ivy Sepulchre*. As well as that, she was a hardworking and conscientious student.

Trish came from a large, close-knit family who lived in a big rambling house outside Bristol. Her mother was a great lady and seemed to accept our relationship quite happily. My only memory of Trish's dad was on the summer solstice at her house where a motley array of friends and relatives played football on the large, rather moth-eaten lawn. I was wearing (I can hardly bear to write these words) a pair of purple flared, velvet loons. They, in the style of the times, had voluminous folds below the knees, but were crutch huggingly tight above. Needless to say, I had managed to bust the zip and, in a golden sunset, lying in the grass but still wearing them, Trish set to work to repair it. Passing by, her dad gave me a rather strange look, obviously fearing the worst.

By this time Steve Durkin had moved to Wales, and bought a tiny cottage, the Nook, in Brynrefail, the little village at the bottom

^ *Trish aged 20 after her Foundation Course.*

end of Llyn Padarn where I stayed on my infrequent trips to Wales. On one occasion, which Steve often referred to as the 'Brynrefail tsunami', Trish and I managed to cause a small tidal wave in the bathroom that fused all the electrics in the cottage. I don't think any further explanation is either necessary or desirable.

In the years since leaving college, Steve's life had become a bit of a mystery to me. Back in 1964 he had a terrible motorbike crash that nearly cost him a leg. His recuperation was long and painful, and he developed an obsession with climbing *Cenotaph Corner* to prove to himself that he had completely recovered. When he did it he seemed to lose a lot of his drive and self-motivation. Years later he used to refer to his time in the Nook as his Lost Years and, after the fashion of the time, he certainly appeared to me to have more or less dropped out. I fear that by now I was far too full of my own ambitions to take too much notice of his state of mind. On my visits we tended to play the same game with variations of 'What's it all about?' and 'Why are we here?' If we ever found the answers, we had forgotten them by the next morning.

While the Foundation Course year drew to a close, Trish applied to and was accepted on the Theatre Design Course at Nottingham, one of the best of its kind in the country. I had spent the last two years painting or attempting to paint various rock-climbing scenes, but the only one I rated was the aforementioned one of Paul Nunn at Cheddar. I had also become quite keen on still photography and had leaned to make black and white prints in the photography department. But I could never get completely involved in photography. However technically well done, I was always slightly disappointed with the results.

Then two things happened. After teaching now for eight years I was due to have a year's sabbatical (a privilege long gone). Only one was awarded to each Faculty and as I was the only applicant I got it: a whole year off with full pay. I had been thinking about filmmaking and had occasionally helped students shoot Super 8 film. Knowing no more about it than they did, any help was limited. But there was something about film that intrigued me, far more than still photography, though I couldn't put my finger on it. I decided that a film course would be the best way of spending the year on the frankly dubious basis that it would broaden my teaching skills and possibly go some way to resolving my own creative dilemma. With the help of Bill Beech I was accepted on the Film Course at Sheffield — where else?

Inevitably, Trish and I would go our own ways. I was very conscious of exploiting my position as a lecturer and felt it was important to let her go. So I wasn't a complete bastard. We gradually lost touch, though years later I visited her on my way

125

back from Wales where she and her husband lived near Llangollen. Shortly after that she moved to Market Harborough and disappeared from my life.

Back in the summer of 1973 I was so fixated on my coming year in Sheffield that nothing else seemed to matter. It was the beginning of two decades of non-stop ambition. Trish escaped by a whisker, for within a year I had become a self-centred and at times a quite devious and driven person for whom the words 'bastard' and 'complete' were probably quite appropriate.

Chapter fifteen: A Great Effort

When I started my one-year postgraduate film course at Sheffield I remembered Bob Burn saying, in some bewilderment, that as I was technically incompetent at making anything more complex than digging a hole, he failed to see why I should have picked film, an activity that demanded high levels of skill and know-how across a wide range of disciplines. I could only agree with him. But most of my feelings of inadequacy were dispelled when I met Barry Callaghan, Head of Film at Sheffield. Barry was one of the most patient and kindly of men — ever tolerant of students' behaviour and with a wonderful knack of encouraging you at the very moment when you wished you had never set eyes on a strip of celluloid in the first place. For a year he put up with me, as did his fellow lecturer Paul Heywood. I will never be able to repay all the help and kindness they showed me.

Many years later Barry moved to Leeds where he ran the Film School at Leeds Metropolitan University. By sheer coincidence, my eldest daughter, Gemma, was his secretary for a year. She, too, has fond memories of Barry who also rated her very highly. Tragically, Barry died of a heart attack in 2008. Generations of students and staff attended his funeral to pay tribute to the man who had inspired so many to make films.

Back in 1973, long before the advent of video, let alone high resolution digital technology, 16mm film was the medium to be mastered. Barry wanted us all to experience the multi-discipline of filmmakers. We worked on each student's film, running sound on one, camera on another, lighting on a third, as well as directing/producing/editing a film of our own. Whereas in one short year nobody was going to excel in any one discipline, by the end of it you should know how a film is made, from a proposal to begin with, to a finished print at the end. There was an awful lot to learn in between. Inevitably, I wanted to make a climbing film of some sort. It took me the first few weeks of the course to work out what I wanted, and how. The first little exercise I did was to go out into Derbyshire with a clockwork Bolex camera, and a 100-foot roll of film (about three minutes long). A technician, Tony Riley, filmed me from two angles as I twice soloed an easy route on Stanage.

Tony Riley was a climber and still photographer who had already co-operated with Paul Nunn in producing the photos for Paul's compendium *Rock Climbs in the Peak District*. Tony was, and is, a technical perfectionist and seemed ideal to be cameraman on any film I made. It was the beginning of a partnership that would eventually take us to the Trango Tower in the Karakoram, and to Ben Nevis to make what I always think of as my favourite film, *The Bat*.

127

Back at college I edited the results. I was absolutely transfixed. Even with no sound I found that by cutting long shots and close ups together, you could be almost infinitely inventive, making a sequence so convincing that it made the whole more than the sum of the parts. I can't explain the elation of just joining a few bits of film together. I felt at the time that that was what I wanted to do — that this was my way of fulfilling whatever potential I possessed. Later in the course, with the addition of sound, music and effects to make the mix even richer, I couldn't imagine ever doing anything else. From the first day of editing my own film, painting ceased to figure and would stay that way for nearly 30 years. I ate and slept film for the whole year. There was nothing to rival it except… except…

When I arrived at college on the first day with Bill Beech, at whose house I was staying, I caught a glimpse through a window of a woman with long dark hair descending the stairs from the Film Department. "Who the hell is that?"

"Oh," said Bill, "that's Fran Hegarty."

"Christ," I croaked, in despair, "give me a break."

Need I say more? She was married with a small child, Irish-born, but her family had moved to Glasgow where she went to art college.

If ever I fell for a lost cause this was the one. I was besotted, but knew deep down that nothing would come of it. The snag was that initially I had some cause for hope. At a fancy dress dance at the college Frances turned up, almost unrecognisable, in a blonde wig. At the end of the evening we danced together and suddenly, apropos of nothing, she murmured: "What are we going to do when you go back to Bristol?" As sentences go it was hardly up there with great literary declarations of undying love, but in the circumstances it probably ranks number one as the most exciting sentence I had ever heard. (Although come to think of it, running a close second must be the phone call I received many years later that started, "Hi Jim. This is Joanna Lumley." But that's another — even shorter — story.)

So, despite the ever-present nagging heartache for Frances, I had to get on with the course. I have always been an avid reader and, of course, I had read most of the climbing literature around. I had always been impressed with the tortured prose and poetry of J Menlove Edwards, the great rock-climbing pioneer of the 1930s, particularly in Wales.

Edwards, an unhappy and unfulfilled homosexual, had written several articles for The Climbers' Club *Journal*. They were dense, complex pieces of work, far removed from the understated laconic Oxbridge-dominated writing of the time. One article

Pause, stand on th scree edge and look back.
You who too hastily — Watch carefully again
There is the cliff, its Eastern incline steep
With turrets there and there: How well I
Know them. When we were climbing there
Do you remember, far from that tiny earthwork
You remember, stretching, then upon the slab:
How powerful the fingers? ...
And then that other day, rock wet, wet everything,
How on that bare wall on the right,
Where from the stance a craftsman riskily ...

And there again, still on that Eastern slope,
Day after day repeats, day after day
The clouds pass over, or the wind occurs,
Or snow. Sparse growth on it, on this
Dull cliff, dead or asleep or living,
But the thoughts return.

Or am I mourning for the dead?
And is it you? You, where
That stream of sunlight shows
The texture. You. Watch
Carefully again: there it is
Steep and solid there, broken more
Here over on the left. Yes
It is you, you only.
And on your form the dusts will come
Thy walls do lichen grow.

On with your coat: walk jauntily
And turn your back: be gone
Over the springy turf: so
Should we celebrate departure.

Menlove Edwards – circa 1937

^ *Drawing based around Menlove Edwards's poem 'Pause' — one of the last drawings I did before film dominated my life for the next 25 years.*

had already become a classic: 'A Great Effort'. It was a painfully honest account of a solo climber failing miserably on a climb that he feels he should find straightforward. It was set, probably, on some small crag in the Ogwen Valley. I thought it would be a good subject for a film. Most climbing films and TV outside broadcasts of that era tended to glorify stars like Joe Brown, Don Whillans and Chris Bonington, who, in various ways, downplayed their own considerable abilities. They all used self-deprecation and modesty to deflect the hero-worship heaped upon them by commentators like Chris Brasher. Despite being a climber himself, Chris Brasher was in a constant state of awestruck sycophancy, which I suppose made for good television, but didn't tell the viewers much about the nature of the activity he was describing. Edwards's articles could hardly have been more different if they had been written in Urdu.

Having decided that 'A Great Effort' would be the basis for a

129

film, the problem of location became increasingly urgent. Tony and I spent a few weekends in Wales, visiting the locations of many of Edwards's routes: The Devil's Kitchen, Clogwyn y Grochan in the Llanberis Pass, and Lliwedd. Though 'A Great Effort' was clearly written about a climb on a much smaller crag, Lliwedd had an old-fashioned grandeur that fitted the article, epitomised by Edwards's own route, *Central Gully Direct*, a loose and serious Hard Very Severe that even in 1974 had had only a handful of ascents. I went there with Bill Beech and in some trepidation, led the long crack pitch, finding an ancient rusty piton about halfway up, a relic possibly from the first ascent in 1938. Despite its inaccessibility high on a crag that was an hour's walk from the road, it seemed to fit the article perfectly, and it became the location for what I hoped would be a fitting tribute to one of the great Welsh climbers.

The first problem was to find a format for the film. I decided that instead of a straightforward period recreation, I would climb the route as a modern climber, and intercut the live action with stills we made especially for the film. I hoped that by doing this the essential timelessness of the article would be preserved

The stills entailed having my hair cut drastically short, wearing an old sports jacket, baggy trousers, a white cricket sweater and either nailed boots or plimsolls. Then Tony and I went to Wales and ran through what we hoped would be the scenes in the movie, producing over 200 still images that could be intercut with the moving image more or less at will. I really didn't know if this idea could work at all. The whole filmmaking business was an endless set of questions that could only be answered by first-hand experience.

^ *Me dressed as Menlove Edwards.*

Meanwhile, my confidence was increased slightly by working on other students' projects. One was set in a graveyard near Rotherham. I was cameraman on the shoot which necessitated horribly early starts, and filming in the pouring rain. All good experience but, given my lovelorn state of mind, really depressing.

Since my summer trip with Paul to the Alps, we had become friends, and one evening I went for dinner with Paul and his wife Hilary and met a striking blonde lady called Laraine. A few nights later she turned up in the pub and we started going out together. At first, I didn't know she was one of Fran's ex-students; what Laraine didn't know was the depth of my feelings for Fran. Fran herself, when she found out, seemed to think that I was just an old lecher and refused to believe my protestations to the contrary. Laraine was understandably upset, and I wondered how I had managed to get myself into such a mess, where whatever I did or said would upset someone, including me. Despite an unpromising start, it was a volatile relationship — Laraine always wanting more than I was prepared to give, and my feelings were hopelessly split between futile ones for Fran and an increasing entanglement with Laraine. I also had to make a film.

In February we set off to Wales to try and shoot the film in a week. In those days you could ring an RAF weather centre in Bawtry who gave you a comprehensive analysis of the weather. The forecast for Snowdonia was fine, dry and cold with freezing levels at around 1000 feet. The high pressure should last for at least four or five days, so off we went to stay with Steve in the Nook.

I had been determined to make the shoot as simple as possible. We were not going to use 'sync' sound as the whole film would be using only narration (voice over), music and effects, so there was no need for a sound recordist. In the end we could reduce the numbers to just two — Tony Riley and me, for all but one day of the shoot.

After two days, we had filmed the walk up to Lliwedd. Edwards had described walking in some detail, 'Three hundred yards, then a rest. Three hundred yards, then a rest. During the last war it was explained to me that the British soldier marched by stages and it has been my chief method since. It is easier. Some people prefer to go up hills at a steady 10 miles an hour, as if they were an army tank cruising, or Scott driving sledges in the Antarctic. I do not'.

In his original article, all the climbing action (or inaction) probably occupied only about 20 feet. I felt we had to show some real climbing and so we filmed an elegant Edwards climb that led up to the foot of Central Gully. This was *The Sword* and is graded Very Severe 4c, but the only tricky bit is at the bottom and I had climbed it two or three times already. Mildly gripped, I was prepared to solo it, which I did, finding it quite easy as the camera rolled. Above the awkward start the climb takes the crest of a smooth ridge and looks very elegant. It provided Tony with a beautiful long shot and ensured that there were at least a few minutes of real climbing in the film.

For the crux, which all takes place in the dark confines of Central Gully, I employed two helpers, Bob Dearman and Martin Barnicott, who were responsible for making sure we didn't kill ourselves. Both were excellent climbers and rigged the section to be filmed. For the first time I realised that when filming in a position of high risk and the camera starts rolling you suddenly lose touch with reality. In war zones cameramen have occasionally filmed their own death, so oblivious are they to danger. High on Lliwedd with a drop of 500 feet below, Tony and I were completely reliant on Bob and Barney's skill in, not just making it safe, but concealing any of the gear from the prying lens.

We completed most of the filming on the fourth day, all shot

131

under cloudless skies and freezing conditions. On the last day, which was to be the scene of failure and retreat, clouds moved in and the temperature rose. It couldn't have worked out better and after one more long day in which we not only filmed, but also carried all the gear back to the road, exhausted but incredibly pleased with ourselves, we drove back to Sheffield.

It took the rest of the academic year to edit the film and lay all the different tracks. An important ingredient was the inclusion of two of Edwards's poems, 'Pause' and 'You Rock, You Heaviness'. Both are sad reflections on climbing and unrequited love. 'Pause' is actually written about Lliwedd. They served the function of both embellishing the prose and, at the end, slowing down the story. The film ran to 18 minutes. I suppose if it was made today, which is most unlikely, it would be about four or five minutes with no poetry or musical interludes. An old colleague from Rotherham, Derek Allport, did the narration, and my brother Phil, who had followed family tradition by studying piano and composition at the Royal College of Music, wrote haunting piano pieces that beautifully reflected the mood of the film. Finally, in two long and anxious days, Tony and I did the 'neg cutting' ourselves, a labour of love that was intricate and had to be done perfectly as any mistake could completely wreck the finished print. At last it was done, and the result looked stunning when we saw it projected onto a big screen for the first time.

Unbeknown to me, but to my great delight when I found out, Barry Callaghan showed the film to the producer of a BBC 2 programme devoted to student films, *The First Picture Show*. Not only did they like it, they showed the whole film. I could hardly have hoped for a better start for my new obsession. The year in Sheffield was not just a success, it was a life-changing revelation. At last I felt that after the dreadful loss of confidence two years earlier, I had actually achieved something and, more to the point, it did combine my two interests, art and climbing. What would come next? I thought. Would *A Great Effort* be a one off, or could it be a stepping-stone to greater things?

there

Chapter sixteen: An Opportunity of a Lifetime

My return to Bristol was a huge anticlimax. Nobody seemed remotely interested in what I had done and I was mildly irritated that, as far as teaching was concerned, I might as well not have bothered.

Though the Photography Department (part of Graphic Design) had some basic film gear, it was never used, and was not likely to be. In the end though, this was a blessing in disguise as I found that the quickest way to lose motivation in a subject is to teach it. (My view entirely, not a universal truth.) If Bristol Poly was happy to have sent me on what, in reality, was a year of self-indulgence, who was I to question them? But I did feel very strange leaving Sheffield, with all its intrigues, and start teaching on Foundation again.

One big difference was that, in my absence, an ex-Fine Art student, Caroline White, who had completed a postgrad course at Chelsea College of Art, had been appointed to take my place for the year. With the sort of cunning that I could only admire, Caroline managed to stay on full-time, and a long friendship developed.

I rented a room in whatever flat or house Caroline lived in, and over the years stayed with her for longer than with any other woman, which says a lot for celibate relationships — for that was the basis of our long friendship. How or why she put up with me for so long is a question only Caroline can answer, but it certainly made my life in Bristol much richer and far more interesting.

During my visits to Wales I had become friendly with Mo and Jackie Anthoine who knew Tony Riley. Though I have written about Mo before, I have never really managed to do him justice. He was quite the funniest man I have ever known. He was the most outrageous person who, above almost anyone else, I was most privileged to know. I can only write this last bit because he is dead. If I had ever admitted it during his lifetime I would have had to endure a variety of withering comments that would have reduced me to shame and embarrassment. Some of the difficultly in writing about him is that the printed word, however accurately recorded, just doesn't do Mo's humour justice.

Anyway, before I get too star-struck, Mo, an inveterate expeditioner, had spent the summer of 1975 driving to and from Pakistan and attempting to climb the iconic Trango (the Nameless Tower) in the recently opened up Karakoram range. Martin Boysen, Joe Brown, Ian McNaught Davis and Dave Potts made up the team. The expedition had failed when Martin Boysen got his knee stuck in a crack high on the Tower and narrowly escaped with his life. Mo desperately wanted to return and finish the climb. When Tony and I heard about it, we equally desperately wanted

^ *Joe Brown.*

to go with him and film it. Mo's advice to me on pre-expedition training was: "The best that you can do is sit in a warm oven eating shit sandwiches."

We would be going to Trango again with Joe Brown and Martin Boysen, and also with Malcolm Howells. For an average climber like me, brought up in the 60s, Joe was simply the biggest name in the climbing world. The routes he did on gritstone, in North Wales, on TV spectaculars, set him apart from everyone else, including Chris Bonington (on his own admission) and Don Whillans (who could never accept it). I think there were two reasons for this, apart from the simple truth that, as a rock-climber, he was by far and away the best. The first was that in the 60s the climbing media was only just beginning to find its feet. Until *Mountain*, then *Crags, Climber and Rambler* and later *High*, found their voices, you were as likely to read about Joe Brown in the daily press or see him on TV as anywhere else, and then only infrequently. Consequently he was more of a legend than a reality and the myth around him could grow unchecked, almost in a vacuum. Secondly, Joe's deadpan Mancunian humour and personal charisma was increasingly fashionable, not unlike The Beatles, with whom Joe shared a similar working-class background.

In his autobiography *The Hard Years* he even compared himself to the Fab Four. 'Crew interested me because he was more concerned with the consequences of what I had done than trying to put me on a pedestal like an idol. My trouble was that I felt no responsibility for the consequences… The Beatles didn't set out to dominate the pop world. They made a sound that everyone liked. If the reception had been otherwise the sound would have been just the same. That was how it was with me'. It is hard to agree wholeheartedly with the comparison: The Beatles strove and changed as a direct result of their success. But the interesting sentence is 'I felt no responsibility for the consequences', which, of course, is very similar to some of the difficulties The Beatles brought upon themselves — notably Lennon's unfortunate throwaway about being more popular than Jesus. Rather like the appearances by The Beatles, which were carefully rationed, so Brown's popularity was somehow enhanced by the infrequency of his appearances on TV and in the climbing media.

^ *Jackie and Mo Anthoine.*

Compare Joe to, say, Ron Fawcett in the 80s, or Jerry Moffatt, Catherine Destivelle and Ben Moon in the 90s, all of who seemed to feature in every edition of the monthly magazines and produced their own videos, and you can begin to see why the legend of Joe Brown was so strong and enduring. The others only lasted as long as the magazines were interested and the videos remained playable. To emphasise this, an early climbing book devoured from Ealing Public Library was *Snowdon Biography* by Wilfrid Noyce and Geoff Sutton. In it was a full-page photograph captioned 'Joe Brown on the East Buttress, Clogwyn Du'r Arddu'. By modern standards it is a flat grey snapshot with a tiny figure on the near vertical skyline. It is impossible to see who it is or what he is doing, but the image, more than any other sticks in my mind as the epitome of the impossible and the sheer boldness, and loneliness of that little figure is still burned into my imagination. A modern, high definition photo, like those plastered all over the magazines, just wouldn't have the same resonance. Similarly, an ancient photo in Eric Shipton's autobiography *Upon That Mountain*, misleadingly entitled 'Shaksgam Granite Peak', had long been a fantasy image. It was, of course, Trango.

The idea of going on an expedition to the Trango Tower, the mountain that for me, more than any other single peak in the world, was the most beautiful, desirable and alluring, was almost beyond my comprehension. To be going with Joe Brown and Martin Boysen, was roughly the equivalent of playing football with Bobby Charlton and George Best, or cricket with Len Hutton and Don Bradman. For Martin Boysen was only just behind Joe in the fame and charisma stakes. Martin from Tonbridge (though born in Germany) had started climbing as a schoolboy. He was a tall

137

^ *Martin Boysen.*

rather arrogant lad in big spectacles. He was streets ahead of us and whenever we saw him climbing we realised just how brilliant he was. I remember on an abysmal wet day at Harrison's, sheltering under an overhang when Boysen, wearing sloppy Wellington boots, soloed nonchalantly up *Stupid Effort*, a 5b route that even when dry was beyond my capabilities. Without even vaguely knowing him, I decided I didn't like him much.

Since then Martin had risen to greater things — extreme hard new routes in Britain and the Alps, and distinguished himself on the South Face of Annapurna, the first of the many successful Bonington expeditions. He had just returned from the successful Everest South West Face (The Hard Way). A faulty oxygen set and the loss of a crampon had deprived him of the summit where, sadly, filmmaker Mick Burke disappeared in a storm. I only met Mick once, in a pub just before he left for Everest, with Tony Riley. We tried to pick his brains without much success. Martin, who had suffered on Everest, wanted to go back to Trango possibly even more than Mo, and had a score to settle.

It was actually Malcolm Howells, the fourth member of Mo's team, who put me in touch with Chris Lister and Allen Jewhurst. Both worked for Yorkshire Television and they were already thinking of forming their own independent company, Chameleon Films. We made a sort of ramshackle agreement with them, the first of many, and begged film gear from anyone who would lend it. Tony would drive overland with Mo and I would fly out with Martin and Malcolm. (Joe was already in Pakistan, trekking with his wife Val.)

And so began the first of around 15 visits to Pakistan, India, Nepal, China and Tibet. What are the memories of that first wonderful expedition? The most evocative are undoubtedly the smells, not all of them pleasant: the fumes from the cheap fuel pervading the atmospheres of Rawalpindi; the evening scent of bougainvillea growing in the Embassy properties in Islamabad; the dire stink of excrement and worse that you could find anywhere in the sub-continent; the body odours of the porters, unwashed and mixed with the cooking smells of rice, ghee, onions, lentils and chillies, and most vivid of all, the wonderful sweet smell of burning juniper that the porters used for their fires. Even the slightest sniff of this and I am back at Payu campsite on the walk-in. If only the smell could be bottled...

And the sights? Martin, our resident pyromaniac, forever blowing the embers of campfires into life; Mo, giggling at any misfortunes that could befall anyone at any stage of the expedition, like Tony Riley's appalling blisters on each heel that he acquired after only a day or two of walking. Then there was the sight of Joe,

^ *Trango Tower.*

happy with a cigar in his mouth, making deadpan comments that were impossible to disagree with, and Malcolm our self-appointed doctor, dispensing words of wisdom and aspirins regardless of his own diagnoses. And, of course, dominating everything, the first sight and impression of the Trango Tower itself.

In Fosco Maraini's classic book *The Karakoram*, which is actually about the first ascent of Gashebrum IV, Maraini describes the Trango Tower thus, 'The Nameless Tower (20,528 ft), a superb shaft, rising between the First Cathedral of the Baltoro and the Trango Peaks. Not only is it still unclimbed (1857): no one has ever got near it'. This scarcely does it justice. The quote is, as far as I am aware, the first time it was referred to as the Nameless Tower. As it is undoubtedly part of the Trango Group, the Trango Tower would seem to be its logical name. Galen Rowell in his book *In The Throne Room of the Mountain Gods* also calls it Nameless. Later he made the first ascent of the Great Trango Tower next to it, pointing out at some length that it is higher than Nameless, though only apparently by a few metres. As none of the Trango Group is renowned for their height, this seems to be hair-splitting. What, by any reasonable standards is true, is that the Trango Tower is one of the very few free-standing rock spires in the world that command such a mind-boggling sense of awe that it borders on disbelief. The Towers of Paine, Cerro Torre and FitzRoy in Patagonia are its only real rivals. When I first saw the Tower perched at the top of the repulsive couloir that is its first line of defence, I very nearly fell over backwards. With binocular vision it appears more slender than most photographs and, of course, far, far bigger.

Despite patchy weather, the second Trango expedition climbed the mountain in three weeks of almost non-stop action. To my disappointment I didn't figure much in the climbing. Tony was fitter and acclimatised better than I did, and there really wasn't room for two of us on the climb. But friendships were forged that continue to the present day. I have to confess I still find it amazing that, 34 years on, I am friendly with Joe Brown, and that Martin and Maggie Boysen are always amongst the first people I invite to a party or barbeque. Tony now lives in the Lake District and we still work together occasionally. Malcolm lives in San Francisco, but I am quite sure that if, or when, I see him again we will carry on where we left off. Only Mo, that brilliant shooting star, burnt out and died of a brain tumour a few days after his 50th birthday. He, probably above all my other adult friends, actually gave me the confidence to develop into the person I now am. He, along with Al Rouse and Paul Nunn, is in my thoughts every single day and the pain of losing them never disappears completely.

Since 1976 many much harder climbs have been made on Trango and on the almost inexhaustible supply of granite walls of the Karakoram. At the time it was seen as a breakthrough, along with Pete Boardman and Joe Tasker's route on Changabang, which probably eclipsed it. It was a route that pointed to the future, but done with the materials belonging to an age of climbing that, although we didn't know it at the time, we would soon come to be seen as old-fashioned. We had no Gore-Tex, no Friends, and no modern high tech nuts. We climbed in big boots, used heavy pegs, including bongs, and had no freeze-dried food. But the four lead climbers produced around 1000 metres of high standard mainly free climbing, and some very precarious aid pitches. Unlike, I regret to say, many later expeditions, Mo was scrupulously honest in describing the details of the climb. It remains a source of irritation that so many modern accounts of expeditions are frankly misleading, if not downright dishonest.

Though Joe Brown and Martin Boysen were undoubtedly the two biggest stars of both Trango expeditions, Mo Anthoine was the driving force. Without Mo it is doubtful if either trip would have happened, even though it was Chris Bonington who had first got permission to attempt Trango in 1975, before the South West Face of Everest commanded his full attention.

Mo was a superb leader, though he always denied it, and a climber with, in his own opinion, a rare ability: "A lot of climbers who lead E5s and E6s at sea level, are horrified when they go to high altitude and can't put one foot in front of another. I'm just the same at 20,000 feet as I am at sea level — not brilliant, but good enough."

He was also a good enough aid climber and produced a couple of pitches high on the Tower in which he had to drive pegs between a funnel of water ice and rock, and move up quickly before they popped out. Above all, Mo had a personal vendetta against Trango, which he shared with Martin. The knee jam episode of 1975 had obviously hit them both hard. Martin kept his ambitions pretty much to himself, but Mo was totally tuned to getting to the top of what he called 'that immaculate pile of rock, the best climbing that any of us had ever experienced'.

Mo expressed his love of climbing in his own inimitable way: "Climbing and sex are complete opposites. You spend ages trying to avoid climbing, getting scared, and dreading the moment when you start a hard pitch. But afterwards you feel brilliant — the world is a richer, rosier place. But with sex, you spend most of your life thinking about it, looking forward to the act itself but, once it's over, you feel sad and let down." I don't think Mo seriously believed that, but it does give an insight into his unique view of the world.

The Trango expedition was, by a long way, the happiest and funniest I have ever been on, and my overwhelming memory is of laughing. It gave me a taste for adventure, a love of the world's great mountains, and a lifelong affection for the people and places of the Indian sub-continent. And that's not bad for a first trip.

^ *Chris Lister (left) and Allen Jewhurst, the two most influential figures in my film career.*

141

Chapter seventeen: If at first you don't succeed, try, try, and fail again

Questions I have been asked over the years tend to be repetitive. "How do you have a crap at high altitude?" is probably the most frequent. (Answer: "Quickly and carefully.") Far more interesting is: "How do you adjust from the excitement of a trip to boring old everyday life?" If I had an office job, or was a sales rep in a Ford Mondeo, I'm sure that the question would be relevant. But in the autumn of 1976 the combination of working on the Foundation Course, travelling to and from Sheffield to see Laraine, and to Leeds to work at YTV, gave me a constantly interesting and varied life. I worked four days a week in Bristol, then part-time on Fridays in the Fine Art Department at Sheffield. Normally I would spend one day of the weekend editing with Chris Lister and Allen Jewhurst, and the other one climbing. Now, looking back, I can see that Laraine got a pretty raw deal. By comparison with most of the Sheffield climbers who went away just about every weekend, I wasn't too bad. Often Laraine and I would go to Wales for the weekend, but it was all about me really.

^ *Gemma on one of the visits to Malvern to see Mum.*

Becky and Gemma playing in Malvern. >

One thing that wasn't all about me was the relationship I tried to build with Gemma and Becky. Long after Ali and I had finally divorced during my year in Sheffield. She had been just about the perfect mother to the girls and after we separated she never stopped me seeing them, or did anything to harm their relationship with me, quite the contrary. Over the years Ali and I have stayed friends and often phone each other when the girls have any problems. I have always loved visiting them and though the guilt of leaving them has never gone away, it has been offset to some extent by the pleasure of watching them grow up. Whenever I could I took them to see Mum ('Elliegran') in Malvern, though I know Mum would have loved to see them more often. And every year we enjoyed camping at Sennen Cove, near Land's End. I did occasionally take the girls to visit friends in Sheffield or Bristol, hoping to bring some normality into my relationship with them. Years later they told me that they always dreaded these visits because they never knew where they would be spending the night. Gemma once asked me what I thought would have happened if Ali and I had stayed together. The answer, I'm afraid would be that we would have probably split up.

142

^ *Becky, Mum and Gemma.*

In Leeds the Trango film slowly took shape. It is a film that I have great affection for, but I am the first to admit that it is deeply flawed. The reason is simple. Before we left we had begged 'short ends' of film from anyone who would give them to us, like the BBC in Bristol, YTV and Sheffield Film School. These came in 100 foot 'daylight' spools, but were often not rolled together tightly enough and in loading them into the camera in the harsh light of the Karakoram, much of the footage had bad 'edge fogging', bursts of red or orange down the edge of the frames and sometimes all over them. Consequently the film was never technically good enough for a TV screening and, as we often joked, would have worked better as a radio documentary. But it was another steep learning curve for me. Watching Allen Jewhurst and Chris Lister working on the film, I realised that I still had an awful lot to learn. They decided that in order to cover the first expedition with Martin Boysen's epic knee jam incident, we would have to film him telling his tale. This was done in a pub in Leeds where we all spent time getting suitably relaxed. By the time the cameras rolled, Mo in

143

Chapter seventeen: If at first you don't succeed, try, try, and fail again

particular was well away, and as Martin recalled the gory details of cutting through his climbing breeches with a saw-edged piton, blood gushing everywhere, Mo's laughter sounded quite demented. In America, when it was shown at the Telluride Mountain Film Festival, the bewildered audience thought that the whole film was some sort of strange episode of *Monty Python's Flying Circus*, which I took as a huge compliment.

Almost as soon as I had returned from Pakistan, driving back overland with Mo, Martin and Tony, I was invited on another trip, this time to the Kishtwar range in Northern India. Paul Nunn had been invited to join a team from the Reading Climbing Club by Geoff Tier, probably the club's leading light. Paul also wanted to invite Bob Toogood, a vastly experienced climber and caver from Sheffield, and it was Bob, Geoff and I who drove overland in the summer of 1977. We travelled in a Sherpa van loaned to us by British Leyland. This is a sentence that makes me feel my age, and is probably quite unintelligible to anyone under 40, as both the van and its makers have long since gone to the graveyard of great British industrial dinosaurs.

For those who wonder why expeditions took their gear overland, the reasons are simple. First, air fares were more expensive in those days, second, the style of most expeditions needed far more equipment, and third, it was still possible to travel freely through Iran and Afghanistan before politics took over the former and war decimated the latter. Part of the deal with British Leyland was to film the journey and I still see sights on the news taken from the same positions as I filmed all those years ago. But now the pictures are littered with burnt out tanks, or show roadside explosions.

Once again I said my goodbyes to Laraine and the girls and plunged myself into three months of expedition mode. I have never actually considered myself to be much of a traveller. Given the amount I've done this does seem a little odd, even to me, probably because 'real' travellers write erudite reams about history, flora, fauna, archaeology, anthropology, etc. It's not that I'm not interested, but I do tend to be a bit of a spectator. Perhaps the role of filmmaker precludes any more wholehearted activity. On this journey I can't remember anything of any note until we reached Turkey and Istanbul. Here we had a morning looking round the Blue Mosque and a visit to a hippie shrine, the Pudding Shop, where I had been the year before with Mo and eaten delicious cakes, but shunned the other more exotic fare on offer. I dreaded the next section to Ankara where lorries battled it out for supremacy over anyone else foolish enough to share the same road. It wasn't any better this year, but once we got into Eastern Turkey we began to feel the strange timelessness that, though still in the

Middle East, heralds the first intimations of Central Asia. Seeing the hazy bulk of Mount Ararat just before the Iranian border was the landmark that I had been looking forward to, and I filmed the van driving through desert with the mountain in the background.

One of the less pleasurable events of the overland drive is border crossings, and from Turkey onwards they became progressively more stress-provoking. Drug smuggling was the main hazard, more so on the return journey, but you can't be too careful, particularly of being used as an unwitting 'mule' by smugglers planting packages on the van to be retrieved once past the border. The other time-consuming problem was the sheer quantity of goods we carried. An officious customs officer could hold us up indefinitely by demanding to see a tin opener in box 13, or an ice-axe in box 24. Luckily for us, Geoff Tier was himself a master of bureaucratic zeal, and on several occasions he managed to outwit his opponents by arguing with them so persistently that they lost interest and waved us through. There is no doubt that to take an overloaded van of expedition gear through over a dozen border crossings means that you are almost bound to be breaking the law in some way at every border.

When we returned from Trango we had completed the journey from Islamabad to Chamonix in just six days, which meant Iran and Afghanistan had only taken a day each. So I was understandably keen to spend a bit more time in these countries, particularly Afghanistan, which after only the briefest of acquaintances, I had found quite the most exciting country we passed through. The landscape was extraordinary, the cities, Herat, Kandahar and Kabul, mysterious and enticing. But first there was Iran, which I found on a second visit disappointing and far more westernised than Afghanistan, with huge posters of the Shah of Iran plastered everywhere. They wouldn't be around much longer as the Shah himself was deposed two years later. Iran, after flirting with the 20th century, settled for the Ayatollahs and the Middle Ages. Not that we could have known that at the time, as we battled with traffic in Teheran, but there was no doubting that the country was in a state of tension.

We arrived at the Afghan border. As I am writing these words on June 21st 2010, the lunchtime news is announcing the death of a Royal Marine, Richard Hollington, the 300th soldier to die in Helmand Province, south of Kabul. I think back to our arrival that evening in Herat, sitting in a hotel courtyard with the heat of the day still radiating off the white plastered walls, sipping cold lemonade and watching the sun sinking into the desert. What has happened to this lovely country? Why did the British in the 19th century, then Russia and America, and now Britain

^ *Filming the van in Afghanistan.*

and America again, try to occupy a country that simply does not want to be occupied? Afghanistan has the misfortune to be placed in a sensitive position, vulnerable to Russian occupation from the north, and, in the Victorian age, colonial occupation from the British in India to the east. Here was the scene of the Great Game of espionage, double dealing and manoeuvring for political domination of vulnerable borders. But no one has ever managed to hold Afghanistan, a country of proud tribal allegiances, whose first love seemed to be of long-standing feuds that could only be settled by revenge and murder. It says a lot that the nearest anyone has ever come to uniting the country is by attacking it. Today the fight is between Britain and America against the Taliban, who like so many terrorist organisations before them, seem to be impossible to wipe out. It does seem futile to try to 'democratise' Afghanistan and then beat an orderly retreat, as is the stated aim of two British governments. You don't have to be a clairvoyant to predict that the country will soon revert once more to its tribes and warlords.

Meanwhile, more and more British and American soldiers (as well as a few from our other allies) will have lost their lives, and the threat of terrorism in Britain and the States will be as real as ever.

Back in 1977, the three long-haired, dishevelled men in sore need of a wash could sit with their lemonades without a care in the world, listening to the amplified wail of the muezzin echoing around the evening air calling the faithful to prayer. The drive had gone well, with no breakdowns so far, and in a few days we would be greeting old friends in the British Embassy compound in Islamabad, where we would have unlimited access to showers, a swimming pool and cold beer.

Many people would consider the road to Kandahar and from there to Kabul to be boring. True, it is a more or less straight road across a desert and to be driving is deadly dull. But for the passengers the landscape is full of subtle changes of colour, texture and tone, with blue hills in the distance emphasising unlimited space. Vast tracts seem to be completely unoccupied, but

Chapter seventeen: If at first you don't succeed, try, try, and fail again

I remembered the year before stopping for a few hours' sleep next to the van in apparently a totally empty landscape to find that in the morning my flip-flops, placed carefully under the fleece I was using as a pillow, had disappeared. Whoever had seen the van stop and turn off its headlights must have walked miles for this bit of treasure and miles more to vanish without trace. I was impressed.

This time we were taking it slowly; a night in Kandahar and two in Kabul where we had to get some piece or other of the van mended. Not only am I technically illiterate, I simply can't remember what it was. It meant going into the covered market to get a new one made where we were warned we would almost certainly be murdered. I have to say that I enjoyed myself immensely and, whatever it was, was replaced with the minimum of fuss. So long as our problems were simply mechanical I was confident that they could be mended or replaced. Indeed, if we had taken the whole engine into the market, I am sure we could have had a replacement built from scratch in a day or two.

We were soon on our way again, this time to get down the Khyber Pass and into Peshawar in one day. Once through the Pakistan border without incident, it was only about three miles to the head of the pass, and into the sinister village of Landi Kohtal. This is inhabited by Pathan tribesmen, armed to the hilt with rifles of various vintages and quite often, wicked, curved knives that were not just for decorative purposes. As we drove slowly through the crowded lanes, we were surrounded by silent, hawk-eyed men all glaring at us. Suddenly we realised it was the middle of Ramadan and Geoff and I were smoking. Hastily we stubbed them out. There are not many places in the world that I have been relieved to get out of alive, but Landi Kohtal is one.

As we drove down the Khyber the sky ahead was filling with colossal anvil clouds and in the distance a grim, black horizon was broken with flashes of lightning from the monsoon, still rampant on the plains of the Punjab. I shot some film in the pass, conscious that we were not alone. Occasionally we saw a motionless figure on the crest of a ridge, rifle in hand, watching…

A day later we were relaxing in the British Club in Islamabad, or rather Geoff and Bob were. I was driving back to Peshawar hell for leather to retrieve the movie camera, which by an astonishing act of stupidity (even by my standards) I had left by the roadside in the Khyber Pass. It had been handed in to a hotel, and the owner had rung the British Embassy to see if anyone had lost one! A miraculous story and one that comprehensively demolished my dark forebodings that everyone in the Khyber was about to steal the clothes off our backs.

While we were in the luxurious comfort of the British Club

148

we heard the first garbled versions of a story that later became famous. On the first ascent of The Ogre, Doug Scott had broken his legs, Chris Bonington his ribs and Mo Anthoine and Clive Rowland had been involved in the protracted retreat/rescue from just below the 7285 metre summit. Over the months I got to hear the story first-hand from almost all the expedition members and wondered if they were all talking about the same events. It was a phenomenom I was to experience all too vividly in 1986 after the disastrous summer on K2, when I, too, had a story to tell.

We sat round the Embassy pool for two blissful days. I remembered that after the Trango expedition we all had to wait a fortnight in Skardu for a flight to Islamabad after which, suitably washed and shaved we turned up at the Club for the longed-for swim. Joe Brown warned us that, after nearly two months in each other's company, our language had deteriorated: "There'll be wives and children around the pool, so be careful." We each dived in and silently mouthed our delight until Tony Riley forgot, and surfacing from the deep end with a blissful expression on his face, he shouted: "Oh, fucking great!" Joe was appalled: "Oi! Watch yer language, you cunt!"

We spent one night in Lahore before crossing the border into India the next morning. I don't know quite what I was expecting — herds of elephants and bejewelled maharajahs perhaps. Actually it was more colourful than Pakistan, mainly because women were now more in evidence. Our first stop was at Amritsar, to visit the famous Sikh shrine, the Golden Temple. Then it was just a matter of driving down the Great Trunk Road, avoiding bullock carts, pedestrians and cyclists milling all over the place, to arrive in Delhi in the middle of the night. It was hard not to feel that this was journey's end, for we would be spending a week or so in Delhi before the last leg up to the mountain village of Kishtwar. But, here we were, all in one piece, with the rest of the team due to fly out in a couple of days.

Delhi — What can I write about Delhi? It would be easier, I'm sure, if I was a city-hater or a city-lover. But I am ambivalent. Apart from my childhood in London suburbia, I have always probably subconsciously done a deal with myself. Cities are fine so long as I don't have to spend more than a few nights in them or can escape to the country quickly. Manchester, and especially Sheffield, are all easy to escape from. But I have had the misfortune to be stuck for a lot longer than I wanted in Lima, Santiago, Delhi, Hong Kong, Islamabad and Kathmandu. The attraction of all of these places has quickly palled and, in so doing, tarnished the memory of what I'm sure are far more interesting places than I am prepared to admit. Kathmandu is for many people an endlessly fascinating

149

rabbit warren of bazaars, temples, bars and restaurants. But if, like me, you have been stuck there on three separate occasions for weeks at a time waiting for a plane, the novelty quickly fades.

So it is with Delhi. On my first visit, with Geoff and Bob, we quite enjoyed the sights: the Red Fort, Janpath Market, the strange astronomical observatory built for Jai Singh, the Maharajah of Jaipur, and the imposing but faded grandeur of Lutyen's government buildings and palaces. Inevitably though, we would retreat to the shade of a restaurant in the fading elegance of Connaught Circus where we could sip cold drinks and watch the world go by. The rest of the team arrived and we were ready to go the mountains, we being the Brits. Unfortunately our Liaison Offices had not arrived in Delhi, and we were not supposed to set off without him.

At the risk of upsetting both the Indian and the Pakistani armies, I think a word of criticism is called for. Both the Indian Mountaineering Federation and the Ministry of Tourism in Pakistan insist that army officers accompany expeditions. The regulations in each country are labyrinthine. The reason given for their presence is to make sure the expeditions behave themselves (i.e. don't spy) and conform to all the myriad rules laid down. The LOs are also issued with a full set of free personal equipment by the expedition, though as far as I know none of them have ever been known to climb. But they often have wildly unrealistic ambitions and on every expedition I have been on with an LO it has been a long and tactful process to disillusion them. Also expeditions often have to spend days or weeks wasting money and time before one is allocated. I know that the armies in this part of the world are busy people (mainly fighting each other), but the numbers of LOs needed are tiny and, if you are going to insist on having them, it seems only fair that they are ready on time. Maybe expeditions should just heed the words of Kipling (misquoted), 'Here lies a man deceased, who tried to hurry in the East'. Rant over.

As we couldn't all fit in the van, we would have to travel up to Kishtwar separately in any case. So leaving Paul and the others, we set off again, first retracing our steps, through the Punjab then up into the wooded Himalayan foothills, to arrive two days later in one of the most attractive mountain villages I have visited.

Despite having a split population of Moslem and Hindu, Kishtwar in 1977 was a tranquil place, with some beautiful intricate wooden houses, an ornate mosque and a lovely maidan or village green, on the edge of which was a Dak bungalow. These useful little buildings date from the days of the Raj and were designed for the use of travelling officials. Looked after by a chowkidar

150

(caretaker), they still provide cheap, basic accommodation for travellers like us.

Once again we waited for the rest of the team to catch us up. I may as well admit here that our expedition failed in 1977 and (perhaps unwisely) I returned again in 1979 with Paul Nunn, Tony Riley and John Yates. What happened on the mountain was fairly similar on both trips, though Paul and John got a lot higher in 1979, and were stopped on a long summit ridge in the face of bad weather.

Compared to the Karakoram, the walk along and above the foaming Chenab River could hardly have been more different. Instead of the arid sun-scorched deserts and abject poverty and squalor of the inhabitants of Braldu Valley, here were cool forests alive with birds and monkeys and comparatively affluent villages. Ominously though, the river was being used for logging higher up the valley and at the time it was almost clogged with tree trunks, a harbinger of deforestation to come.

On the second expedition John Yates and I walked up the Bhut Nullah (valley) towards Machail, the last village before Base Camp. We were both going well and, in attempting to double stage, had to bivouac in a clearing beside the river. It was in this idyllic spot that an almost biblical scene was enacted. A group of nomads with a large flock of goats, presumably from Tibet, each carrying a light load of salt in tiny panniers, arrived as it got dark. John, on his first

^ *Me descending in a storm on the first Barnaj expedition.*

^ *Barnaj, the South Summit.*

^ *Tony climbing a hard, water ice gully.*

^ *Tony Riley, co-cameraman on three films.*

Himalayan expedition, thought they might rob or murder us as we slept. In fact, they couldn't have been friendlier. Amongst them was a girl of, I guessed, about 16. She was incredibly beautiful with huge flashing eyes and a regal bearing. The headman noticed my fascination and tried to explain something to me. It took a few minutes to realise that he was trying to sell her! I tried to imagine taking her into my favourite pubs in Bristol and Sheffield. She was phenomenally dirty and reeked of wood smoke. But oh, those eyes! John and I ended up sleeping in the midst of the nomads round the dying embers of their fire. When we awoke they had gone.

After the success of the Trango expedition I imagined that Barnaj would be a much easier proposition. If we had reasonable weather this might have been true. As it was, each trip was stopped by prolonged storms. As the mountain was a mixture of rock and ice, and long snow slopes there was an increasing avalanche danger. On the first trip four of us, Geoff Tier, Paul and Geoff Smith huddled together in two tunnel tents for three days of non-stop snow. On the fourth morning Paul called from the other tent: "What are you thinking about, Jim?"

"My life."

"So am I, chappie, let's bugger off." On the second expedition, climbing with Tony

Riley, we were caught in virtually the same spot. This time we didn't wait and retreated after only one night.

It was on the return journey on the second trip that I have to confess a shameful episode. We knew that we had to spend a long day in the confines of an overloaded Indian bus, followed by a night in an equally ghastly train to Delhi. On the way up we had travelled with another expedition. Pete Minks was a member and it was he who gave me a piece of hash to eat. The train journey was a breeze and I awoke relaxed and oblivious to the squalor that the others had to endure. So John and I decided a repeat performance might make the bus journey more bearable. Pete had given us quite a large lump for just such an eventuality. The snag was that neither of us had a clue as to how much was necessary. I decided to err on the generous side and we simply broke the thing in half, which we washed down with a cup of Indian tea at the local Kishtwar café.

At the first light of dawn we boarded the bus and I tried to fit my knees into the tiny space available. It was excruciatingly uncomfortable, but at least, I thought, oblivion would soon overtake me. For about an hour nothing happened. John, who is only about five foot four, was similarly unaffected, but not so cramped. The bus follows a deep gorge and is often perched hundreds of feet above the river, risking head on death with Indian lorries which have no intention of giving way. I shut my eyes and suddenly saw a skeleton in a flapping mackintosh running in front of the bus. Opening my eyes, the plunge to the river seemed to be thousands of feet below. Closing them again and the skeleton reappeared. Christ. Next to me John started up. He is from Staffordshire: "Fookin 'ell', oh, fookin, fookin 'ell," was the sum total of his vocabulary for the next 12 hours. So began the bus journey from hell. Both of us suffered appalling hallucinations and on the one occasion when we stopped for lunch, in a town that we thought was in Mordor, we got totally lost and couldn't find the bus until Tony guided us back inside. Apparently we had only strayed a couple of yards away.

It was I think in the afternoon when I opened my eyes as the bus slowed right down. We were crawling along completely surrounded by goats. As I tried to comprehend what was going on I found myself staring at the nomad girl standing right beside the bus. Separated by only a pane of grimy glass we made eye contact. Then she gradually slipped away and was gone. In my drug-raddled brain it was the most tragic episode of my life and I seriously contemplated asking the driver to let me off, but fortunately my powers of speech had deserted me. I nudged John who managed to open one eye at the goat-filled environment: "Fookin 'ell" was his not terribly original comment.

153

We arrived at Jammu railway station in the dark and had a couple of hours (or was it days or months?) to wait. Indian railway stations are pretty grim at the best of times. Now it was a scene from Dante's *Inferno*. John and I had to cling together and were terrified of getting lost. Somehow we managed to get our gear and ourselves onto the train and finally found the oblivion we had sought. In the morning I woke on the carriage floor inches away from a live hen. Mercifully this one was not a product of my imagination (it had shat all over my T-shirt) and apart from the odd flashback I was now over the worst. In Delhi we met up with Pete Minks again. He offered us another lump to cope with the flight home. It wasn't a big decision to refuse. The thought of having a bad trip at 30,000 feet was too awful to contemplate. Lesson learnt: never again.

After the first Barnaj expedition, Chris and Allen at Chameleon once again edited the film, which British Leyland had funded. It was a much slicker presentation than Trango, and if I had the opportunity to change one thing in my creative life it would be to make the Trango film with the experience of Barnaj behind me. Then I think it would have been a memorable effort. British Leyland seemed to like it and it was shown at the Motor Show at Earls Court. When Geoff Tier rang and asked if they would provide us with our own print of the film the answer was that that was the least they could do! "In that case, what is the most?" asked Geoff innocently.

I haven't written extensively about the climbing on both expeditions, basically because there wasn't a lot. But compared with Trango, where I was out of my depth, I acquitted myself reasonably well on both the Barnaj trips. The second one was a change because this time I wasn't making a film. This, and a trip to Peru in 1985 with Geoff, were the only expeditions where I could climb for its own sake, until, many years later, I climbed with Ian McNaught Davis in Chile, South Africa and Kenya. Here I almost made up for those expedition years when my role as cameraman really precluded doing much real climbing. But those days were still a long way off. In the meantime, rock-climbing at home became almost obsessive and nearly every weekend saw me in North Wales or Derbyshire or further afield in the Lake District or Cornwall.

Chapter eighteen: Putting the Art Before the Course

When I returned to Bristol from the first Barnaj expedition, Dennis Curry had taken early retirement and Neil Murison (he of the pale face and hangover) was now running the Foundation Course with wisdom and tolerance. The next years were, to my mind, the best we ever had and Neil managed to create just the right balance between full-time staff and some excellent part-timers filling the gaps in our still rather Fine Art-based expertise. Bristol attracted huge numbers of applicants and our course could only accept between 50 and 70, which seemed about right for the 400 or so applications every year. Unlike most universities, and probably now unlike most Foundation Courses, we set great store by the interviews, which took up most of the Easter term. Essentially, we were looking for the creative potential of students who, in the main, were doing A-Level Art. Which, with the best will in the world, is not very imaginative. On top of that we constantly had to compare students who obviously had excellent teachers and/ or facilities and those who hadn't. Often we would see three or four pupils from the same school. Sometimes their folders would be almost identical, though I don't think we ever caught anyone actually cheating by bringing someone else's work. But it did make it very hard to decide whether to accept all or none of them. One of the most frequent questions was: "How much of this folio is course work and how much have you done yourself?" On one occasion a pupil from a well-known girls' school turned up with something like 15 GCSEs (all grade 1) and predicted five As at A-Level. Sadly, she hadn't the faintest evidence of any creative input at all and we had no choice but to reject her. I had to field the outraged phone call from her headmistress and try to explain why a more academic activity like Art History would suit her better.

There were many moments to treasure doing these interviews. The confidential report was often unintentionally (or maybe not) hilarious. 'She sits a horse well', was all one headmistress could bring herself to comment. 'This student is pure evil', wrote a headmaster when I was at Rotherham. Intrigued, we gave him a place. He was. On one dark February afternoon whilst interviewing with Nev, I fell asleep, slid off my chair and shot under the table, ending up entangled in the legs of a very bewildered girl who, mercifully, had an excellent folio. We offered her a place there and then with a clear conscience. And on a famous occasion an interview had somehow been arranged on the very last afternoon of the Christmas term at about 4.30 pm. Caroline was the one member of staff sober enough to do the interview, and was embarrassed halfway through by the sound of snoring coming from under the table. It was, well, you know who it was, wrapped up in a sleeping bag and dead to the world.

Perhaps the most excruciating interview was actually one of my own. By some curious circumstance I was still at the top of the basic lecturers' pay scale, the only lecturer Grade B left in the whole Polytechnic (possibly the whole world). When this was eventually noticed I was called to the new Director's study 'for a chat'. Neil would be there as well: "Don't worry. It's just tea and biscuits and you'll be fine." So one afternoon I drove over to the main Poly building at Coldharbour Lane ('Colditz' to every student who passed through) and knocked on his door. "Come." (I don't know about you, but there always seems to be something not quite right when the person on the other side can't bring himself to say "in".) Dr Birch, for it was he, was a tall man with iron-grey hair and a matching beard. "Good afternoon, Mr Curran. This is a very important day for you, if you are to rise to the senior echelons of staff." (Eh? I was only trying to catch up with the other 99.9 per cent.) "Perhaps," he continued in his portentous manner, "you could outline your aims and ambitions over, say, the next five to 10 year time span?"

"That," I replied, quite cleverly I thought, "rather depends on the next five to 10 minutes." Why, when dealing with authority do I have the overwhelming urge to be facetious? I glimpsed Neil standing behind Dr Birch, holding his head in his hands. The interview limped on until the final doom-laden question: "I am always impressed at the technical expertise shown by all the staff down at Bower Ashton — but sometimes I wonder about the intellectual rigour and discipline they display." Unsure of whether this was really a proper question I replied, quick as a flash: "Don't worry, I'm pretty crap at the technical side as well." After that, the interview petered out somewhat and I was shown the door. Eventually Neil emerged: "Well, you'll be amazed. You got it! All Birch managed to say was, 'I suppose every faculty needs an eccentric and you've got yours in Mr Curran'. " I was quite flattered.

Over the years my own teaching style had developed, and looking back to Rotherham days, I felt I had probably been too dictatorial and judgemental. Now I tried to set open-ended projects and set a lot of store on individual tutorials. It was during one of these, with a more than usually obstinate lad who couldn't see the point of any of the projects set him (not just mine) and wanted to do his own thing, that I suddenly put my finger on his problem. "The trouble with you is that you want to put the art before the course." It goes without saying that, while I was convulsed with my own brilliant play on words and couldn't wait to tell Neil and Caroline, he just looked blank. Oh come on, raise a smile — please,

I thought, to no avail. But as I've said, those were the glory days and every year we seemed to get most, if not all, our students into the college of their choice.

Despite the success of the course, very few years passed without some sort of conspiracy to close the whole thing down. This was usually a plot hatched by Fine Art, hoping to expand their empire. On one occasion, Big Nev Aston, who was about six foot seven and in his youth trained as a discus thrower for the Melbourne Olympics, found Ernest Pascoe from Fine Art armed with a tape measure sizing up one of our three studios. Nev picked him up at arm's length and carried him back to his office where, shaken but unhurt, Ernest plotted his next move. What was absurd about these take-over bids was that, because our course was not actually a degree course, there was no set number of students we could accept, and the more we had, the more cash we could generate for the whole faculty. It took years for that particular penny to drop. Then, abruptly, we were told to double our numbers, which spelled the beginning of the end for me, though that day was still a long way off.

Since returning from Barnaj in the autumn of 1977, I had given a lot of thought to the next film project. What Trango and now Barnaj had taught me was that however exciting and demanding an expedition is, the filmmaker has little or no control over the outcome. If I needed any more persuading as to the truth of this, I went on a very low-key expedition in 1978 to climb and film a small(ish) mountain on the Choktoi Glacier in the Karakoram. There were just four of us: Dave 'Pod' Potts who had been on the first Trango trip, Malcolm Howells, who had been on the second, Barry Whybrow and me. We were dealt a hammer blow even

before we left England. Nick Estcourt had been killed in an avalanche on K2, only a week or so before we were due to leave. Nick had been a close friend of all four of us and, in retrospect, we probably should have just packed it in. As it was, we spent our last night before departure in The Railway in Hale, with a deeply grieving Carolyn Estcourt and Chris Bonington who had rushed back from

< Choktoi Peak — probably still unclimbed.

157

Pakistan to be with her. Why we persisted in going on our own trip is a question I asked myself frequently at the time.

The mountain was hard, the weather dreadful and the only memorable part was the return to Skardu. Most people don't realise that once an expedition has failed (or, indeed, succeeded) any lingering team spirit tends to evaporate rapidly as thoughts of home start to intrude. If there is any chance of getting home first (thus automatically acquiring bragging rights in perpetuity), then most climbers display a degree of cunning and ruthlessness that might well have proved more useful on the mountain.

Abandoning our attempt, we set off on the long journey home, but had hardly gone a mile before we bumped into four eminent American climbers who had just failed on the North Ridge of Latok 1 in the same storm that had stopped us. Jim Donini, Michael Kennedy, George and Jeff Lowe had got higher on this great Karakoram ridge, the 'Walker Spur of the Himalaya', than any of the subsequent dozen or so expeditions. At the time of writing it is still unclimbed.

When we met them, all four were exhausted and crippled with monstrous loads. Despite this, they were aiming to double stage back to Askole (the first village on the walk out) and reach Skardu two days later to catch their flight back to the US the following day. We were unsure whether to be mightily impressed or utterly cynical. However, two days later, as the four of us sat happily paddling our feet in a little stream, George Lowe, whose voice sounds uncannily like Mickey Mouse, approached: "Hey," he greeted us. "How come you guys going slowly are going quicker than us guys going quickly?"

We arrived in Askole together and then made a joint decision to walk over the Skora La, a high pass infrequently used, but cutting a couple of days off the walk out. The next day, halfway up to the pass, we met another expedition. This was an all-woman team led by Jackie Anthoine, Mo's wife, and comprising Marion Wintringham, Brede Arkless and Anne Redman. They too had failed on their peak, Bakhor Das, in the same storm. They were all far more organised than our motley crew and Marion was carrying a bag that looked suspiciously like a handbag. "A haandbaag?" said Malcolm. "On the Skora La?" I don't imagine Oscar Wilde has often been misquoted in this part of the world, and it will be some time before it happens again, but it made us laugh. Now that there were 12 of us (or 15 if you include Liaison Officers) it was increasingly obvious that getting to Skardu airport first was imperative, for it was unlikely that all of us plus our gear would get on the same flight. So began a game that owed a lot to the Tour de France. Every so often a small group would surreptitiously break

> *The Backor Das team L to R Brede Arkless, Jackie Anthoine, Anne Redman and Marion Wintringham.*

away, leaving the *peleton* plodding behind. But inevitably the leaders would be reined back by the pack and the leadership changed frequently in the next couple of days without anyone managing to keep the Yellow Vest for more than a few hours. Strangely no one ever admitted their devious plans.

When we breasted the crest of the Skora La, we descended a hideously steep and rotten hillside to the most squalid Balti village I have ever seen. Our arrival coincided with a spectacular thunderstorm with hail and rain and lightning. In the middle of this a stream draining a glacier high on the opposite side of the valley suddenly turned into a torrent. We watched aghast at an apocalyptic vision, as millions of tons of boulders, mud and water belched out of low cloud cover and smashed down next to the village. Livestock was swept away, though amazingly none of the buildings were damaged. The porters managed to pull our loads to

159

safety, but it was a frightening episode and quite the most powerful demonstration of natural forces that I have ever witnessed.

The next day we had to follow the valley through a succession of narrow gorges, some only a few metres wide, and dripping mud from high on each wall where the torrent had driven its way through. Though it was a much better day, it was hard not to keep glancing over your shoulder to look for another mud avalanche which, had it occurred, would surely have killed us all.

The Americans had formed another breakaway sprint, but this time, in trying to follow a high route out of the gorge, had outwitted themselves, and ended up spread-eagled along an almost vertical wall of dried mud. "It was probably the scariest moment of the whole trip," Jeff Lowe told me later. Eventually, four rather rueful Yanks caught us up just in time for yet another river crossing.

All told, we crossed the same swollen stream about 15 times that day. If we all linked arms and nobody lost their footing, all was okay. Often Jackie, the smallest of us, was swept off her feet and pulled almost horizontally by the two alongside her. In all my time on expeditions, river crossings always seemed to be the most likely way to end it all, and it was with huge relief when we suddenly emerged into the poplar trees and beautifully irrigated oasis of Shigar. Here a jeep drive took us to Skardu. Needless to say we all arrived together, there were no flights and we were all stuck there for over a week — an improvement on the 14 days on the Trango expedition. Rumour had it that the Americans managed to pull rank with a phone call to Senator Edward Kennedy who, in turn, pulled strings for a PIA Fokker Friendship to take them back to Islamabad, plus Jackie and Pod. Even so the plane was struck by lightning and I was quite happy to wait for better weather and a safer ride.

As far as filming went, the expedition had been a complete write off, and Chameleon never even bothered to get the footage processed. I couldn't blame them. I felt even more strongly that a film more like *A Great Effort*, that could be scripted and planned in detail, would be a much better bet. While dreaming my life away at Skardu airport I had a kind of eureka moment and flew back to England with my brain spinning. What I had in mind would be far harder to make than *A Great Effort*, but seemed to me to have all the ingredients I was looking for to become a really exciting climbing movie. Roll on Ben Nevis and *The Bat*.

Chapter nineteen: The Bat and the Wedding

When I had been thinking about my first film I had come across one of the iconic pieces of writing about rock-climbing, amongst the best ever written. 'The Bat and the Wicked' by Robin Smith described the first ascent of that climb on Ben Nevis by Smith and a young Dougal Haston. At the time it had seemed a hopelessly over-ambitious project to film but now, four years on, in 1978, I thought it might be a feasible proposition. A major stumbling block had also resolved itself. The climb was done in 1959. Robin Smith, probably Scotland's best young climber, was killed in the Pamirs in 1962, while Dougal had gone on to achieve fame and glory on the Eiger Direct, Annapurna South Face and Everest South West Face when he summitted with Doug Scott. Until Haston's death in 1977 in an avalanche above Leysin in Switzerland, it would have been difficult to have a climber to act the part of Smith and to have Haston playing himself, only 20 years younger. To have another actor/climber taking the part of Haston would also have seemed strange. Sad though his death was, the problem was now solved and I began to see how a film could be made.

Three things attracted me to the project. First, and most important, was the quality of Smith's writing. It was very much of its time and influenced by the Beat generation of writers and poets. Smith, a highly intelligent and gifted writer, was a philosophy student at Edinburgh University, still developing an original style, and, compared with so much university writing of the day, it positively crackled. The second big attraction was that Dougal Haston had also written about the climb — and in a few significant ways the two accounts differ. There was obviously tension between the two, and I wanted to juxtapose both men's perception of the same events. Finally, to film a classic hard rock-climb on one of the steepest and best bits of rock on the highest mountain in Britain was an obvious challenge, though I was under no illusion as to how hard it would be. Ken Wilson, perhaps the most vociferous and forceful voice in the climbing world, then as now, told me dismissively that it would be quite impossible to translate Smith's writing into a film. He obviously thought I was riding for a fall; the thought had also crossed my mind.

Unlike *A Great Effort*, when Tony and I had the time to make a thorough reconnaissance, filming on Ben Nevis would have to fit in with five people's busy schedules. Rab Carrington would be playing the part of Robin Smith and eventually I persuaded Brian Hall to be Dougal Haston. Al Rouse was my first choice for the Haston role, but he couldn't fit it in around his guiding commitments. Paul Nunn would be our safety officer and, once again, Tony Riley and I would be filming together. For Brian and Paul this was to be the

^ *Rab Carrington who played Robin Smith.*

^ *Paul Nunn at the foot of Carn Dearg Buttress.*

^ *Brian Hall who played the part of Dougal Haston.*

first of many film commitments — Brian in particular has made a large chunk of his career around a huge range of projects from TV documentaries to high budget feature films. Tony and I were already involved, and only Rab spurned the dubious attractions of the silver screen to form his own company making sleeping bags and jackets. 'Rab' gear now has an international reputation.

So at the beginning of July 1979, with the generous help of a grant from Yorkshire Art Association, the five of us set off in a borrowed Volvo for the 'Big Black Ben, sitting in the clouds in the huff and bucketing rain'.

We had to camp in the Allt a' Mhuilinn next to the Scottish Mountaineering Club hut right under Carn Dearg where we would be filming. The SMC had refused our request to use the hut, claiming, absurdly, that we would cause 'gross inconvenience to the hut users'. As the hut was locked and empty for almost all our stay, the only 'gross inconvenience' would be to ourselves which, as most of us had reciprocal rights to use the hut anyway, seemed a strange logic. So we camped, cursing the rain, the bogs and the SMC as we made two carries of film, food and camping gear up from the car park.

Amazingly though, the God of Filmmakers was on our side and, though it rained almost everywhere else in Scotland for the next week, the Ben remained dry, if constantly threatened by lowering cloud which gave the whole film a terrific atmosphere. Tony and I took it in turns to either film on the climb, or from the ground with

162

a telephoto lens. As we approached the two key pitches we had an alarming ascent up 150 feet of fixed rope to get into position. The rope hung way out from the rock which overhung about 20 or 30 feet, and upward progress on Jumar clamps involved wild spinning on the rope. I did most of it with my eyes tight shut, and I think the others did as well.

The whole shoot seemed to be virtually trouble-free, despite the logistical problems. The script called for three falls: a big one from Brian (Haston) and two smaller ones from Rab (Smith). They were the centrepiece of the story and had to be as authentic and spectacular as we could make them. In fact, Brian's fall was way over and beyond the call of duty as he fell over 50 feet, almost into the lens of Tony Riley's camera. When he returned to the tents that evening he was in shock and retreated to his sleeping bag. We weren't much better.

To our mutual delight we managed to complete the shoot, apart from a short scene in a pub, in just five days. Little did I know then that the editing would take the best part of a year. Such is the pace of modern life that within a week of shooting on Ben Nevis, Tony, Paul and I were in Delhi, and Rab and Brian in Kathmandu. As far as I remember, the next time we all met up was at the first Kendal Mountain Film Festival in 1980.

It wasn't until I returned from the second Barnaj trip that I started to grapple with the editing. Two things were obvious. Unlike the three previous films, we actually had too much climbing footage, and the original article by Smith needed a lot of simplifying to make it intelligible to a cinema audience. For instance, Smith refers to three attempts to climb the route with two partners. I cut that to two attempts and, with silent apologies to Dick Holt who was with him on his first exploration of the lower section of *The Bat*, he went as well. Even so, the editing was a real labour of love. I got used to walking into college by 6.30 to start work on the Steenbeck editing machine, which gave me three hours before the students arrived.

When I had returned from Barnaj for the second time, Laraine finished with me and, far too late, I realised that I wanted to be with her. I persuaded her, against her better judgement, that we should get married. It was probably a last ditch resort for us both. The story of the wedding and honeymoon has, over the years, become a minor saga in its own right. Chris Bonington has requested I tell it on at least two occasions at expedition Base Camps and even Laraine herself has heard it and laughed. So here goes…

We were married in the Sheffield Registry Office on December 22nd and had a small family lunch in a Derbyshire restaurant. The

163

^ Laraine and me on our wedding day.

evening 'do' was for all-comers and was at The Moon in Stoney Middleton, the much loved Derbyshire pub that for years was the centre of Peak District climbing, like the Padarn Lake in Llanberis, or the Clachaig in Glencoe.

By the time the evening was in full swing, both Laraine and I were well away. At some point I attempted to make a speech. What happened next was a subject of controversy, which has only just been resolved. Laraine intervened and made a speech herself, culminating in her sitting on the wedding cake. Ever since she claimed it was I who did this, and ever since I have denied it, with less and less conviction. Maybe she was right. Then in January 2010 I attended the funeral of Chris Astill, known to everyone as Shilling Rabbit (another story for another day). Tragically, he had been killed in an avalanche in Torridon and a large number of shocked mourners turned up for his funeral. At the wake afterwards in a Nottingham pub I met many people looking uncannily like people I knew 30 years ago, but older. Strangely enough, they seemed to think the same about me, and one familiar face suddenly turned to me and said: "I've not seen you since your wedding day. Do you remember the do in The Moon when your wife fell in the cake?" I think I punched the air.

The rest of my wedding remains a blur but we did have a drunken, pointless and vitriolic row on the way home. Laraine got out of the car we were in and disappeared into the night. I was never quite sure what happened to her, but with no house keys I spent the night on Tony Riley's floor in a borrowed sleeping bag in front of an electric fire. At some point in the night, the bag started burning. I awoke in a mass of charred feathers. Doug Scott had given us both white muslin Nepalese prayer scarves to bring us good fortune. Mo Anthoine, who woke me up, observed that, as I was still wearing mine, I was lucky to be alive.

I found my way back to Laraine's house and eventually we set off for our honeymoon in Chamonix. We barely spoke until the following afternoon somewhere near Geneva, when she suddenly said: "You'll be hearing from my solicitor," which seemed to break the ice a bit, and by the time we reached Cham we were just about on speaking terms. We drove into town at seven, the time I had arranged to meet Al Rouse in the Bar Nash. We would be staying with Al and his French girlfriend Gwen in her apartment. Just as I found a place to park in deep, fresh snow, Laraine decided to put her face on, which I knew wouldn't be a quick job, so I went ahead and walked through the doors of the Nash, kicking wet snow off my shoes. Inside the floor had fair-sized puddles of melt water. Al wasn't there, but a French friend, Catherine, or Cat, a climber and ski instructor was: "Ah, Jeem, it is good to see you — but why are you 'ere?" I explained I had just got married. "No, no, it is not possible!" She grabbed me and started a friendly wrestling match, when, of course, we slipped in a puddle. She was sitting astride me still laughing in disbelief when Laraine walked in… Back to square one.

Apart from the honeymoon element, we were in Chamonix because Al was planning to do a new winter route on the Grandes Jorasses and I was to film it. This would involve me learning to ski properly to get to the foot of the face. Al generously included his offer of ski lessons for Laraine, who hadn't the slightest interest. As the weather was vile and there was never any chance of even looking at Al's route, we confined ourselves to skiing in a local park, mainly on wet slush.

It would be nice to say that Laraine took to it like a duck to water — it was more like a newborn foal to custard. Added to which, she was wearing an old pair of Gwen's ski boots which she said were far too tight. Al explained patiently that they had to be reasonably snug, but when we finally managed to prise them off, her feet were covered in blood. At least this time Al joined me in the doghouse. As for my own skiing, I did improve a bit but, like many climbers, I still favoured the 'straight line until you crash' method of descent. Parallel turns were always as foreign to me as quadratic equations were when I was 16. After a few days, Dave Wilkinson, a Birmingham-based climber arrived. He was on his way to Courmayeur to see his girlfriend, but a French lorry drivers' strike had closed the Mont Blanc Tunnel. The only space available for him to sleep was in the tiny vestibule of Gwen's flat. Laraine and I were on the floor of her sitting room, and Gwen and Al were in the only bedroom.

At last relations between us thawed to the extent that we managed to consummate the marriage. Like most French apartments, the central heating thermostat was set high enough to bake bread, and when the deed was done I whispered to Laraine through parched lips, that I would make us both a cup of tea. "If you're having a brew, I'll have one as well." Dave's stentorian voice came from only inches away, as once again the matrimonial temperature dropped like a stone, though for the life of me I couldn't work out why this particular debacle was my fault.

We set off for home on New Year's Day after a particularly splendid evening in the Nash. It was a long, bitterly cold drive across a frozen and deserted France, and by the time we got north of Paris it was dark, snowing hard with every service station shut, and the petrol gauge well in the red. By a quite brilliant piece of driving, (he claimed modestly) I managed to persuade the car all the way to Calais by driving in the highest gear possible and caressing the accelerator with the gentlest of gentle pressure. When we got there the ferries weren't running and we had a miserable bivouac in the car. When, next afternoon, we finally reached Dover and I pulled into the dockside filling station, I nearly cried in relief. Then it was just a long flog up the M1 to home where we found Laraine's house frozen solid.

I spent the evening lighting paraffin stoves, turning all the gas fires on full, and eventually managing to boil a kettle. Armed with a hot water bottle we fell into bed, exhausted. After 10 minutes we were just warming up when there was a horrible crunching sound from the bathroom as the ceiling collapsed, bringing a huge cascade of ice cold water flooding the upper floor and kitchen below. Anyone passing Langdon Street at about one in the morning would have been startled to see a large, nude man hacking at the snow-encrusted pavement with an ice-axe, which at least had been easy to find, unlike the stop cock which I eventually unearthed and turned off to halt the deluge.

The next day we managed to get a plumber to sort us out. When he left, Laraine called me up to the bathroom where the bath had been pulled an inch or so away from the wall. I pushed it back, there was a horrible crunch as a pipe snapped and another icy deluge flooded the kitchen below…

After this unpromising start, our marriage went from bad to worse.

Chapter twenty: Pilgrimages to Pembrokeshire and the Death of my Mother

In 1980 while I was not editing *The Bat*, I had a sudden upsurge of interest in rock-climbing. Here is a strange conundrum. In my own eyes I was only ever an average but competent climber. Because of my participation on high profile expeditions, non-climbing friends assumed I was far better than I knew I was and any attempt to enlighten them was taken as false modesty. By comparison with the whole body of British climbers I suppose I was, at my best, a reasonable performer, but in the rarefied circles I associated with for a lot of my career, I was tolerated as someone to hold the ropes, make jokes and generally be encouraging to my leader. I was, I think, roughly the equivalent of a semi-pro footballer, a club rugby player or a minor county cricketer; not bad, but certainly nowhere near as talented as the world-class climbers in whose elite world I was privileged to be just a bit more than a spectator. So I have found myself at the other end of ropes attached to Joe Brown, Don Whillans, Martin Boysen, Henry Barber, Chris Bonington, Al Rouse, Doug Scott, Joe Tasker, Ian McNaught Davis, Jim Fotheringham, Rab Carrington, Paul Nunn and many others. I feel proud to have followed in their footsteps and even, on occasion, led them up some of my favourite test pieces. I hope that is a reasonably fair assessment.

During the Easter holidays a huge crowd of climbers descended on the camp site at Bosherston in South Pembrokeshire. Here, new routes were crying out to be done on the steep limestone sea cliffs. They had been partly explored by a knowledgeable few and had suddenly found favour with the magazines and the masses. Even I could mop up a few of the easier pickings. For two or three years, Easter at Bosherston was *de rigueur* if you wanted to be in with the in crowd. The year 1980 was a special one; probably more new routes were made than ever before or since, and we had some wonderful evenings recounting our adventures in the St Govan's Inn where, as Rab Carrington observed: "Anything less than three new routes a day doesn't count!" which was as good a piece of pub bullshitting as anything anyone else came out with in a long weekend of intense competition.

Hardly had I returned to Sheffield, and a few days of gritstone climbing when Jim Perrin abducted me back to Pembrokeshire to attempt a new route he had spotted on the imposing Mewsford Point. Laraine, needless to say, didn't come on either trip. She didn't want to and, apart from a few holidays in Cornwall and Wales, didn't really take to camping. But I find it difficult to understand how selfish I had become. Just saying so doesn't make any difference and nothing I can say or do now can undo my behaviour in the past. Laraine wanted what she considered a normal marriage. Weekdays in Bristol and weekends in Sheffield didn't fit the bill,

particularly when climbing and filmmaking was involved.

Jim and I bivouacked in the Bosherston car park and set off early on a cloudless day for the crag, which is only accessible for a few hours at low tide when a tilting ramp of limestone is uncovered. Unusually for a sea cliff, you can then step back and see the whole cliff. Our proposed line looked desperate to me. I wondered why Jim had put his faith in my climbing ability after only a couple of outings at Easter on the more amenable Crystal Slabs, and a few gritstone routes since.

I was never too sure about my feelings for Jim Perrin. We both shared an obsession with Menlove Edwards, on whose biography Jim had been working for what seemed like years. He was extremely well-read and a brilliant, if erratic, writer. Because of our mutual interest and some similarity with our names, people often got us confused, to my amusement and his irritation. He was quite obviously a very good climber, far better than I, but unlike, say Paul Nunn or Joe Brown, he didn't seem to have any sympathy for, or understanding of, his partners — me in this case. I felt his climbing was very much for his own self-fulfilment and I was just a portable belayer, a feeling that grew stronger as the day wore on.

After a stiff little pitch to a good ledge, Jim and I were belayed under a smooth, overhanging, leaning groove which looked desperate. Jim made several tentative attempts to climb it, placing four or five tiny wire runners in a thin crack and climbing down on a tight rope from each one, making sure they were secure but also making them harder to remove. I felt that this climb was far too hard — if Jim was climbing right up to his limit, how could he expect me to follow him? I prayed he would give up, and return with someone like Pat Littlejohn who would be well able to follow, or actually lead it. But Jim persisted and at last got up the groove and onto the steep and somewhat easier ground above. He climbed out of sight, but I could still hear the reassuring click of karabiners and feel the tell-tale jerk of the ropes as he clipped more runners. I assumed he would belay as soon as possible, but my heart sank as I continued to pay out the ropes. Eventually they came tight. Jim was well out of earshot. Below, the ramp had disappeared on the incoming tide and waves were seething and sucking around the base of the cliff. I felt lonely, exposed, and very frightened. The ropes tugged incessantly and reluctantly I started to undo the belay, freeing a few more feet of rope. It was all too obvious that Jim was still climbing and that I had no choice but to follow, hoping that he would soon find a belay.

In the last few minutes I had managed to form a cunning plan of sorts. The problem was that as the groove overhung slightly, and was tilted to the right, there was a very real danger that as I

< First ascent on Flimston Slab
— Brass in Pocket.

removed the well-placed wire runners, they would suddenly jerk out and I would almost inevitably swing off and out. If I lost contact with the rock we were both in real trouble. There was obviously not enough rope to lower me and even if there were, I would probably miss the ledge and end up in space. If that happened there was a strong possibility that we would both die. There was, of course, the temptation to just unclip the rope from all the runners, use them as handholds and abandon them, incurring the wrath of Jim, but, in fact, it didn't make much difference to my predicament. As the groove was both overhanging and leaning to the right, the biggest jerk came when I unclipped the tight rope from the runner and I instantly started to swing. The wires actually came out with a bit of fiddling, and I retrieved them all. But there was no way I could free the ropes and the wires without flying into space, so this is what I did.

With a spare line sling I managed to fix a prusik loop to one of the ropes. As I reached each jammed wire I used a prusik loop as a portable handhold. It was precarious, and twice I all but lost contact with the rock. Eventually, and almost sobbing with relief, I reached better holds at the top of the groove and a big sling that I clasped with both hands. The ropes were almost cutting me in half, and presumably doing the same to Jim, but after a few more moves came the longed-for slackening as Jim found a belay somewhere beyond the top of the crag. There was no chance of him hearing me as far below huge waves exploded against the crag and the wind got up. But now, as I moved up the steep wall, the ropes were taken in normally, and I could climb properly at last. It was, of course, a full 150 feet to the top, and I passed several points where Jim had left good runners, and I cursed him for not belaying much earlier. The last 20 feet involved precarious climbing over vertical rubble and avoiding a huge loose block. Apart from *Coronation Street* in the rain, I have never been so glad to reach horizontal ground and the welcome sight of Jim belayed to the remains of a rotting flagpole. Then, with all the fright and effort behind us, we were exultant.

Driving home and re-living the climb, I felt that I had acquitted myself rather better than Jim would ever know. Many less experienced climbers might have freaked out completely faced with my predicament on the stance, with the knowledge that Jim was still climbing. I had hit on possibly the only solution of climbing the crux groove without lurching into space.

So Jim had his new route and we were both still alive. He called it *The Voyage Out* and it is graded E2 5c, which is quite respectable by any standards. But above all, it was a real adventure, albeit rather bigger than we bargained for. Jim wrote a good article about it for The Climbers' Club *Journal*, and it even got a mention in the anthology *Extreme Rock* in which he stated that 'the loneliness and seriousness of the place really came home to us'. So a gripping day went into the memory bank, and there it stayed for 11 years.

During the summer term it became quite obvious to Laraine and me that our marriage would never work. I was more upset about this than I cared to admit. At about the same time Mum, who since her breast cancer in 1953, had basically been in good health, started losing weight, and it was no real surprise to find the disease had come back, this time in her spine.

By now *The Bat* was nearing completion and I brought Mum down to Bristol to see it, still on the Steenbeck editing machine. I sensed that she might never see the finished film, and during the autumn she slowly deteriorated. Both Phil and I tried to see her as often as possible and I vividly remember driving away from Malvern one Sunday evening and stopping in a lay-by. Suddenly I admitted to myself that she was dying, and there was nothing that anyone could do about it.

On top of worrying about Mum, a major event was to take place in October. I had become involved along with Brian Hall, John Porter, Al Evans, Ian 'Sherpa' Roper, Ian Wall and Phil Ham, in getting together ('organising' is too strong a word) the first Kendal Mountain Film Festival. This was a chaotic, alcohol-fuelled shambles, a far cry from the sponsored, high publicity, money-driven giant it has become today. Nobody made any money (no change there, you might say, quite rightly) and though everyone had a great time, it was obvious that if we were to do it again it would have to be more structured. It was, but that's another story.

As far as I was concerned the highlight was the premier of *The Bat* which I finally picked up from a London film laboratory on the Thursday before the festival got underway on Friday. It was due to be shown in a non-conformist chapel we had hired on the Saturday afternoon. We had blacked it out with bin-liners covering the windows. Halfway through the morning we were told that there would be a wedding at midday, and it all had to be pulled down! Afterwards we tried to replace it all, but the church was far from dark and stray shafts of sunlight played across the temporary cinema screen. To add to that, in front of a full house, the projectionist had threaded the film incorrectly and to my horror it started ripping. Suddenly, I blew my top. "Stop! Stop! I refuse to show the film under these conditions. I'll show it this evening when it gets dark." About 300 disconsolate festival-goers were let out onto the streets of Kendal while I wondered what I had done. Since I had picked up the finished print I had not actually seen it myself. I had no idea whether or not all the sound tracks were synced up correctly and whether the neg cutters had done their job properly.

So when the time came, the church was bursting at the seams as news of the afternoon fiasco spread. I was a mass of nerves and prayed that just for once, nothing would go wrong. Just for once, nothing did, and the film got a standing ovation! I have little recollection as to what happened next and woke up in an armchair in someone's house. I was completely unaware that I had been booked into a hotel, and that there were several Jim Currans sharing my room. The festival had, after all, been a huge success but it was two years before we could summon up the energy to do it again.

Meanwhile, real life carried on and, as autumn turned to winter, Mum's health grew worse. Soon after the festival she had a series of small heart attacks and I spent a week in Malvern doing what I could to help. Cousin Chris was there and so was Uncle Wilfred. At about the same time I had to have a wisdom tooth removed. I didn't realise, until the dentist asked me if I had arranged to have a week off college, how big a job this was. I spent the night in my Bristol flat, drugged with painkillers in a sleeping bag in front of a gas fire (no conflagrations this time). In the morning, whenever I awoke, there seemed to be Beatles music on the radio, particularly John Lennon singing 'Imagine'. Eventually it penetrated my addled brain what had happened. I have always associated Lennon's death with Mum's a few weeks later, and those sad, simple chords still remind me of her. I had visited her in hospital the evening before she died but decided to drive back to Bristol. At half past seven in the morning the phone rang and I was filled with remorse that I hadn't been there at the end.

Wilfred conducted the funeral and she was buried in the nearby Malvern cemetery. A few weeks later Phil and I performed the last sad duty, to clear out her flat. It was horrible task, dismantling her life, sharing out her possessions and throwing so much away. But it had to be done, and at the end the only item we both wanted was a pair of nail scissors. We put them in the middle of her empty sitting room and retreated to opposite corners. Someone counted to three and we both dived for them. I won and I still have them.

Chapter twenty one: "Aye-aye-aye Kon-gur!"

^ *Chris Bonington.*

There have been, I think, surprisingly few genuinely life-changing moments in my 67 years. One was the showing of *The Bat* in Kendal, for the direct result was that I went to China with Chris Bonington.

I had known Chris for a few years, initially through the Bollin Primary School in Bowdon, where Gemma and Becky had been in the same classes as Mathew and Tom Estcourt. Nick Estcourt was a climber I first met in the Alps in 1964 and he introduced me to what were commonly referred to as 'the Altrincham All Stars': Martin Boysen, Malcolm Howells, Dave Pearce, Chris Bonington and, of course, Nick himself. Chris's children, Rupert and Daniel, also went to the Bollin, as did all the All Stars offspring, causing one of them to comment after a children's party: "You know, Mummy, so and so's Daddy? He isn't a climber!"

Chris was soon to move up to the Lake District. My friendship with him, I am under no illusion to reveal, was initially based on the fact that because I worked in Bristol, he knew I could always be lured away from college to climb in the Avon Gorge when Chris was in the vicinity on his annual lecture tour. Quite often, after an afternoon's climbing, I would help out with the lecture (this was before the days when Chris had his own roadie) and on several occasions ended up staying with Bob and Pat in Banwell. At least twice he persuaded me away for a weekend and I remember climbing *Mousetrap* with him, a classic route on Craig Gogarth in Anglesey, and on another occasion doing several hard routes in Borrowdale before hitchhiking back to Bristol.

The opening up of peaks in China and Tibet had been rumoured for the last two or three years, and I had no doubt that when it happened Chris would be at the head of the queue for permission. He was, but it was not, as I had expected, for Everest, but an unknown mountain in the Chinese Pamirs called Kongur. At 7719 metres, it was one of the world's highest unclimbed peaks.

Now, 30 years later, it is difficult to explain to younger climbers the huge attraction of having the opportunity to visit, let alone climb, behind the Bamboo Curtain. Quite a lot was known about Chinese Sinkiang and Tibet, but it was almost all in the books that had been written before the Second World War. Explorers like Younghusband, Sven Hedin, Shipton and Fosco Maraini and, of course, all the pre-war Everest books, were well-thumbed tomes. Since no expeditions had been allowed since the late 30s, and even then they were almost exclusively to Everest, it was impossible to imagine the colossal potential of virgin peaks and exploration of whole ranges that were barely heard of outside the hallowed portals of The Alpine Club and the Royal Geographical Society.

So when, in 1980, Michael Ward, (who had been a doctor

on John Hunt's successful Everest expedition in 1953) Chris Bonington and Alan Rouse got permission to explore the Kongur region, practically nobody had a clue where they were going, and that certainly included me. (When they returned, the close-knit climbers in Sheffield were underwhelmed by Al's slightly dismissive and humorous account of his time in the company of the two men, both old enough to be his father.) Michael Ward would technically be the leader of the main expedition, which also included three other doctors, for the expedition would also combine climbing with medical research.

I had been promoted to the 'A' team. I would be:

1) going to China (brownie points galore)

2) with Chris (more points)

3) Pete Boardman, Joe Tasker, and Al himself (brownie points off the scale).

Since the disastrous honeymoon, Al and I had become friends. Tragically, not long after that visit, Gwen had been killed in Chamonix skiing off piste and a shattered Al had returned to England to try to rebuild his life in Sheffield. He had since started a new relationship with Hilary Ramsey, a nurse who had lived in Bristol and had been the girlfriend of Arnis Strapcans, a brilliant climber who had himself been killed on Mont Blanc attempting to solo a climb on the Italian side of the mountain. Both Al and Hilary seemed devoted to each other.

On Kongur, Al and I invariably shared hotel rooms, and each other's company whenever we could. Both of us had a similar, slightly anti-establishment sense of humour, and often found it hard to take some of the more curious edicts of our Chinese hosts as seriously as we should have. My relationship with Chris at that time was strangely similar to my facetious dealings with Dr Birch in Bristol. I could sense that Chris often seemed to be exasperated by my apparently casual manner, but I found it almost impossible not to come out with flippant comments. Al had his own problems with Pete Boardman, who found his incessant story-telling increasingly irritating as the trip progressed. Al's problem was later compounded by his performance on the mountain. He had led an unsuccessful expedition to Everest's West Ridge in the winter of 1980-1 and had returned thin and exhausted by his efforts. I felt that neither he, nor Joe Tasker, who had been with him, ever really recovered. Certainly Al's reputation as one of Britain's foremost exponents of bold Alpine style climbing, was not helped by his almost permanent sore throat which reduced his bull-shitting to a hoarse whisper. His pace on the hill was much slower than Pete's, who was by a long way the strongest member of the party. Pete and Al partnered each other, possibly to keep Pete and Joe apart,

< Chris on Fool's Paradise*,*
Gowder Crag, Borrowdale.

175

^ Old men in the market in Kashgar.

for they would surely have put Chris and Al in the shade. At 47, Chris had reason to be slow, and I thought Joe was quite cunning in climbing with him, when any weakness on his part would be less noticeable.

Once we reached Beijing, on an almost empty 747, the new boys had their first impressions of China. The drive from the airport to the city centre was extraordinary. There were hardly any cars, millions of cyclists, not a single sign in any western script, and no advertisements at all. This all took some getting used to. Awful to admit, but the huge advertising hoardings that litter the approach to Central London from Heathrow, do at least cheer the place up. Our huge hotel was basic but comfortable, and in the few days we spent there we did the usual tourist things, including the Great Wall, the Ming Tombs and, of course, the Forbidden City.

I had been invited on the expedition to make a documentary, a daunting task to undertake on my own. On this trip perhaps more than any other it would have been great to have a sound recordist, for all the sights and sounds of China were obviously going to play a bigger part in the finished film than the more familiar settings of Nepal or Pakistan. Recording sound as well as film was almost impossible, and even using the camera was far harder than anywhere else I have worked. The problem was that, however strange and interesting we found China, the Chinese found us even more fascinating. Once the camera was unpacked, vast crowds of spectators materialised out of nowhere and it was impossible to film anything other than a crowd of gawping spectators. Sometimes I even had to revert to walking along, holding the running camera at my side, in the hope that I could get a few shots without causing a riot. Using a tripod, which is what I wanted to do, was just a joke. Maybe because of this, Chris seemed to think I wasn't doing my job, and I was on the receiving end of quite a few pointed comments, which didn't do my self-confidence any good at all. This reached its nadir in Kashgar when we were taken to see the old British Consulate where Eric Shipton had served briefly after the war. This was now a lorry drivers' hostel. This was followed by a visit to the Concubine's Tomb where one of the many wives of the Emperor Qian Long was reputed to be buried. I dutifully shot rolls of film at both these venues, though neither was visually exciting. Then, completely unannounced, we were taken to a junior school where ornately dressed children sang and danced to the accompaniment of local stringed instruments. Ethnic or what! And I had run out of both film and tape. Chris was understandably unsympathetic and I was pissed off with myself, and the fact that I never seemed to be told from one moment to the next what was going to happen. Al, who had been here the year before, had a

176

reasonably good idea what to expect, but it was too little, too late for Kashgar.

After we left Kashgar we drove round the edge of the Great Taklamaken Desert. Not all the way round obviously, but for 100 miles which was far enough to confirm that it was very big, about 126,000 square miles, and made of sand. (If I'm honest we knew that already, having flown across it a few days previously.) Then we started climbing up a long valley called the Gez Defile. We were actually following the old Silk Road, one of the great trade routes of the world. The main strand linked Peking (now Beijing) with the Mediterranean. The one we were following went to India. Though called the Silk Road, the routes enabled the transport of goods both ways: perfume, spices, slaves, knowledge and even the bubonic plague travelled this huge transcontinental network. All we could see were the remnants of a rocky track that our modern Landcruisers criss-crossed on a road that wasn't much better.

The road, which was actually the Chinese end of the Karakoram Highway, brought us out at the tranquil expanse of the Karakol Lakes. It was strange to think that if we carried on we would end up in Gilgit, whereas we had flown right across China and back again, to end up only a couple of hundred miles from Trango, K2 and the rest of the Karakoram peaks.

Here the views were very different. Instead of steep-sided valleys and jagged peaks, there were vast views of brown dusty hills and peaks that looked more like the Cairngorms, reflected in the turquoise lakes. It was, I suppose, the archetypical Central Asian landscape and was almost identical to thousands of Tibetan vistas, but in 1981 it was all new to most of us. These panoramas seemed to cry out for paint and canvas more than cine film. Much later, I was pleased to see, in a review of the finished film in *Mountain* magazine, that I had brought a 'painter's eye' to the landscape.

Flattering, but, in fact, almost impossible not to.

When we got established on the mountain I was paired with a man that everyone else seemed to think was a most unlikely partner. David Wilson was the political adviser to the Government in Hong Kong and had been 'borrowed' by us as he was a fluent Chinese speaker and an enthusiastic (and

< David (now Lord) Wilson.

^ Wild horses on the Pamir plateau.

very fit) hill-walker. He was an urbane old Etonian, who Al Rouse was convinced was a Russian spy! Or rather he tried to convince me that he was and we both enjoyed the pretence. David himself was the epitome of the British diplomat and he pretended not to notice Al's scurrilous fantasies. We really hit it off on the hill and a friendship was born, both with David and later with his wife Natasha, that has lasted nearly 30 years, during which time his career progressed to being appointed Governor of Hong Kong and then to be Master of Peterhouse College, Cambridge. Now Lord Wilson of Tillyorn, David sits on the Cross Benches of the House of Lords and is as active as ever. Though our paths don't cross often enough, it is always a real pleasure to see him, and I would like to think the same is true for him.

I was delighted to climb a small peak on the South Ridge with David that the others had given a rather unflattering name, the Pimple. At around 6200 metres it was an altitude record for me and, I was rather pleased to find out later, about the same height as the Trango Tower, to which it bore no resemblance whatsoever. We camped on its rounded summit as it commanded a superb view of the South Ridge that the Gang of Four, as I had christened Pete, Joe, Al and Chris, would be climbing. As well as the view, it was also the most exposed camp site you could possibly imagine. In the two days we spent there, the wind, which seemed far more prevalent on Kongur that any other mountain I had ever been on, was mercifully almost absent. In a full-blown gale, I wondered

^ *Kongur, the summit pyramid from our camp on the Pimple.*

whether we would have simply been blown into oblivion.

The expedition gave me frequent, and sometimes disturbing, insights into the world of top mountaineers. For Chris, Pete and Joe and to a slightly lesser extent Al, success was everything. I sometimes thought, with Pete and Joe in particular, that the expedition book was also as important as the reality of the climb itself. But their commitment to that was frightening. When the first attempt on the South Ridge failed, many expeditions would have called it a day, for we had already been away for six weeks, and the four climbers looked shattered after spending a week on their attempt. But after only three days' rest they were off again, this time for 10 days, before they returned, exhausted but successful. Although I was hugely impressed, it was a world that I wasn't going to be a part of. It seemed to me that such commitment carried with it risks that, even if I had been physically able, were substantially greater than I could ever justify.

Here, again, is a conundrum. I have spent the best part of 25 years going on expeditions to big mountains, as well as lesser trips to South America, Africa and Russia. All of these required an acceptance of risk far higher than, say, rock-climbing in Britain, or even the Alps. Just travelling in the Karakoram or Himalaya, whether it be trekking or driving, or flying in light aircraft, is hazardous enough. So having accepted a higher level of risk than most, why should I baulk at those who go a step further? I suppose I can sort of justify it by saying that the proof of the pudding is in the eating. Pete, Joe, Al, Nick Estcourt and Paul Nunn are all dead, and represent a high proportion of my adult friendships. The 'B' team, on the other hand, are largely, but not completely, unscathed, although, of course, they owe their very existence to the 'A' teams. So maybe I struck a kind of balance – dangerous, but not too dangerous. Undoubtedly I have been lucky. I escaped a boulder avalanche in the Trango Couloir by a hair's breadth, survived several solo trips on skis up and down the Savoia Glacier on K2 — a profoundly stupid thing to do — and, on my last serious climbing expedition to the Kinnaur region of India, avoided drowning in a glacial torrent by sheer good luck.

Is it possible, I have often wondered, to justify such behaviour? There is no doubt at all that a minority of the human race mainly, but not exclusively, young and male, need to test themselves — by war, by sport (a safer substitute) and by so-called 'adventure' activities: climbing, canoeing, potholing, off-piste skiing, etc. The world would be a drabber place without them (apart from war obviously) and in Western society at least, these activities and those who pursue them seem to be generally admired. Until, that is, they go wrong. Ever since Queen Victoria wondered whether mountain climbing could be made illegal following the Matterhorn disaster, the general public and the media have either thrown up their hands in horror when disaster strikes — or praised the unfortunate victims to the skies. Scott of the Antarctic, Mallory and Irvine, Donald Campbell, Pete Boardman, Joe Tasker and Al Rouse were all given posthumous accolades, despite many reservations about the wisdom of their actions, while Alison Hargreaves, the sailor Donald Crowhurst and Everest eccentric, Maurice Wilson, got the thumbs down; Alison because she was a mother of two children and the other two because they were unacceptably mad. The ambivalence to risk is probably best illustrated in the current attitudes to Health & Safety, with local authorities being forced to offer 'safe' adventures, and being hauled over the coals when there is an accident. All of which, I have to say, leaves me none the wiser.

Many years after the Kongur expedition I saw uncut interviews with Gemma and Becky, by now in their late 20s. In front of a camera, they opened up, and it was hard viewing for me as they revealed childhoods that were constantly punctuated by the deaths of their school friends' fathers and increasing fears for my safety. "Really," Gemma said, "we just spent most summers waiting for 'that' phone call." And Becky made the telling observation that whatever transient fame the media confer on their dead heroes, the families have to cope with bereavement for the rest of their lives — a sentiment eloquently summed up by George Mallory's son John in 1999: "I would so much rather have known my father than to have grown up in the shadow of a legend, a hero as some people perceive him to be."

^ *Carole Innocent.*

Chapter twenty two: "Down, Down, Deeper and Down"

When the British Airways 747 pulled up at the gate, disgorging a travel-weary and hungover Kongur expedition who blearily waited for their luggage to emerge from Baggage Reclaim, I realised that the high I had been on for three months had largely evaporated. Before I left for China I had been going out with an ex-student from Bristol with the unlikely name of Carole Innocent. It wasn't the affair of the century, but when she met me at Heathrow and drove me back to Bristol, she told me she had met someone else, which was a bit of a blow, but hardly surprising, given my long absence. Carole subsequently married (someone else), had two children and lived in the Lake District before that all ended in tears. She now runs a successful art gallery in Bristol called Innocent Fine Art. We are still close friends and have set several dates by which time, if neither of us has remarried, we will settle for each other. Most, if not all the deadlines have now expired, but with the optimism of the truly foolish, we both hope something better than each other will turn up. Not too difficult for her — highly unlikely for me. I digress.

Anyway, back in Bristol with not much to show for the last three months, except some film rushes that I was really pleased with for all of two days, I felt myself slipping into what soon became the worst depression I had ever experienced. It was not helped by the fact that there was to be no place for me on Chris's next Everest expedition, on which I had pinned a lot of hopes. Al too had been dropped. My exclusion tipped me further into a mire of self-doubt and loneliness, but it was probably even worse for Al, for whom a professional climber's life seemed to have been snatched from his grasp.

Two contrasting events happened in the autumn, which scrambled my brain even more. The first was an invitation for the whole Kongur team to a reception at Number 10 Downing Street by Dennis Thatcher. It was an informal event that seemed to attract dozens of hangers-on, some, but not all, from the climbing world. The Minister of Sport was there, as well as several MPs who, as far as I could see, had nothing whatsoever to do with any kind of sport, let alone mountaineering. But I have to say it was an enjoyable event and an honour to step through the famous door. Afterwards we all went for a dinner at which Al and I felt ill-at-ease, given our impending absence from the team on Everest.

Hardly had I returned to Bristol when the news came that Al Harris had been killed in a drunken car crash. Al had long been a legend for his hedonistic lifestyle in North Wales, since his arrival in the early 60s. He had started climbing on sandstone and I first met him at High Rocks where he fell off soloing and landed on

^ *Al Harris.*

my head. He had pursued a life of pleasure-seeking decadence in Llanberis and Deniolen, and his parties were legendary. I had always enjoyed his company, but not the excessive drug-taking and shoplifting that were almost inseparable facts of his life. He had been a brilliant rock-climber but that had been overshadowed by the rest of what, in the end, became a rather forlorn and desperate existence. His death seemed inevitable and was utterly irresponsible (a head-on crash with two young passengers; Al wasn't wearing a seat belt). His funeral was a grim affair at Bangor Crematorium under leaden skies. It is a cliché to say that a part of our youth died with him, but on this occasion it was true — an end of an era and clearly not one to help my mental state.

My depression was, I am sure, caused largely by delayed grief at Mum's death, which I had suppressed in the euphoria of going to China, and a similar reaction at the failure of my second marriage. The two events merged into one ghastly downward spiral of regret. Halfway through the Christmas term my self-confidence was at an all-time low and my teaching was badly affected. It is hard to remember the unhappiness of this time, which seemed to be all pervading and lasting forever. I was drinking far too much and virtually chain smoking. My nerves were utterly shot to pieces. I have a terrible memory of playing darts one lunchtime, when I was so out of control that I literally couldn't throw the darts as far as the board, and I remember the humiliation of picking them up off the floor, and the embarrassment of Ned and Nev who probably didn't realise how far gone I was.

When, much too late, I went to the doctor, he promptly signed me off work and sent me to see a psychiatrist at the Bristol Royal Infirmary, as well as, inevitably, prescribing me with anti-depressants. I have spent several periods of my life with these drugs and still have no strong feelings about them. I have always found them easy to stop taking, but have never really worked out how much good they do. Certainly, they seem to numb the feelings somewhat, suppressing the really piercing sadness, but they never remotely seemed like 'happy' pills which, I suspect, don't exist, or if they did, would be highly addictive.

As for the psychiatric help, I went to see a man at the hospital every month for about six months, at the end of which he told me that I needn't come again. I had no blinding revelations from him except for his casual observation that humans were surprisingly resilient to one disastrous event, but completely vulnerable to more than one. According to him, a widow appears to cope well with the loss of her husband, but when her budgie dies two months later, she cracks up completely. This made sense to me, as it was similar to my situation, but he could offer no cure except the old one — time.

182

Since 1981-2 I have had several more bad depressive episodes. Sadly, they have become harder, not easier, to cope with. The only thing I have learnt is to get to the doctor earlier in a vain attempt to head it off at the pass, but it doesn't work. Or if it does, it is only marginal. I have found that depression itself can be addictive. By this I mean that when, after weeks, or more likely months, there seems to be the faintest of faint hopes that it might get better, there is a strong temptation to reject that hope and stay wrapped in the protective cloak of misery. The logic goes that if you allow even the slightest chink of light into the darkness it will almost certainly be a false dawn and you will be plunged back into an even darker place. To get better requires an astonishing amount of willpower, even courage, and probably explains why some people commit suicide when they have apparently started to recover. The theory is that they have also recovered the will to destroy themselves.

Another horrible part of depression is the realisation that many, if not most, of your friends, don't want to know. I realise now that when it strikes (hopefully never again, but I am not holding my breath) there are probably only two or three people I can turn to who can do me any good at all. It helps if they are fellow sufferers. One very close friend explained to me that, because she has never had depression she simply couldn't imagine what it is like, and couldn't understand why it is impossible to 'snap out of it', or 'pull yourself together'. Actually, the words 'can't understand' are not strictly accurate. The understanding is there, but it is only a kind of academic acknowledgement, not an emotive one. Strangely enough, as the woman concerned will feature later on, I may as well reveal that she is a care worker, who in her everyday professional life shows exceptional understanding, helpfulness and involvement with her concerns for the old and needy. But not, alas for me when I am depressed. Boo-hoo.

During the worst winter months, I spent time in Leeds with Chris Lister at Chameleon, editing the Kongur film. He was also depressed and I remember one day looking at the Steenbeck editing bench with reels of film and sound snaking their way in between half-empty bottles of whisky, an overflowing ashtray and several half-empty plastic cups of coffee. The film itself, however, is fairly upbeat without any hint of the feelings of the two miserable old gits who were putting it together. The major snag was that we could never make it stretch to the hour slot on YTV (actually 52 minutes with time out for adverts). It seemed to be at its best at about 45 minutes, a non-existent time-slot for any channel. In the end it was stripped down to just 28 minutes — the half hour slot — which really upset me at the time, as a lot of what 'ethnic' material I had managed to shoot was binned. Looking at the finished print now, I am forced to admit that it is probably a better film for all its brevity. In those days of processed film it was far too expensive to produce more than one version. Today, with digital video images and editing, it is comparatively easy to produce as many versions as you want, which is a mixed blessing for long-suffering editors.

One weekend in January, I was staying with Paul and Hilary Nunn in Sheffield after a week's work in Leeds. The phone rang and Hilary answered it. "Jim, it's Neil from Bristol with bad news." Big Nev Aston had been found dead at his home in Nailsea, outside Bristol. Since I had worked on his house in Pensford, his marriage had foundered and he lived on his own.

I returned to Bristol determined to try to go back to work, which, now that Nev had gone, left a big hole in the Foundation Course. Many of the students went to Nev's funeral, which I have to say, was the worst I have ever attended. This was not just because his death seemed so sad at only 47, but also because the vicar who conducted it took it upon himself to constantly rebuke the congregation for basically being Godless heathens. For reasons that seemed unclear at the time, and totally bonkers now, he compared the price of refrigerators in Russia with those in the West. There was, I seem to remember, some strange point to be made about materialism versus communism, but it had nothing to do with Nev. I left the crematorium as angry as I've ever been (I was not alone in my fury), and many of us drowned our sorrows in the college bar, which at least made us feel properly sad. Rather more appropriately, we later organised an exhibition of Nev's spare and understated low relief paintings and very austere black and white photography. This seemed a more fitting tribute than that ghastly funeral. We owed it both to his memory and to the students on the course, to make the rest of the year as good as we possibly could, and in doing so I suppose I managed to lift my own spirits a bit.

We took the students away on a field trip to Pembrokeshire at the end of May and I was sitting next to my tent on the Bosherston camp site listening to the car radio when it was announced on the six o'clock news that Pete Boardman and Joe Tasker were missing on Everest. No doubt at all what 'missing' meant. A week later, I was up in Sheffield seeking out Al's company. Both of us had, in the months before the expedition, predicted the sort of scenario where Pete and Joe would go it alone and meet with disaster. Our forebodings were uncannily accurate, and we both felt obscurely guilty for having had them. Twice now, expeditions I had high hopes of being part of had ended in tragedy, for I had been terribly disappointed not to go to K2 in 1978 when Nick Estcourt had died. I don't imagine that our presence on Everest would have made much difference — we might have made it rather more light-hearted but, equally, Al could have died as well. Once again, our presence at the memorial services for Pete and Joe were awkward affairs, far worse for Al than me.

There was no doubt that we were both badly shaken by a succession of deaths in the late 70s and early 80s. Expeditions had become a way of life for some of us, but already a way of death for far too many. Pundits have drawn parallels with going off to war, and I can see what they mean. But, of course, an expedition is a voluntary affair. Or is it? There is no doubt that, throughout the 80s, going on expeditions was a very addictive pastime. So much so that it was hard to say no. Like going to war there was a lot of self-delusion about; 'it won't happen to me', or even worse, 'it won't happen to my husband/wife, she/he is too careful and responsible to die on a mountain'.

After the Kongur expedition and the events surrounding Everest, you could say that I was disillusioned with the way my life was going. Even when the depression lifted, I was still lonely, but climbing was still my raison d'etre. I could see no alternative to my rather schizophrenic way of life. This, after all, was not unique — many climbers hold down good jobs and spend every available opportunity travelling all over the world pursuing their obsessions. I feel comfortable in their presence, as I do in the company of artists. My friend Caroline White once said that the only people she could really relate to were her fellow artists and climbers. Both seemed to be compulsive risk takers; artists in pushing the boundaries of their work, which was primarily cerebral, and climbers who, though their risks were physical, made similar mental demands in their execution. I would also add that, although an outsider might consider both groups irresponsible, self-destructive and amoral, many artists and climbers live their lives to a code of self-imposed ethics that can be surprisingly strict. Or am I trying to detect faint echoes of my Catholic upbringing?

Perhaps the one thing that helped my recovery was buying a house. When Mum died, the house in Ealing was valued and Phil and I had half each. It never seriously occurred to me to buy a house or flat in Bristol. Despite having worked there for the last 10 years, I never really felt it was my home. It dawned on me that I could, more or less, live anywhere and although Sheffield was the obvious, and inevitable destination, I did spend a weekend driving around North Wales. Steve had bought the Nook at the end of the Padarn Lake; Mo and Jackie were in Nant Peris. Why not follow their example? It was probably a good job it was scything down with rain that weekend and, horribly disillusioned, I drove back to Bristol in the Sunday evening resolved to live in Sheffield. I have to say that, for most Bristolians, the idea of a holiday home in Sheffield (for that was how many viewed it) was seen as eccentric at best, or completely barmy, for hardly anyone in Bristol could believe that anywhere 'oop North' was only about three hours drive away. So when the cash eventually materialised, I bought a new Ford Escort Estate (the first and so far only new car I have ever owned) and found a delightful little end terrace in Nether Edge. All seemed well until my mortgage request was refused as the walls had been reinforced with tie bars. I was bitterly upset, but within a month another terraced house in Nether Edge came on the market, which was actually a much better bet. It cost the princely sum (in 1982) of £16,000, and I paid half up front to give myself a tiny mortgage. When I moved in, the woodwork in the whole house had been 'decorated' in bright red or lurid green. It was so grim that I spent most of the next few holidays decorating and in so doing found that I was developing a homing instinct. Since my split from Alison I had become semi-itinerant. I've lost count of the number of addresses I had in Bristol, even allowing for longer stays in Caroline's various flats. I almost took pride in the fact that my sum total of possessions could be stored in the back of my car.

So now, settled for the first time in years, and actually beginning to feel house proud and at home in Sheffield, it was only natural that I should find a new girlfriend — living in Bristol, of course.

Chapter twenty three: Old Friends

Cass Lane was an art teacher in a large comprehensive school in Keynsham. She lived in Bedminster, not far from Bower Ashton, and was a regular in the Wednesday evening sessions in the Port of Call on Blackboy Hill where Bristol climbers congregated. She was still going out with a climber who was working in the oil industry in Turkey and was away for months at a time. It probably wasn't the noblest thing I ever did, but I couldn't help but try to justify it by thinking that if you choose to live most of your life away from your partner, this is an ever-present risk. After all, it had happened to me more than once.

Cass is a tall blonde woman with a personality that the word 'extrovert' barely describes. I spent great weekends with her in Sheffield with Al and Hilary, who she had known well from Bristol. Even better, my two girls became very fond of her and, to my delight, we had an idyllic holiday camping in Cornwall at Trevedra Farm campsite. Here, in the company of Paul and Hilary Nunn and their children Louise and Rachel, we had the sort of classic Enid Blyton-style holiday of beaches, swimming and surfing, plus climbing in the morning with Paul at Bosigran or Chair Ladder. I have lost count of the times I have camped at Trevedra, and they do tend to merge together in my memory, but the first one with Cass and the girls was the special one.

Gemma and Becky, now 13 and 11 respectively, were growing up to be intelligent and self-assured. They both went to Altrincham Girls' Grammar School where Becky later became Head Girl. What I loved about them both was that, from their earliest days, they were genuinely good company. Gemma always treats me with a kind of longsuffering tolerance. (What am I saying? She could be, and still is, on occasion, as critical and intolerant as anyone.) She once said that she couldn't help treating me as a rather gormless younger brother. And Becky is so well-balanced and measured that I often find myself asking for advice about all manner of things, including my own relationships, which I don't think is all that common between father and daughter. I am very lucky. (I was going to say 'blessed', but don't think I could write it without feeling slightly nauseous.)

Between 1982 and 1986, Cass and I were as close as anyone I have ever lived with. She was incredibly tolerant of both my climbing and my to-ing and fro-ing from Sheffield. I took her to Wales several times, to the Kendal Film Festival, to North West Scotland, and to Jersey on a strange 'family' outing — so called because we travelled on a railcard that enabled several unrelated adults and two children to travel to the Channel Islands at a fraction of the normal fare. Here, in the company of Al Rouse,

^ *The climbing team on Jersey: Richard, Bill, Ian, me, Al and Phil.*

Richard Haszko, Phil Burke, Ian Smith and Bill Dark, we had the opportunity to run amok in an area where hardly any climbs had been done. It was the equivalent of going to Cornwall in the 1940s and there were routes of all grades waiting for first ascents. Ian, Bill, Richard and I went for the easy and middle grade options, while Al and Phil competed for the hardest. Al won, with his masterpiece, the three-star *Tax Exile* at E5 6a. But at different times we all climbed with each other and in the week or so we spent in Jersey we claimed 20-plus new routes between us, and Cass and the girls had an unexpected summer holiday at Easter.

Cass took everything in her stride and I can hardly remember a single cross word between us. Like so many other relationships, the long shadow of K2 in 1986 eventually caused our split, but that, as we all lay in the sun on the beach in Jersey, was still well over the horizon.

Mention of Cornwall and Cass reminds me of Don Whillans. So much has been written and argued over the reputation of one of Britain's most charismatic mountaineers that it is probably impossible now to change the way people remember him. This is either as a working-class climbing genius whose life was an uncompromising battle against the climbing establishment, or an overweight, unhappy, lazy, middle-aged drunk whose moments of fame were long lost in the mist of time. It is hard to think that Don has been dead for a quarter of a century.

Jim Perrin's biography *The Villain* wasn't published until 2005, a full 20 years after Don's death and, for all its painstaking research, seems to me to give a badly skewed version of his latter years. Perrin, who constantly compares Whillans unfavourably with his hero, Joe Brown, gives the impression that once Don lost interest in British rock-climbing, which has been the central *raison d'être* for the author, Whillans's decline was uninterrupted until the fatal heart attack in a friend's house in Oxford in 1985. I was lucky to get to know Don quite well during his last five years, and saw a much more rounded (literally) personality. On the world stage, it is true that his greatest success was summitting with Dougal Haston on the South Face of Annapurna in 1970, but in the next

^ *Cass interviewing Don Whillans during a climber's 'drag' beauty contest at a Buxton Confernce.*

^ *Don Whillans, holding court in my Sheffield home.*

15 years he was hardly idle. He climbed Denali (Mount Mackinley), Kilimanjaro and Mount Kenya, and made expeditions to Patagonia, the Karakoram (Broad Peak) and Guyana (climbing Roraima, Conan Doyle's 'Lost World') and Venezuela.

As important to Don were his other interests: tropical fish (with diving trips to the Red Sea), sky diving (hard to imagine) and, in his last years, a revival of interest in rock-climbing, nowhere near cutting edge, but easy classics that he had never bothered with in his prime. I was flattered that he often sought me out for these little trips down memory lane and we climbed in Cornwall, Anglesey and Derbyshire. He also climbed the Old Man of Hoy with another old friend, Derek Walker. On all these outings Don was great company and, although no day out was complete without a trip to the pub, I would never have described him as an alcoholic. Maybe he was. Technically, drink certainly shortened his life, as did smoking (other people's cigarettes), but the decline described by Jim Perrin is one I don't recognise. I found Don's 'hard man' exterior was all a bit of a front, and deep down he was capable of great friendship and loyalty. He never had children, for whatever reason, which might have made him a different person, but he often let his guard slip with other people's. I remember him playing football with very young kids at Trevedra Farm and looking faintly embarrassed afterwards, when he realised that we had been watching.

He was certainly fond of Cass, 'The Giraffe' as he called her, and behaved impeccably in her presence. He once arrived in Bristol to give a lecture and stayed at her house. I have a wonderful memory of Cass blocking the front door as he tried to push his motorbike

189

^ *Don seconding on* A Dream of White Horses.

into her hall. "Get that thing out of my house!" she hissed through tight lips, and Don meekly wheeled the bike into her front garden. I'm not sure that he didn't actually mumble an apology.

I regret that I never saw Don climbing in his pomp as a young man. The nearest I got was watching an appallingly grainy old video at Joe Brown's house. It was the only surviving footage of the first BBC Outside Broadcast on Cloggy (Clogwyn Du'r Arddu) when Joe, Don and Ian McNaught Davis joined French star, Robert Paragot, to climb a combination of the routes *Llithrig* and *Pigott's* in vile weather. Most of the video was a succession of grey shadows moving through what looked like Demerara sugar. At one point the mist cleared for a few seconds and a tiny figure, resembling the modern climbing phenomenon, Johnny Dawes, skipped across the screen with twinkling footwork and the kind of gymnastic movement that I have only ever seen occasionally in bouldering competitions on artificial climbing walls. It was, of course, Don, and it was hard not to feel sad that such a talent was lost forever. The best 'live' climbing memories I have of him are in Cornwall on an ascent of *Diocese* at Chair Ladder and on Anglesey on *A Dream of White Horses* on Craig Gogarth. During the latter I was able to observe him every inch of the way. It was a bit like watching Mohammed Ali sparring long after he retired, or an old Test Match cricketer playing in a club charity match — still impressive but watching tinged with regret that such a huge talent had become a shadow of its former glory.

Probably the most frequent climbing partner I had in the early 80s was Paul Nunn. As well as making two expeditions and a film together, we climbed together frequently all over the country. Paul was vastly experienced. In the 1960s and early 70s he had been at the cutting edge of British rock-climbing. He was a member of the much admired Alpha Club whose members included Martin Boysen, Richard McHardy, Clive Rowland, Pete Crew and Bas Ingle. Paul had put up new routes all over the country, particularly in Derbyshire, the Lakes and North West Scotland.

Paul was strong as an ox, and incredibly cunning, both in his climbing and the rest of his life. He was the opportunist par excellence, and even on the wettest weekend away it would be unusual if Paul didn't find some obscure crag that had remained

^ *Paul Nunn.*

dry enough to climb. Consequently, though I did dozens of hard routes with him, they were often either routes on crags on which he had already done the classic lines, or in places I had never heard of. Occasionally he would take pity on me and we would do three-star climbs like *Kipling Groove* on Gimmer Crag, *Mercury* on Carn Gowla in North Cornwall, *Ogof Direct* in Cwm Silyn, and *Desolation Row* and *Thin Wall Special* at Bosigran, as well, of course, as hundreds of classic gritstone climbs.

Paul was nicknamed 'Captain Unreliable' by his Sheffield climbing friends. What seemed to be a firm arrangement to go to, say, Borrowdale for the weekend, Paul would consider to be one of many options. On several occasions I would wait, rucksack packed, on a Friday afternoon for hours, before ringing up Hilary and finding he had departed the evening before to somewhere entirely different. You couldn't stay angry for long, for as often as not he would turn up unexpectedly (probably having let someone else down) and you would embark on one of Paul's Magical Mystery Tours that might take in three or four venues, several pubs (in which Paul would be treated like a local) and possibly a visit to some stately home that Paul was studying as part of his thesis in economic history.

Paul was a mine of information, a lot of it so esoteric that it was quite impossible to know whether or not he was making it up. He had a formidable intellect and, even after a number of pints of beer, could hold and dominate at least four arguments at once with different people, rather like a chess master playing against several opponents simultaneously.

As a mountaineer Paul was supremely competent, and also quite cautious. I always felt

< Paul climbing one of the great classic routes of Stanage, Ed Drummond's Wuthering.

^ *Paul Nunn.*

that if he were killed, then I would give up climbing. Paul did everything possible to reduce the danger. Joe Brown and Mo Anthoine were similarly canny, yet it was Paul who eventually ran out of luck. Strangely enough, the year before his death I had already made the decision to stop serious mountaineering, fearing exactly that which was to happen to Paul.

Of all my friends who have died in the mountains, Paul is the one that provides the most and the best memories. Of a magic evening at Shining Clough where we did most of the classics of the crag as the sun set over Manchester and the Longdendale reservoirs. Of a gripping day on the Lleyn Peninsula, climbing a long rickety route with the curious name of *Fantan B* in a snowstorm, when Paul's mountain experience saw us through. Days of winter climbing on Ben Nevis and in Glencoe, finishing in the dark and just making it down to the pub for a last pint. And so many evenings in our local pub, The Byron when, in the company of locals like Rab Carrington, Geoff Birtles, Joe Simpson, Richard Haszko, Mike Richardson and Steve Bancroft every Thursday evening was an event in its own right. With jokes, point-scoring and arguing, every evening was different and in that company if you weren't on your game you could sink without trace. Fittingly it was in The Byron when I last saw Paul who was due to leave next day for Haramosh 2 with another old friend from Hayfield, Geoff Tier. I bought Paul a final whisky and walked home. As I turned the corner at the end of the road I heard Paul's great guffaw rend the night air as he made some absurd point that only he could understand. Did I actually say goodbye? Can't remember. Does it matter? He is gone, and left an unfillable void and that's that.

Chapter twenty four: A Gringo Not a Sahib

One of the unexpected bonuses of having a home in Sheffield was a growing love of walking. Like most climbers, I had always regarded the walk to the foot of the crag as a necessary evil. But on the Trango expedition, which involved over 50 miles of walking to Base Camp, there was every reason to try and enjoy it. On Barnaj, where the walking was through lovely wooded countryside, this wasn't difficult. Since then I have become more and more addicted to walking, and I even once tried to walk the Pennine Way before an Achilles tendon flared up and I had to give up after completing nearly two thirds of its 270 miles.

^ *Geoff Tier.*

In 1985, Geoff Tier and I went on a very low-key trip to Peru and with his friend living in Lima, Andy Maskrey, did the first ascent of a mountain called Palomani Tranca in the Cordillera Apolobamba north of Lake Titicaca. At 5633 metres, it was hardly the find of the decade, but it gave me as much satisfaction as any mountain I've ever climbed. Free from any film commitments and climbing with friends purely for pleasure was something I had been in danger of losing. Two things struck me about the Andes. The first was that without Chepi, Andy's Peruvian girlfriend who was half-Indian, we would have been lucky to get anywhere near our mountain. Gringos in Peru do not command the respect (if that's not too strong a word) that the Sahibs still just about do in the Himalaya. The second was my unfortunate tendency to compare the Andes with the Himalaya. I suppose the first visit — in my case to Trango — becomes a yardstick. Even earlier, I had compared the Lake District to North Wales which for years I saw as a kind of spiritual home. The point is, of course, that they are all different. The high altiplano around Lake Titicaca is superficially like the Tibetan Plateau. But it is not the same at all, and I have slowly learned to try and accept the unique characteristics of every area I have visited. If you look for just comparison and similarities, what's the point of going there?

After we returned to Puno on Lake Titicaca to meet Geoff's wife Barbara and her friend Liz, we still had plenty of time to walk the Inca Trail to Macchu Picchu. This must rank as the best and most enjoyable walk I have ever done, mainly because I was

probably fitter than I have ever been, before or since, and also completely acclimatised. For Geoff and me walking the Trail meant we were actually at a much lower altitude than we had spent the last month. For Barbara and Liz, of course, it was far more tiring and Barbara in particular found it very hard work. This description is of the Inca Trail as we found it in 1985. Since then you have to have a guide and be part of an organised group.

We travelled from Puno to Cuzco on one of the great railway journeys of the world. For most of the 386 kilometres the track never drops below 3500 metres and reaches 4321 metres at its highest. Oxygen bottles are kept on the train for the unacclimatised. Cuzco is now a vaguely hippyish destination and you can't go for more than five minutes without hearing those bloody pan pipes playing 'I'd Rather Be a Hammer than a Nail'. What with ponchos and those silly, woolly patterned hat things that have ear muffs, to say nothing of the guinea pig stew, I soon found that my boredom threshold was not at its best.

We spent a fair amount of time admiring Inca stonework, which is undoubtedly impressive. But I could never understand the rapturous admiration given to their clean joints. Tourists took squillions of photographs of them with cameras that would have your average Inca fainting with admiration and incomprehension at their precision. Given that virtually every tourist arrived on a Boeing 747 or its equivalent, I was thankful that the Inca slaves had nothing to do with putting them together.

In fact (developing a rant), it always seems odd that skills that have been superseded by new technology are given so much adulation. Chippendale would have been completely gobsmacked at the insides of any laptop, and the craftsmen labouring over the stained glass of Chartres Cathedral would be blown away if they could see an IMAX film. What is surely the magic ingredient of all these manifestations are their aesthetic ingredients where, arguably, the Inca or medieval craftsmen score higher on the scale than the sophistication of utilitarian technology. Skill is just a part of it. Of course, ancient skills are not the only things that get the semi-mystical treatment. Ley lines do, as well as the ludicrous 'mystery' of crop circles and how they are produced. I can think of dozens of examples of Renaissance and Islam craftsmanship that must have tested the technical ingenuity of the makers to their limits. Trampling a few lines and circles in a wheat field, armed only with a stake, a long piece of string and a plank doesn't seem to me to need a great deal of intrinsic skill, beyond the ability to fool some of the people some of the time. And ley lines! When I was young, we had comic annuals in which we had to 'join the dots' to find 'Rupert's friends'. Any Ordnance Survey map has enough material

< Andy (R) and me on the descent of Palomani Tranca, our tracks are clearly visible from the summit.

195

to make any shape or line you want; ditto star signs. (End of rant.)

I wouldn't like anyone to think that I didn't like Peru. I had just done a smashing climb with Geoff in a remote area, and I probably found the return to civilisation a bit of an interruption, knowing that we would soon be off again. Luckily (and I use the word advisedly), there was a rail strike in Cuzco, which dissuaded everyone from going to Macchu Picchu. With a bit of lateral thinking, we managed to use a bus, then a lorry full of English archaeologists to get us to the start of the Inca Trail at the kilometre 88 point where you would normally get off the train. I said 'luckily' because we then had the whole of the Trail to ourselves — no other groups and consequently, no thieves, who haunt the trail to rob the hapless trekkers. We heard that a whole party of Frenchmen and women had recently been robbed and had arrived at Macchu Picchu stark naked. If this is true I have to say that I would have paid good money to witness it, and can't imagine it happening to a nicer nationality. (Maybe a bit harsh this, but I have always found French trekkers and expeditions appallingly insensitive to their surroundings, leaving litter everywhere without a second thought.)

But, fully clothed and in splendid isolation, we rambled over the first high pass and had all the camp sites along the way to ourselves. I thought that some of the more remote ruins, like the wonderfully named Winay Wayna, were actually more interesting than Macchu Picchu. They were certainly unspoiled and I loved the way they were just emerging from the depth of the jungle that had engulfed them. There seems to be a kind of universal feng shui that places temples, castles, churches and monasteries in the 'right' places. Obviously some of the criteria for their siting must be strategic, but on the Inca Trail every ruin seemed to be placed exactly where you thought it should. God, I don't believe this — I'm going all New Age myself now.

The last few miles of the trek were along the most extraordinary path I have ever travelled. It was built protruding over a colossal drop to the Urubamba River and is made of branches and layers of smaller twigs and vegetation. Because of the forested hillside and dense undergrowth, the sense of exposure is diminished, but there are a few places where you feel that if you fell off you could land in the river thousands of feet below.

The last night's camping before Macchu Picchu is in the ruined buildings of Intipunku where, as dawn breaks, you get the classic view of the ruined city that graces hundreds of posters. In fact, nothing quite prepares you for the reality. As we had got up early we had a couple of hours' peace and quiet amongst the ruins before, strike over, the first rail tourists arrived, grinding

^ *Macchu Pichu.*

up the zigzag road from the station in fume-belching old buses that shattered the silence. Behind Macchu Picchu is a mountain called Huayna Picchu which looks uncannily like the Dru from Chamonix, but a Dru encased in trees and jungle! A steep path and steps leads to the top and I amazed myself by running up and down in under half an hour in an exuberant celebration of fitness and acclimatisation. It marked the end of a wonderful trip, for it only remained to force our way onto a train to return to Cuzco, and then fly to Lima and home. Cass came to meet us and, hating to break our celebratory return, told us the news of Don Whillans's death the week before. It was the first of several horrible returns to Heathrow. Even today I hate walking through the Green Channel and out into the real world, remembering when the protective embrace of an expedition was abruptly shed and, vulnerable, I had to face life on my own.

Chapter twenty five: K2 Tragedies and Traumas

When I returned from Peru the summer was not over by a long way and in Sheffield I found Geoff Birtles, editor of *High* magazine, having one of his periodic revivals into hard rock-climbing. We had a magic few weeks during which a fit and light version of me at last got up *The Sloth* at the The Roaches. On the beautiful buttresses of Cratcliffe Tor I managed to follow him up *Fern Hill, Boot Hill, Suicide Wall* and what I thought was the hardest of the lot, *Five Finger Exercise*. Who knows where it might have ended, but Geoff, leading *Regent Street* on Millstone Edge, fell off and absentmindedly grabbed the rope and gave himself a very nasty burn across the palm of his hand. This put paid to his climbing for the year and, soon after, I had to turn my attention to making a decision. Al Rouse had got permission for K2, the second highest mountain in the world, in 1986 and wanted me to come along and make a film.

It would be quite untrue to say that I had premonitions of disaster from the very beginning. In fact, any misgivings I had were based more around the fact that I would be 43 years old, and that Chris Bonington had been toying with the idea of driving to the Caucasus in a couple of Volvo estates. The thought of a film à la British Leyland was quite attractive. But the idea never took off (though we did go to Russia seven years later) and after a lot of dithering I decided that, if we could get a film off the ground, I would go to K2.

Problems abounded. Al was in a terrible state of mind when his relationship with Hilary ended, a fact that Al found impossible to accept, even when Hilary got engaged to another climber, Chris Hamper. Al, who had been a bit of a childhood prodigy in maths and chess, seemed to find his emotions desperately hard to cope with. Probably remembering my bad time four years earlier, Al turned to me for advice and it would not be exaggerating to say that I became a cross between an agony uncle and resident guru. I remember Al arriving at my house some mornings before eight, already having smoked a full pack of cigarettes and desperate for someone to unburden himself to. I don't know if there was ever anything I said that helped, but 20 years later, going through the worst emotional trauma of my life, I could have done with someone I could endlessly confide in. Basically, Al was horribly lonely, a fact that I realised, far too late and all too well, when I would have thought I was old enough to know better.

The story of events on K2 in 1986 has been the subject of several books, including two of my own and there is no point in re-telling the story except in the broadest terms. My own involvement in the last multiple tragedy was peripheral almost until the end. But for those unfamiliar with K2, here is a brief and very simple

^ *Geoff Birtles leading* Five Finger Exercise *and me seconding.*

description of the most relevant features. From the glacier at Concordia, the point where K2 first comes into view, it appears as a classic child's drawing of a mountain — a pyramid with three of its great ridges visible. (In fact, it has six ridges.) The far left-hand one is the West Ridge. In front of that is the South West Ridge, the so-called 'Magic Line'. On the right is the Abruzzi Ridge, the line of the first ascent and the most popular route on the mountain. The Abruzzi is a mixed snow and rock ridge that leads to the Shoulder of K2, at around 8000 metres. This is a snowslope almost flat at its base where Camp 4 is situated, rising increasingly steeply as it nears a huge band of ice cliffs (séracs) at the top. The route goes up a narrow gully (the Bottleneck) and then traverses left under the séracs before it is possible to climb straight up the long snow slopes to the 8611 metre summit.

Al had picked a team of hot shots (at least, that's how most saw themselves) in the expectation that he would be given permission to attempt a new route on K2, a line to the left of the Abruzzi Ridge that later became known as the Basque or Česen route. This was a line that would have been ideal to attempt Alpine style, which

199

> *Geoff leading* The Sloth *at The Roaches, the author looks on apprehensively.*

was Al's proven and preferred way of climbing, as he had already shown on Jannu, Kongur and Broad Peak. Instead, he was given the long unclimbed North West Ridge which forms the border with China. This seemed unlikely to succumb without fixed ropes and camps, a 'seige' that none of his team favoured (apart from me, for it would give me a far better chance to get film high on the mountain). But Al and the team were stuck with a route that required great teamwork and self-sacrifice, neither of which were forthcoming.

Slowly, our expedition fell apart. Brian Hall went first with a knee problem that had flared up on the walk-in. Then John Porter left, anxious about his job, and seeing no likelihood of an imminent summit attempt. The rest of the team gave up on the North West Ridge, opting for an illegal but quick ascent of the Abruzzi, which also failed. In the end only Al had the commitment

^ *Alan Rouse as I remember him.*

to stay for one last effort and I, with a mixture of determination to get a finished film, and loyalty to Al, decided to stay on, though I desperately wanted to go home.

The summer had already seen several disasters. Two Americans, John Smolich and Alan Pennington, died in an avalanche attempting the 'Magic Line'. Then Maurice and Liliane Barrard disappeared on the descent from the summit after an Alpine style ascent of the Abruzzi Ridge, which had taken far too long. Wanda Rutkiewicz, the famous Polish climber, became the first woman to climb K2, just before Liliane. Then another Pole, Tadeusz Piotrowski died on the descent of the Abruzzi after making a new route on the mountain with Jerzy Kukuczka. Then, appallingly, only yards from safety, solo climber, Renato Casarotto, died in a crevasse fall, despite a concerted effort to rescue him.

Many people have questioned how, in the light of all these terrible events, anyone could have even considered carrying on. It would, after all, have been completely understandable if everyone acknowledged the terrible death toll, packed up and went home and to be fair, most of the survivors of expeditions where there had been deaths did just that. Our expedition gave up too, but mainly because of our own lack of success. It is noticeable that on Everest in 1996, and again on K2 in 2008, the same kind of thing happened, only even worse, with climbers carrying on after and in some cases, even during, tragedies on the same route on the mountain. Descriptions of climbers walking past dying members of other expeditions seem unbelievably callous. Whatever the circumstances, one cannot help believing that morals and ethics have suffered a sad decline since the heroic efforts of, say, Charlie Houston's team in 1953, attempting to rescue the stricken Art Gilkey.

I think in 1986 we had to some extent been sheltered from the worst effects of the tragedies by having a Base Camp about half a mile away from the normal K2 Base Camp. But Al had an overwhelming ambition to be the first Brit up K2. This was largely based on a long-held desire to eclipse Pete and Joe, who had failed twice on K2 and had been instrumental in dropping him from the Everest expedition in which they had met their deaths. More

201

^ *The first view of K2, still plastered in winter snow and ice.*

immediately was the knowledge that Hilary and Chris would be getting married on August 10th. Most of us were invited, and I think Al would have found it too painful to return empty-handed.

To complicate matters even more, Al, who had begun an affair with an ex-art student called Deborah, had left her pregnant, with the baby due around the time of our return, a prospect he found quite impossible to deal with. Al's life at home was in such chaos that I felt when the K2 expedition also fell apart, Al lumped the whole lot together. Curiously, looking back now, when just the two of us were left, feeding a bonfire of burning rubbish, the fire seemed to have a symbolic resonance with him. Perhaps he felt that he had burnt his boats, almost literally, and now it was just a simple confrontation of man versus mountain. Al impulsively teamed up with a Polish woman, 'Mrufka' Wolf, a member of a strong Polish team also attempting the Magic Line. For whatever reason, she felt that she stood more chance of getting up K2 with Al than with her team-mates.

By this time there were several remnants of attempts on the mountain. As well as the Poles and Al, Kurt Diemberger and Julie Tullis were attempting the Abruzzi. So were a Korean expedition, and an Austrian one who, at Base Camp, had been so antisocial that they had cordoned off their tents with climbing ropes. I felt that with such a strange polyglot collection on the Abruzzi, international co-operation would be absolutely essential. If not, the whole house of cards would tumble. It did.

202

In the light of what happened, there is no point in concealing the fact that Kurt, Julie and I had a bit of history. Kurt was a living legend, doyen of many expeditions and the only person since the death of Hermann Buhl to have claimed the first ascent of two of the 8000 metre peaks, Dhaulagiri and Broad Peak. He was partnered by Julie Tullis, married to Terry, who was for many years the guardian of Harrison's Rocks. They used to run a café in Groombridge called the Festerhaunt, but at that stage I never knew them well. Kurt and Julie had been together as 'The Highest Film Team In the World', with T-shirts to match, since 1981. They were very coy about the nature of their partnership and even Terry seemed to collude in keeping everyone guessing.

They had turned up unexpectedly at an early Kendal Film Festival and asked if Kurt could show some of the uncut rushes of their recent expedition to Nanga Parbat. We squeezed them in and Kurt overran by nearly an hour, and then asked for a £200 fee, which we paid in the knowledge that, yet again, the festival was losing money. Later they turned up in Bristol and, with a huge amount of wangling, I managed to persuade the Graphics Department to allow them to work on editing their film, which they did for three days before leaving without a word of thanks. The Head of Department, who didn't know either of them from Adam, was livid with me, quite justifiably so.

Since then they had been to Everest, K2 and climbed Broad Peak, narrowly avoiding death in an avalanche on their descent. At K2 Base Camp, Al, trying to be friendly, asked Julie if she was interested in doing a series of lectures in Cheshire libraries, which he had done the previous winter. "I only do big public lectures," was Julie's dismissal of one of the leading lights of British climbing. She told us how annoyed she had been when Jenni Murray on BBC *Woman's Hour* had told her they had one thing in common — neither of them had climbed Everest. This was a story that I would have been inclined to keep to myself. Their presence undoubtedly added to Al's motivation to get up K2, for if Julie had done so, and thus claimed a first British ascent, and Al had gone home, his humiliation in his own eyes, would have been complete. All of which didn't bode too well for the ascent of the Abruzzi. Al, in a praiseworthy desire not to be seen to be taking advantage of the expeditions that had already put in a lot of work fixing ropes and establishing camps, was at great pains to be independent in every way possible, apart, of course, from using the fixed ropes which were almost impossible to avoid.

If every expedition had been able to stick to its original plan it is possible that everyone would have been able to clear the Shoulder of K2 by August 4th, and be well on their way down when the

203

worst storm of the summer hit the mountain. But crucially, a day was wasted on the August 3rd when the Koreans made their summit bid and the occupants of Camp 4 on the Shoulder — the Austrians, Kurt and Julie, Al and Mrufka — chose not to follow them for reasons that are still not totally clear. There was an arrangement between the Koreans and Austrians about a shared tent. This was not adhered to and meant overcrowding on the night of August 2nd. This apparently left Al and Mrufka without a decent night's sleep and their subsequent postponement of a summit bid. I can't help wondering whether there was not a bit more to the story than that, for an article of faith with Al was that you should spend the absolute minimum amount of time at or above 8000 metres (the approximate height of Camp 4). But whatever the reason or reasons, the fact remains that Al and Mrufka, Kurt and Julie, and the three Austrian climbers spent August 3rd at Camp 4 in good weather. It was a decision that would cost four of them their lives.

On the evening of the 3rd came another unforeseen problem. Three of the Polish team on the Magic Line summitted late in the day and started to descend the Abruzzi. One, Wojciech Wröz, was killed when he abseiled off the end of a fixed rope. The other two, Peter Bozik and Przemyslaw Piasecki, both exhausted, got down to the Shoulder where they added to the overcrowding problem. Al apparently slept half in, half out of his tiny two-man tent.

However, on the 4th, Al proved to be the strongest, breaking trail to within 300 feet of the summit when the two Austrians, Willi Bauer and Alfred Imitzer, caught him up and took over the arduous job for the final stretch. Mrufka had been left floundering in Al's wake and on his way down he persuaded her to give up and they returned to Camp 4. Earlier at Camp 4, Bozik and Piasecki had tried to persuade the third Austrian, Hannes Weiser, to go down with them. Weiser had given up on the summit early that morning, saying that his wet gloves would lead to frostbite. Weiser told them he would wait for his friends and in doing so made a mistake that would cost him his life. Also, by using food, fuel and tent space, he made the subsequent plight of the others even worse.

Later in the day Kurt and Julie summitted. The exact time has become a matter of bitter controversy. On the descent, just below the summit, Julie fell, dragging Kurt with her. They fell around 300 feet and were lucky not to fall over the huge sérac band above the Bottleneck. They suffered a miserable bivouac and spent much of the 5th in a white-out trying to find Camp 4.

Here, the weather, which had been deteriorating since the afternoon of August 4th, broke down completely and the seven climbers crammed into three tents that became two when Kurt and Julie's tent collapsed. Julie Tullis was taken into the Austrian tent where, during the night of the 6th or 7th, she died. Kurt, in Al and Mrufka's tent, was devastated. The storm didn't let up until the morning of August 10th when, despite high winds, there was enough visibility for the Austrians, Kurt and Mrufka, to set off down. Al was too far gone to move and was left semi-conscious in his tent. Of the five who left Camp 4, only Kurt Diemburger and Willi Bauer made it down.

During the storm my role at Base Camp started by simply taking radio messages from the Polish climbers on the South West Ridge. It developed into becoming an interpreter to the Polish, Korean and Austrian teams and their Liaison Officers. English was the only common language and I felt, as the events unfolded on the mountain, that while each climber obviously had a personal tale to tell, I probably got a better overall picture of events. Though I was just as prone to making mistakes as anyone else, I could at least try and understand how events affected everyone. For instance, when Bozik and Piasecki got back to Base Camp there was a big 'discussion' with the Koreans about how Wojciech Wröz had died abseiling off the end of a Korean fixed rope. Emotions were running high and it wasn't easy to persuade the Poles (who actually had no right to descend a different route from the one they had just climbed) that the mishap on the ropes in the dark was not just a tragic accident.

When, on the evening of August 11th Willi Bauer, on his last legs, made it back to Base Camp, I set out with three Polish climbers to Advance Base at the foot of the Abruzzi. In the middle of the night I found Kurt descending the last long snow slope. His first words to me were: "I have lost Julie." We managed to get him into a tent and warmed him up and the next day got him back to Base Camp where, during the next few days, I heard the terrible story.

Eventually I left Base Camp, on my own, and started the long walk home. I was aware that my life would never be quite the same again, but I had no idea of the years of controversy and recrimination that lay ahead. As I looked back at K2 for the last time, bidding a silent farewell to Al, I did actually think that, having been there, I might be spared some of the anguish of family and friends at home who could never have a body or a funeral to enable them to grieve properly. I was quite wrong. Even now, nearly 25 years later, the scars are all too easily opened up. As I walked down the long Baltoro Glacier, I was aware that I had a huge responsibility to get the story right.

Grief, I found out on my return from K2, affects people in

^ Kurt Diemberger at Base Camp after his ordeal at Camp 4.

different ways. Anger is not infrequent, neither is a desire to 'own' the deceased and to resent anyone else's involvement. Blame, guilt and denial are common. Simple sadness is often hard to come by. In the months following the deaths of Al, Julie, Mrufka and all the others on the mountain, I was often plunged into near despair by Kurt Diemberger, who managed to display in interviews, lectures and writing, each one of the reactions listed above, and who wasn't afraid to use every means at his disposal to undermine anyone who had the temerity to offer a different opinion.

Soon after my return I drove up to Caldbeck to stay with Chris Bonington. He, more than anyone, knew what I had been through at Base Camp, having had the same protracted and agonising wait when Pete and Joe had disappeared on Everest. It was Chris, more than anyone else, who urged me to write a book and in his company I could begin to tell the story with a degree of objectivity. Chris and Wendy were both very supportive and helped me through those first dark days.

Something that I found strange on my return was probably quite natural. This was that almost everyone I met for the first time felt they had to tell me exactly where they were and what they were doing when they first heard the news. Poor Gemma was on her own when she saw on ITN that both Al and I were missing. (This, of course, was long before satellite and email communications.) Eventually Matthew, her stepbrother, took a phone message and told her: "Your dad's okay, but he's ill in bed." Puzzled, it took a few phone calls before she realised that 'ill in bed' meant 'in Islamabad'.

The members of a British expedition to the North East Ridge of Everest heard over the BBC World Service that there had been a terrible accident on K2 and that there were no survivors. Apparently a rather stunned silence in the large Base Camp mess tent was broken by Mo Anthoine, who observed that if, indeed, it was true, then Jim Curran must have been killed by a falling rhododendron!

Back in Bristol, Cass was also full of sympathy and sadness at Al's death. Quite naturally, but I thought, with bad timing, she wanted a far deeper commitment from me than I could give at that time and, with regret, we split up. I was given unpaid leave of absence to write a book with an advance that more or less covered my college salary. I had until the end of March to deliver the first draft.

A month after my return, we held a memorial service for Al, a harrowing occasion made worse as I had to give the last tribute. I was a nervous wreck by the time I stood in front of a packed church and tried to do him justice.

Even before the memorial service, Kurt had phoned me from his hospital bed in Innsbruck, asking me not to use the footage I had shot, actually at his request, of him on a stretcher being carried that last mile or so back to Base Camp: "It makes me look as though I was rescued," was his puzzling explanation. I couldn't imagine what he thought the Poles and I had been doing for those last 24 hours. In all the time we spent together at Base Camp waiting for a helicopter to take him and Willi Bauer to Skardu, he hadn't said thank you to anybody and I wondered whether, even then, he was looking to come out of the whole grim business without a single sign of weakness of any kind.

Later he gave an interview to Dennis Kemp, an old friend of Terry and Julie, which was published in *Climber*. In it he put the blame for the tragedy firmly on the Austrians, who had brokered a deal with the Korean expedition about sharing a tent and then gone back on their word. I found this curious as neither Kurt, Willi nor the Koreans had ever mentioned the problem at Base Camp. Kurt also seemed to change his mind about when he and Julie reached the summit. Not, as he originally told me at 7pm, but between 5.30 and 6pm. But he confirmed the later time to an Australian Broad Peak expedition whose doctor had looked after him at Base Camp.

I cannot emphasise too strongly now, as I did then, that I originally had no reason to doubt Kurt's story. Willi Bauer, who speaks no English, gave an interview to a Polish climber, Krystyna Palmowska, at Base Camp which, by and large, tells the same story.

There are a few minor differences, but in my book *K2: Triumph and Tragedy* I tried to emphasise the common ground and, in fact, went out of my way to avoid any discrepancies and even omitting one or two of Willi Bauer's more pointed criticisms of Kurt's behaviour. But to no avail. Kurt wrote a letter to the 1988/89 *Alpine Journal*, complaining bitterly about anyone who had dared to question his story, and made several thinly disguised swipes at me. The first I knew about the letter was when I saw it published. Nobody thought to ask me if I wanted to reply. What I still find laughable is his assertion that Willi Bauer's memories were clouded by the altitude, which Kurt affirms, affects everyone but not, apparently, Kurt himself, who remains the sole repository of the truth.

Diemberger's own book, *The Endless Knot*, was published in the UK in 1991 and is a harrowing and emotional account of the disaster. But it is also puzzling and fragmentary, and does little or nothing to clear up the outstanding controversies. All of which is such a shame because, had Kurt's original account that he gave to me at the time been left to stand, most of the subsequent bitterness and suspicion would probably never have occurred. Sadly, Kurt's whole career has been badly flawed by his own one-sided accounts. The events on Broad Peak and Chogolisa, where the great Hermann Buhl met his death, have thrown up bitter controversies and received very similar criticisms. Kurt has done very little to help his own cause. For instance, in Katowice at a Polish film festival, Kurt gave a lecture (in English) to a highly emotional audience about the events on K2 and forgot Mrufka's name, referring to her throughout as: "The Polish girl"! When, at the end, a member of the audience asked in perfect English if Kurt felt any responsibility for what had happened, Kurt said he couldn't understand the question and left the stage to an awkward and hostile silence. He has frequently signed copies of my books with instructions to read his own to understand the 'true' story. Very sad.

For me, all this, plus editing the K2 film, made the winter of 1986-7 extremely fraught. Long evenings were spent with Geoff Birtles and Paul Nunn, endlessly discussing K2. I think now that feeling the responsibility of writing the book and film, and answering endless questions from friends, climbers and journalists, actually stopped me from going through a normal grieving process. I lived on a knife-edge for months, hardly ever allowing myself to give way to my emotions. I have only two memories of breaking down. Once, I was staying with John Porter in the Lake District when I cried myself to sleep, and the other was driving into college and catching sight of a cloud formation that reminded me of the approaching storm on K2, causing me to pull up at the roadside until I could get it together to continue. Oddly though, I didn't suffer from full-blown depression, just a huge sadness that has never entirely disappeared. Above all, I missed the Al Rouse that I had grown so close to in his last five or six years. Even now, I wonder how he would respond to current events, and I find it almost impossible to understand that for him it all ended in delirium, crying out for water that wasn't there, on August 10th 1986. I think of him on every anniversary, his youth and humour and, until the last couple of years, his zest for life. I always thought that Al surfed the leading edge of a huge wave that threatened to overwhelm him. But when it finally broke, I found it impossible to accept the inevitability of that total wipe-out. For years I dreamed he was still alive, sometimes dreams that were so vivid that it was almost a relief to wake up.

Going back to college in the summer term of 1987 was difficult. Two questions kept coming up. The first was the old one — how to readjust to life in the Faculty of Art and Design after the events of the last year. I still trotted out the same old answer; that it was an interesting and stimulating job that was so different from sitting in a freezing cold tent halfway up K2 that I could immerse myself into college life quite easily. Only this time my words lacked conviction. The following six or seven years I spent in Bristol slowly became less and less attractive. My own feeling, that I had not much left to offer as a teacher, undoubtedly caused some of it, but also the job itself was becoming less stimulating as the Faculty entered an age where financial accountability and course structure increasingly threatened the creative basis of everything in art education that I held dear. And beneath it all was the endless shadow of K2.

The other question was succinctly put to me by Ali when I returned from Pakistan: "Will you give up climbing after what has happened?" At the time I was quite shocked. Giving up wouldn't change anything, wouldn't bring anyone back to life and would leave a huge hole in my life. As Geoff Birtles put it: "Take the word 'climber' away from the words 'Jim Curran' and what have you got left?" So, after K2, there was never a possibility of giving up, but as I had foreseen on the way back from K2, nothing would ever be the same again.

Chapter twenty six: More Old Friends

In the summer of 1987 I took Gemma and Becky for a short camping holiday to Chamonix. It was their first ever experience of big mountains and I shared their thrill when, almost at journey's end, we caught our first view of the Bossons Glacier with a band of low cloud above it. "Look at that!" They were unimpressed. "No, not the glacier — above the cloud!" There, high above the car at a neck-craning angle was the sunlit snow dome of Mont Blanc. It's not often that a father can impress his daughters, but this was one of those occasions.

We spent a few glorious days walking and bivouacking (deliberately) on the Mer de Glace and on the paths below the Aiguilles Rouges, admiring the panorama of the Aiguilles, Mont Blanc and the Grandes Jorasses on the other side of the Chamonix Valley. Truth to tell, I didn't ever want either of the girls to become climbers, even though Gemma did spend a year or two rock-climbing and could have been quite good. But I did hope that they would develop a love of mountains and wild places. I think they have, even if they don't often travel to them. Neither of their partners has any real interest and, though Becky in particular loves the north west of Scotland, neither feels strongly enough to spend much time in the mountains. In some ways this is a relief, as it is one less thing to worry about.

When I returned from Cham, I had the chance to go to St Kilda with Chris Bonington and a team of ace rock-climbers led by Pete Whillance. We spent three weeks on this, the furthest outpost of the Outer Hebrides. Apart from demonstrating, quite conclusively, that I am not a sailor, it was a wonderful experience of vast sea cliffs, mountainous seas, fulmars and gannets in their millions, and the strange experience of seeing the remnants of habitation on St Kilda whose people had lived mainly off the sea birds and their eggs. It was a forlorn little outpost of civilisation that ended when the last survivors were evacuated to the Scottish mainland in 1930. Visiting St Kilda was a great contrast to the long drawn out rigours of the Himalayan expedition and, apart from the sea voyage, it was a really enjoyable trip and probably quite therapeutic.

One evening in January 1988, I arrived back in Sheffield after the weekly drive from Bristol. Paul broke the news with brutal honesty. "Mo has been told he's got a brain tumour. They think it's malignant, and they're going to operate."

A few days later, I visited Mo Anthoine in hospital in Manchester. Irrepressible as ever, he told me that as soon as he came round after the operation he did *The Times* crossword puzzle in half an hour. He seemed to think that the operation had been a complete success: "If they've really buggered it up, I'll have to get a job as an instructor at Plas y Brenin!" He was already talking of returning for another attempt on the North East Ridge of Everest in the summer.

Up until the 1990s, going on an Everest expedition was probably an unfulfilled dream for many climbers who realised that

a) it was most unlikely to happen, and

b) even if it did, the chances of actually getting to the top were remote.

How things have changed. Commercial expeditions have opened the doors to virtually anyone with a few thousand dollars to spare and the numbers standing on the summit have risen exponentially, as have the deaths of those unfortunate enough not to have recognised that getting back down is just as, or more important than, getting up. So in one sense, I was lucky to go before the floodgates opened.

Two years after my return from K2, I was invited on Brummie Stokes's second attempt to climb the North East Ridge, the route on which Pete and Joe had disappeared six years earlier. Once again I was going as filmmaker; once again I would be doing this on my own. Mo, regardless of his tumour, was going again, as was Joe Brown. The rest of the team was mainly made up of ex-SAS soldiers, plus the New Zealand climber, Russell Brice.

Quite simply I made a huge mistake. The lure of what was almost certainly the biggest unclimbed route on the mountain was too much for me to resist. But coming only two years after K2 meant that I was never really focused on the trip and our doctor, Philip Horniblow, told me after we returned that I was a classic example of post-traumatic stress syndrome. But how can you say no to a trip to Tibet, to spend time in Lhasa, to travel across the Tibetan Plateau, and to follow in the footsteps of Shipton, Tilman, Mallory and Irvine, up the Rongbuk Valley to the still mysterious north side of Everest? We would be going during the monsoon season, in June and July, the only slot available to us, in the hope that the North East Ridge wouldn't be too badly affected by the heavy snowfalls that would make every other route on the mountain suicidally dangerous.

The expedition got off to a slow start, stuck in Kathmandu because the road link to Tibet, the Friendship Highway, was closed, though Mo had gone on ahead with much of the gear and had been waiting for us for two weeks. Eventually, we flew to Lhasa in thick monsoon cloud cover. At one point a summit appeared briefly through the clouds. An American couple were sitting two rows in front of me. "Gee, that must be Everest." The little grey-haired man in the next row glanced out. "It's Kanch." Though the Americans had no ideas who he was, his voice carried such an air of authority that they didn't argue. Joe, who made the first ascent

211

^ *Me filming at Everest Base Camp in 1993 with Nuptse behind.*

in 1955, carried on reading his paperback.

Before we left Kathmandu I had been eating in a local restaurant and realized that Phil Horniblow was sitting at the next table with his back to me. He was talking to an American trekker just returned from Tibet. It turned out that she was a radiographer. I couldn't help overhearing their conversation. "Hey, you know what? I've just come from Everest Base Camp and there is this amazing, funny little guy sat there, dying of a brain tumour." My heart missed a beat. Philip agreed, saying that he probably only had a few months to live. "I suppose if that's the way he wants to spend his time, then who are we to tell him not to?" How I wished that I hadn't heard them. Everyone else seemed to think that Mo was okay, though I often wondered whether Joe, his long-term friend, knew, or suspected, the worst.

Flying into Lhasa, like catching the train to Lake Titicaca, is probably the worst way of gaining altitude. Though I wasn't ill and only had a vague headache, walking round the streets of the Old City, carrying a heavy Aaton film camera and tripod in the brilliant sunlight, was desperately tiring. A couple of the team helped me for a few hours, then got bored and left me to cart everything on my own. For the first time ever on an expedition, I felt lonely and terribly vulnerable. I was working for HTV and trying to do the sound recording as well. By the time we reached Base Camp a few days later I felt quite exhausted and a stomach bug I had picked up in Kathmandu wouldn't go away.

Unlike K2 Base Camp, or indeed Everest Base Camp in Nepal, at just over 5000 metres we were below the terminal moraines of the Rongbuk Glacier and, because we went in the summer, there was actually grass and a few flowers growing in what was normally an arid waste. Not that it made me feel any better, but at least there was none of the constant stress of living on ice.

I fear that I found the prevailing ethos of the expedition hard to take. It was macho and highly competitive with lots of army terms in common use: 'yomping' (walking), 'scran' (food), 'Ruperts' (officers), etc. Weakness was not tolerated. I wasn't very surprised when Brummie Stokes at Advance Base managed to have a stroke lifting loads on and off yaks before he was properly acclimatised. After a couple of days rest at Base Camp, he did the same thing again, and was lucky not to die. He returned home and carried out the leadership of the expedition via satellite phone from the wilds of Shropshire.

Eventually, I managed to drag myself to Advance Base and even to the Raphu La, at 6510 metres, the col at the foot of the North East Ridge, where I had a brief view of Makalu and Chomo Lonzo before the monsoon clouds moved in. If ever I needed evidence of high altitude deterioration this was it. Even though I was nowhere near 'the Death Zone' (8000 metres and above), I was at ABC at 6400 metres for three or four nights and can barely remember any of it. When, still suffering appalling dysentery, I crawled back to Base Camp, I had been gone for about 10 days. Dr Horniblow took one look at me and sent me back to Kathmandu in a Landcruiser for treatment at the Canadian clinic. This, amazingly, did the trick in just a few days. But when I eventually returned to Base Camp the expedition was over. Harry Taylor and Russell Brice had made a bold traverse over The Pinnacles where Pete and Joe were last seen, and then an epic descent to the North Col and back to Advance Base. A great effort, but no big cigar since they didn't summit.

Back again to Kathmandu where I seemed to have spent most of my life, I shelled out a vast sum of money to get home, courtesy of Air India. My dysentery returned with a vengeance (on the plane to my horror, which made it worse), and later for at least two months afterwards. When it eventually cleared up, I went to see Mo in Wales.

"I see you've become the self of your former shadow," he greeted me. It was one of the last one-liners I heard from Mo, for not long afterwards his tumour returned, and this time there was no escape. He was such a tough little bugger that he wouldn't give in and even in a coma he lasted longer than his doctor imagined possible.

When the inevitable phone call came I was as grief stricken as I have ever been. I drove over from Sheffield to Wales for Mo's funeral on a luminously bright evening. On the little road from Whaley Bridge to Pott Shrigley there is, briefly, a superb view out over the Cheshire Plain. But on this occasion, I could see much further and there, etched against the evening sky, was the tiny but unmistakable silhouette of the Snowdon Horseshoe. I had never seen this before and I have never seen it since.

Mo's funeral was in the parish church of Nant Peris and his coffin was carried the few yards from Tyn-y-Fynnon, his home. The church was crammed to the rafters with friends like me who wept for the loss of a man who had lit up our lives for so long. A huge overspill stood outside where loudspeakers relayed the service. As the coffin was carried out to the cemetery just across

213

the road, 'Land of my Fathers' rang out over the valley. High on the ridge above the village, tiny tell-tale puffs of smoke from the Snowdon Railway rose into a clear blue sky and a faraway whistle mixed with the grand old Welsh anthem that, even at the best of times, brings tears to my eyes. When the coffin was lowered into the ground, Bill Barker, one of the pallbearers, said: "Well, that's the last time you'll be getting a tight rope from me." As we filed past, throwing earth over the coffin, I heard a dull clunk as Joe paused to look down. When it was my turn, I saw that he had dropped a karabiner and sling for him. It was the last straw for me and my tears fell freely.

As for the whole Everest experience, it had been disappointing and it was not made any easier by HTV claiming it as a huge success. It seems to me that anything to do with Everest gets distorted and 'the media' have absolutely no intention of getting their facts right. As a trivial example of this, I have just watched a beautiful film, narrated by David Attenborough, examining the flora and fauna of the whole length of the Himalaya. It started with wonderful rare footage of a snow leopard hunting a deer, a sequence shot in the Karakoram. Then, over a long shot of the Baltoro Glacier and a distant view of Gasherbrum IV the narration stated that we were now travelling east of the Karakoram to the Indian Himalaya. Twenty minutes later, we were in Nepal looking at 'the highest mountain in the world, Everest'. It was the classic view of K2 taken from Concordia.

The HTV film remains the only film I haven't got any sort of copy of, and one that I wish I had nothing to do with. Shortly after our expedition's return I met the great old 1933 Everester, Jack Longland, still sprightly in his 80s at the Alpine Club: "I see your expedition succeeded some way below where ours failed."

Chapter twenty seven: Disillusioned With Work, but the Beginning of Four New Friendships

One miserable dark afternoon in November 1989, I noticed a clapped-out car parked, extremely badly, outside Bower Ashton. A woman with a baby and buggy was going in through the main entrance. Ten minutes later the same woman arrived in the studio where I was teaching, still with the buggy and accompanied by Sara, one of the part-time tutors. I did a double take — it was Annie. She was a student way back in 1976 when I had gone to the Trango Tower.

Annie had been in the Painting Department and could draw quite beautifully. The Head of Printmaking often said that her sketchbooks were the best he had ever seen. She was stupendously shy, and her small-scale work was never appreciated by the painting

> Annie.

> *Annie and Hugo.*

tutors. She came from a creative background. Her maternal grandfather, Roy Chadwick, had designed the Lancaster bomber, and her father, a vicar, was a craftsman who made violins as a hobby. Annie has a fantastic ability as a restorer and can rebuild grandfather clocks, or renovate a Japanese screen with gold leaf and lacquer with incredible skill.

Despite her talents, she lacked confidence and for many years before we met up again, she had rather lost her way. But her child had given her a new lease of life. I remembered that she had the biggest, widest smile I had ever seen. She still had, and the contents of the buggy had inherited it. In fact, I was bowled over by Hugo who gave me a smile that looked as though he had known me all 11 months of his life. He melted my heart, as did his mother. We soon had an on/off relationship (mainly off, if I'm honest) that lasted until I left Bristol but even though she is now married and living near Durham, I would like to think that I have always been there for Hugo. He has amazing musical gifts and went to Cheetham's School in Manchester where he studied the saxophone and piano. He became obsessed with all things to do with Japan and, largely self-taught, got an A in A-Level Japanese and a place at Leeds University. As I write this, he has just returned from a year in Japan

216

and, his enthusiasm for the country undimmed, is returning to Leeds for two more years. After that, who knows? But anyone who can speak Japanese and play Bach on the harpsichord with quite astonishing fluency will always, it seems to me, find a way to earn a living.

Neil Murison had taken early retirement in 1987. We organised a big party for him on the grass outside the studios and after various speeches and toasts the students produced some very impressive fireworks, giving me the opportunity to hand Neil a box of matches and say to him: "Light the blue touch paper and retire immediately."

Neil's departure meant that I was the only one left of the five staff present when I was appointed. Suddenly I felt old. When a young ex-student, Stuart Geddes, joined the part-time staff I told him the ancient joke about the old bull and the young one. Seeing a herd of cows at the bottom of the hill, a young bull says: "Let's run down and have one." The old bull says: "No. Let's walk down and have them all." Stuart always called me the old bull after that and, though we got on extremely well, Neil's retirement marked the end of an era.

He was replaced by Dick Le Feuvre who had been a History of Art lecturer since, well, since a lot of art history was just art. Dick was, by a country mile, the vaguest and most absent-minded man I have ever met. Nothing ever fazed him, and when, frequently, his slides were projected upside down he assumed that his audience would try and turn their heads through 180 degrees. He often had to ask them who the artist was, not as a teacher, but because he had forgotten. He drove an ancient VW mini bus, the one that had a tiny front windscreen, and was beloved of 1960s hippies. It was on its last legs and older than the students that we taught. One day, I told Dick that it really was time to sell it. Dick, rather to my surprise, agreed: "I wrote an advertisement for the *Bristol Evening Post*, and when I'd finished writing it, I read it and thought, ha, just what I'm looking for." On another occasion, returning from a coach trip to Paris with all the students, Dick strode up and took the microphone: "Well, um, Jim doesn't mince his words... but I do." It was on that trip that a female student lost her passport as we were boarding the coach for home. Dick, trying to be helpful, told her: "It's a bit like losing your virginity — you want to hang on to it for as long as possible. Then you'll have no difficulty remembering where you lost it." Needless to say, it turned up under the student's bed, the passport, not her virginity.

Dick's arrival coincided, more or less, with the decline of Foundation at Bristol. This was nothing to do with Dick, but a reluctance on the part of the Polytechnic to value what was one of

217

Chapter twenty seven: Disillusioned With Work, but the Beginning of Four New Friendships

its most successful courses. At the time, I was working on both the Foundation and the Graphic Design Courses and was bewildered at how most of the Graphics staff underestimated not just ours, but every Foundation Course. Yet, every so often, they would get a student applying for direct entry, that is, going straight from school to the degree course by passing Foundation. The penny never seemed to drop as to how valuable that experience had been. If I always sound aggrieved about this, it is because, having spent virtually my entire teaching career working with Foundation Courses and, I think, feeling justifiably proud of my contribution, I know that most of the staff on the degree courses took our work completely for granted. In fact, I often felt that they only just tolerated our presence. I remember one Head of Graphics, who shall be nameless, saying: "You don't need to impress me with your knowledge of art — I know Gainsborough painted 'The Hay Wain'." It was, I suppose, the general negativity and ignorance that got me down. I never really felt that any of the degree areas were doing anything remotely creative or interesting. Indeed, in Fine Art, it was hard to see any evidence of any course structure at all — it just seemed to drift along pandering to students' whims.

By the time I left, 'Brit Art' was in full swing, characterised by installations which actually had been around for some time, in fact, since Marcel Duchamps's famous ready-made urinal that he displayed in 1909. But Fine Art students had long found installation art irresistible, I suspect for two reasons. First it is incredibly irritating; whatever you think of the famous pile of bricks in the Tate, the artists always manage to have the upper hand. There never seem to be any grounds on which one can criticise, without feeling stupid or angry. In fact, I always feel that the 'it's not art' argument is very weak. It is precisely because the pile of bricks is art that people get so annoyed. If it were not art, nobody would bat an eyelid, unless, of course, you find that every pile of bricks is an affront to your senses. In fact, I would say that unless something is labelled as art, it is impossible to make any value judgement about it. But once you accept that it is art, you can, of course, decide that it is good, bad or indifferent, or a load of bollocks.

The second reason that installation art is so annoying is that a lot of it is so easily made. I am not suggesting that constructing a model of the QE2 out of matchsticks is a praiseworthy artistic achievement because it is clearly a difficult thing to make, but so much of installation seems so facile — for example, turning lights on and off in an empty room.

Two things seem obvious to me. The first that in any age about 90 per cent of all art, music, literature, poetry, etc. will not survive. What I was going to call 'popular taste', but clearly a bit more than that — a kind of cultural sieve, exists to save the best bits. Secondly, virtually every generation has an establishment that, Emperor's new clothes-like, will worship the phoney and persistently disregard the genuine article. Look, for example, at Impressionism, jazz, film, even pop music. Actually, Impressionism is a good example. The very name was first coined as a term of ridicule. The Paris Salon rejected it out of hand for years. The expression 'throwing a pot of paint in the public's face' is a classic example of ignorant criticism. If you don't understand something, then simply describe how it is made, painted, sounds. Strangely, the 'it's not art' argument is never applied to literature (it's not a book), or film (it's not a film), critics appearing to understand that their comments are only valid when they accept what it is.

In my last years at Bower Ashton I began to feel the old stirrings of the painter in me. Ever since I started painting again in 2002, I have lost count of the number of people who claim to have been amazed when they found out that I could paint. In fact, all through my teaching career I taught life drawing, and always drew in the corner of students' work to illustrate a point. So I never actually lost touch with drawing, which I still believe is the root of whatever creativity I possess. From 'drawing', which means 'thinking' in my mind, to painting is a short step, and it was no surprise to me that when I eventually managed to get started again, it didn't take long to get going.

One of the best bonuses about Bower Ashton is that only a short walk, or run, away is the Suspension Bridge. At the bottom, on the Somerset side, (which is the same side as the college) is a quarried limestone buttress about 30 metres long. Most lunchtimes I could run there, clutching a pair of rock boots and a chalk bag, and traverse along it upping my rock-climbing standard. In the company of Phil Kershaw, a mature student on the Fine Art course, and later with a friend John Warburton, I actually raised my climbing standard in the Avon Gorge, being able to follow (and very occasionally lead) routes of E1 and E2 grade. Eventually, when I had done climbs like *Lich Gates* and *Pink Wall Direct*, I found that unless I could climb better than ever before (unlikely in my late 40s) there were no routes left in the Gorge that I hadn't either done before or couldn't even begin to think of doing.

During the late 80s I became friends with Ian McNaught Davis, or Mac as he is universally known. I had known him on and off since the mid-70s, but felt slightly wary of him. Mac had long been the joker of the British rock-climbing elite. His articles and speeches were hilarious, derogatory and often quite rude. You either loved or hated them. Mac could back his words with deeds.

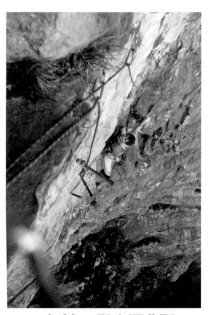

^ *Me on* Pink Wall Direct, *Avon Gorge.*

219

> Mac.

He had been a leading Alpinist in the 1950s and in the 60s had taken part in most of the BBC Outside Broadcasts, always climbing with his great mate, Joe Brown. I felt a bit of a Johnny-come-lately when I came onto the scene after the Trango expedition, and feared he might think I was challenging his position. (Years later, when I told him this, Mac laughed and told me he never even noticed me, a pretty good put down, I thought.)

When we got it together to climb with each other, we hit it off immediately. Even in his 60s and 70s Mac was technically extremely good. He was also immensely strong and though I led most of the time, I always knew that if I couldn't get up something, Mac would probably succeed. More to the point, we made each other laugh all the time.

After a few routes in Wales, Mac suggested a quick trip to the Alps via the sandstone boulders of Fontainebleau. Great, I thought, but was a bit wary about spending time abroad with Mac, whose solution to any problem was to 'hose money at it until it goes away'. "Don't worry," said Mac, "I'll pay the big bills, you pay the small ones." It was a brilliant system (especially for me) because it meant I could feel I had contributed something to the holiday, and it has been our method ever since, for which I owe Mac my

220

deepest thanks.

We set off from Mac's Kensington home in his sumptuous Mercedes convertible, Mac confidently wending his way through south London on what I assumed was a route he knew well. Suddenly, he swore: "Christ! I'm driving down to Harrison's Rocks!" After that hiccup, the journey was uneventful and we reached Fontainebleau in the evening. Mac is a fluent French speaker — I rely on half-remembered O-Level which is basic to non-existent. Mac, who is nothing if not a man of the world, confessed to my surprise that he hated going into a hotel he hadn't previously booked, fearing rejection, and would get his wife Loreto to do it for him. So I always had to go to reception and ask for two separate rooms followed by Mac who, once he felt secure enough, could talk the hind leg off a donkey.

Fontainebleau, 'Font' to devotees, is a frequent weekend destination for many southern sandstone habitués. The rocks take the form of dozens of boulders and soloing is the norm. I had been there occasionally and not particularly enjoyed the climbing.

But Mac, who had once worked in Paris in the1950s, knew the rocks well, and was aware that to get the best out of them you have to follow the intricate guidebook layouts, solving as many as 30 problems, colour-coded according to difficulty. When you have found one at a level you can cope with, you simply follow the dots of colour on each boulder, taking in every imaginable bit of technique. By the time you have finished, your body feels as though it had been through a mangle; every muscle has been stretched in ways you didn't know they could be.

After two days, I was begging for mercy, so we drove down to Switzerland, to the Furka Pass where a scene from *Goldfinger* was filmed. We wanted to climb an easy classic, the South East Ridge of the Gross Fürkahorn. As we were two gross old Fürkas it seemed a reasonable proposition. Here, climbing in rock boots on perfect granite, I realised just how much I had missed in my early Alpine visits, encumbered by big boots and heavy 'sacks — no wonder we had so many bivouacs. Well pleased with ourselves, we wandered over to Zermatt, where we fancied climbing the Zinal Rothorn. This involved a gruelling hut walk and a night where my snoring kept everyone awake, including me. With hardly any sleep, we failed miserably and walked all the way back to Zermatt where we booked into the first hotel we came to. A dour Swiss girl was at the reception. "Passports?" We had left them in the car. "ID?" Mac snapped: "No, that's why we fought the war and you didn't." As usual in Switzerland money won the day. After walking down about 4000 feet of paths, our knees were knackered, so much so that when we had a competition to stand up from sitting in a chair without using our hands and arms to push, we both failed miserably.

Our next projects were foiled by torrential rain and after a wet couple of days we decided to drive back to Fontainebleau to have another body-wrecking session. Then we went home and I was conscious that, even with our arrangement, it had been an expensive outing. As I unlocked the front door the phone was ringing. "This is Barclays Bank." Christ, they haven't wasted any time. I was just stammering out my excuses for spending their money when the voice said: "No, it's Barclays Bank Mountaineering Club. Will you speak at our Annual Dinner?" I was so relieved I would have done it naked with bells on my... "Sorry to tell you we can't actually pay you." I suppose that was because I had been busy spending their money (as if!), but I agreed with some relief. So after 10 days of ostentatious richness, I went back to normal penury. But it had been a really smashing holiday, and was the first of many even better adventures with Mac over the next few years.

As well as Mac, my other regular climbing partner was Mike Richardson who I dubbed 'my common law husband', as he had married (and subsequently divorced) Laraine. Mike's climbing career had blossomed in his late 40s and early 50s. He had been a fanatical cyclist, which had rivalled his dedication to rock-climbing. As a climber, Mike was apparently quite fearless and could (and did) solo routes on gritstone that were very near his technical limit. I hated watching him go, like a bull in a china shop, at some gritstone horror but despite several close shaves, and some very impressive jumps when things got out of hand, he never came to any harm. We climbed a lot together — in Derbyshire obviously, but also a lot in Wales where we shared leads on *Plexus*, *Diagonal* and *Black Spring*, all on Dinas Mot. Later we climbed on the magnificent *Great Slab* of Cwm Silyn where we also did the three star classic *Crucible*, one of the very best routes in Wales.

Mike was easily the worst second I ever climbed with, impatient, intolerant and easily distracted, so it was much easier to let him lead. I felt that he had grown up in the shadow of Paul Nunn, but as he got older, Mike climbed harder and harder. He was, and is, a great bird-watcher. Often looking

^ *Mike Richardson.*

out over Derbyshire on some late summer evening as the shadows grew, he would say: "God, I'm going to miss this when I'm gone." Then, out of the blue, he developed the unusual illness, Myasthenia Gravis, a kind of wasting muscular illness. Not a killer, but one that forced him to give up climbing. When climbing ended, he became an obsessive twitcher, prepared to travel vast distances to look at some hapless feathered friend who had been blown thousands of miles off course.

In later years, my regular climbing partner in Bristol was Tony Iveson. Tony is a tall man, about six foot five, with a schoolboy's face, making him look absurdly young. We particularly enjoyed climbing in the Wye Valley at a small crag called Shorncliffe. It was desperately difficult to find, lurking in the densely wooded hillside near Tintern Abbey, but once found, it had some superb single pitch routes on perfect, sound grey limestone, just the right side of vertical, where you could pretend you were a brilliant rock athlete. Mo used to describe this sort of climbing as: "You show me good holds and I'll show you good technique," and climbing on its delightful pocketed walls it was, indeed, possible to display delicate footwork and stylish movement.

Often, we were joined by Stephen Venables, when he could grab a quick few hours on a Wednesday evening. He also loved Shorncliffe and there was always time for a quick pint with him before he drove back over the Severn Bridge to his home in Bath.

I had first come across Stephen Venables in Kishtwar when he got on the same bus as Paul and me after the first Barnaj expedition (not the one where I was stoned and only semi-conscious). Shortly after this I had been judging the photos for the Kendal Film Festival. This was done 'blind' — not with our eyes shut, obviously — but with no knowledge of whose pictures were whose. Stephen's photos were of such uniformly high quality that he easily won the 'best folio' category. Then, in 1986, when I was Chairman of the Boardman Tasker judges, his book *Painted Mountains* was the winner, though I had no idea of the controversy that this would cause (years and chapters) later.

Looking back on the Bristol years, I did have a brilliant time, for many years and made long-lasting friendships. Quite why I never felt settled there is not easily answered. Perhaps it was because I could never identify with what I called the Clifton Trendies. These were an amorphous group of wannabe artists, writers, poets and musicians who frequented the pubs of Clifton, but, it seemed to me, indulged in far more talking and drinking than actually doing. Sheffield, and of course Leeds, where I did most of my film work, always seemed to have a more focused, gritty determination to get things done. Maybe this was an illusion; maybe it was just

223

because they were both colder and windier than muggy old Bristol. Whatever the reason, I always felt, and still do, that whenever I drive into Sheffield from Derbyshire, or arrive by train at Sheffield Midland Station, that I want to get cracking on whatever project I am involved with. I could never feel like that in Bristol and am quite prepared to accept this is largely in my head. Strangely, and I think quite independently, Gemma, who went to Bristol University, felt exactly the same way and since she got her degree has only been back once in the last 20 years.

Chapter twenty eight: Curran versus Perrin

During the 1990s I was involved in a protracted saga of litigation that provoked an astonishing amount of vitriol and ill-feeling throughout the British climbing world. During, and ever since that time, I have remained silent and only now, 20 years later, am I prepared to comment on the issues involved, and I do so with some trepidation. However, as my side of the story has never been made public, I think it is now time to do so. Before I start, I must make it quite clear that the magazine with which I took issue, *Climber and Hillwalker*, has since been sold, is now called simply *Climber* and is now under new management and control, with whom, obviously, I have absolutely no quarrel.

My problems with the magazine concerned the writings of Jim Perrin who, over the years, has contributed to all the British climbing press. He is, without doubt, one of the most talented writers around; some would say the best mountain writer in Britain. His biography of John Menlove Edwards remains his masterpiece and it deservedly won the Boardman Tasker Award for Mountain Literature. But Perrin's writing has, in my opinion, been flawed by a streak of bitterness and vitriol, and over the years many of his contemporaries have been at the receiving end of wounding comments or jibes, often made about events apparently long gone and forgotten.

When Jim Perrin joined *Climber and Hillwalker* after an acrimonious departure from *High* magazine, it became apparent from his column that he felt that everything that came out of Sheffield (where *High* was based) was bad news. His magazine had also coined the phrase 'the Sheffield Mafia', referring to a nebulous group of elderly climbers who apparently exercised a malevolent influence over climbing politics through the pages of *High* and *Mountain* magazines. What started as a tongue in cheek joke in the pages of *Climber and Hillwalker* soon began to be referred to as an accepted fact.

Over a period of two or three years I grew progressively more irritated at Jim Perrin's snipings, but refused to rise to the bait, though I became increasingly puzzled as to why I was being singled out. I could only assume it was due to my friendship with *High* editor, Geoff Birtles, though I still don't know if this really was the case. Then in March 1991, Perrin wrote an article explaining what it was like to climb with some of the greats of British rock-climbing: Joe Brown, Don Whillans, Johnny Dawes, Martin Boysen and Ron Fawcett. It was, I thought, a rather sycophantic piece, but at the same time implying that Perrin himself was in that league. Towards the end of the piece, and quite out of the blue, he also wrote about the worst climbers he'd ever climbed with and named

Joe Tasker, Nick Estcourt, Alex McIntyre and me. I was astounded that he could cite Nick, Alex and Joe who were, of course, all dead, and almost flattered to be named in their company, except that the words he used about me were, 'in an incompetence league entirely on his own — Big Jim Curran who once put the fear of God into me on a first ascent in Pembroke by starting up the 5c crux before I had managed even properly to belay on the top of the crag'. He was referring to our first ascent of *The Voyage Out* which we had done in 1979.

I was bemused, hurt and baffled when, 12 years later, Perrin made his comments in *Climber and Hillwalker*. Others were more shocked than I was, and pointed out that, as a climbing cameraman often employed by TV companies, I could have a problem with insurance. The word 'incompetence' and phrase 'put the fear of God into me' could be cited as evidence that a TV company should not have employed me if, in the event of an accident, blame was attached to me. The article seemed to have been read by lots of people and when I was accosted in a Bristol street by a climber I scarcely recognised, and asked why Jim Perrin seemed to be carrying out some kind of vendetta against me, I reluctantly decided to at least seek legal advice.

Alison, my first ex-wife, was now married to a QC, and it was he who recommended a young solicitor, Rhory Robertson, who worked for a firm called Swepstone Walsh in Lincoln's Inn Field. His opinion seemed to be very reasonable. He thought it was clearly a libellous statement that could be damaging to future employment if it were not retracted and a full apology printed. His words were to the effect that, while it wasn't exactly the crime of the century, a solicitor's letter should do the trick, plus a few hundred pounds for my trouble and anxiety.

I was appalled when *Climber and Hillwalker* immediately refused to apologise and horrified when they then employed Peter Carter-Ruck and Partners, the celebrated libel lawyers frequently lampooned in *Private Eye*, to fight their case. I imagine the magazine assumed that I would be quickly frightened off by the big guns and they were almost right. The problem was that, from the very beginning, cases like this cost a lot of money and I couldn't afford to lose. I felt that with each exchange of letters I was getting more and more committed — I simply couldn't back out and lose what was for me a huge amount of money. The magazine, of course, and Jim Perrin, were covered by insurance and could go on fighting without any personal financial risk at all. I still had a small sum left over from my mother's will which I'd kept for a rainy day. And this seemed to have just arrived.

Over the months the letters from 'the opposition' became

more and more eccentric and wide-ranging. Initially *Climber and Hillwalker's* main line of defence was that the remarks were meant to be a joke, but, as they then spent a great deal of time and effort trying to justify them, it seemed that even they couldn't see the funny side. In a tacit acceptance that the problems with Perrin and me went back a long way, the magazine then introduced a new and sinister element into the case.

In 1986 and 1987 I had served on the judging panel of the Boardman Tasker Award for Mountain Literature and was chairman of the panel in my second year. During that year I had been shocked to find out that Jim Perrin had questioned my integrity in judging a book by John Barry on the events on K2 in which I had been involved the previous year. I offered to resign immediately but my offer was refused, and my two fellow judges supported me, as did the Committee of the Boardman Tasker Award whose members included Chris Bonington, Dorothy Boardman and Charlie Clarke.

It is worth pointing out that my then full-time lecturing job at Bristol Polytechnic regularly involved assessing the work of art and design students. This is an activity that might seem to an outsider to be a particularly subjective activity and one prone to prejudice, favouritism or personal animosity. In fact, after nearly 30 years of both participating in and observing assessment procedures, I am still impressed by the way in which we, the lecturers, could make judgements that, while not always unanimous, rarely varied significantly, and were supported by the external assessor who had no prior knowledge of previous grades. So the idea of my personal integrity being under suspicion was one I bitterly resented and refuted. It could even be used against me in my college life.

It came as a major surprise and shock when *Climber and Hillwalker* produced a copy of a letter that Jim Perrin had sent to Chris Bonington which not only questioned my judgement over the John Barry book, but, worse, accused me of influencing the judges the previous year in order to ensure that an author who was also a contributor to *High* magazine won the award. As Perrin himself had won the award the year before that, when he was still working for *High*, it would be two out of two for the magazine he now despised.

I must admit that when I saw the letter, which had been sent to Chris Bonington, Dorothy Boardman and the then Secretary of the BMC, Dennis Gray, I was mortified. How do you refute something for which there is absolutely no evidence one way or the other?

What had happened was that I had read some, but not all, of the books submitted for the 1986 BT award, then gone to K2 on what had been a far longer expedition than I had expected.

When I eventually returned, all the books had been submitted and my two fellow judges, Bill Murray and Al Alvarez, had tended to favour a book by Walt Unsworth on the history of Mont Blanc. I thought the book workmanlike, well-researched and written, but inevitably based on second-hand experience. The book that stood out for me was one by Stephen Venables called *Painted Mountains*, which described intense, first-hand experiences on two Himalayan expeditions. The writing was fresh and, to my mind, the book was a far greater creative achievement than Walt Unsworth's. I pointed this out to the other judges who, to my delight, both agreed and Venables duly won the BT award. At the time I had no idea or even interest, in whether or not Venables was going to work for *High* magazine, my mind being fully occupied with the enormous tragedies on K2 that year, and the imminent task of writing my own book on the subject, as well as producing a film.

Now, five years later, I was made aware of all the undercurrents of suspicion and ill-feeling that I had been blissfully ignorant of at the time. I simply couldn't think that anyone in their right mind would believe that I would risk fixing an award for someone I knew, but not particularly well, and who, like many other climbers, was going to write a column in one of the three British climbing magazines. I was frankly baffled. But I was on a steep learning curve and Rhory explained to me that, while I was suing Perrin and the magazine for libel over a couple of sentences, they would use anything to question my integrity. I became very depressed and anxious, wondering what else they would manage to dredge up.

There were, though, some good signs. Rhory kept asking *Climber and Hillwalker* to settle out of court and at one point they offered to put a small sum into court as a compromise. But there was no offer of an apology, which was all I really wanted, and in any case, the sum was so small that I could still end up out of pocket. I decided to fight on, though by now I was losing both weight (no bad thing) and sleep. As Rhory kept telling me, the important thing was to keep your eye on the ball, and on the allegations that I was in 'an incompetence league entirely on his own'. We had some fairly impressive witnesses who were prepared to refute this. Among them were Paul Nunn, Joe Simpson, Chris Bonington and Ian McNaught Davis, all of whom had climbed with me often enough to know what they were talking about. While I would never claim to be anything other than an average performer, I had over 30 years' experience and was well able to look after myself in a wide variety of mountain environments.

The date for the case to be held was arranged. I was beside myself with worry for by now I was arranging to re-mortgage my house to pay the solicitor's and barrister's fees. If I lost, I would have to sell everything, as I would then be faced with the legal fees from both sides. Rhory (and common sense) suggested that this was highly unlikely, but once a case goes to court, anything can happen. Two weeks before the trial, Rhory took me round the High Court and we stood in the actual court where it was to be heard. It seemed quite small and very intense; even the lighting gave it a sense of drama and seriousness. I didn't know whether to be appalled or encouraged and tried to imagine being cross-examined by a hostile barrister. I just couldn't understand why the opposition were going through with it and prayed that they would offer a decent out-of-court settlement.

Throughout all this time, the climbing rumour factory had been working overtime. Popular myths were that Mac was paying all my bills for me, that I was doing all this at the behest of *High* editor Geoff Birtles, (who, in fact, had always tried to warn me off taking legal action) and that I wanted to see Jim Perrin bankrupt (quite absurd, since, as explained earlier, all his *Climber and Hillwalker* costs were fully insured). What was undoubtedly true, though, was the fervent wish that the whole business would suddenly just go away which, only days before the case was due to be heard, it did.

What happened arose out of a terrible tragedy. Andy Fanshawe was the BMC's National Officer. He was a talented climber and a very promising young writer. I didn't know him well but had met him first at K2 Base Camp when he had turned up with a team of young activists attempting the traverse of Chogolisa, an ascent they completed in fine style. I had supplied a rather good photo for Andy's book and, though we never climbed together, I always enjoyed his company and boundless enthusiasm. It all stopped suddenly in March 1992 on Eagle Ridge, Lochnagar, when Andy suffered a horrendous fall and was killed outright. Hundreds of friends and family attended his memorial service and afterwards, over a pint, I found myself talking to Stephen Venables who asked me how the libel case was going. Strangely enough I had never thought to involve Stephen in any way and it never occurred to me that he could be of much help. It wasn't the right time or place to discuss it and I just said something to the effect that I thought it was a bit rich that Stephen's book, which I still admired hugely, had been dragged into a legal battle, and left it at that. I drove back to Bristol with an overwhelming feeling that Andy's death made my battles seem trivial and pointless. But they were real just the same.

When I got home to Sheffield at the weekend, I found an envelope with a Bath postmark. It was a letter from Stephen enclosing copies of two letters he had received from Jim Perrin when Stephen was considering working for *High*. I read them, absolutely thunderstruck; I couldn't believe what was before my eyes. For here was Jim Perrin wooing Stephen Venables and praising his book to the skies. Not only did he think it should win the Boardman Tasker Award, but he, Jim Perrin, was prepared to try to influence the judges to make sure the award didn't go to Walt Unsworth. He finished by expressing his hope that, for a second year running, the award would go to one of the *High* writing team. How Perrin could have carried on his defence knowing that these letters might still exist is something I shall never understand.

It doesn't take much imagination to realise that after this monumental own goal, *Climber and Hillwalker* settled the case in my favour within days, and I was pleased to receive an apology and substantial damages. Sadly, references to the case continued to be made by people who should have known better, somehow implying that I, who had risked everything in fighting on my own against a large publishing group, was undermining the right of free speech in climbing writing. The whole episode left a nasty taste in my mouth, and it is something I would never dream of going through again if I could possibly help it. But when it happens and you find things in print that are seriously damaging to your reputation, you sometimes have to stick your head above the parapet. I certainly don't regret what I did, only the protracted worry and stress it incurred. I certainly found out who my friends were (and weren't) and I am eternally grateful to those who were also prepared to stand up in court and defend me. But I'm glad they never had to.

Chapter twenty nine: Two Little Trips (And the End of the Road in Bristol)

I t would be true to say that my trips to Everest and to K2 had, in their different ways, left me disillusioned with the climbing world, filmmaking and also expeditions. It all seemed a far cry from those wonderful days on Trango and I felt I wouldn't be too upset if I never went on another expedition. Then, in the summer of 1990, I was asked to go on a rather curious little adventure. Richard Else, a producer at the BBC in Newcastle, was making a series of six half-hour programmes about the history of mountaineering. One was to examine the role of politics and nationalism in Himalayan climbing, first comparing the earliest expeditions to Nanga Parbat, when the British pioneer Mummery disappeared, then contrasting these with the huge German expeditions in the 1930s overtly propagating the Nazi cause, which in turn were compared with the successful first ascent of Everest, coinciding with the Coronation of Queen Elizabeth. Finally the grand old man of American climbing, Charlie Houston, would talk about his altruistic view of mountains and his two K2 expeditions in 1938 and 1953. Chris Bonington would cover the British efforts and Sigi Hupfauer the German ones. The programme was to be filmed at the foot of the colossal Diamir Face of Nanga Parbat.

I was thrilled at the prospect of meeting Charlie Houston. After my K2 book was published he had written me a very kind letter. The events of 1986 on K2 contrasted with those in 1953 when his small team made a heroic effort to rescue Art Gilkey who had developed phlebitis at their highest camp at just under 8000 metres. I was eager to talk to the man whose exploits, both on K2 and in the world of mountain medicine, I had long admired.

I met him at Heathrow and was almost too shy to say hello. It was obvious that he didn't suffer fools gladly. But as our little expedition progressed and we walked up the Diamir Valley towards the mountain we started to talk. At Base Camp, Charlie was breathless and convinced he was coming down with pulmonary oedema. As he was undoubtedly the world's greatest expert and had done most of the research into how and why it develops at high altitude, it was hard to disagree with him. After a day filming we set off down the following morning. According to Charlie, who frequently told the story thereafter, I saved his life by helping him down the steep trail that led to a more reasonable altitude. Though I hate to contradict him, the truth was that I took advantage of a golden opportunity to talk to him about K2. Charlie and I had already discussed the possibility of my writing a second book, telling the history of K2. Now, here was one of the very great names associated with the mountain and I had his undivided attention for three days!

231

Chapter twenty nine: Two Little Trips (And the End of the Road in Bristol)

It was the beginning of a long and fruitful friendship. I visited Charlie twice at his wonderful home in Burlington, Vermont and he came over to England three times, to the centenary Climbers' Club dinner, to the International Festival of Mountaineering Literature at Bretton Hall, and to the Kendal Mountain Film Festival. On each occasion he stayed at my house. In between visits we frequently rang each other and I often searched out his opinion as I wrote the book. Charlie died in December 2009 aged 96. I find it hard to believe that I had the huge privilege of knowing him, and being able to call him my friend.

Another little trip was in 1993, the 40th anniversary of the first ascent of Everest (and coincidentally my 50th birthday). Chameleon films in Leeds had been commissioned to make a history of Everest, and once again I was invited to be Base Camp cameraman, this time in Nepal. Chris would be fronting the film again. After our rocky start on Kongur, we now got on really well. Because we knew each other's foibles, we were both far more relaxed filming together, and I felt that, though Chris is basically quite shy and doesn't enjoy doing pieces to camera, he was getting better and better at it.

That was a trip that took two weeks from Heathrow and back, which meant that we trekked in to Everest Base Camp far more quickly than is really advisable. So much so that Simon Wells, who worked for Chameleon, developed cerebral oedema at Pheriche, a village two days below Base Camp, and only the presence of a medical centre and a Gamow Bag, an inflatable canvas tube that can bring the air pressure up to somewhere near sea level, saved his life. Allen Jewhurst, my sound man, Mark Stokes, and I made it to Everest Base Camp while Chris, who had a bad head cold, stayed at Kala Pattar. When we got there we found Rebecca Stephens, soon to be the first English woman up Everest. Allen thought it would be a good idea to interview her to bring the history right up to date. The interview with Rebecca was a rather stilted affair as she was preparing for her summit attempt. With the outcome uncertain, the interview was full of "ifs" and "maybes". If we had arrived a few weeks later it would have been a very different story. Rebecca, quite rightly, was fêted by the British media, going overnight from complete unknown to flavour of the month.

Getting back to college, only just over a week after leaving Everest and the Khumbu Glacier, was a bittersweet occasion, for this was the last time it would happen. Since Neil had taken early retirement a few years previously, I had got progressively more disillusioned with my job. The student numbers had doubled and my role wasn't much more than an admissions tutor, which seemed to take up an inordinate amount of time. The Christmas term had

Chapter twenty nine: Two Little Trips (And the End of the Road in Bristol)

seen me suffering recurrent nose-bleeds, high blood pressure and other symptoms of stress. I applied for early retirement at the very early age of 50, knowing I would be giving up a significant proportion of my pension. I hoped that if my reduced pension could be added to with lectures, film fees and the odd miniscule book royalty, I should be able to keep body and soul together. After all, my biggest monthly expenditure was driving to and from Bristol to Sheffield to earn it!

So, after 23 years at Bristol, and nearly 30 in art education, I was preparing to live without it. I was expecting to get quite emotional on my last day and wondered what sort of surprise the staff and students had planned. It was certainly a surprise, for the answer was nothing at all. When it dawned on me that there was to be no send-off, I got in my car, said: "Fuck you Bristol Poly" (which it wasn't, because it was now masquerading as a university which I still can't take seriously), and drove out of the Faculty car park, never to return. No tears. No regrets. I even had to buy my own leaving present.

and everywhere

Chapter thirty: Fifty Not Out – Celebrating Freedom

Part of my reasoning for leaving Bristol was that I reckoned I had about 10 more years to do all the big outdoor things I wanted to do. If I carried on until I was 60 or 65, I would have a much bigger pension, but might not be able to do any of them. This, as will become apparent, could have been amazing foresight, but was, more likely, just luck. So, at only 50 years old, I thought I'd better get cracking.

Chris Bonington had been toying with the idea of climbing the Seven Summits — the highest mountains on each continent. As he had already bagged the most difficult couple, Everest and Mount Vinson in the Antarctic, and had also climbed Kilimanjaro with his two sons, the remainder would have been quite straightforward. I was never totally convinced that he really wanted to complete the set, for even in the early 90s quite a few people had already done it, and it was beginning to look a bit like a glorified package holiday for climbers looking for a world-wide tick-list. It was in a different league from climbing all the 8000 metre peaks, another much harder, but to my mind, rather more pointless collection. But in 1993 Chris seemed keen enough and Richard Else, the BBC producer with whom I had gone to Nanga Parbat, thought it was worth the gamble of filming the ascent of Elbrus, the highest mountain in Europe, in case he ever made a documentary of all seven summits. My own view was that at last I could go to Russia and the Caucasus, the trip that hadn't happened in 1986.

Chris would be climbing with Jim Fotheringham, and also taking with him his long-serving (and suffering) secretary Louise Wilson and her husband, Gerry. Louise, together with Wendy Bonington, had been the powers behind the throne of Chris's complicated life for years and Chris wanted her to experience a trip away. She and Gerry were seasoned walkers and climbers. I always thought of Louise as Miss Moneypenny in the James Bond stories and wondered if, without her rock-solid presence at home, our trip would degenerate into chaos if anything went wrong. Chris shrewdly solved the potential problem by giving Louise all the decision-making she wanted.

Jim Fotheringham had been with Chris on several trips, notably when they did a hard new route on Shivling in the Garhwal Himalaya. Jim is a dentist living in Brampton near Hadrian's Wall. His enthusiasm for climbing, whether it is cragging, Alpine or Himalayan, is almost as great as Chris's. Meeting him at Heathrow wearing a pale lightweight jacket and a trilby hat, I thought he looked like Our Man in Moscow and wondered if his ice-axes were also machine guns.

We flew to Moscow and the following day down to the exotically named Mineralnyye Vody. This translates as Mineral Water, which

^ *Jim Fotheringham bouldering at Burbage.*

doesn't quite have the same ring. The flight was in a huge Russian plane which had the most colossal cabin with a ceiling about 20 feet high — I'm not sure that it didn't have chandeliers as well. In flight sustenance was an apple and a glass of water, served by Rosa Klebb who starred in *From Russia with Love*. I looked to see if Miss Moneypenny recognised her, but she was too well-trained and remained quite impassive. 00Jim also stared through her but I noticed him checking her shoes for concealed poisoned blades. I bit into my apple cautiously but it didn't explode, so I took a chance and finished it.

Our next step was a three-hour drive that took us to the Itkol Hotel in the Baksan Valley where we would be based throughout our stay. It is hard to avoid clichés when describing the valleys of the Caucasus. Stunningly beautiful, relatively unspoilt and on a slightly grander than Alpine scale, they also have a few of the most hideous, tumbledown, unfinished hotels, cable cars and chair lifts I've ever seen. Mercifully, the break-up of the Soviet Union has put a stop to development.

Climbing in the Caucasus varies from the simple Alpine-type ascents (but mostly from high camps, not huts) to higher and more remote objectives that are almost Andean or Himalayan in scale. We started gently with a walk up the exquisite Adyslu Valley to the Green Bivouac, a meadow below the Jankuat Glacier. The 'B' team, Richard, Louise, Gerry and I would climb together, while Chris and Jim had more ambitious leanings. Accompanying us were three Ukrainian climbers who rapidly became more than guides. Sasha Vasko, our interpreter, was 22 and took his job seriously, often looking worried and perplexed at the antics of his charges who he clearly, and with some reason, suspected of suffering from collective senile dementia. Vochka Gosbach spoke little English, which didn't matter. He is one of the best ice-climbers I have ever seen. Often ignoring crampons and using only one axe, he possesses incredible poise and agility, plus total self-confidence. Sergei, who had organised the whole outing, looked, with his shoulder-length pop star haircut, high cheekbones and piercing eyes, like the lead guitarist in a supergroup taking time off from his world tour. Despite their enviable fitness and collective knowledge, skill and experience, they were genuinely pleased to stage these 'adventures' with us.

Our first little foray was up a huge pile of scree and snow patches. It was distinguished only by the fact that we all carried far too much gear and that I managed to put my salopettes on back to front. After suspecting terminal loss of motor control due to alcohol and age, I realised that after about 3000 feet of agonising ascent my inability to stand up was due to the fact that I'd also got my double boots on the wrong way round (I mean on the wrong feet, not back to front, which I hope would have been spotted earlier). Eventually I abandoned my ridiculously heavy rucksack and decided to go just a little bit further before calling it a day. I suspect we all played similar ploys, for eventually we ended up on top of the mountain, Via-Tau (3820m), not bad for a Tuesday afternoon, given that we had only left Moscow on Saturday morning.

The next day was set aside for the nursing of elderly squeaking knee joints and the day after we went up Gumachi (3810m), a good easy snow plod with a nice rocky summit ridge. From there we spotted Chris, Jim and Sergei as they returned from their climb on the harder and more impressive peak of Jantugan and Cheget-Tau. On the way down, Sasha suddenly intoned the warning that became the motto of the holiday: "Be werry careful, our adwenture is not yet over." We returned to the valley with smug grins as the weather broke.

Next, Chris and Jim planned to try Ushba. I knew it was beyond my abilities and that even getting to the Ushba Plateau was quite a serious outing in its own right, but was pleasantly surprised when Vochka insisted that we could all go through the Ushba Icefall as it was in good, and relatively easy, condition this year. My enthusiasm was tempered by the guidebook times, six to seven hours to the 'German Bivouac' and six to eight hours the next day through the icefall. Now was the time to heed the advice in the Elbrus tourist brochure, 'What can be more wonderful than to reach the summit and feel its height? But to achieve this, one has to nail hooks into rocky walls, cut steps in the ice, lower himself into crevasse and hang on a rope over a turbulent river… This can be accompanied

237

by brave, courageous people called mountaineers who have fallen in love with mountains for life. But before taking the ice-axe in hand they must check if the rope is strong enough to rope them together'.

The first day was hell as we carried heavy 'sacks up the interminable Shkelda Glacier, dominated by the colossal Shkelda Wall on one side and curiously named Railway Workers' Peak on the other. I had been intrigued by the Soviet names of some of the peaks and glaciers: Chemists' Peak, Trade Union Peak, Mongolian People's Republic Peak, all had an austere and antique charm that I hoped wouldn't be changed.

Despite some time-wasting dithering, we had guessed wrongly with the weather. Next day dawned fine, but as we approached the steepest section of the icefall, ominous lenticular clouds formed over the Tolkeinesque Shkelda Peaks. By the time we had negotiated a complex crevassed area and plodded slowly up to the plateau, visibility was almost nil and soon it was snowing lightly, then heavily.

"It's getting better, isn't it?" asked Richard, a touch anxiously in the middle of the night. Before I could answer, a blinding flash and almost simultaneous clap of thunder sent my heart on a quick tour of my lungs, throat and mouth. "If you say so," I muttered and curled up in the damp paper bag we were lying in, wondering if the metal 'A' poles keeping it up would be any more tempting as a potential lightning conductor than the four or five spiky summits surrounding us.

It was no better as dawn broke but by late morning it seemed to clear up a bit. I surprised myself by sounding very keen on doing a short climb and the West Ridge of the West Peak of Chatyn-Tau

^ *Ushba, from Elbrus.*

^ *The South East Ridge of Pik Schurovsky.*

was only a stone's throw away and about 300 metres higher than we were. Our mass ascent was notable only for what an ex-wife once described as a slight entrecote between Chris and me over an ice screw. This was quickly resolved, the summit gained and even though our evening meal would not, I knew, be the sizzling contretemps steak of my desire, our descent, masterminded by Vochka, passed in such a blur of speed that I am quite unable to describe the system we used. Suffice it to say that it mainly consisted of running down, facing out, while clipped into a rope that at any second would come whistling past with a diminutive Ukrainian attached to the other end laughing quietly to himself. The technique, if it can be called that, seemed to have a potentially fatal flaw in it somewhere but, like all good conjuring tricks, was performed too quickly and smoothly to spot.

Our return to the plateau was marked by a quite stunning evening. Sunbursts through clouds, plumes of spindrift blowing off Ushba and a magnificent view down the Shkelda Valley to bubbling clouds clearing around Mount Elbrus.

Next morning was the big one as Chris, Jim, Sasha and Vochka left early for the North East Ridge of Ushba North. Our rosy sunset had let us down and great streamers of dirty cloud were already sliding over the summit towers of Shkelda as they set off. Within an hour it had clagged in completely I expected them back at any minute, but their failure to do so explains, in part, why I have never been a top class mountaineer and Chris and Jim have (okay, okay, so talent counts as well).

Eventually, Gerry, Louise and I decided to go and have a little look at Pik Schurovsky whose imposing North Face we had skirted on our way to the Ushba Icefall but whose South East Ridge provides another relatively easy route. Its main attraction is that it offers the classic viewpoint of Ushba's twin summits. On our ascent we had the all too familiar classic Scottish winter viewpoint of about 150 cubic metres of snow-filled maelstrom. No amount of wishful thinking revealed even the faintest glimpse of Ushba (to my chagrin as official camera-person).

We returned, imagining Chris and team already back and packing to descend, but it wasn't until just before nightfall and the first little nagging pangs of worry (surely they wouldn't have used the same kamikaze method of descent as yesterday) that we heard distant shouts and eventually spotted four welcome specks on the last ice slopes above the plateau. They all looked tired and Chris described how they had pressed on all day, thinking the weather was never quite bad enough to turn back. Eventually they reached a point probably only 50 metres or so from the real summit where Vochka declared that: "This would be our summit for today". Their descent had been as rapid as the day before but it worked, as a quick head count proved. It was far too late to descend any further, so I resigned myself to another wet night in the paper bag.

A grim dawn was the precursor for a monumental and gruelling descent. I was dreading the icefall but nothing untoward occurred, other than an amazing circus trick by Vochka who, in order to check that Richard had clipped into an abseil correctly, suddenly jumped from the top of a fragile ice pinnacle on which he had been nonchalantly balancing, across the gully down which we were abseiling, on to almost vertical ice the other side and landed on his front points with no more fuss and effort than you or I would use to get up and put the kettle on. I actually doubted the evidence of my own eyes, but Chris confirmed that it had, indeed, occurred.

Our return to the Itkol Hotel coincided with the return of a group of Elbrus trekkers. These included Cameron McNeish, editor of *The Great Outdoors* and he and I formed an unlikely musical and drinking partnership later that evening, using a borrowed guitar and half-remembered chords to Beatles songs.

And so, between us we had climbed seven respectable peaks in just two weeks, which only left Elbrus. Our sports plans worked out that both we and the trekkers set out for Elbrus together after a curious night in 'the Barrels', a set of ugly, unhygienic but warm, purpose-built pre-fabricated cylinders that had originally been designed for use in Siberian oilfields where they could be easily positioned by helicopter.

A funny thing had happened to me on my way from the top of the cable car to the Barrels. I was suddenly accosted by two

Me with the two girls in swimsuits. >

stunning near-naked females who demanded to be photographed with me. They appeared to be modelling swimwear while I looked like an advert for an old folk's home and the episode remains a curious mystery which, had not Gerry taken a photograph, I might simply have put down to the effects of altitude.

Next day, our progress was aided, I have to confess, by a ride at some ungodly hour in a Snocat which, for a mere seven dollars each, gained us a useful chunk of welcome height. Then, abruptly, we started the long, long plod through the cold night, cramponing up a mixture of iron-hard ice and gritty névé.

"This is the most surreal start to a day I've ever had," was Jim's verdict, but dawn brought its own reward and the first rays of sun dispelled any thought of climbing Elbrus being boring. The mountain itself may be, but the views are sublime. Set just north of the Caucasus, the old volcano commands a panorama of the whole of the central range with Ushba's twin peaks dominating the horizon. Elbrus also has two peaks separated by a col about 250 metres below the higher West Summit. Louise, going strongly

241

^ *Loreto in the Valley of the Moon. The volcano, Licancabur, can just be seen as the pyramidal peak on the skyline directly above Loreto's head.*

and surely, led Chris, Gerry and me up the final slopes on to the summit plateau and towards the final pyramid.

Our arrival was marked both by the blowing away of a pall of mist that had draped itself over the final slopes and by an embarrassing and unexpected desire to weep. The 360 degree panorama was simply breathtaking.

After a leisurely picnic just below the top, it was time for the descent. The interminable cramponing down easy-angled water ice and melting snow set me thinking. In fine weather, Elbrus is an exercise in simple endurance and acclimatisation (in which our sojourn on the Ushba plateau had paid handsome dividends), but in poor visibility it must be a real test of navigational skills with small margin for error. In a full-scale storm it would be a nightmarish place.

On our last night, nursing a clutch of bruised toenails, and knees that collapsed just going downstairs, we celebrated in style. Chris announced: "I'm going to be *really* abstemious tonight and just stick to champagne and vodka." Nevertheless, it was a fine end to our 'adventures' and time for the story to end as well, but that would mean not telling you about Cameron on our return to Moscow: "Take me to the Urals," he ordered a bemused coach driver on our way home from a banquet. Next morning an ashen faced Cameron faced me over breakfast: "Where are the Urals anyway?"

In the autumn of 1993, still slightly bemused by the fact that I didn't have to go back to Bristol, I celebrated my freedom by taking

242

Mac up on another great offer. This was to fly to Santiago, visit Mac and Loreto at their seaside home, and then fly up to northern Chile to the Atacama Desert and perhaps climb a volcan or two.

Loreto is from Santiago, and her elderly father was still alive. It made sense for them to have a holiday home in Chile — and what a home it was! It backed onto a beautiful rocky beach where Mac had worked out a Fontainebleau-like bouldering circuit. The house itself, airy, light and spacious, had its own swimming pool in the extensive gardens.

Once there, it took a bit of willpower to move on. After a week we dragged ourselves away and flew up to Antofagasta, a mining town, that Mac and I, always reverting to a childish sense of humour, renamed Antofaghastly. Loreto was with us for the first week or so and, in a hired Toyota pick-up truck, we drove up to San Pedro de Atacama at 2436 metres.

Here, in an oasis village at the foot of Licancabur at 5919 metres, we explored the curious Valley of the Moon; petrified salt frozen into surreal rock formations and half enveloped by graceful sand dunes. A couple of hours' drive away were shallow salt-water lagoons supporting thousands of pink flamingos. The whole area was as hypnotic as any landscape I have ever seen. Though the Atacama Desert is apparently the driest place in the world, with no rainfall recorded, the combination of mists drifting in off the Humboldt Current and snowfall on the highest volcanoes that drain into the desert, gives life to an environment as harsh as anywhere in the world.

When Loreto returned to Santiago, Mac and I, with virtually no Spanish between us, drove north to Arica, the last city before the border with Peru. Arica has a huge fishmeal processing plant and unfortunately this is all too obvious to those with olfactory sensitivities. But Mac and I were more interested in driving inland, up to the Lauca National Park. Here by the shores of Lake Chungara we looked out at billowing snow clouds over Parinacota (6330 metres), which carried far more snow than Licancabur. The lake was only at 4600 metres, but it was an awfully long way, both horizontally and vertically, to climb Parinacota and, in any case, we probably would need ice-axes and crampons, which we hadn't got. As we had driven up to the lakes in a matter of hours, we had a couple of grim nights camping, due to my snoring and the effects of the altitude. In the end we managed to walk up a small hill called Guaneguane, at just over 5000 metres. It had magnificent views and emphasised that, in our present state of acclimatisation, we were unlikely to get up anything much bigger. Temporarily, and rather unusually for Mac, we didn't quite know what to do next. Then Mac had a brainwave. "If we drive back to San Pedro, we've just

243

^ *Licancabur.* got time to have a go at Licancabur and get back to Antofaghastly in time for our flights back to Santiago."

This was music to my ears for, ever since I had seen a large poster of the volcano at Mac and Loretto's house, I had really wanted to climb it. On our first visit we had no chance but, now that we were fitter and more acclimatised, it seemed a realistic proposition. Two things nearly stopped us. The first was that, unbelievably for two intelligent (ish) and well-travelled men, we contrived to nearly run out of petrol in the middle of the featureless desert road from Arica to the turn off to San Pedro. The second was that I was driving in a haze of heat, sun and sand along the endless road when, unseen by me (but increasingly and horrifyingly real to Mac), the Toyota and its contents very nearly collided with a vast diesel locomotive, pulling trucks about two miles long on a single-track railway that crossed the road diagonally with no warning signs. Mac had seen the train encroaching for about 10 minutes and couldn't believe that I hadn't seen it. At last Mac yelled a warning and was drowned out by a withering blast on the diesel's klaxons as thousands of tons of steel clanked by only feet away. I caught a glimpse of the driver shaking his head in disbelief as he looked down on us from on high: "Sorry about that. Thanks for pointing it out."

Back in a little hotel in San Pedro we discussed how we would try and climb Licancabur. Unknown to us, there was a trail of sorts from a high col, which would have made the whole thing much easier. But seen head on from San Pedro we could see, at around half height, what appeared to be a terrace and a small snow patch, which might make a good bivouac site. I suspect, in retrospect, that

244

Mac relished the idea of some off-road driving to get us as near the foot of the mountain as possible. Mac had a lot of off-road driving experience in Arica and was really good at it. So that was the plan.

We were blissfully unaware that we were driving into an area previously occupied by the Chilean army, worried about possible border disputes with Bolivia. We found dozens of used cartridge cases and were told later that there were still unexploded mines around, which might well have made us use a different route (including, of course, the super direct to oblivion). But ignorance is bliss.

We drove as far as Mac's considerable skill would let us and then realised it would be quicker to get out and walk. We walked all afternoon under a cloudless sky and unrelenting heat, allowing ourselves five minutes every hour for a quick rest and a glug of precious water. The longed-for terrace and snow patch were hidden from us and we plodded upwards over endless scree and boulders, becoming increasingly tired and irritable. At last, in late afternoon, we stumbled into the terrace. This was made of large, sharp boulders, with nowhere flat enough to unroll a sleeping mat without considerable excavations. At least the old snow patch gave us much-needed fluid for brews and a meal of sorts.

Because we were so near the Equator, darkness fell suddenly at six. We settled down for the night. Mac had been coughing badly for the last couple of days, now it was keeping me awake. As it began to get light Mac told me he hadn't slept a wink, and was worried that he might develop pulmonary oedema. He said he should descend immediately, but urged me to have a go at soloing the mountain. Against my better judgement, but reluctant to give up on what had become a bit of an obsession, I decided to go for it. Mac could go back to the truck and wait. I gave myself until 2pm to get to the top; about seven hours up and four all the way down. A quick brew and some chocolate, then with a full water bottle and a camera, I set off.

At first, I seemed to gain height quickly unencumbered with a rucksack. I followed a rocky, rotten rib that was like climbing slates in a Llanberis quarry (not on slate, that's a different story altogether). Every step was precarious but, by concentrating on each move, the time sped by and soon, on another windless day, it got hotter and hotter.

As I slowed down, time speeded up and the hours passed without any apparent height gain. I could judge roughly from the uniform angles to my left and right that the top was still a long way off. Midday came and went, then 2pm. I stopped and looked round. Surely I must be getting near. Away to my left I could see into Bolivia and the bright green Laguna Verde. Stubbornly, I ignored the deadline and carried on. Two-thirty came and went, then at 3pm it suddenly flattened out and I could see right round the rim of the volcano and down into the crater where a small pond smelt strongly of bad eggs.

When I left Bristol, I told Annie's son Hugo, then aged four, that I was going to try and climb a volcano: "Be careful you don't fall down the little hole at the top," he warned. I asked him what was down there? "Dragons and flames," he asserted confidently.

The summit cairn was only a few yards away. I set off, camera on auto-timer, placed it on a flat rock and posed self-consciously. It was perfectly still and in the afternoon sunshine shadows were forming on the surrounding hills and volcans. Away in the distance I could see the oasis of San Pedro and beyond it, the convoluted Valley of the Moon. It was utterly silent, so much so that I was aware of my own heart beating. I wished Mac was with me and could share this moment. I was also aware that I was now at just under 6000 metres and a little way out on a limb. Looking down I could just spot the snow patch and a tiny speck of red that was my sleeping bag. Come on, Curran. Let's get out of here.

All the way up I had skirted a huge scree slope that was so unstable that upward movement was almost impossible. Now, trying to run down it, I found that it had turned, miraculously, into immoveable piles of solid conglomerate. After falling flat on my face twice, I felt a jolt of real worry. It would take forever if I had to scramble down the whole way, probably longer than it took to climb up. I hit on a solution of sorts.

By traversing onto a section of scree that seemed marginally looser, I kicked around until I started a small rock avalanche. Then I jumped onto it and, by lying flat, both the avalanche of scree and I got rolling sedately downhill in a huge cloud of dust. Progress was erratic but I was losing height slowly. I felt like a pope at his funeral.

^ *Me on the summit of Licancabur.*

^ *Me in the headlights after the scree running descent.*

At last, in late afternoon, I regained the bivouac site and packed up as quickly as I could. From here on I would have to walk and scramble down the interminable boulder fields that had driven us mad on the way up.

Inevitably, I couldn't find the easiest way we had used on the way up, and dusk was quickly encroaching. At last it flattened out and I got my head-torch out and flashed a couple of times in the direction I thought the truck would be. To my relief headlights immediately pierced the darkness as Mac returned the signal. It was still about a mile away and now, in total darkness with a fading head-torch, I stumbled and groped my way towards journey's end.

Suddenly I was there and Mac took a flash photo of me looking as though I had spent the summer cleaning out Hope Cement Works in Derbyshire. Mac had become increasingly worried and

247

began to fear I had had an accident. As the truck jolted back towards San Pedro, I told him my story. I was wheezing like a leaking concertina, and when we reached the hotel I ditched all my ripped Gore-Tex gear into the nearest bin.

We found a restaurant still serving food and, far more important, beer and I began to rehydrate — one bottle of beer to about three glasses of water. Then bed, too tired to sleep and still wheezing. I relived the day over and over, until I fell asleep just before it was time to get up.

Only five days later I was sitting down to an Alpha Club dinner in Buxton on a cold November evening: "Been anywhere interesting recently?" enquired someone. Well, I thought, if this is retirement — I want more.

Two weeks later, I was climbing in the Wye Valley with Tony Iveson and Stephen Venables, recounting my adventures to a slightly sceptical audience. I was as fit as a butcher's dog from the waist down, but arm and finger strength were practically non-existent: "Let this be a lesson to you," advised Stephen kindly. "All this mountain climbing is just another step down the road to old age and decrepitude. You'll be joining the Austrian Alpine Club next and learning to yodel."

This, coming from the man who made a new route on Everest without using oxygen, and who had subsequently fallen down Panch Chuli, was advice I could not ignore. I resolved that next year I would try, yet again, to get back to a decent level of rock-climbing. The only problem was that I was already half committed to an adventure I had been angling for since I had first met that iconic figure who has grown to be the public face of Indian Mountaineering, Harish Kapadia.

Chapter thirty one: Bombay Mix

In 1994 Harish Kapadia was a cloth merchant living in what we must now call Mumbai — though Harish himself still occasionally calls it Bombay. Over the years this indefatigable, plump, jolly little man has probably totted up more expeditions to the Indian Himalaya than anyone else, living or dead. His knowledge is encyclopaedic and he has written innumerable books. For anyone wanting to find an unexplored nook or cranny that Harish hasn't been to first, they are essential reading.

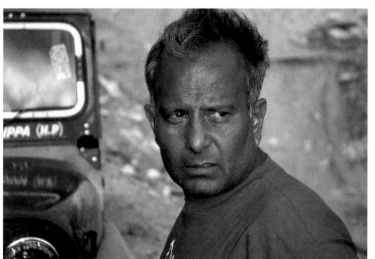

Harish Kapadia.

Pete Boardman once wrote that to go on a Bonington expedition 'is one of the last great imperial experiences that life can offer'. To go on one of Harish's trips gives you a unique insight into post-Imperial Indian culture that would be quite impossible for an all-British party to experience. (And if Chris goes as well, you couldn't have it any better.)

I first met Harish at one of the Buxton Conferences organised by the BMC. Harish was with Paul Nunn, who in 1991, to my ill-concealed envy, had been with Harish to Chang Kumdan in the Eastern Karakoram. Harish, Paul and I were soon laughing together and I met him and Paul again in The Byron. Once again, I was charmed by Harish and when he left we had a vague understanding that at some point I would go on a trip with him.

And so it came to pass that in 1994, Harish and Chris Bonington put together a joint Indian/British expedition to the Kinnaur Himalaya. The British team was Chris, Paul, Jim Fotheringham, Jim Lowther, Graham Little and me. Harish had chosen Divyesh Muni, Muslim Contractor, Kaivan Mistri and Vijay Kothari. Our objective was an unnamed peak of 6553 metres in an area near the Tibetan border. A British expedition on its own would have no chance of getting permission, but the beauty of going with Harish is that he can get you into places that you didn't even know were places. I was expected to make a film, but initially we had no sponsorship, which would make the whole venture horrendously expensive. An old climbing friend of mine, Duncan Sperry, worked for a communications company called Veriphone. To my surprise, they decided to sponsor us. In India, Godrej, a huge Mumbai company, sponsored the Indian climbers. Chameleon decided they would back a film, and suddenly we were in business.

Before I left Sheffield I had gone to the bank to pick up some dollars. As the bank clerk counted them out, she said, without

249

looking up: "Off up the Orinoco again, are we, Mr Curran?"

Chris, who was President of LEPRA, was going to fly out to Mumbai a week early and visit leper colonies in southern India. I flew out with the potential to lose what sanity I still possessed, by extricating all our baggage from Indian customs. We stayed with Harish and his wife, Geeta, in their tower block flat in an area of Mumbai where, since the advent of Bollywood, property prices had rocketed.

Getting mountaineering equipment out of Indian customs is as labyrinthine a process as freeing hostages in the Middle East. The customs set up traditional lines of defence.

1) The goods do not exist.

2) Even if they do, you will have to find them yourself.

3) The offices are shut for the day.

4) Tomorrow is the start of a two-week holiday.

5) The joker in the pack — you have not got the correct forms.

This card can be played whenever there is a possibility that the kit is on the verge of release. Luckily, a friend of Harish's, Rashmi Shah, a startlingly attractive young lady, was on hand to help. In fact, she more or less took over negotiations when my legendary patience failed after about two hours. After only two gruelling days wandering around the stiflingly hot customs sheds, looking for the proverbial needle in a haystack, we got the gear out and loaded it all precariously on a clapped-out, flatbed lorry. Riding shotgun on top of the tottering mass of boxes and holdalls, I repelled borders all the way back to Harish's flat and the downing of several long, cold drinks. I was reminded of a story Charlie Clarke had told me of trying to free gear from the customs for a trip to Kishtwar years before. At last the agent Charlie had employed to pay all the necessary bribes approached him. "Mr Clarke, I have very good news. Your equipment will definitely be released tomorrow at 11.30 prompt... or perhaps a little later."

As we unloaded the lorry and stacked the boxes safely in Harish's stairwell, Chris looked at me: "You know you really are a bit of a team player."

"That's what comes of playing cricket and rugby as a schoolboy," I replied, probably rather smugly.

When Chris was in Hyderabad doing his LEPRA work, Harish sorted out a few diversions for me. One was to go with him and Geeta to an experimental play about the meaning of life, spoken in Urdu, which, for all but the first five minutes, I slept through. Then I spent a curious day visiting Vijay Kothari's velvet factory on the outskirts of Bombay. This was like going back into Dickensian London. In a rundown building, vats of steaming velvet and dye were heated by gas-burners, all of which were linked by a maze of decaying rubber tubing, patched and worn, and a truly horrifying fire hazard. "We have not had fire for several years," said Vijay proudly. Returning in the ubiquitous black and yellow taxi through miles of ghastly slums, I reflected that expeditioning certainly gave you some strange experiences. It was funny to think that the day I had just had was part of the same activity that saw me climbing on Stanage on a sunny Sunday afternoon.

Harish is a devoted train-lover and when the rest of the team arrived we all caught the night train to Delhi. Here, lying in an air-conditioned carriage on semi-comfortable bunk beds, we trundled through the night occasionally being woken in dimly lit stations with the characteristic "Chai-ee!" call of the tea vendors with their tiny ceramic cups that you throw away once you have drunk the sweet milky cardamom-flavoured tea.

Arriving in Delhi in mid-morning was a shock. It was searingly, take-your-breath-away and burn-the-hairs-in-your-nostrils, hot. Chris and I had to give a lecture to Delhi members of The Himalayan Club. Somehow the deed was done and, wrung out with the heat and nervous tension, we departed from Delhi on another night train to Kalka.

Here was the jewel in the crown of Harish's journey — the rack railway up to Shimla. This masterpiece of Victorian engineering design was built to make the journey for officials, memsahibs and children of the Raj to escape the heat of the plains, going up to the administrative capital of India in the summer months. The

little diesel train chattered out of the station and quickly started climbing through green forests. Monkeys jumped off the line at the last moment, and impassive turbaned railway workers stood and watched as we clanked past.

Halfway up, we stopped at an immaculately kept little station. "Breakfast time," announced Harish joyfully. And so it was: eggs, toast and unlimited chai. I wouldn't have been surprised if Lord Curzon himself had walked in with his Victorian entourage. Burping contentedly, we re-boarded the train for the last leg.

Shimla was, I thought, a rather sad shadow of its illustrious past. As the train arrived, it almost looked as though we were arriving in a Surrey village in the North Downs. But the illusion didn't last long. The town seemed to be falling to pieces and the grandiose European architecture was rotting away. Even so, you could sense in its decay faint echoes of tea dances and British gentility as the unbending rituals of the middle classes were enacted thousands of miles away from home.

There was no time to explore, for Harish had arranged a bus up the Sutlej Valley to where our walk-in started, up the Tirung Gad. The valley was the setting for much of Kipling's *Kim*, but now it is heavily industrialised and much of it looks more like the Rother Valley than the romantic vision of India that Kipling conjured up. By contrast, once we left the roadhead, we were into an area where we could only go with our Indian friends. It was quite the most enchanting walk I had ever experienced. A well-worn path led intricately up the valley bottom, skirting granite boulders and some immense Yosemite-style walls, some over 1000 metres high. The

whole area would have made a great venue for a rock-climbing holiday and I wondered whether, in 50 years time, climbers would just be happy to come here to rock-climb, as was already happening in similar situations in the Alps. Chris actually started fantasising about coming back with rock-climbing star Johnny Dawes, but the idea never took off.

It took three days of leisurely walking to reach the head of the valley, spoiled for Paul and me by the usual stomach ailments.

< *Geoff Birtles*

252

I was particularly annoyed, as Chris had invited Geoff Birtles to come with us to Base Camp and I, veteran traveller that I am, had warned him about drinking contaminated water. On the bus I had absent-mindedly opened a bottle and swigged it before I noticed that the seal was already broken.

Geoff had arrived in Mumbai in the middle of the night with the rest of the team and they had taken taxis to Harish's flat. Geoff, on his first visit to the sub-continent, had been horrified at seeing whole families sleeping by the side of the road, and found the culture-shock of India hard to take. He certainly cheered up on the walk in, particularly when he realised that Paul and I were leaking like sieves from every orifice.

Rangrik Tungma is a little monastery reputed to be 700 years old. Here we split up to recce the various approaches to our mountain — actually a whole massif with four or five subsidiary peaks. I went with Harish up a steep hill behind the monastery. We gained height quite easily, given that we weren't really acclimatised. At the top of the hill I was surprised to find a beautifully made cairn. Harish was excited: "Jim sahib — here is relic of your forefathers. It is from Great Trigonometric Survey of India. I don't expect any European has stood here since it was built." I was impressed and actually quite moved. The GTS had plotted the whole of India in the 19th century, almost incidentally measuring the relative heights of Everest, K2 and Kangchenjunga to within a few feet. Using no more than a plane table, trigonometry and a small army of dedicated surveyors, they produced quite incredibly accurate heights and distances. These have changed very little to the present day, even using satellite and laser technology.

Despite the fact that the easiest way up our mountain was probably another couple of days' walk up to the foot of the northern flanks, it was too close to the Tibetan border to get permission, even though we were a joint expedition. We had to settle for a western approach with a steep ice wall to gain a long summit ridge.

Once we established our Base Camp, Geoff and Geeta who had also come with us, prepared to go home. But not before the Great Cricket Match. Here, on a rough and unready pitch, the addicts of the game — Geoff, Jim Lowther, me, Muslim, Divyesh — played against some of Harish's handpicked porters. Hasingh (junior) proved to be an elusive left-handed spin bowler and the porters, predictably, ran rings around us. Of course, we said sniffily, they were far better acclimatised. Harish, the greatest cricket lover of all of us, looked on approvingly. Luckily nobody got injured and next day, after wishing Geoff and Geeta a safe journey home, the serious business of climbing a mountain started (about time too, I hear you say).

^ *Kinnaur cricket match.*

For some reason I acclimatised quite well and managed to just about keep up with the all-star team. The crux of the climb, the ice wall leading to the North East Ridge, proved a bit of a wake-up call. That, combined with a few days of bad weather and Chris having a bad chest infection, meant that all of us with intentions of climbing the mountain arrived at the foot of the wall in more or less the same state of readiness.

Given that nine of us had designs on the summit, we all felt that the ice wall needed fixed rope. (I was probably more relieved than anyone else.) In fact, the wall took three days to climb and it would have been pointless to do it Alpine style. It enabled me to jumar up the ropes and get some good footage of Paul leading. It was the first time I tried filming myself giving a running commentary by holding the camera at arm's length and talking at it. These days, it is so common that no one notices, but in 1994 it did seem to be quite a novel approach.

Two days after Chris and Jim Fotheringham completed the wall, we were all crammed into four tiny two-man tents dug into the very crest of the North East Ridge. This was, by a long way, the most dramatic camp site I had ever occupied. Huge drops on each side of the tents fell away to dizzy blue depths. It was the stuff of nightmares, though when you were actually in the tent, it seemed quite normal. Chris and Jim's tent faced Paul's and mine, and a few metres away Jim Lowther and Graham had, with a bit more cunning, dug their tent into the angle of the snow slope, which

^ On the long snowslopes to the top camp.

seemed much more secure. Tomorrow would be summit day, we hoped, though I had severe reservations. I had been desperately tired that day, climbing to about 6000 metres. Over the years it seemed that this was to be my height ceiling. On K2 I had got a bit higher, and much the same on Everest, but 7000 metres was just out of my reach. (It was out of all our reaches on this trip, for the mountain was only 6553 metres high.)

After only half a rope length the next day, I knew the game was up. Each step seemed to take every ounce of strength I possessed and there was no way I could carry on for 550 metres. So Paul tied on to Muslim's rope and I retreated to the tent where I prepared for a long wait.

It was an absolutely stunning day, with views out over Tibet and across to the mountains of Gangotri where Kamet sat on the horizon looking remarkably like K2. It is not often that you get the chance to simply look and think in fine weather on a high mountain. Normally you are either trying to get up or down, and in the bits in between you are either trying to go to sleep or trying to wake up. Here, in absolute silence, I spent the day consciously absorbing the sight. I was also making a big decision. Now 51, I couldn't delude myself that I could even vaguely keep up with world-class performers. Graham Little and the two Jims were at the height of their powers and Chris, now 60, was still going incredibly well. So was Paul, who in the past had seemed to have the same sort of problems with altitude as I had.

Looking down, I could just pick out the tents of Advance Base, a world away. I have to say pangs of fear gripped me. Had I pushed myself too far? Could I get down safely?

The answers the next day were yes and no. The successful team had arrived late, but tired and triumphant. In the morning, after kicking steps downhill for only one rope length, I felt quite shattered. By the time we had descended to the fixed ropes, I was finding it hard to stand up, and once I started abseiling I was barely in control. Almost sobbing with relief, I sat in the snow at the foot of the wall. Harish had sent a porter to take my rucksack back, but, even without it, I was walking like a drunk. Halfway I stopped, utterly exhausted, and sat on the dry ice of the glacier. Above me was a hanging sérac, and I was directly underneath. If it falls, it falls, I thought. But it still took me about half an hour before I could get up and make it back to the safety of the camp.

With only a couple of hours' walking down to Base Camp, I thought that the chances of me having a brush with the Grim Reaper were now slim. But as I followed porter footprints on old snow on the bank of a deep fast flowing glacier stream, I could have sworn I saw a grey-hooded figure with a scythe — no,

255

obviously not — it was Chris with an ice-axe. But I still fell into the icy stream and was whisked along at ever increasing speed towards certain death when the foaming water went under the ice to re-emerge just above Base Camp. Providentially, a jammed boulder half blocking the torrent enabled me to escape, shaken and chilled to the bone. Definitely, definitely too old for this game, I told myself. We called the mountain, by the way, Rangrik Rang, after the monastery at its foot. As Geoff Birtles could now say: "Rangrik Rang, but you were out".

For Paul and me, there was a second half to this trip. Chris and company went home, while Harish and his Indian team got permission to go beyond the 'Inner Line' towards the Tibetan border. Harish waved his magic wand and we got on the permit. Two days later we found ourselves driving towards Spiti via the village of Poo. (I enjoyed writing that sentence.)

Our objective this time was the slightly higher peak of Manirang at 6593 metres. We approached via a wire crossing the Spiti River, suspended in a ramshackle wooden box. Then we walked up a steep hillside to the strange village of Mane. I say strange, for not only did it have satellite TV, on which we watched bits of Wimbledon and Formula One Motor Racing, as well as ancient episodes of *Neighbours*, but also the place was unnaturally silent. It took a little time to work out why. Then the rupee dropped. Of course! No dogs. Apparently the headman had got so fed up with the incessant all night barking, he had had them all shot.

Unintentionally, I spent an extra day in the village when a crippling pain flared up in my foot. Eventually a huge amount of ibuprofen cured it, but it would be several years before this problem, which occurred every few months, was diagnosed as gout! Dragging myself reluctantly away from the women's final (which Navratilova won yet again), I hired a man to carry my gear — I was getting used to the Kapadia/Bonington way of life — and, after a long day, caught the others up at the foot of our rather ugly looking mountain which had already been climbed twice.

Despite my resolve to give up, the prospect of what seemed to be an easy ascent lured me back into the ranks. Will I never learn? Three days later saw Paul and me teetering around at 6300 metres on deceptively easy angled water ice that seemed to stretch all the way to the top, and certainly all the way down to oblivion. It was self-evident that even if Paul combined with Divyesh Muni, the best of the Indian climbers, and we pooled all our ice-climbing gear to cope with the conditions, it would still be a close run thing. We managed a precarious reverse down the evil ice slope and I, with Harish and Muslim bowed out gracefully to leave Paul and Diviyesh to try and get to the top. This they did, in a long day of

< A thought-provoking camp site.

257

^ *One of the biggest avalanche scars I have ever seen opposite Manirang.*

climbing as precarious as our attempt, but this time all the way to the top, with some delicate and dangerous abseiling to round it off. Once again, I had failed at around 6000 metres. This time would be the last.

But it had been the best expedition I had been on since the first great trip to Trango. I felt it was time to call it a day, and perhaps get some more of my own climbing in on lower peaks. For Paul, getting to the top of two good mountains meant that this was easily his most successful expedition. But if I could see the writing on the wall, I doubt that Paul thought for an instant that his time was up, and neither did I. We never discussed it and I'm sure that whatever I may have said would have made absolutely no difference. But, as with Al Rouse on K2, maybe I should have tried.

Chapter thirty two: African Double Top

After my ventures on Licancabur and Mount Elbrus, I felt a certain affinity with climbing volcanoes, so, when Mac suggested another little outing to climb Kilimanjaro and Mount Kenya over the Christmas holiday of 1994, I was immediately enthusiastic. I had always fancied a trip to Africa but, apart from a short visit to the Atlas Mountains with Tony Iveson, which I thoroughly enjoyed, I felt, irrationally, that Morocco didn't really count whereas Kenya undoubtedly did.

Mac is an old Africa hand, and had lived and worked there in the 1950s before becoming the computer and media tycoon of later years. We flew to Nairobi and caught a bus down to the border with Tanzania. Halfway, we had our first view of Kilimanjaro. At 5895 metres its vast bulk rose majestically above the plains. The snows of the summit looked high and remote. It remains one of the best long-distance views of any mountain I have ever seen.

I had a bit of unfinished business with Kilimanjaro, for I had been asked by Chris Bonington, still on his improbable quest for the Seven Summits, to go with him and his two boys, Rupert and Daniel, to climb the mountain via the Credner Glacier; a far more interesting route than the voie normal which is not much more than a walk. Irritatingly, I had managed to get such severe tendonitis in my heel that I had to pull out.

Mac and I wanted to climb this route for two reasons. First, because it involved crossing the crater at the top of the mountain. Second, and more important, we would spend a lot longer on the ascent, as we would be traversing round the mountain at the halfway point, giving us valuable acclimatisation. I had a theory that it made more sense to spend time on Kilimanjaro before going to Mount Kenya, which at 5199 metres, is nearly 700 metres lower. But climbing on Mount Kenya is technical and we wanted to enjoy it. I couldn't help thinking (and still do) that Mount Kenya is a far more worthy objective. I think Mac felt the same, though we never discussed it.

Our ascent of Kili followed the normal route from the village of Marangu as far as the wide saddle between Kibo, the highest point, and Mawenzi, a sister peak but significantly lower mountain in its own right. Here, in the company of our obligatory porters, we veered off the main drag and started traversing. It was a hot cloudless day and our progress was slow. Suddenly we came across a solitary trekker, dressed in full wet weather kit. Wondering why people feel they have to wear every bit of expensive Gore-Tex they possess, we rounded a corner and within yards, the weather changed completely. Moisture-laden mist drifted silently around us, the temperature dropped and within moments we were digging into our rucksacks for the self same waterproofs.

259

^ *Kilimanjaro, one ski pole, no axe, rope or crampons.*

We spent the next couple of days stumbling around the mountain with no visibility and soaked to the skin. It would be another long day to reach the foot of the Credner Glacier and our porters suggested that we ascended the Arrow Glacier which was apparently only just above us. This would enable us to cross the crater and, given the state we were all in, seemed a reasonable compromise.

That night was the wettest and coldest I have spent in a leaking tent since early days in Wales. Mac and I shivered in sodden sleeping bags while the rain, now turning to sleet, then wet snow, was unbroken.

At some unearthly hour we forced down a brew and some soggy bread and set off up an easy angled névé into the grey dawn. Our porters had assured us that we didn't need axes or a rope. As the glacier gave way to a rocky buttress, they suddenly produced both for their own use. I hoped they had some sort of divine faith in our ability to solo. Actually, it wasn't any harder than, say, the Bristly Ridge on Glyder Fach in North Wales. But it was still a bit unnerving to balance up blocky, square cut rocks covered in fresh snow, armed only with a ski pole. If you fell off, you would probably kill yourself, so we did our best not to.

Mac, who was then aged 66, was undoubtedly a lot stronger than me. He has a phenomenal constitution, never apparently suffering hangovers, and able to rock-climb to a high standard even after little or no preparation. On odd trips to Harrison's with him, I was

260

impressed at how neatly and craftily he still managed to top-rope climbs of at least 5c difficulty. Now, on our summit day, he was always ahead of me and I was finding it hard going at over 5000 metres. But at least the weather was clearing, or we were climbing out of it, for glimpses of the crater rim seemed quite close, and soon I could see our porters relaxing on flat ground. Thankfully, we pulled out into the sunshine and looked around.

Even with global warming, the crater is an extraordinary place. Ice cliffs glistened in the hot sun, and underfoot was either ash or ice. It was a bit like wandering through a Salvador Dali painting: ice pinnacles melting, fumeroles smoking, and a strange inability to judge how far or near anything was. Perhaps because of this we allowed ourselves to be conned by the porters. We had assumed that we would, at some point, gain the rim leading to the summit, still 100 metres or so above us. Suddenly we realised that we had walked past it and now, late in the afternoon, we were at Gilman's Point, the place on the rim of the crater where the main route of ascent/descent arrives. Our head porter said that crossing the crater was the same as reaching the top, which it obviously wasn't, but we were too tired to argue, let alone go back along the rim. So we began to descend the interminable scree slopes that I seriously doubted whether I would have had the patience or energy to ascend. At last, hot, sweaty and almost completely exhausted, we reached the Kibo Hut (or huts, for there was the large main one and several odd tent-shaped smaller ones). It had been a very long day. Next day we walked easily down to Marangu to the comforts of civilisation: a hot bath, a proper meal and a certain amount of beer.

We needed a few days' rest and decided to do the tourist thing of visiting the Ngorongoro Crater to look at the wildlife. The crater is a natural sanctuary, a huge bowl of an extinct volcano, 2000 feet deep and covering 100 square miles. The fertile plains in its base are home to an estimated 25,000 animals, including the Big Five: elephants, lions, rhinos, leopards and hippos — in other words, every animal you could wish to see (though Mac complained at the absence of polar bears). For two or three days we were just gaping tourists. What I hadn't realised — or rather, hadn't been bothered to think about — was that these animals were genuinely wild. They weren't performing for us and were just doing their own thing. I particularly liked the hippos, squelching around in their muddy pond with every indication that they were in hippo heaven. Giraffes glided through the long grass, elephants crossed the road in front of us with total disdain and at last we saw a family of lions. Bloated after a kill, the female stretched out half asleep. The male made a desultory attempt at a bit of 'how's your father', to be repulsed with a throaty growl. "That's lion for 'I've got a headache'," Mac observed to the amusement of the people sharing the back of the open Land Rover we were perched on. Very little (nothing) separated us from becoming the lions' next meal, and I thought how ironic it would be to emulate the fate of my namesake in Hilaire Belloc's Cautionary Tale.

But all the enjoyment couldn't last and, after just one night in Nairobi, we hired a Toyota pick-up truck and headed north in the rain to Naro Moru, the jump off point for our intended climb on Mount Kenya.

We were pleasantly surprised when we awoke the next morning to a cloudless sky and saw the characteristic spiky silhouette of the massif jutting above the eastern horizon. I couldn't believe that the weather would last for the four days we would need to walk in and do the climb, but, if nothing else, we'd got one spectacular long-distance view of the mountain.

Perhaps because we were well-acclimatised and reasonably fit, the approach, via the infamous Vertical Bog, the Mackinder Hut, and the semi-derelict Austrian Hut, seemed fairly painless. I had imagined the Vertical Bog to be a battlefield of sorts, tilted through 90 degrees, and was relieved to find a gently inclined swamp. We had clear views of the Diamond Couloir. Global warming has reduced it to an evil runnel of dirty ice with an ominous gap at its base. I was glad we had no intention of climbing it.

In Nairobi we had contacted Ian Howell, an old climbing partner of Mac's. He had strongly recommended that we bivouacked in the eponymous Howell Hut on the marginally lower summit of Nelion. He explained that, from there, we would get better views from the top first thing in the morning and could take our time to do the route in comfort. This, I think, was his tactful way of saying we were unlikely to get up and down in a day, which was certainly correct.

So it was that dawn on yet another fine day saw us slithering cramponless across the hard, frozen snow of the Lewis Glacier to the foot of the climb. Up close, the elegant architecture of the mountain seemed surprisingly broken but, once we'd started, we found that the rock was generally sound and enjoyable to climb, though route-finding on the bottom half was quite difficult.

Quite early on we came across an incredibly ancient piece of bleached rope, reputed to be a relic of the first ascent in 1899. Could it really have survived for nearly a hundred years? Our meanderings had taken in various time-honoured features such as the Keyhole, the Rabbit Hole and the One o'Clock Gully. None were particularly difficult, apart from when I climbed an arête to avoid an awkward-looking chimney crack and failed to spot an easy traverse at the top, which meant I climbed an unnecessary little overhang and earned Mac's justified disapproval. I was wearing rock shoes, gambling on the whole climb being on rock. Mac sensibly wore boots and carried a short hammer axe. From the Austrian Hut, Nelion had appeared to be snow-free but as we gained height, old snow patches started to appear and streaks of old ice filled some of the cracks. Memories of Lliwedd, all those years ago.

The weather was still settled, with wisps of innocuous cloud drifting up the valleys. We were level with Point Lenana, shamelessly hyped as the 'third summit' of Mount Kenya by trekking companies anxious to make a mountain out of a molehill.

After crossing a snow-filled gully, we arrived at the foot of De Graaf's Variation, a long corner crack that, in good condition,

provides the crux of the climb. It looked steep but straightforward and I could see several protection pegs in place. After about 10 metres I decided to climb without my 'sack, which I hung on a peg. Delightfully unencumbered, I carried on, revelling in a really enjoyable pitch. At the top I belayed happily, knowing that the rest of the route would be easier.

Twenty minutes later I brought up Mac in a fury, cursing my stupidity as, while hauling them up, I'd managed to get the 'sacks stuck under overhangs and tangled in rope. Suddenly I felt tired. Mac led up to a broken arête around which we climbed to make a descending traverse across a gully. The atmosphere changed abruptly. It became cold and gloomy, and the bed of the gully was seamed with ice. Climbing at 5000 metres didn't help, even though we'd been almost 1000 metres higher on Kilimanjaro.

Mac led everything, as I was too tired to lead through by the time I had followed a pitch. One pitch in particular still sticks in my memory. Mac climbed a steep wall to avoid cracks bulging with water ice. It felt much harder to me than

< Mount Kenya.

^ The summit of Nelion — Mac swears that he didn't notice the position of the metal cross.

anything else on the route. I was impressed.

Above, the granite walls stretched away, catching the late afternoon sun playing on what I hoped would be the summit. Mac climbed on, almost scrambling. He shouted down that there were only two or three more pitches. Wearily, I followed. As I joined him I found with great relief that he had been kidding — the summit was only a few metres away. I plodded shakily across almost flat ground in a tangle of ropes and slings to the glistening aluminium biscuit tin that is the Howell Hut. Inside it were rotting pieces of foam, frozen snow, and some dubious remnants of ancient dried food. It felt like a five-star hotel, even though there was only just room for the two of us to stretch out.

We wriggled in and within minutes were in our sleeping bags, melting snow for the first of many brews, then preparing a meal of sorts. Soon we had made the cramped interior our home and crashed into dreamless sleep.

^ Bivouac in the Howell Hut.

We awoke early to a freezing, stunning dawn. Below us was a fabulous panorama across Kenya, though a cloud ceiling blocked the 'ultimate' view to Kilimanjaro, over 300 kilometres away to the south. While I brewed up our remaining tea bag and tried to swallow a piece of stale bread, Mac found the hut book in which we made the first entries since August. He wrote a fantastic description of our breakfast: bacon, liver, sausages, quails' eggs, salmon kedgeree, fried bread, black pudding, coffee, toast, and marmalade. Months later it provoked a bewildered climber who had spent a miserable night in the hut to ask me how we managed to carry up all that food!

We scrambled the few metres to the highest point of Nelion

264

and looked across at Batian, now so close we could almost touch it. But to gain those final 11 metres would mean crossing the Gate of the Mists, which seemed out of the question — bits of old fixed rope disappeared into hard, frozen snow, its rocks were rimed with hoar frost, verglas gleamed evilly — it would have taken hours. We settled for retracing our steps. It took several hours of abseiling and down-climbing to reach the Lewis Glacier. Apart from getting the ropes well and truly jammed and having to re-climb a pitch to free them, it passed uneventfully. But, in the late afternoon sunshine, re-crossing the glacier was a desperate affair and we floundered through slushy, waist-deep snow. At last, it was done and we walked unsteadily down the path to the MacKinder Hut. Behind us the last rays of the sun turned the mountain gold. Already it was becoming a memory. Deep down though, I felt a sense of fulfilment.

Hugely satisfied, we slept late and next morning watched in amazement as an awesome wall of cloud and snow billowed over the mountain like a breaking wave in a surfer's nightmare. We fled down the Vertical Bog in mist and drizzle to regain the roadhead. Behind us the vast expanse of damp forested hillside once again disappeared into a lowering cloud base that looked as though it had been there forever.

A few days later, after a bleak and rather lonely Christmas Day in Nairobi, we were on a flight home. "Come on, be honest," said Mac, "when we arrived, what did you think we would actually do?" I thought for a moment: "What I really wanted was to get up Mount Kenya, but I didn't think we had more than a 50-50 chance." Mac was more forthright: "I didn't think we would do either of them." Technically, I suppose he was right — we hadn't. But as far as I was concerned we did. Crossing the crater on Kili was a unique experience and climbing Nelion wasn't a bad effort for two old farts. I reminded Mac of the trekking team we had met on our way down from the Mackinder Hut: "Have you climbed Point Lanana?" enquired a rather striking German lady. She commiserated with what she obviously thought were two unfit, overweight old men who replied that they hadn't climbed Lanana, but after a suitable pause, admitted that they had climbed Big Brother next door. She looked at us in ill-concealed amazement: "You mean… with ropes?"

Chapter thirty three: I Chose to Trek

A group of us used to go to the Quiz Night in The Abbey pub in Woodseats where Pam Beech lived, as did her friend Pam Gleadall (Pams 1 and 2). One evening in the autumn of 1994 they were joined by a blonde lady, not conventionally beautiful (long face, big teeth), but with smiling blue eyes that somehow radiated fun and laughter. These middle-aged ladies later became known collectively as 'The Old Spice Girls'. I saw her again at a party at Geoff Birtles's home and asked her out for a drink. Sue Coonan (for it was she) said yes, but later asked Geoff to tell me she had changed her mind, a bit of a blow to my attempts to be a middle-aged Lothario. The next time I saw her I was nursing a leg in plaster having broken it in Scotland. It was Pam Beech's birthday and we were celebrating in another Woodseats pub. She came over to me, said she owed me an apology, gave me a quick peck on the cheek, and that was that. Except that that wasn't that, though it took another couple of years for the full impact of the woman to hit me.

I was slightly unsure of what I would do if, as I had decided on Rangrik Rang, my expedition career was really over. So when Steve Berry, who runs Himalayan Kingdoms, a Bristol-based trekking company, asked if I would like to lead a trek in the summer of 1995, I thought, why not? Let's give it a whirl. This was probably not the best motivation for a new activity and my commitment was not helped when, climbing with Paul in Scotland, I broke my leg descending an icy slope after completing what would prove to be Paul's last winter climb.

The trek I was given was to Zanskar, south of Ladakh, one of the longest and hardest treks around (though nowhere near as difficult as one to the K2 Base Camp). It also had 12 members, the maximum number before two trek leaders are necessary. Both these factors, combined with the after-effects of a broken leg, contributed to the general feeling of apprehension as I greeted my team at Heathrow. The only time I had met them before was on a 'getting to know you' walk in the Cotswolds some weeks before, when my leg was still very weak and sore. About half the team turned up and seemed pleasant enough, but the walk did little to ease my misgivings. I wished then that I had the courage to withdraw but it was probably too late to find a replacement.

We spent a day and a night in Delhi then took an internal flight to Chandigarh and then a coach drive, first to Menali and then over the Rotang Pass to the start of our trek. Within the first three days we had to cross the Shingo La, a pass at just under 5000 metres, so I couldn't help worrying. Hardly anyone in our party had been this high before and I felt it was far too early to commit ourselves to the crossing, beyond which, while not so high, we would be trekking for days without either losing much height or finding any escape to a road if anything went wrong. A helicopter rescue was a remote possibility, but no more than that, and it would take at least two days to organise. I prayed that nobody would suffer from pulmonary or cerebral oedema.

Two of my team were a Scottish father and son. The lad was only about 16 and obviously extremely fit — a classic case for oedema I thought, remembering Simon Wells on the Everest trek two years before. Sure enough, the lad woke up on the second morning with a splitting headache and, as we all ground up the unending path to the top of the pass, he went more and more slowly.

The first, last, and best bit of advice I was given about trek leading was simple. Bring up the rear. That way if anything goes wrong you will be walking towards it. So on the Shingo La my worries grew with each step. Everything told me to go down with the boy and spend a day or two resting to enable him to recover. But that would mean splitting the team and then trying to catch up. If there had been two leaders it might have been possible. Against every bit of judgement I pressed on, hoping that once over the col he would recover.

When we got there I found another of my charges looking decidedly off-colour. She was a lady from South Wales and, frankly, I had my doubts as to whether she should have been accepted for the trek. The problem is simple. The trekking companies hate turning people away but for a trek like the Zanskar one you have to be reasonably fit. Of the 12 people under my care I thought that about half weren't really up to it (and that didn't include the 16-year-old who, two days later, had made a complete recovery). So, once away from the roadhead, the hapless trek leader is stuck with whatever he has been given. My problem, I was finding out quite quickly, was that I should have been either:

a) a lot nicer, or

b) a lot nastier; I could never quite decide which.

Sometimes my instincts were to give people a no-holds-barred bollocking when they did something stupid, like the couple that found a broken jola bridge. These are made of intertwined birch twigs and in the Western Himalaya and the Karakoram are still used today, though they are gradually being replaced by the wire and pulley affairs which are doubtless safer but feel just as precarious. Anyway, spotting one that was clearly disused, these two amused themselves by swinging around over a lethal river, dicing with certain death had anything snapped. The same couple took great delight in scree running, safe enough in Britain, but asking for trouble here, miles from any possibility of rescue, where even a sprained ankle could mess up the whole trek. But if I did give them a full dressing down it would probably poison the atmosphere for the whole trip. Equally, when my charges needed encouragement, sweetness and light from me, I was probably too grumpy to give it.

Halfway through the trek we visited the Phuctal monastery, an amazing building: half-cave, half-fort, nestling in an almost vertical cliff. It was probably the most charismatic of all Buddhist monasteries I have ever visited and you could hardly imagine a more spectacular setting. Climbing the stone steps up a steep, dark tower I was amazed at what I thought was a projected slide. In fact, it was just a slit in the thick stone walls through which a group of irrigated fields and cultivated apricot trees were visible. In the darkness they positively glowed with an unearthly green luminescence. The whole monastery looked as though it was a film set for *The Lord of the Rings* which is, I know, a philistine cliché, but I can't find the words that do the job any better.

A couple of days later, just when everything seemed to be going well, the trek was stopped. The reason? The villagers of Padam had a list of grudges against the government — lack of schools, hospitals, roads, etc — that had been promised but nothing had happened. The villagers decided to stop all trekking teams in the area from proceeding. It was a simple but effective ploy. I spent a day trying to negotiate a way through, but even bribes had no effect. One of the trekkers suggested sneaking through the village in the middle of the night. Almost as if he was reading our minds, the local policeman, who was nothing if not switched on, told us that if we disobeyed an official ruling, the members' travel insurance would be null and void. Whether or not this was true, nobody felt inclined to put it to the test, so there we were. Stuck.

I hated the thought of retracing our steps all the way to the start of the trek and discussed with our sirdar (head porter) what it was possible to do. After hours of negotiating, we thrashed out a plan; to go back a day then go over a little-used pass that would bring us out onto the Menali-Leh road. A bus would take us to Leh, the end of our trek, where we would spend four or five days instead of the two nights as originally planned. We would miss about half of the journey through Zanskar, but there was no alternative.

A couple of very attractive German girls were similarly stuck, and asked if they could join us. As they had both recently qualified as doctors it seemed a good idea. A day after our enforced rest day, we got going again. The Welsh lady had spent the whole day sunbathing, despite several warnings that at nearly 4000 metres she would regret it. She did, and so did I. The day we crossed the pass she went more and more slowly. Eventually, she hitched a precarious ride on one of our donkeys and wobbled off leaving me miles behind on my own. As I reached the little col at the top of the pass, the trekkers gave me an ironic cheer. As for the Welsh lady, she had fallen off the donkey near the top and thought she had broken her arm. "It hurts when I do this," she groaned, trying to lift her arm up. "Well," said one of the German girls, "don't do it." I asked her if she had heard of Tommy Cooper but got a blank look.

Strangely, although the trek had been severely curtailed, the next two days were the most enjoyable, walking gently downhill through wild, uninhabited country. One evening a herd of Ibex grazing on the hillside above our camp came closer than I thought possible before taking flight and gliding effortlessly up the hillside.

When we reached the road we waited for the usual grinding Indian bus to trundle us off to Leh. At one point I was chatting with a trekker when the bus stopped at a small rockslide. She had been suffering with the inevitable stomach upset and, still chatting gaily, she squatted unselfconsciously by the bus. I thought how amazing it was that three weeks ago she would no more dream of doing this in the middle of Bristol, where she was born, than fly to the moon. Does trekking make you loosen the bonds of civilisation, or does it help your tolerance and acceptance of the human condition? Puzzling over this, I got back on the bus and we carried on our way to Leh.

Leh is the former capital of Ladakh and, in appearance and culture, looks more Tibetan than Indian. The ruined palace, still with streamers of prayer flags fluttering, is built in the same style as the Potala Palace in Lhasa, and was built at about the same time in the 17th century. Leh itself is surrounded by the mountains of Zanskar and Ladakh and is set in the Indus Valley.

Now we were here I had to find ways of keeping the team occupied until we were due to fly back to Delhi. We spent one day engaged in what was optimistically called 'white river rafting'. As the Indus here is wide and sluggish 'brown' was more appropriate and I was amused that the pilots of the two inflatables we had hired aimed for any patch of rough water they could find to give us a very tame thrill. (Is that a contradiction in terms?) But for me it was curiously satisfying to know that if we kept on paddling we would reach Skardu in Pakistan.

Another day we spent visiting local monasteries. Not for the first, or last, time I found that Buddhist monasteries reminded me of St Benedict's. True, the Buddhist monks were recruited as small boys and St Benedict's didn't have huge horns bellowing out over Ealing Broadway. But the ritual seemed similar with its combination of devout prayer and complete irreverence. The music, with its ensemble of drums, gongs, oboe-like instruments, horns and chanting, seemed at first to have no discernible form, but regularly the group would reach a crescendo of noise to drive the evil spirits away. It was strangely compulsive listening. On two later visits to Lhasa I got to look forward to hearing the monks in the Johkang Temple. Every monastery seemed to have at least one monk with a phenomenally deep bass voice, almost a growl, and I wondered how they were trained to produce that awesome sound.

As the days passed, slowly the weather turned and it rained non-stop. Flights to Delhi were cancelled. Shades of Skardu airport, I thought, knowing that our schedule depended on catching the flight and then, the same day, leaving Delhi for home. Any cancellation could have ferocious knock-on effects, for Delhi flights were hopelessly over-booked during the trekking season.

On our last evening I overheard some of the team discussing something they had been told. Alison Hargreaves was missing on K2. Some of the women were critical of Alison, a mother of two small children, risking her life. Even at the end of our trek they seemed oblivious of the risks they had run themselves. Not, of course, as extreme as K2, but much, much higher than anything they had previously experienced. I felt sad, but resigned. I had seen Alison before she left and wished her well. Now she was yet another K2 statistic.

The day we left, the rain had eased off, but when we reached the airport there was a huge jostling crowd of tourists and locals who had been stuck for days. My heart sank, but we had an agent in Leh who was made of sterner stuff: "Mr Jim," he said unforgettably, "please use elbows, but no fists." Somehow we fought our way through to the most thorough security checks I've ever experienced and, at last, with a huge sigh of relief, the Air India 737 hurtled off down the runway. It seemed to take forever to lift off — but I had forgotten we were at over 3500 metres. A few minutes later I glanced out of the window. We were still only a few hundred feet up and as we streaked over houses I could see people looking up as we thundered past.

Delhi airport that evening was another vision of hell. An American businessman ahead of us in the queue had been turned away. He was almost in tears: "I have confirmed this goddam flight three times and they still won't let me on." He had all my sympathy, particularly when our man in Delhi produced the magic boarding passes! Then, one last hurdle; halfway down the pod onto the plane, an official demanded to see my pass. My heart sank: "What for?" "So that I can upgrade you." I nearly kissed him. Consequently when we landed at Heathrow the next morning I had had quite a good night's sleep. "Never mind," I told my little team, "you can't win them all."

As we waited for baggage reclaim I was talking to the lady from Bristol, who had recently been divorced. "The worst thing is knowing that there won't be anyone here to meet me." As we pushed our trolleys into Arrivals I replied: "Well, the only reason anyone would be here to meet me is if there was some really bad news." Hardly had the words left my mouth when, to my delight, I spotted my brother Philip and his wife Heather, Gemma and Becky, and Mac of all people. "Hey, what's all this? Great to see you …" My voice trailed off as I registered their faces.

"Oh, Jim — what can we say? It's Paul Nunn and Geoff Tier."

^ *One of the beautiful cantilevered bridges on the walk-in to Sepu Kangri.*

Chapter thirty four: Africa Again

The shock very nearly knocked me off my feet. I can understand how, on being given bad news, ladies swooned, and gentlemen felt the ground give way beneath them. Mechanically I said my goodbyes to my trekking team, and let myself be led, at first to Phil and Heather's language school on Ealing Common, and then driven up to Sheffield. At home, jetlagged and overwhelmingly sad, I did what I always do in desperate times, I drank whisky and played old Beatles tracks very loudly.

That evening I walked round to see Hilary and the following day drove over to Hayfield to give Barbara Tier what little consolation I could. Both women were putting on a brave face. For Hilary it was what she had always dreaded but half expected since marrying Paul, who once told me that he didn't imagine that he would reach 30, let alone 53. Barbara was utterly stricken and unprepared. Geoff had always climbed at a more than decent standard, but was a strictly amateur weekends-and-holidays climber compared to Paul, who had been on expeditions every year since I could remember. Both Barbara and Hilary asked me to speak at their memorial services, which were to be held on successive days. These were arranged immediately before I was due to fly out to South Africa to give three lectures and do some climbing. I couldn't have felt less like going, but it was a commitment I felt I had to fulfil.

The Mountain Club of South Africa had always remained anti-apartheid during the dark days of the Vorster regime and now, with the new government headed by Nelson Mandela, the club was hosting the Annual General Meeting of the UIAA, the International Mountaineering and Climbing Federation, roughly the equivalent of FIFA which represents football. Mac was a vice-president of the UIAA at the time and he suggested that, in exchange for free flights, I would lecture in Johannesburg, Durban and Cape Town. I could be taken climbing by club members, as well as Mac himself when he could escape from the interminable meetings that such bodies feel are essential for their own survival. It was a little trip I had been looking forward to, but now, with the deaths of two close friends, I couldn't imagine that I would enjoy it at all.

Geoff's service was held in Hayfield parish church, and Paul's in the Hallam University Lecture Theatre. Both were highly emotional occasions and I felt drained and numb when I got on the overnight flight to Johannesburg. All I wanted was to rest and sleep, but Mac and I were met off the plane by a skinny, bronzed man, ominously clad in shorts and walking boots. He explained that we were going climbing before my first lecture at the university that evening. My heart sank even lower, but there was no refusing him. The walk,

^ *Seconding around* The Eye of the Needle.

to a steep gorge, took over an hour. The climb he chose was called *The Eye of the Needle*. It wasn't too hard, but our guide spurned the use of our new(ish) rock gear and produced an ancient piece of string that looked like Joe Brown's famous mother's washing line, but long after he had stopped using it. As the crux pitch was a poorly protected traverse around an overhanging nose of rock, I imagined the consequences of a fall and a snapped rope. Shattered, I finished the pitch and, already late, we started the walk back to the car. I was dehydrated and almost passing out through lack of sleep as we drove back into Johannesburg and to the university where about 200 students had been waiting patiently for hours. With a last spurt of adrenalin, the lecture actually went well, and soon after I collapsed into someone's spare bed and slept for 12 hours.

After a couple of days we flew to Durban where I did a repeat performance. With a few days to spare, we hired a car and drove north to the Drakensberg Mountains. These reminded me of the Pennines but on a gigantic scale. Mac and I walked up to a hut where, still desperately tired, I spent a day sleeping whilst Mac went for a long walk round the edge of a plateau. A group of club members arrived at the hut and, at last somewhat revived, Mac and I spent the evening exchanging climbing stories with them. For the first time since arriving back at Heathrow, I felt my spirits lifting.

When we returned to Durban we stayed with a Scottish couple and their young family. They were desperate to return to the UK but knew that their beautiful house was almost worthless under the

273

present political climate. When we left I was shocked to realise that the wife was weeping silently. We could swan in and out of their lives, but they were stuck. Like the days I had spent freeing our gear from Indian customs, I felt again that climbing has led me into all kinds of human situations, far removed from the simple rigmarole of rock-climbing. Whether good or bad, happy or sad, I was living a rich and privileged life. Don't forget it, I told myself sternly as we flew off on the last leg of our trip to Cape Town.

It is self-evident that Cape Town, nestling under Table Mountain, is one of the most beautiful cities in the world. But, as usual, I found the city only moderately interesting. Once again I had been assigned a climbing partner, a young teacher from one of the schools in the city that had produced several South African cricketers. His brief was obviously to sandbag me, for despite me telling him that I wasn't climbing well, he took me to a strange granite dome, only a couple of hundred feet high, and proceeded to lead me up a truly desperate route: a thin vertical crack, followed by a friction traverse on minimal handholds. Protection on the traverse was almost completely absent and, had I come off, I was faced with a huge pendulum. At one point both feet slid off and only some frantic pedalling kept me on the rock. In England it would have been graded at around 5c, which was way beyond my comfort zone that year, which had only seen me break a leg and go for a long walk. I was not best pleased when I reached the stance but was relieved to know that, in the arbitrary way of modern climbs, this was the lower off point. My tormentor had, like our friend in Johannesburg, spurned the use of my ropes. When he fixed the abseil I was unconvinced that the doubled rope would reach the ground. Sure enough, as I slid over a bulge, I could see that the ropes were almost 30 feet too short: "Oh, for fuck's sake," I groaned, at the prospect of an unnecessary epic.

I know my brain cells are disappearing at an alarming rate, but however hard I try I just can't remember how we managed to extricate ourselves. As I'm still alive, and don't recall breaking both legs, we must have done something right. Over the years I seem to have become quite good at escapology. Don't ask me how.

As the prospect of another climb was set against the offer of a visit to a winery there was no real contest, and I spent the rest of the day enjoying the fruits of the vine. Next morning Mac was free and we caught the cable car to the top of Table Mountain. Armed with a guidebook that describes the approach to the climb from above, we stumbled on our choice of route quite by chance. Though it was little more than a classic Very Severe, I can't remember such a sensational position. The climb starts in the bed of a gully and traverses out horizontally above a truly monumental

274

overhang. At the very end is a belay position that was as sensational as anything in the Dolomites. Far below, the buildings of Cape Town were laid out like a map. Forty odd years of climbing hadn't cured me of the sheer horror of our position — yet as soon as I started climbing, everything slotted in to place and the holds appeared in the right places. In fact, once I had persuaded my brain that we were not on the verge off calamity (every knot simultaneously coming undone, a major earthquake, both of us deciding to end it all), it was actually quite easy and before long we were back at the summit plateau, enjoying a cool beer before sliding effortlessly down in the cable car to the fleshpots of Cape Town.

After my last lecture there was time for just one more climb. My flight home was due in the evening, but I wanted to do one route that started from the foot of the mountain and we set out on a long rambling VS that followed, more or less, the line of the cable cars, which zoomed overhead as we climbed. The final pitch actually ended up perilously close to the top station and officials shouted at us to get out of the way. (A couple of years later I heard that a girl had been killed by a cable car, which doesn't bear thinking about.)

At a hut on the plateau the Mountain Club of South Africa were celebrating the end of the UIAA meeting. A Land Rover was there with all my luggage, and only a few hours after reaching the top of Table Mountain, I was wheeling around it in a 747 in the setting sun. I remember one of Mac's lighthearted maxims, 'Always try and do the route on the mountain that dominates the view. Then in your old age you can say — I climbed that'. Now, 15 years later, whenever I see the famous backdrop of Table Mountain, I find myself thinking just that. Next day I was back at Heathrow, this time without any bombshells to contend with, and returned to Sheffield where Paul and Geoff's absence was as painful as it had been when I left.

On face value the trip had been a success. But I have to say that I was left with very mixed feelings about South Africa in general, and the Mountain Club in particular. My three lectures had been given almost exclusively to white audiences. The only blacks were the technicians who helped set up the lecture. The Club's most famous black member, Ed February, had not been around. My hosts were, to a man, welcoming and attentive, but even amongst the so-called liberal, white middle-class, it was not difficult to sense that many of the old attitudes had not changed. It seemed to me that the white minority were clinging to the past and that one day they would inevitably be shown the door. It hasn't happened yet and I can only hope I'm wrong. But I did feel that I had gone to

South Africa under the illusion that I was part of the celebrations of the formation of a multi-racial state, which still seemed a long way off, and that's the most tactful way I can put it.

In the winter of 1996-7 I was made aware of another Bonington extravaganza planned for the spring. When Chris had first visited Tibet on the ill-fated Everest expedition in 1982, the team had flown from Chengdu over eastern Tibet to Lhasa. Chris had photographed a range of mountains stretching away to the north, with one peak dominating the view. Since then Chris had often mentioned his 'Secret Mountain', Sepu Kangri, and in the summer of 1994 he had at last made a reconnaissance with his old friend, Dr Charles Clarke.

I had been to Kongur with Charlie, but hadn't got to know him very well. He lived in Islington with his formidable, funny and charismatic wife Ruth, a renowned child psychiatrist. Their house had become a stopping off point for expedition climbers on their way to or from expeditions: Pete and Joe had been the most frequent visitors. Charlie is a distinguished neurologist but most climbers know him as an expedition doctor. On Kongur, where there were four specialists in high altitude research, I hadn't fully appreciated his skills, but he had successfully treated Chris who had developed pneumonia, so much so that Chris was able to climb the mountain with Pete, Joe and Al Rouse, all much younger than him. Until 1995 I always felt slightly uneasy in Charlie's company. His Harley Street manner and dry humour took some getting used to. And initially I was in awe of Ruth, who seemed able to effortlessly put everyone down, particularly, of course, Charlie.

Chris had got permission for a full-scale expedition, which was slowly taking shape. John Porter, who I knew well from Kendal Film Festival days, Jim Lowther, who I had been with on Harish's trip to Kinnaur, Jim Fotheringham, ditto, and Charlie made up the team. Duncan Sperry, who had been instrumental in raising the sponsorship for Kinnaur was going to be in charge of the state-of-the-art communications we would be taking, and it seemed too good an opportunity to miss out on filming a range of unknown mountains in Tibet, so Chris asked me as well. If Paul had not been killed he would probably have once more come as my minder.

But hang on, I hear you say. You were supposed to have given up expeditioning. That resolution didn't last long. What changed your mind? Come to think of it, why was it okay to go to Tibet and yet still you have a guilty conscience about South Africa?

I rather wish I hadn't written that last paragraph, and I am tempted to leave it out. No, I can't. I've raised questions that I need to answer. To question one, I was far more interested in going to Tibet as a filmmaker than as a climber. Chris had shown me slides

276

of the approach to Sepu Kangri which I found quite entrancing. After my first experience of Tibet in 1988, on Everest, which I felt was a personal disappointment — both in my own performance, but also as an experience I hadn't committed to emotionally — I hoped that returning to an almost unknown area would be more rewarding. I think (I hope) I made it clear to Chris that I had no expectations or ambitions to climb above Base Camp, apart from helping out with carrying gear if needed. I reassured Gemma and Becky that I was not getting involved in proper climbing which they, after the deaths of Paul and Geoff, were far more concerned about than I realised at the time.

As for the hypocrisy in entering Tibet, an oppressed country, I felt that the premise for going was very different from my trip to South Africa. I had no illusions about the Chinese occupation, but didn't think that my going was of any significance to the Chinese. Indeed, even the exiled Dalai Lama has approved of tourism in Tibet, if for no other reason than to see what it's like.

Once again no TV company was interested in financing a film. Even Chameleon, who had post-produced the Rangrik Rang film which was shown on Yorkshire TV, couldn't get interested. So not only was I going on yet another expedition as a one-man band, but I was doing it with no backing whatsoever. I had been here before, but at 54 years old, I felt I was getting a bit long in the tooth to undertake such a speculative venture. However, before I returned to China I managed to fit in three more little adventures, and a wholly unexpected TV project.

Chapter thirty five: Patagonia, Yosemite and visits to Pebble Mill

Once again Mac came up with another good idea for the Christmas break of 1995. This was to go trekking and possibly climbing in Patagonia. I had always dreamed of going down to the bottom of South America and seeing the Towers of Paine, Cerro Torre and FitzRoy, but it was out of the question while I was teaching. With only two weeks at Christmas and New Year it wouldn't be worth the huge air fare to get there. Now time was no problem, but expense certainly was. Then came an unexpected solution. On my first trip to Chile I had met Rodrigo Jordan, one of Chile's leading climbers. He was planning to lead an expedition to K2 in the summer of 1996. The sponsors were Lanchile, the national airline. Rodrigo suggested I came to Santiago to give a lecture to team members in exchange for a free flight from the sponsors. All I would have to find was the airfare from Santiago to Punta Arenas and the normal living costs.

The only snag was that I would have to fly out a week before Mac and Loreto to give my talk and then kick my heels in Santiago. Yet another enforced stay in a capital city with not much to do. I felt lonely and then depressed as Christmas approached and I was almost as far away from my children and friends as I could be.

We were going to Patagonia with Derek Walker. Derek was a Patagonia aficionado. He had been with Chris Bonington and Don Whillans on the famous Towers of Paine expedition in 1962 and, later on, was headmaster of a small British school in Punta Arenas for several years. In 1967 he had attempted The Fortress with Ian Clough. Derek was our own private guide and historian.

When my spell of solitary confinement ended we spent Christmas itself at Mac and Loreto's Pacific home, then we all flew down to what Mac always called Punt Up Your Anus.

It really did seem like the end of the world as we stood gazing out over the Magellan Strait towards Tierra del Fuego. Already we could feel the ever-present wind that could make climbing impossible for days, even weeks. It had a relentless power and, still in my state of depression, I wondered what I was doing here.

Three days later we got out of a minibus at the edge of Lago Sarmiento to get our first feel of the Paine Massif. After taking a couple of steps Mac, Derek and I were blown flat on our backs! We didn't really have a coherent sports plan, though Derek was keen on climbing one of the Cuernos (Horns), an iconic peak a long day's walk along the side of the Lago Nordenskjold. The weather was vile and we camped in woods next to some bedraggled Chilean lads. We asked them how long they had been there: "Since the beginning of December," was the rather gloomy answer. (It was now the beginning of January.) "And how much climbing have you done?" "About 20 minutes."

278

We did manage one short walk on one of the very few fine days, when we had the classic view of the Towers of Paine. The Central Tower, sunlit against a cloudless sky, looked really magnificent and I wondered how Chris and Don must have felt on first seeing it. For Derek, almost every square metre around here was redolent of the events of 30-odd years ago and it was great hearing the stories we already knew, but now seeing exactly where they occurred.

I don't know how keen Mac and Derek were on actually doing a climb, but deep down I knew that I was:

a) too old,

b) no good at aid climbing,

c) not prepared to spend the remainder of my life waiting for a spell of good weather which might never arrive.

To my relief it didn't take too long before the others agreed and we gave up any further thoughts of climbing. Even walking in squally, driving rain wasn't much fun and when Mac proposed hiring a pick-up truck and driving into Argentina to see Cerro Torre and the other legendary giants, we all said: "Yup, bring it on".

So it was that we set off on a long drive across the rolling pampas to the village of Chalten, where we arrived in (yes, you've guessed it) wind and driving rain. We stayed in a refuge where I manage to conjure up two or three meals on an outside barbeque.

Loreto had been impressive both as a strong trekker and a really good companion. So long as she felt she was getting the best of whatever was going she was quite prepared to rough it with us. But her boredom threshold was not great. After two days in the refuge in vile weather, the only thing to do was read books. Mac, Derek and I were quite happy. Loreto became increasingly bored. On the third day she cracked: "Jim, tonight you are not cooking — I have spoken to the guardian and he will cook us steak and chips."

"Oh great." Mac and Derek looked up from their books. "Jolly good."

An hour later Loreto was still unsatisfied: "Mac, shall I ask the guardian to make soup?"

"Please yourself," said Mac.

"How about you Jim?"

"I'm easy."

"MAKE YOUR MIND UP! You never make a decision about anything."

"Okay then — let's have soup." Loreto stalked off to the kitchen and returned almost immediately. "Well, it's too late now, thanks to you." Mac and Derek buried themselves in their books, while I bit my tongue.

At last the sun shone and we walked up the approach to Cerro Torre. It was a beautiful day, and strolling along sandy paths

279

^ *Cerro Torre.*

through little wooded glades it was impossible to believe that the weather could ever be anything but perfect. But when we got our first close-up view of FitzRoy, Poincenot, Cerro Standhart and Cerro Torre itself, we were all jaw droppingly silent. The ice plastered to vertical grey granite walls was unlike anything I have ever seen before, but even without their ice mushrooms were as, or even more spectacular, than the Trango Towers. Once again I was all too aware that these mountains were totally beyond my abilities. But I was glad to have seen them.

In the spring of 1996 I had an offer I couldn't refuse. BBC2 ran a weekly countryside programme called, rather obscurely, *Tracks*. The programmes were made in Birmingham in the now defunct Pebble Mill Studios and they were the forerunner to the present *Countryfile*. I was asked to make a set of short (around five minutes) sequences that showed rock-climbing as neither a how-to-do-it feature, nor as a superstar activity, but from the perspective of an ordinary climber, doing climbs around Britain. I chose climbs at Bosigran in Cornwall, Stanage Edge in Derbyshire, Craig Gogarth in North Wales, Gimmer Crag in the Lake District and Suilven in North West Scotland. All these, bar the last, were obvious choices and I could have made similar lists over and over again. Suilven was a bit unusual. I had driven past this charismatic little triple-summited mountain many times on my way to greater things, and vowed to climb it one day. The problem was that it has quite a long approach. It is over five miles just to get to the foot of the mountain. To climb Suilven, traverse the three summits and walk back, makes a long day. But I had done this solo recently during a lecture trip to Inverness and Aviemore. I managed to bag Suilven and also Stac Polly which necessitated some brisk driving to make the venues. Now I fancied a return to climb a rock route on Suilven, so I included this in my list.

I had recently bought myself a new digicam, and it gave excellent TV quality pictures. A cynical old vision mixer at Pebble Mill suggested, as we looked at the rushes, that it would be a lot easier if I used one, instead of the cumbersome old cameras that, at the time, the Beeb were convinced were the only ones fit for purpose. I explained that he was watching the results of the self same digicam. He was impressed.

The project had the blessing of John King, Head of Programmes at Pebble Mill (and the father of wildlife cameraman Simon King). He was keen that I should integrate my drawings with the moving footage, which I did, rather tentatively. I didn't know it at the time, but the germs of my future work were born in this project.

< *The classic view of the Towers of Paine.*

Something I found out very quickly is that telling a simple story in five minutes is not as easy as I had thought. Every shot has to count and, after shooting the first couple of programmes, I realise why Hollywood directors are hired to make high quality commercials. I had climbed and filmed with Mike Richardson at Bosigran where we climbed the old classic *Doorpost*, and also with him on Gimmer Crag where we did a lovely, but not terribly well-known route. In Wales, I left the climbing to a husband and wife team. Bruce French was a Nottinghamshire and England wicket-keeper. Before he retired he was already a good climber, but climbing was restricted by his playing commitments. Now free of these, he pushed his second interest to become a very good rock-climber. To my surprise he hadn't done *A Dream of White Horses*, one of the great, easy classics of Craig Gogarth, and one of the most photogenic climbs around. When we climbed it I could have done with a second cameraman, as I had to run around to the finishing belay and film Bruce as he climbed confidently and quickly, as did his then wife Elaine. Since then Bruce's climbing has gone from strength to strength and he has also become England's wicket-keeping coach, earning him high praise from the players and the media.

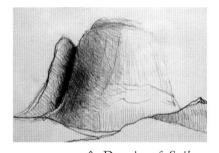

^ *Drawing of Suilven.*

This left only Suilven, the eccentric choice, for which I co-opted Tony Iveson, my old Bristol climbing partner. Over the years we had climbed a lot in the South West, and had two memorable Scottish winter weekends when, whilst giving lectures in Glencoe and Fort William, we had wonderful days on the Aonach Eagach Ridge, and Tower Ridge on Ben Nevis. Hoping that our Scottish luck would continue, we drove up to a campsite near Lochinver and set out early for what we knew would be a long day.

In fact, when we got to the mountain, we climbed only one pitch before the heavens opened and, frustrated, we opted for the ridge walk that I had done only months before. Despite the showers, the views on the ridge of sea, moors and lochans and clouds was sublime. Of the little features that the BBC showed, Suilven was visually the best of the five and made the point that failure is something that has to be accepted. In fact, I thought we had pulled off something really worthwhile out of the ashes. On the long walk back, we had to walk round the slopes of Loch Fionn. I suddenly remembered Mo, years earlier, telling me about climbing with his wife Jackie on Suilven. Describing the walk in, he said that not only was it a long way, but at one point they were walking away from the mountains. "What was worse was that at one point on the way back, we were actually walking towards Suilven." I remembered his words as we did exactly the same thing and laughed at the memory of the man who had brightened up my life for 15 wonderful years.

If you were brought up, like me, on a diet of early *Mountain* magazines, you may understand my misgivings when, for the first time in June 1996, I lurched out of a car hire parking lot at San Francisco airport, aiming for the correct strand of the spaghetti complex of freeways that leads to Yosemite Valley. I remembered stunning black and white photos of soaring walls, flared cracks and holdless slabs on which gaunt, hollow-cheeked hard men like Warrren Harding and Royal Robbins stared, wild-eyed, over bottomless voids. They obviously were never frightened.

Why then was I, in the last throes of middle age, heading for this Mecca of world rock-climbing? The answer lay with my companion. It was all Mac's fault. Ian McNaught Davis is a devout — now what is the word? 'Americaphile'? 'Yankophile'? (I've just rung Mac: "What do you call someone who likes all things American?" "A complete prat.") Whatever. Mac was on his 130-something trip to the States and has climbed and skied extensively, from the Gunks in the east, to the Valley in the west. He assured me that we were heading for a feast of easy classics, tailor-made for our declining powers. I wasn't totally convinced, and felt the first pangs of fright rising in my chest.

Two days later, in Tuolomne Meadows, my worst fears were realised. An Achilles tendon injury, originally acquired playing geriatric pub cricket in Sheffield, had flared up on an innocuous little route on Lambert Dome. The weather was awful (it was actually snowing gently), and I was tempted to cut my losses and go home. Then Mac, inspired, suggested a drive down through Death Valley to Las Vegas and a couple of days climbing on the sandstone of the nearby Red Rock Canyon.

Las Vegas was, even to an old cynic like me, a bit of a shock. I could cope with most of its garish excesses, but the sight of all those blue-rinsed, semi-transparent old ladies endlessly feeding the slot machines was beyond my comprehension. I am still haunted by them. Couldn't someone explain that they weren't ever going to win?

After a gruesome night in a cheap motel, which it obviously wasn't, we took the local climbing guidebook's advice and got a fantastically cheap midweek deal in the Las Vegas Hilton (no kidding). We wanted to do one really excellent climb and after the drive and a day off, my ankle had miraculously improved. We chose a route called *Tunnel Vision*. It was 800 feet long and graded 5.7, well within our capabilities, or so we thought. It was, in retrospect, an eccentric choice on the grounds of shape alone, as it consisted mainly of flared chimneys and various unspecified subterranean ramblings.

Many years ago, when I was merely fat, Mo Anthoine had

^ *It may have been coarse cricket but I still kept my left elbow up, a lesson learnt at St Benedict's 30 years earlier.*

inveigled me into climbing the detestable *Monolith Crack*, a party piece he had perfected in his days as an instructor at Ogwen College. Like Winnie the Pooh on his ill-fated visit to his friend Rabbit, I had become inextricably stuck. It was only Mo's ability to make me laugh that caused some strange convulsion of stomach muscles that enabled me to wobble up, like a fart in the bath, to break surface with a sigh of relief and a vow to never, ever, go near such a route again. Now, in a kind of ecstasy of self-delusion, we stood at the foot of what appeared to be about 10 *Monolith Cracks* stacked up on top of each other. Anyone in the State of Nevada could have told us we were about to make a silly mistake. I knew I was going to get very frightened.

After two or three relatively easy pitches, Mac set off on what was to be the lead of the trip, up an imposing flared chimney that looked horrifyingly unprotected. Eighty feet of squirming brought him to a point where the chimney narrowed and both walls overhung. Mac was worried: "If I can get some decent protection you can lower me off — this is absolutely desperate." After fiddling around for ages, the unwelcome news fluttered down that it was useless. Not trusting it, Mac climbed a few feet higher and at last slotted in a perfect nut. "Might as well carry on now," he muttered before shooting up the last 20 feet to a belay and a whoop of delight — from him, I scarcely need add, not me.

Strangely, though, I climbed through the lower constrictions quite easily. I had watched Mac carefully and, knowing I was even bigger than him, managed to unlock the combinations without too much trouble. Relieved, I started the steep moves at the top. I was appalled. What Mac had made look easy, I found to be the living end. Apoplectic with fury, fright, wasted energy and the desertion of every bit of technique I had ever possessed, I was hauled on to the ledge by Mac, only for him to have to endure a tirade of abuse instead of the congratulations he richly deserved. He heard me out: "Oh Jim, I do enjoy your company," was his disarming remark, accompanied by a beatific smile, as I subsided into grumpy silence.

Above this, the climb was easier, though increasingly peculiar, as we climbed through a weird landscape of sandstone features vaguely reminiscent of the Old Man of Hoy. We arrived at the pitch that gave the climb its wholly appropriate name. Mac's lead again, and he disappeared into the bowels of the earth behind a monstrous flake. Eventually a faint shout, followed by a piercing whistle, jerked me back to reality. I disentangled the belay and set off to see what was coming next. Or rather not to see, for I was immediately plunged into inky darkness. As the ropes led upwards I followed, wondering where I was going, until I could hear Mac somewhere up to my left.

284

> *Mac on the first pitch of* Tunnel Vision.

"Walk along the ledge."

"Oh, really?"

"Well, I think it's a ledge."

"It doesn't bloody well feel like one."

Blindly, I groped, shuffled and slithered towards his voice. Suddenly there was a flash as Mac took a picture, which later provided us with the only visual evidence of the whole pitch. I emerged into daylight on the other side of the flake. After that, two long pitches led to the top and partial satisfaction, for the route description of the descent was incredibly complicated. Amazingly though, we got it right for once and a couple of hours later the blue-rinsed old ladies in the foyer of the Hilton were treated to the sight of two grinning, dust-encrusted climbers in torn shorts and bloody T-shirts, carrying ropes, boots and racks of gear to the lift.

^ *Only when we got home could we see the ledge lit up by Mac's flash.*

285

^ A misleading but impressive view of Half Dome. Snake Dyke *goes more or less up the centre of what is actually a huge slab.*

In the London Hilton we wouldn't have made it through the door. Here we could have carried ice-axes, worn crampons and full down suits and nobody would have batted an eyelid.

Two days later we were back in Yosemite and Mac's master plan was revealed. *Snake Dyke* is a route on Half Dome and Mac had failed to get to the bottom of it with his son Simon several years previously. Ominously, it was again graded 5.7, which seemed to cover a multitude of sins.

Half Dome, seen from the viewpoint of Glacier Point, is a wonderful but wholly misleading sight. The huge, apparently vertical, blank face in front of you is, in fact, a slab set at a reasonable angle and easing all the way to the top. But Glacier Point is a great place to get photos to impress your children and girlfriends (as if).

We decided to bivvy near the foot of the route and plodded up the Half Dome trail past the impressive Vernal and Nevada Falls in the heat of the afternoon, carrying as usual, ridiculously heavy 'sacks. Our prospective bivouac site was not exactly cramped — about three acres of flat ground, but Mac and I stayed reasonably close together, enough to assuage our terror of bears, but far enough apart for Mac not to resort to extreme violence at my snoring. (In the middle of the night at one camp site, Mac had seriously considered tying all the guy ropes of my tent to the hire car and towing me out of earshot.)

Just before we settled down, we were surprised by the arrival

286

^ *Mac leading the crux of* Snake Dyke.

of three young super-fit Californian climbers, two youths and a girl. They explained that they were off to do a nocturnal ascent of *Snake Dyke* to celebrate a Blue Moon. I, for one, was unaware that such a thing existed outside popular songs, but was informed that this occurs when there is a full moon twice in the same calendar month. Tonight would be such an occasion and, what's more, would happen in a cloudless sky.

They invited us to join them, which we declined without too much trouble, and wished them well before settling down to sleep in what, as the moon rose, seemed like broad daylight. As usual before a big climb, I was bundle of nerves and didn't sleep a wink, though Mac disagreed and said my snoring was enough to keep every bear in the Valley well away. At dawn (which was not noticeably lighter that the rest of the night) we set off and I could easily understand how Mac and Simon had got lost, particularly as they had strayed into an area of fallen trees blown down in a storm. This time we found the trail, which led deviously to the foot of the route, which was still in shadow.

What can I say about such a superb climb? Like all classics it takes the easiest line through a huge area of much harder rock. It is never much more than good British VS but, and it is a 'but', the protection is minimal. Those who shudder at the mention of the word 'bolt' should get themselves on the upper pitches, which are probably no more than Severe, but have only one bolt runner between each bolted stance; there is no natural protection at all. The climbing is exactly the same standard, move for move, but it feels much harder as the fall potential grows, particularly if, like Mac, you fail to notice a protection bolt and climb past it giving a possible 100 metre fall, plus rope stretch, if you come off just below the stance. It would be like sliding down a colossal cheese grater. Even if you weren't killed, you could be sprinkled over several plates of spaghetti.

In fact, Mac was climbing really well, as he had done the entire trip, whereas I had long succumbed to the 'Oh-God-what-am-I-doing-here?' syndrome, a question that was not difficult to answer as far as the view was concerned. What a stupendous place! Once you are above the valley, Yosemite is as wild and beautiful as anywhere. Here, the views across to Glacier Point and down towards the unmistakeable profile of El Cap, now actually below us, were sublime.

As we gained height the angle eased. Suddenly, in the middle of a long run-out, I made an amazing discovery: I could stand up and walk! After another pitch we unroped, but kept our rock boots on to the top, for a slip here would be both embarrassing then, shortly afterwards, terminal. The last few hundred feet seemed to take forever. It was scorchingly hot and windless. I was puffing, but, of course, Half Dome is nearly 9000 feet. Could I be about to succumb to the lowest ever case of pulmonary oedema?

Eventually we arrived at the flat summit, along with dozens of hikers who had flogged up the Half Dome Trail and braved its extraordinary and rather frightening line of ladders up the final few hundred feet. Descending them, against the panic-stricken hordes coming up, was interesting, with one severe case of hysterics to contend with, but luckily, Mac quickly calmed me down and the descent passed off without further incident. We were happy and fulfilled.

The fright quota for the holiday had been realised and we could go home with a clear conscience. Later I read the account of the first ascent in Steve Roper's excellent *Camp Four: Recollections of a Yosemite Rock Climber*. As you may imagine, it was a bit of an anticlimax to find it described as 'a perfect beginner's climb'. As Mac and I had almost a hundred years of climbing between us, our egos were slightly bruised. But hey — I will never be a hollow-cheeked, wild-eyed hard man.

Chapter thirty six: Sepu Kangri – One

T he first time I stayed in Lhasa in 1988 was in the indescribable Lhasa Holiday Inn, a stupendously ghastly building that, at the time, was far from completion, or perhaps was already falling down. It was cold, the food was dire and nothing worked. I hated it. On their Sepu Kangri reconnaissance in 1996, Chris and Charlie had found the exquisite Khada Hotel in the Tibetan Quarter, only a short walk from the Barkhor, the old market surrounding the Jokhang Temple.

When we arrived the following year, after the two-hour drive from Lhasa airport, and pulled into the little courtyard to be greeted by the hotel staff in traditional Tibetan dress, I felt that the omens were already good. All our rooms were beautifully decorated with intricate Tibetan motifs. Although the thin air of Tibet was as big a shock to the system as it had been the first time, Chris and Charlie were so laid back that despite the huge list of Things To Do, I never felt the pressure that in 1988 that had precluded any kind of enjoyment. I knew all the team and the competitive edge was wholly absent.

This year, armed with a lightweight digital video camera, I could actually enjoy Lhasa. What's more, the camera was not so different from the ubiquitous tourist cameras and for once I could film without the irritating crowd of gawping onlookers buggering up every shot. It is a strange phenomenon but I always found, when shooting a documentary, that it you didn't get on top of it on the

^ *The Potala Palace, Lhasa.*

289

very first day, it was hard to make amends. This time, as we left Lhasa I knew we probably had a good five minutes of edited video from over an hour of footage shot.

We travelled in style in two Landcruisers en route for Nakchu, billed as the highest city in the world. This may or may not be true, but it is surely the highest ugly city in the world. The previous year Chris and Charlie (aided by their resourceful interpreter Pasang, who was with us again this year) had cunningly driven through the city and camped a few miles beyond it, a ploy we repeated this year. At well over 4000 metres we endured a bitterly cold night on the Tibetan Plateau. We awoke with headaches and were all, in varying degrees, tired and grumpy. It was here that we observed a pilgrim, prostrating himself full length at every step, presumably on his way to Lhasa, over 100 miles away. Strangely, though it never crossed my mind at the time, the pilgrim and his monumental journey of faith and self-denial became a motivating force four years later when I started a long solo bike ride from the Shetlands all he way down to Land's End.

There was still a lot of winter snow on the Plateau and we had to drive over several 5000 metre passes. On the last one, the Shar La, I was particularly pleased with the telephoto footage I shot of our heavily laden lorry groaning up the icy ruts at the top of the pass. Shot on a tripod, it involved a slow zoom out to keep the lorry the same size in the frame. With only one chance, I was aware that at this height, being almost completely unacclimatised, it would be all too easy to mess up. From here it was downhill all the way to Khinda where our walk started.

Compared with K2 this walk-in was a doddle. Compared with Everest from Tibet it was a gruelling epic. (The Everest walk in is less than 50 metres!) This one was a leisurely three days' walk, at first up the beautiful Chih-chu valley to Samda monastery. The walk involved two crossings of the river by wooden cantilever bridges. The valley was quite small and the walking easy. The monastery is actually not Buddhist, but Bon, a pre-Buddhist religion that is still practised in Tibet. It is animistic and shamanistic, but to the ignorant eye (mine) it is identical to Buddhism. The only difference I could see is that you walk round the chortens en route the opposite way to Buddhist ones. As I could never remember which way to go in Nepal, I was totally confused here and still don't feel confident enough to ask which was which.

Beyond the monastery, a long day for the unacclimatised led to the first views of Sepu Kangri: Chris's Secret Mountain. It sat at the far end of a long lake, Sam Tso Taring, which was completely frozen over. So the last three miles of the walk were easy and

^ Dawn on Sepu Kangri.

absolutely horizontal as we tramped along the ice which, as it clearly supported yaks, should easily be thick enough for us. At the end of the lake were a few ramshackle single-storey houses, the permanent home of an extended family of yak herders. Here was our Base Camp.

The more I think about it, the more I think that our Tibetan friends must have thought that time travellers were visiting them. Their environment was, even by Tibetan standards, more like the Stone Age or, at best, a medieval community like St Kilda in the Outer Hebrides. Here their lives were almost completely bypassed by the 20th century. Suddenly, in a riotous outbreak of coloured Gore-Tex, computers, video cameras and mysterious packages of ropes, spiky things attached to boots made of goodness knows what, pale men, some obviously giants, appeared out of nowhere and set up home only a few metres away. True, they had already had some warning when Chris and Charlie visited on their recce the year before, but it is hard to imagine what they thought of us. Here, more than any other expedition I have been on, I was actually aware that once again I had dropped into someone else's life, but not just life — their culture, their whole existence. We had nothing much in common and the only really useful things we could give them were medicine and rope. The former, as our time at Base Camp lengthened, grew increasingly important.

As we unpacked and revealed more and more goodies to our bemused neighbours, Chris was in near despair. His box containing all his climbing gear was missing. I'm afraid that experienced Bonington watchers didn't pay much attention to his predicament. Chris's capacity for losing things was legendary and we imagined that the missing box would eventually be unearthed. The new boy, John Porter, helped him search whilst Chris, almost in tears, had given up: "Chris," sighed Jim Fotheringham, sounding like someone's long suffering father, "what's that you're sitting on?" Crisis over.

During our first week or so at Base Camp, we saw the comet Hale Bopp on clear nights. I had been impressed with the sight in England. Here, at around 5000 metres with no city lights, the sight was spectacular as it blasted through space. Looking through binoculars, as the frozen lump of rock trailed remorselessly across

the skies, it made me feel horribly lonely — don't ask me why.

The to-ings and fro-ings on the mountain have been described in great detail in the book *Tibet's Secret Mountain* written by Chris and Charlie. My role in that trip was peripheral at best, but I do recall looking at four specks inching their way up a long snowslope apparently beneath a hanging sérac, and seriously wondering why they were doing that. It was a bit like a lapsed Catholic watching the faithful queuing for confession. After 40-odd years of climbing mountains I just couldn't see the point of it any more.

This was in stark contrast to watching Charlie as he dealt with the worst medical crisis in his expeditioning career. The problem was not with one of us, but with one of the yak herders, Tsini. She was ill and Charlie was asked to examine her. He found a lump in her abdomen that was causing her terrible pain. Charlie diagnosed an ectopic pregnancy, which would normally require surgery — impossible to perform here. If the problem was

< Tsini.

^ Charlie with Kharte, Tsini's grateful husband.

left to take its course it could mean death. Charlie, availing himself of satellite technology, rang a gynaecologist consultant in London who confirmed Charlie's diagnosis and advised strongly against an operation, but suggested a course of painkillers and antibiotics. Charlie gave her injections of diamorphine (that's heroin to you and me) and gradually Tsini recovered. Backing their horses both ways, her family called a monk from Samda monastery who I filmed in the smoky interior of the house as he chanted and beat his drum. Slowly Tsini recovered and Charlie's reputation grew.

As an observer I found the whole protracted event deeply moving. Both Charlie and I found Tsini incredibly charismatic, with a dignity and beauty that were beyond description. I don't think it is any exaggeration to say that we both came to love Tsini and her family. Certainly now, when I remember Sepu Kangri, Tsini is the first person I think of. Is she still alive? What did she think of the strange, grey haired man who had saved her life? It must have seemed to her that she had been the recipient of a miracle. Charlie was certainly revered and when we returned in 1998, his fame had spread far and wide.

For return we did. Persistent foul weather stopped any real summit bid in 1997 and it got warmer and wetter by the day. The lake was slowly melting. Pasang interviewed one of the yak herders who, he said, knew when it was unsafe to cross it: "How could he tell?" we asked.

"He has fallen in," was the reply.

293

All the way back to Lhasa, then Kathmandu, then home, Chris and Charlie were planning to return. I was incredibly frustrated as I knew I had the makings of an interesting documentary and was deeply reluctant to give up, even though the thought of returning to the same place twice in two years was unappealing. I let Chris know that I wanted to come back to finish the job and hoped that in a year's time I would be suitably motivated. I remembered the words of Mark Twain, 'There is probably no pleasure equal to the pleasure of climbing a dangerous Alp; but it is a pleasure strictly confined to people who find pleasure in it'. In the meantime, another much more exciting adventure arrived, almost out of the blue.

I say 'almost' for this was a project that had simmered away on the back burner for the last two years. But it came as a mighty surprise when, not long after I returned from Tibet, I got a phone call from my old friend, TV producer Chris Lister: "It's on. Can you come up to Orkney in two weeks?" Bloody hell, Chris. You've done it.

Chapter thirty seven: Hoy

'It' was the reality of making a TV documentary about Catherine Destivelle soloing the Old Man of Hoy. It was an idea born out of frustration, when Chris Lister and I had had our latest proposals rejected out of hand by various companies, including BBC2, who had almost, but not quite, accepted one I was inordinately proud of. It was so good I can't remember for the life of me what it was.

I certainly had a bit of history with the Old Man of Hoy. I had climbed it once, properly, back in 1983 as part of a charity event. This plan was to climb 100 routes in 10 days, starting with the Old Man, and finishing at Land's End. I did all the climbs with a Fine Art student from Bristol, Phil Kershaw. Paul Nunn had joined us on Hoy. Since then I had made a little five minute short for HTV in 1994 featuring septuagenarian Mike Banks who, at 72, had been the oldest man to climb the Old Man. (He returned in 2000 to do it again at 78, having briefly surrendered his record to a 75-year-old. This provoked Chris Bonington to think about a bid himself when he gets to 80 in 2014, which he has probably forgotten.)

^ *Catherine Destivelle.*

So this would be my third visit to the Orkneys, an area I had fallen in love with on my first visit and even now, 27 years later, it is a passion that shows no sign of abating. Every time I sail across the Pentland Firth on the St Ola car ferry and see the weathered Old Man standing next to the huge red ramparts of St John's Head, my heart leaps and I feel I am coming home.

And what about Catherine Destivelle? In the 80s she had been one of the most famous climbers in the world. Only Reinhold Messner could challenge her, and films of her soloing in the Verdon Gorge and elsewhere had made it into mainstream British TV. Even now I get asked: "Do you know that beautiful French girl who climbs with no ropes?"

It had taken Chris Lister months of patient negotiating to line up Catherine, the crew and, of course, the film deal with the Discovery Channel. Like playing with a giant Rubik's Cube, every time Chris got one side correct, something would invariably go wrong with another. At last everything clicked with only three potential problems. One, we would be filming in the height of the midge season, not to be taken lightly. Two, the birds would still be nesting. Three, Catherine was pregnant. In fact, the weather was so

^ Phil Kershaw, the first time I climbed the Old Man in 1983.

constantly windy and foul that even the midges gave up. The birds had to be endured, though Catherine was always wary of them. As for Catherine's pregnancy, well, it never seemed to affect her, apart from a compulsion to eat fish and chips — not a serious problem on Hoy.

I can't remember ever starting a film suffering so much stage fright. Most of it was misplaced, but initially I did wonder how Catherine would cope with it all; climbing on the sandy, slimy rock in lousy weather, working with an English crew and, unlike all her previous films, making one that was not her own idea.

The reality was that it could not have been easier. Catherine was the epitome of the professional. As a climber she was superb, which, of course, we knew already, but her attention to detail was impressive. As a performer she could not have been better: calm, articulate, eloquent and, while not exactly a stand up comic, wryly humorous when it was needed. Her English was almost perfect. One day, when the weather was really appalling, she was interviewed at great length, first in English, then, as we were making a French version, in her native tongue. Surprisingly, she later told me that she found the French version nowhere near as good as the English. The problem was, having given a perfectly good answer to a question, she found herself translating her own words into French, and this made it sound very stilted.

As the days sped by (we shot the whole thing in only five days including the interview) we all became friends. I had known Catherine for a lot longer than the rest, but it was a good sign when she could discuss Harry Ramsden's fish and chips restaurants with

^ *Catherine on the crux being filmed by Gavin Crowther.*

Nick Lyons, our ever patient sound recordist. And on a memorable evening in the Youth Hostel in Rackwick Bay she opened up to all of us and told us what it was like to be famous. She said that a lot of her fans had quite unrealistic opinions about her, that she hated being touched, and that occasionally, when she didn't live up to expectations, hero-worship could easily turn to anger.

I genuinely think that Catherine enjoys her infrequent climbing trips to the UK. Of course she is still recognised, but there is still a bit of traditional British reserve, which means she can sit in a pub without being mobbed. On quite a few occasions I have seen climbers almost going out of their way to ignore her. I am sure Catherine is grateful for this, but a naughty little bit of me wonders how long it would take before she missed the attention.

Now, 13 years later, Catherine and Erik Decamp are divorced and Viktor, their son, is a teenager. Catherine is now in her 40s — as beautiful as ever and still climbing brilliantly. She is no longer the pin-up girl she used to be, but has a maturity and charisma which is, to my mind, even more attractive. My week with her and our little film team was one I will treasure forever. It was the first time Chris Lister had ever come with us and I can still see his slight figure huddled in the rain and wind on the cliff top opposite the Old Man as he produced the documentary that we both knew would be a winner. For some months past I didn't think he had looked very well, and was not completely surprised when he was later diagnosed with lung cancer.

^ *Waiting at the first stance gossiping with John Whittle.*

Back in Leeds, my favourite number one all-time great editor, Barry Reynolds, edited the programme. It was he who had made the K2 film so special, and he came up trumps again with *Rock Queen*, our not terribly original title for Catherine's efforts.

Before I leave the Old Man (not forever) I must mention our safety crew, John Whittle and 'Cubby' Cuthbertson. Both of them are climbers in their own right. Cubby, in fact, has been right at the forefront of Scottish climbing, both winter and summer, for many years. But they also have a long and distinguished role as safety officers in innumerable documentaries. *Rock Queen* was, for me, the stand-out project where camera crew needed looking after, and they did it brilliantly. In addition to making sure Gavin Crowther, my co-cameraman, and I didn't fall, jump or push each other off the Old Man, they were also more than willing porters. On top of that, they were both great company. One afternoon John and I were waiting for hours on the first stance, while a party of three made a laborious ascent of the Old Man. With nothing better to do we indulged in scurrilous gossip about anyone and everyone, including our fellow crew: "Very interesting that," said Chris Lister that evening, "you forgot to turn your radio mikes off!"

Chris Lister was determined that we celebrate in style on the last evening and had booked a table for 11 at the only restaurant on Hoy. It turned out to be a huge room, entirely empty except for our table. It reminded me of a school canteen. The waitress stood by shyly, a bit forlorn.

"Um, can we see your wine list?"

She looked stricken: "We have only 10 bottles in at the moment."

"Oh well, better bring 'em all out."

The meal was okay in a basic Scottish kind of way and we were determined to relax and enjoy it. Suddenly, to my horror, Chris called for silence and announced that, as the whole exercise was my fault and I was used to after-dinner speaking, I'd better stand and say a few words. I was nonplussed. I couldn't think of anything to say ay all. Then from the recesses of my mind came a story I had once read of a banquet given in, I think, the Lycée Palace by General de Gaulle for Harold Macmillan, presumably after some grim diplomatic negotiations over the Common Market had gone wrong. Apparently, after one particularly chilly silence Dorothy Macmillan had leant across to Madame de Gaulle and asked her what was the most important thing in life? "A penis," Madame replied with conviction. There was a thunderstruck silence. Then General de Gaulle came to the rescue. "She means 'appiness." I recounted this and proposed a toast "to 'appiness" and sat down quickly. Erik told me that his only regret was that the story would not translate into French. Catherine, when she occasionally rings up from France still giggles and wishes me it.

When everything was in the can, we returned to the mainland with a couple of days to spare before Catherine and Erik were due to fly home, and I drove them round the north-west coast of Scotland, the most stunning coastline in the world. Still buzzing with the knowledge that we had done something special the couple of days passed in a rosy glow. I dropped them off at the airport and looked for signs for the M74 and the South. As I pulled onto the motorway it started raining and I realised that I was blinking back tears — of what? Joy, tinged with sadness that is was all over, the best week's filming I had ever had. Or come to think of it, would probably ever have, given my old age and decrepitude.

298

Chapter thirty eight: Tibet for the Last Time

^ *Sue Coonan.*

Back to unfinished business. Somehow, we had to get a proper deal if I was to go back to Tibet in 1998. If anyone, having read all these pages, still thinks that making climbing documentaries is one of the most exciting jobs in the world, I will disillusion them one last time. Only about one in 10 ideas bears fruit. From a proposition to a deal signed and sealed with a television company, is a protracted nightmare. Phone calls, emails and faxes (not many, even then) followed by trips to London, hours wasted in corridors waiting to see the wrong person. ("It's not me you should be talking to. Let me see if I can get hold of Tristram… He'll see you next week, if that's all right?") The amount of collective time and money wasted knows no bounds. No wonder that these days more and more films are made independently on tiny budgets.

Chris Lister's health was deteriorating and Martin Belderson, who had been director on *Rock Queen*, did most of the wheeler dealing. What he wanted to do was a set of eight programmes, a 'drama doc' to be shown on successive nights. Perhaps 'docu soap' was a better description. In addition to extensive coverage on the expedition, with little digi-cameras issued to all the climbers, crews would film wives, girlfriends, parents and in my case, daughters while we were in Tibet.

At home my life was in its usual mess. On Sepu Kangri, I had given myself a good talking to. I was still smitten with Annie, who had moved from Bristol to Shropshire. Hugo was, as Gemma once observed, my surrogate son. I resolved on my return to England, to do something about it. We had a short visit to Disneyland Paris, in which Hugo was in seventh heaven, while Annie seemed to find me a complete pain and on our return we had a fall out that was to last years.

Crestfallen and hurt, I floundered around. Then Sue (she of the not wanting to be taken out for a drink) became the centre of my attentions and would stay that way for the next 10 years. I fell heavily in love — a love that I always knew deep down was one-sided. But not long before I left for Tibet again, Sue told it to me straight — that I was a good friend but nothing more. She had a strange way of demonstrating this and in the several weeks before I left we had a secret relationship that, looking back on it, seemed rather strange. But I was in bliss, and naively hoped she felt the same for me. When I left Sheffield I was convinced that this time I would return to the sort of domestic happiness that I hadn't had for years.

So, once again, we flew into Kathmandu and then to Lhasa. Two indications of how I felt; first on the way from the airport to the Tibet Guest House, where I have always stayed in Kathmandu,

I noticed we were going a different way from normal. "Big road works," explained Scott Muir, who had flown out a week earlier. On his first Himalayan expedition, and almost young enough to be my grandson, Scott was still blown away by the sights and sounds of the East, whereas jaded, cynical old Curran only noticed road works. Then on the flight to Lhasa, the third time I had done it, I didn't even bother to look out of the windows to spot Everest. I didn't like myself for this and knew my attitude was all wrong.

What I did notice as we approached Lhasa, was that it was a very different landscape from the one I had grown used to. Very heavy rain had caused major flooding and the brown plains of Tibet were riven with streams and rivers, and the whole place looked more like Holland. The drive to Khinda was a saga of muddy obstacles, and the beautiful cantilever bridges on the walk in had been swept away, necessitating Tyrolean traverses, swinging wildly over the still swollen flood waters, and pulling (or being pulled) across in a sit harness. The idyllic walk of the year before was now a lot more gruelling and, feeling in any case that this was a job of work that needed finishing rather than the adventure into the unknown, I arrived at Base Camp resigned to the next few weeks, rather than relishing the new challenge of making the 'socu dope', as I was prone to call it.

It is curious that approaching the end of my film career, I had at last got a director and crew to make life easier. I got on very well with Martin, who was eager to show that he was the director. Consequently, my suggestions weren't often heeded and it seemed to me that we were shooting far too much footage. In the end we had something like 80 hours to edit into a mere four hours of finished video. The problem was that, however accurately this was logged, it was quite impossible for the editor to remember everything and I was disappointed that quite a lot of the best footage never saw the light of day. But that was still a long way off.

This year Jim Lowther, Jim Fotheringham and John Porter all pulled out of the trip, to be replaced by the aforementioned Scott Muir, Graham Little and Victor Saunders. Both Scott and Victor in particular became very keen on shooting video on their little camcorders, and this year we had a secret weapon in Greig Cubitt from Independent Television News. He was to send reports back to ITN via satellite link. He was utterly professional, enabling all our various bits of gear to work despite some stroppy yaks' efforts to destroy them by total immersion on the walk in. When all his gear was set up we could view our own rushes before Greig edited three-minute reports. (It was apparently cheaper to have editing gear at Base Camp, rather than sending long unedited chunks of footage via the satellite.) The happy result of this was that being able to view their own footage, the learning curve of the climbers was quite impressive — from home movie wafting around all over the place with the camera to well-framed static shots by the end of the expedition. Even though I played a kind of anchorman role at Base Camp, I could see that my usefulness was becoming more and more peripheral. Once again, Charlie Clarke and I were thrown together. Our tents were within chatting distance and both of us could find endless amusement in the doings of Chris and the team. I remembered Charlie's comment at the end of the first expedition when yet another snowfall hit our camp and Chris suddenly decided that the weather was picking up at last. Charlie murmured to me: "I wonder if I could be the first doctor in the world to get someone sectioned via email?"

^ *Charlie the dentist.*

Now Charlie was in his element, treating patients who had covered vast distances to ask to be cured, which sometimes was sadly impossible. One day a group of really sinister horsemen approached. I was quite apprehensive: "Christ, they look like the Rolling Stones after a month on heroin and vodka." Charlie spotted the source of the problem, an old man with advanced cancer eating into his jaw. Warning us to keep well away, for they all seemed to be carrying diseases of one sort or another, he explained, as tactfully as his translated words would allow, that there was no hope for him and that he needed to go home to die in comfort. Sometimes I thought Charlie had the hardest job of all of us, and I was amazed that his enthusiasm remained unabated throughout the trip. On another occasion, he pulled an infected tooth from a very pretty young Tibetan girl, while I filmed the gory scene. Charlie's only comment was that it was just his luck to have to perform dentistry now that dentist Jim Fotheringham wasn't here.

We had a little adventure that Charlie and Martin Belderson enjoyed more than me. While Chris and the other climbers rested after their first unsuccessful attempt on Sepu Kangri, Charlie, Martin and I took time off to go down to Samda Monastery to witness the Devil Dances. We felt a bit like teenagers allowed out on a Saturday night to a school disco. We arrived at the monastery at the same time as a heavy fall of wet snow. While several monks tried feebly to clear it from the main courtyard, I filmed inside the

^ Not a natural rider.

monastery as monks tried out their array of frightening masks, practised their dance moves and generally got themselves into a state of pre-match euphoria. We had been given a room for our stay, and were fed on the dreaded Tibetan tea, salted with rancid yak butter, as well as bits of dried yak. This was a combination that reduced me to a dreadful state — leaking from every orifice and feeling like death. To Charlie's shame and my despair, he had forgotten to bring any medication at all. It was probably this that later provoked my comment that the only way to get any doctoring on the trip was to be young, Tibetan and beautiful, all criteria that I failed to meet.

I will draw a veil over how I passed the next 24 hours. Suffice to say that Martin filmed Devil Dances while I groaned, retched, shat and shivered. (Even now I can make myself feel quite nauseous just thinking about it.) When we returned to Base Camp I was so weak I had to travel by Tibetan pony which, given the state of my nether regions and my total lack of ponymanship (is that a real word?), was a mixed blessing.

I recovered quite quickly when the good Doctor Clarke resumed his duties. Since I had arrived on a pony I can only assume he must have elevated me to honorary Tibetan status. The climbers set off for what would be the last attempt on the mountain and once again we could only wait and hope.

Celebrating my return to health, I went for a walk one afternoon, taking the camera and tripod to shoot some reflections on the lake lit by a low sun. As I filmed, a herd of yaks ambled into the frame. The herder kept them together with well-aimed stones that wouldn't have disgraced a Test match fielder. As I finished the shot I realised it was Tsini. In the evening light she came and sat

303

next to me looking me full in the eyes. It was a strange moment. She looked puzzled. We both smiled a bit, and then the moment, whatever it was, passed. What was she thinking? Come to think of it, what was I thinking? There was undoubtedly a shared experience despite the huge gulf between us. Charlie, I know, was even more affected. I walked back to the tents, wondering, yet again, how I came to be in this far-flung corner of the world, communicating with these wonderful people whose lives had briefly entangled with ours.

That evening we heard on the radio that Chris had dropped out of the summit team and, as dusk fell, he arrived, all in, at Base Camp. Doing my duty, I filmed him as he admitted tearfully, that he was holding the others back. Chris is well-known for crying easily and I have to admit I do too. I gave him a very weepy hug, which Martin filmed. Both our shots were later edited together in the finished film, which I still find both moving and embarrassing in equal parts.

High on the mountain, Graham Little opted for a solo ascent of a subsidiary peak and a very dodgy descent that he survived seemingly more by luck than judgement. Then, from their top camp, Scott and Victor missed out on the summit, but only by a couple of hundred feet as the clouds rolled in and visibility on a featureless snow slope made the last little stretch unjustifiably dangerous.

So the expedition had failed again. In his prime Chris would, I'm sure, have been bitterly disappointed, but now he was able to treat it philosophically, though deep down I'm sure he was sad to fail on this, probably his last, major expedition. For Charlie it was slightly different, as he was later to write, '...these three trips, above all others, had made me feel that I had enjoyed a life that had been truly my own, that no one can take away. I think I shall remember them when I die'.

To our great relief, Victor and Scott descended in one piece, and then for the last time we dismantled Base Camp, watched silently by our extended family, to whom we gave everything we didn't need, including, to their obvious delight, quite a lot of spare rope. At last, with much cursing, the yaks were loaded and it was time to go. The Tibetans looked on impassively. I choked back tears and then took the first steps towards home. This was the end of an era for me. I knew that it marked the curtain call of my expedition career. Now I was counting the days before I would see Sue again.

In Lhasa I decided that I would buy a decent present for her and visited a Tibetan artists' group. About a dozen men sat painting incredibly fine and detailed thangkas, wall hangings describing the Wheel of Life, with amazing skill and incredible detail. With impressive lack of will power, I ended up buying three.

We flew back to Kathmandu on a brilliant clear morning, with spectacular views of Everest as we drifted over and past the huge Kangshung Face. Once again I took little notice. After only one night in the familiar Tibet Guest House, we flew back to Heathrow. I had volunteered to take the film gear back to Sheffield, then Leeds, and hired a car at the airport. Then I rang Sue to tell her what time I would be back. There was no reply. I felt the first qualms of icy dread run through me. Totally jet-lagged I was stopped by a motorway pile-up and car fire only miles from my turn-off and actually fell asleep, to be awakened by frantic hooting from behind me as the traffic started moving. It was a cold October night when I let myself into my house at 2 am — far too late to ring Sue. But I went to bed full of foreboding. Please, not again, I thought.

Chapter thirty nine: Floundering Around

^ *John Porter.*

Within a week my worst fears were realised. Sue had fallen for someone else. I was heartbroken and spent a great deal of the following weeks drunk, or in tears, or both. Which made absolutely no difference. On top of that, I had been commissioned to write Chris Bonington's biography. This should have been a welcome distraction, but writing a book is just about the loneliest activity I can think of, outside of going to jail. By contrast, editing film is an intensely social activity, normally involving three or four people working closely together. Painting pictures is lonely, but at least you get instant feedback, whenever you or anyone else enters the studio. With writing, all you have are those words on paper that concern you at the moment. For example, on this book I have now written over 100,000 words, but I can't re-read them every day. So if, as I do, I aim to write 1000 words a day, it is hard to do a great deal of socialising and friends, quite mistakenly, feel I ought to be left alone.

Today is a good example. It is Sunday November 14th, Remembrance Sunday. It is now 2.20 pm, and I haven't actually spoken to anyone else at all since Saturday evening. It will not be unusual if I don't make contact with anyone until tomorrow morning, when I go to the gym. I am also writing about an episode in my life that caused me a lot of pain. So I'm not exactly full of the joys of spring at the moment. If anything unexpected happens, like a phone call, I'll let you know.

As well as the Bonington book, John Porter, Brian Hall and I had decided to bring back the Kendal Mountain Film Festival. This time it was going to be bigger, better organised and, like other similar festivals around the world, heavily sponsored. It was all those things, but somehow we never made any money out of it, and our middle-aged stress levels were probably quite dangerous. I once joked to John, who at the end of one festival, had dark rings round his eyes like a panda through lack of sleep, worry and alcohol: "If you snuff it, I'm going to write on your tombstone, 'He Burned the Kendal at Both Ends'." Despite feeling grim all the way through the festival, there was no doubt that it was a great success, and since then it has been a big fixture in the climbing world.

In 2010 it is still going strong, though John, Brian and I have all, more or less, lost involvement in it. The festival was a big part of my life, but unlike John and Brian, I never had the remotest interest in the financial side of it. As Arts Director I was responsible for choosing a painting exhibition, and some of the photography. I also had the dubious privilege of previewing most of the films, and selecting an interesting and varied programme.

306

^ *Becky and baby Patrick.*

^ *Gemma in Spain.*

So at the end of 1998, I was left with a half-finished, or half-started biography, a broken heart, and a passing involvement with the production of the Sepu Kangri film. I mentioned before that Gemma and Becky were interviewed on camera while I was away. Despite the popular perception that 'reality' programmes are completely false and contrived, there is a long tradition of one-to-one interviewing in which the presence of a camera actually reveals stark and sometimes uncomfortable truths. So it was with the girls, who spoke eloquently and far more frankly to the camera than they ever had done to me. I had originally had no qualms about whether or not they should do the interview. Now I even had doubts as to whether I wanted it shown. But we had all gone into this with our eyes open and agreed to accept whatever came out. It did underline forcibly that I couldn't put them through, in Gemma's words: "Another summer waiting for that phone call."

Speaking of phone calls, no one has rung and I haven't quite made my 1000 word target, but I'm going to bed.

Monday November 15th. Thinking about last night, I realise that I have now written six books, and barely mentioned them in this, the seventh. As most authors, including me, are often quizzed about the nitty-gritty of writing a book, I will try and describe my own procedure, if it can be called that.

I wrote the Trango book for the simple reason that if I didn't, no one else would, and the story of the first ascent was worth a bit more than an article in *Mountain* magazine. It was written in all sorts of bits of spare time and I remember writing during a coffee break in the Foundation Course staff room with constant interruptions from phone calls, students and staff. For some reason I have always been able to cut myself off from my surroundings. It was writing Trango that I worked out a method that I've used more or less ever since. It goes as follows:

(1) Try to write 1000 words, sometimes more, sometimes less,

(2) Next day, re-read and correct these first 1000 words and write another 1000,

(3) Repeat until book is finished.

One comment that is frequently made is that my writing sounds like me talking, the implication being that it is easy to do. Nothing could be further from the truth. As Sue Evans, who puts onto computer all my hand-written crossings out and endless tinkering, would tell you, it is a lengthy and continual business to get it right. Why do I do it all in longhand? It just feels right. I write on one side of lined paper, double-spaced. Small changes go in the in-between lines; bigger ones on the other side of the paper.

Trango: the Nameless Tower was a bit of a shot in the dark and I never expected to write another, but *K2: Triumph and Tragedy* needed writing. *Suspended Sentences* was written as a bit of light relief from K2. Both *K2: The Story of the Savage Mountain* and *High Achiever* were written primarily to see if I could. The second K2 book called for a lot of research, as did Bonington's biography. Neither book came easily to me, and I don't feel inclined to repeat either genre. My respect for historians and biographers has soared, but I don't think I am either. In fact, I know I'm not.

My last book, about a long, solo bike ride, was easily the most enjoyable to write. The only thing I really didn't like was the title, *The Middle-Aged Mountaineer*, which placed it firmly in the climbing category, whereas it was really a travel book. I wanted to call it It's a Long Way from Muckle Flugga, which was thought by the publisher to be too obscure. A year or so later, to my chagrin, the self-same title was used for a book about a motorbike journey. Which brings me neatly to the sticky problem of what to call this book. What is annoying is that you, dear reader, already know, as it will be written in big letters on the dust jacket. So you know something I don't, but you can't tell me, which is bloody irritating because I have already spent many wasted hours trying to think of something erudite, witty and appropriate, so far with absolutely no success.

A rather unexpected consequence arose from my decision to stop expeditioning. I had confidently imagined that once free of all the commitments an expedition entailed, I would be able to concentrate on rock-climbing for fun. Maybe it was my age, maybe a seemingly never ending succession of knee problems, but, like a lapsed Catholic who has stopped believing in God and, therefore, the basis of his religion, I found that without expeditions I couldn't sustain any real interest in endlessly going to Stanage or Froggatt and doing the same climbs over and over again. This wasn't helped by a lack of a regular partner. Since Paul's death I had climbed regularly with Mike Richardson. But now his illness stopped him climbing altogether, and my own commitment was increasingly fragile.

I did, however, keep on walking in Derbyshire, which probably kept me sane. For now I was in the grip of really bad depression. I missed Sue with a horrible intensity. Not just for the obvious reasons, but for her fun, humour and companionship. No one else seemed able to take her place, and I despaired of ever finding that kind of friendship again. I couldn't help thinking back to the time in Bristol, when I had made my 'pact with the devil', as I had come to think of it. I had put my art and climbing above all else and now I was paying the price. Melodramatic? Yes, but still basically true. Too late, I decided to stop being such a self-centred bastard. Tough shit, said the world, you've chosen your way of life, now live with it. But I'm a nice bloke now! Maybe, but women go for bastards, particularly the dangerous ones I fall for. Well, said the world, ain't that just sweet and dandy; a perfect case of the punishment fitting the crime?

If I have learnt anything about depression, it has to be that I can just about carry on working through it. (I have already mentioned editing the Kongur film with an equally depressed Chris Lister.) In early 1999 I had Chris Bonington's biography to finish, and very gradually my state of mind improved enough to take an interest in life, although, as I have said before, I was wary of getting too 'up' as the prospect of a subsequent 'down' was even worse.

I can honestly say that working on Chris's life story was plain sailing. I had expected him to be very vulnerable to any sort of criticism but he urged me to write whatever I thought of him: "The only thing I'll check is facts." He gave me his mother's diaries that I didn't know existed, which gave a wonderful insight into what was a lonely and rather strange childhood. In fact, the first three chapters almost wrote themselves. The hardest part of the book was getting any sort of fresh view into expeditions like Everest South West Face and Annapurna South Face, which Chris's own books had thoroughly described, including the inevitable arguments. There were no exciting revelations or easy pickings to be found there, and I still feel that, though I did my best, this part of the book, which is inevitably a big part, is the least successful. When it was published the greatest reward came from Rupert and Daniel who both said that they found out far more about their dad than they could have imagined. So, with the book finished (together with the Sepu Kangri film), I wondered, for the first time for ages, what to do next.

Two things were apparent. Even without expeditions I felt there was still an adventure left in me, and thus the idea of a solo journey, without using a passport, was born. The other thing, which I could put off, but not for much longer, was a much bigger adventure. I was increasingly thinking about a return to my original discipline, but frankly I was frightened of taking the first step. However, it became more a matter of when, not if, I would start painting again.

Chapter forty: Millennium

I think that my long bike ride from Muckle Flugga lighthouse, the most northerly point in the British Isles, to The Lizard, the most southerly, was born out of a kind of bloody mindlessness mixed with depression. My reasoning was that, as I was already bored and lonely, I might as well do something productive with it. Believe me, I succeeded, because for over two months on the road they were my almost constant feelings. True, there were the odd highlights: meeting Mike Banks again on Hoy as he reclaimed his 'oldest ever to climb the Old Man' record; staying with Jim and Marcia Fotheringham in Brampton near Carlisle; being unexpectedly greeted in Sheffield by loads of friends; staying with Becky and her partner Bob in Altrincham and, finally, my reception in Cornwall from my friends, the Old Spice Girls. All these lifted my spirits, but underneath the feelings of loss never disappeared.

I described the bike ride in a book, and apart from the title, I enjoyed both the writing and, more importantly, the illustrations I made for it. In fact, I had started to do this for Chris's biography and for both books I had produced over 40 drawings. After the cycling book was published, there seemed to be no more excuses left not to paint again. Interestingly, to me at any rate, it has taken two chapters to even start to write about starting to paint.

I know that whenever I get the germs of an idea, it can take months, even years, before I do anything about them. I almost always have fragmentary visions of the kind of work I intend to do. They are only daydreams, I suppose, but they are always very practical regarding things like size, use of colour and, of course, drawing. It was inevitable that I decided to start with some large paintings of the mountain landscapes that had meant so much to me. The first half dozen or so were of K2, the Trango Towers, Chogolisa, Gasherbrum IV and Kongur. Once I had got these out of my system, I thought, I will be able to think a bit more clearly about what to do next.

Inevitably I had to rely on my own photographic records for these early paintings. As I have tried to explain, many painters have used photography in their work, but there is a world of difference between just copying a two-dimensional image and using it for useful information. All the same, I always question my use of photos. Now, when I take pictures with a view to painting, I try to make drawings and colour notes as well. Even better, when time and circumstances allow, I prefer to make, direct from my subject, large drawings or watercolour studies that can be finished works in their own right. This probably worked best on the several visits to my friends Terry Gifford and Gill Round in their home in the village of Sella, a Spanish centre for holiday climbing all year round. Pam Beech also has a house in the same street and, all told, I have visited Sella on some half dozen occasions. Both their houses look out over the village, which is surrounded by ancient terraced hillsides and steep limestone crags. Just sitting on Terry and Gill's roof-terrace, I could work undisturbed all day.

^ *Julian Cooper in front of one of his Kangchenjunga paintings.*

After only two or three paintings, I felt my confidence returning, and with it my technical competence. It is a cliché to say things like, 'You never forget how to ride a bike', but I was amazed at how quickly I got back into the groove. Lakeland painter, Julian Cooper, whose work I have always admired, commented on these first works that the long 30 year gap didn't show, and that in some strange way the ideas had matured with the passage of time. He also said that the paintings looked as though someone much younger made them. (This seems to me to be a bit contradictory, and there were probably a lot of other things he said in between that I can't remember.) Julian is the son of William Heaton Cooper, the renowned Lake District painter. In fact, Julian is the third in the Heaton Cooper dynasty, for his grandfather was also a prominent Lakeland artist. Julian went to Goldsmiths Art School in London and has dropped the 'Heaton' in his name in an effort to be seen as a painter in his own right, rather than inheriting the family mantle. Since I have known him, Julian has put on several major exhibitions in the Art Space Gallery in London. When I first got to know him he was painting large canvases based on a trip to Kangchenjunga. These were followed by the North Face of the Eiger, then the Tibetan holy mountain, Kailas, and most recently the marble quarries of Carrara where the stone for Michelangelo's David was hewn. Each show has left me in awe of his vision and ability. But, despite my jealousy, he has become more than a friend, a mentor.

I had got to know Julian and his wife, Linda, through Terry Gifford, poet, critic and academic. Terry was responsible for 21 International Festivals of Mountaineering Literature, 19 of which were held at his place of work, Bretton Hall College, near Wakefield. Terry had seemingly boundless energy in putting this on annually, and managed to persuade a star-studded cast

311

^ *Me in Sella.*

^ *Terry Gifford.*

to participate. Names as diverse as Catherine Destivelle, Al Alvarez, Kurt Diemberger, Charlie Houston, Chris Bonington, Paul Piana, Doug Scott and, perhaps his greatest coup, Walter Bonatti, were all persuaded, cajoled and, for all I know, blackmailed into attending. My own minor role in the Festival was to occasionally provide low humour and to host the post-festival party. In so doing, some of the greatest names in mountaineering history have entered my house, and many left with a headache and only the haziest idea of what had happened. On another level, Terry and Gill have given me unswerving support in my creative endeavours and I hope I have done the same for them.

Terry and I climbed a fair amount in Derbyshire throughout the 90s, fun climbing on long summer evenings on the gritstone edges, and one memorable trip to North West Scotland when we climbed the best Very Severe I have ever done: *Fionn Buttress* on the remote Carnmore Crag. But the basis of our friendship is to use each other as a sounding board for all manner of our own projects, both of us able to encourage or criticise and occasionally to defuse strongly held opinions. Terry and Gill lived in Crookes, a suburb of Sheffield only 10 minutes away, but have now moved to a smaller house near Ashbourne. We still see each other, but they also spend increasing time in their Spanish retreat where I visit whenever I can summon up the money for a cheap flight to Alicante, and the cheek to rely on their hospitality yet again.

As 2000 drew to a close, there was one truly memorable event. My youngest daughter Becky married Bob.

^ *Terry Gifford on* Fionn Buttress,
Carnmore.

The wedding was held in a hotel near Manchester airport, from where the newlyweds would fly off for their honeymoon the next day. I was banned from seeing Becky until only minutes before I walked her up the aisle. Predictably, when I went into her room and saw her I started crying and so did she, putting her makeup in great danger. Desperately I tried to think of something to distract us: "Becky, your Mum and I decided to tell you today — you're adopted!" This did the trick and with me trying not to step on her wedding dress, we both suppressed giggles in front of the Registrar.

Bob is every father's idea of what a son-in-law should be: a great dad, loyal, supportive… I could go on. His only flaw is in supporting Stoke City, a football club that despite surviving two seasons (at the time of writing) in the Premier League, seems to be almost completely charisma-free. Bob's support is both unreserved and inexplicable (sorry, all you Stoke supporters). Now married for 10 years, they have three wonderful children: Patrick, Sophie and Theo, at nine, seven and two years old respectively. They are a constant source of delight and amusement to me. Patrick is a natural athlete who has had trials for both Manchester United and Manchester City; Sophie is a born actor with what seems like a Curranesque sense of humour (he claimed modestly) and little Theo who is, well, little Theo. I love them all dearly.

Slowly Sue was coming back into my life. She had split up with her partner just before my bike ride and our friendship had blossomed again. This was in no small part due to my friendship with her mother, Mag. She was a wonderful old lady with a wry Yorkshire humour that I could never get enough of. She used to

313

^ *Patrick.*

^ *Becky and Bob.*

^ *Sophie.*

^ *Gemma and Stuart on the day he took silk at the House of Lords.*

^ *Theo.*

come to my Christmas parties, arriving on Sue's arm and dressed to the nines. Then sinking into the depths of a sofa, sipping gin and tonic, and smoking the occasional cigarette, she would pass cryptic comments to everyone who took it in turns to sit next to her. For some strange reason she was very taken with an Emmy Lou Harris song, 'The Wrecking Ball', and she would always request this melancholy song with the plangent chords and tolling bells.

As she grew older, and ever more frail, she reluctantly had to accept that she couldn't look after herself. Sue and her sister Julie were both single, full-time working mothers and found the decision to put her in a care home desperately difficult. She stayed in one for a year or two in the village of Strensall, about 10 miles from her home in York. Sue and I used to visit whenever we could.

On several occasions when I was driving back from the Lakes or Scotland, I would pop in on my own and push her, now in a wheelchair, to a nearby pub garden, where she would enjoy a G&T and a cigarette. Leaving her was always quite heart rending, for we knew that she knew that she was slowly declining. But her wit was as sharp as ever and I treasure the times I had with her.

You don't have to be a psychiatrist to realise that my love for Mag (which it surely was) was bound up with my love for Sue, but also it was a kind of atonement for the death of my own mother. I was always too busy to see her as often as she wanted, and I blocked out a lot of the loneliness that deep down I knew she suffered after Dad died. With Mag, I felt that I was doing what I ought to have done 20 years before.

Mag moved into another home, only yards from Julie's home, and slowly faded away. Seeing her was painful but Sue, who is a care worker, was a wonderful daughter, talking to her, engaging her in conversation and keeping her up to date with family news. Towards the end, I could hardly speak to her without filling up and often, after visiting, Sue and I would both be in tears. One thing I will always remember. This was, that, in a quiet and roundabout way, she told me that Sue and I would never be together. Whether that was just her observation or whether Sue had told her, I never knew. But after Mag's death, Sue told me that she had died happy in the knowledge that I would always look after her: "The only snag is I don't want you to." Oh.

When Mag died, her funeral was held in the parish church at Acomb. It was a simple service and we all coped quite well until the first note of 'The Wrecking Ball' echoed around the church. I don't think I have ever played it since.

Chapter forty one: Why me? Why not?

Rather to my surprise I realised that by the summer of 2002, I would probably have enough work to have an exhibition by the end of the year. The Brewery Arts Centre in Kendal had a rather good gallery (now sadly revamped as an internet café) and as yet nobody was earmarked to show in it during the Film Festival. So I volunteered myself and was accepted (by me). This gave me about four months to produce enough work to fill the gallery.

In addition to the new paintings, I wanted a retrospective element and included the painting of Paul Nunn on *Paradise Lost* at Cheddar, as well as a few watercolours and drawings done in the early 1970s. I also set up a video player and selected tapes of my films. The opening of the show, which was timed to kick off the Film Festival, was a huge success and I was delighted to sell all the big paintings — even though two or three of them were bought by my brother Phil and his soon-to-be wife Heather.

The opening was a wonderful occasion when old childhood friends turned up, like Stephen Oliver and his wife Marcia, Steve Durkin, Robin and Maureen Devenish as well as plenty of more recent ones. Neil Murison, from my Bristol days, gave the opening speech, which was suitably ego-boosting. Rather mysteriously, he said he found my paintings very sexual. I didn't quite get the analogy then (or now), but was quite happy to agree with him. I imagine that two paintings of the Trango Tower could be seen to be quite phallic, but any sexual connotations were far from my mind — at least my conscious mind. What my subconscious was up to was anybody's guess.

Some of the Old Spice Girls, including Sue, came to the opening and, once again, I felt myself becoming hopelessly drawn to her. How can you describe someone who you really love? Her looks are not conventional, but through her personality, she becomes beautiful. She has the rare ability to get on with almost everybody — to think the best of them and to be interested in whatever they say or do. I found her comments about my work disconcertingly perceptive. She could glance at a painting for only a couple of seconds, then spot exactly the weakness that I had been denying myself. I couldn't believe her judgements could be so accurate and, at times, so unexpected.

Between 2000 and 2005 we enjoyed some wonderful outings, which I will never forget. It started in the winter of 2000 when I flew, via Boston, to Burlington, Vermont to see my dear friend Charlie Houston. We drove over to see Bob Bates who had been with him on both of Charlie's K2 expeditions in 1938 and 1953. Charlie always remembered me writing a chapter of my bike ride book lying on his sitting-room floor with his beautiful dog Pooh

^ *Charlie enjoying a stunning sunset.*

^ *Writing* The Middle Aged Mountaineer *on Charlie's sitting room floor with Pooh Bear.*

Bear snuggled up against me. Then I flew down to New York where I met Pam Beech and Sue for a few memorable days in the Big Apple. Before we met up I had pleaded with them that, as they would be staying on for a few more days, we should spend our time sightseeing, and that only when I flew back to England could they do their shopping. So we did the usual tourist things: Empire State Building, the Staten Island Ferry, Central Park, the Frick Collection, MOMA (the Museum of Modern Art) and the Twin Towers…

On our return from the States, weekends with Sue followed: Brampton with Jim and Marcia Fotheringham; London to stay with Charlie and Ruth Clarke and a memorable long weekend when we attended Phil and Heather's wedding in Venice. Gemma and Becky came too, and for three magical days I could pretend we were all a real family. In the summer of 2004 we had another great weekend, staying in Mac's holiday cottage in North Wales with the grandchildren as well as Bob and Becky, and Gemma and her partner Stuart. Happy days.

One of the last outings with Sue and some of the Old Spice Girls was another visit to Sella when I found a fantastic panoramic viewpoint above the village looking at the Puig Campana. In front of it was the wildly jagged, serrated ridge of The Castellets, about three miles long and one that Joe Brown (who else?) and Claude Davies managed to traverse from end to end over several separate holidays. I spent the best part of three days producing four linked watercolours direct from the viewpoint. Later I made a large three-part oil painting of it.

In 2004 Gibraltar celebrated its 300th anniversary of British rule. Don't ask me how, but Jim and Marcia Fotheringham managed to

^ The Rock of Gibraltar, the climb goes up the middle gradually trending left.

persuade the powers that be to mark the event with a climb on the Rock, normally completely out of bounds to climbers.

Jim would climb with Catherine Destivelle, whilst Erik, Catherine's husband, and Victor Saunders made up a second team. All four had designs on new routes on the Rock. We would be making a little film for the local Gibraltar TV station. Jim had first met Catherine and Erik camping in Cornwall on one of the last family invasions to West Penwith. Now it was obvious that Catherine and Erik were unhappy together and it was no surprise when, soon after our Gibraltar trip, they separated.

An unusual role for me was that I would be filming from halfway up the North Face of the Rock, on a flat-topped pinnacle. Access to this eyrie was through the complex system of tunnels inside the Rock. It was the most curious approach; the only similar situation would be the Railway Tunnel Window on the North Face of the Eiger. Here, a precarious ladder, apparently in the bowels of the earth, suddenly ended at a rusty padlocked trapdoor. When it was unlocked you stepped from darkness into the wildly exposed North Face, with a vertical 200 metre drop below you. The first time I emerged into the glaring sunlight I could barely stand up, and looking down made me feel quite faint. By the end of the shoot, I was walking around quite confidently, and set the tripod on the very edge of the abyss. (I did make sure that it and I were properly belayed.)

The Rock had, in fact, been climbed on a few occasions (once by Don Whillans) and Jim's ambition to do a new route was foiled by loose rock and vegetation. From below the Rock appears as a clean, white, just off-vertical wall. From my viewpoint, looking down, it was almost all green — the verdant ledges optically linked in the same way as happens with snow and rock in winter. So, despite my excellent viewpoint, Jim and Catherine were soon forced to climb way over on the left-hand side of the face. Here they were often out of vision, or just tiny figures in my lens at full zoom. Erik and Victor did climb a new route of sorts, almost directly below me, but it was so loose and difficult that when they reached my vantage point they called it a day.

So the climbs were, I felt, rather an anticlimax. Now, my sharpest memory is of exploring the tunnels under the rock which, we were told, were more extensive than the roads on Gibraltar. I also felt that I was really losing interest in climbing films and, as if it needed confirming, far more interested in painting.

Since my bike ride in 2000, I had become increasingly worried about my right knee. I had already had two operations, one on each knee, but my surgeon left me in no doubt that an arthroscopy was only a short term solution for the right knee. I knew I was living,

318

or rather walking, on borrowed time. Even the surgeon's cheerful remark that I had got my knees in such a state through a lifetime of enjoyment, wasn't much of a consolation, and he warned me that this latest operation would only last two or three years, at which point I would almost certainly have to have a complete knee replacement.

But, before that, another more serious problem was beginning to rear its ugly head. Like many middle-aged men, I rarely made it through the night without at least a couple of visits to the loo. My GP at the time was a delightful Indian gentleman. Most consultations featured a chat about our retrospective travels to the sub-continent. He reassured me about my weak bladder, putting it down to my age. Eventually I was unconvinced and changed doctors, signing on at a Health Centre in Nether Edge. I quickly had a blood test (PSA) and got an appointment at the Hallamshire Hospital.

Here, I endured the dreaded finger-up-the-bum examination and was given a biopsy, about which the least said the better. A friend of mine having the same tests asked the specialist whether, if he were to use two fingers, would that count as a second opinion? None of this could conceal what I had guessed almost from day one; that I probably had prostate cancer.

This was confirmed a couple of weeks later by a Professor Hamdy who broke the bad news in the company of a nurse; she was there presumably to either dry my eyes, or stop me from beating him up. Strangely enough, though I knew it was probably a death sentence (though hopefully not for some time), I accepted the news immediately and thanked him for telling me. As I left the consulting room he remarked that most men did indeed thank him. I suppose I felt a bit sorry for him to have to give the bad tidings — after all, I only had to hear it once, whereas he probably had to break the same unwelcome news several times a week.

However, thinking about it now, I really do remain amazed that there was not very much weeping and gnashing of teeth. I was transferred to Weston Park Hospital, and put into the care of Dr Ferguson, a consultant who was able to explain my options (or lack of them) simply and clearly. She told me that my best bet was an intensive course of radiotherapy and a course of hormone implants — an injection into my stomach every three months. Five years later I am still having them.

The prostate gland is about the size of a walnut and its job is to make semen, to help sperm reach the egg during intercourse. When prostate cancer occurs, it is first contained within the gland and the longer it is undiagnosed, the more likely it is to burst. My own was still just about intact but removing the gland was likely to cause it

319

to spread. So the radiotherapy was aimed to bomb it into some sort of submission, and the hormone implants were, in the words of more than one consultant, to 'castrate' me, a phrase I found rather brutal. Chemotherapy was not used, but probably will be in the future, which I try not to think about, as it is the last resort.

The radiotherapy was five days a week for four weeks, during which time I became increasingly tired and depressed. Both Gemma and Becky were wonderfully supportive and one or the other would drive over from Liverpool or Altrincham to be with me during consultations with Dr Ferguson. They gave more than moral support as they:

a) remembered what I had been told and

b) asked intelligent questions.

By contrast, I instantly forgot everything — actually I probably didn't listen, and far from asking questions, was inclined to say how well I felt, even when I didn't. This drove Gemma, in particular, mad: "Why can't you stop pretending you are okay when you know you're not?"

The worst time I had during this period was when the radiotherapy finished. Having been the centre of attention (even though it was only for five minutes daily), I felt abandoned when it was over, and rather unwisely accepted an invitation from Terry and Gill to fly out to Alicante for a few days in Sella. It was a mistake, as I felt desperately insecure and homesick for the whole time. On my return, my next-door neighbour, who was having treatment for breast cancer, showed me a research paper which examined post-treatment care for cancer patients. Rule number one was not to go on holiday and stick to the security of home. Unlike a lot of research, this one (which obviously said a lot more than the one sentence I can remember) made sense. In fact, since I was diagnosed, I have found any travel more than a few days away from home hard to undertake. In particular, flying on my own is almost too stressful to contemplate. Not the fear of flying, itself, which I quite enjoy, but all the check-in rigmarole and waiting around at each end.

My relationship with Sue changed subtly after I was diagnosed. When Mag was still alive I provided a shoulder for Sue to lean on. Now the situation was neatly reversed. So our friendship didn't exactly stagnate, but it didn't really progress either. Nevertheless, I thought about her constantly. In my heart of hearts I knew we would never be a real couple, but I couldn't help allowing myself a little glimmer of hope that eventually I could win her over. Stupid boy, Curran. You should have known that some wishes never come true.

The one thing I could still do during and after the radiotherapy

^ *Guitar and gas fire.*

^ *Cushions on a settee.*

was draw. Harking back to Bristol days, I set about making a series of big, accurate pencil drawings of scenes around me: bookshelves, the TV, guitars, towels hanging over radiators, and some self-portraits. Each drawing took three or four days of concentrated work and altogether I did about 20.

I could lose myself in the concentration needed to produce this work, and following the one single criterion of just getting them right — in proportion, tone and measurement. Nothing else mattered while I was working. At one stage the walls of both the downstairs rooms were covered in drawings. I never sold any and feel that they are so personal that maybe people feel a bit uncomfortable in front of them. Or perhaps they just aren't very good.

I now realise that the radiotherapy took far longer to recover from than I thought at the time. I may as well be frank here. While I was not totally incontinent, for a year or two I wasn't far off, and suffered several humiliating accidents. Slowly things did improve, but even today when any call of nature comes, I don't have much time to obey it. The other problem, castration, is more difficult. Professor Hamdy told me that the bad news would be impotence; the good news would be complete loss of libido, so I wouldn't mind the impotence. Hmmmm...

^ *Bookcase and television.*

still not at all sure I agree with the bit about the good news. The deal, at its most basic is, give up your sex life and live a bit longer with, of course, no guaranteeing that the 'bit longer' is a significant bit to make up for the loss. But I still miss the odd bit of rumpy-pumpy.

Grasping the nettle, while I am on the subject, my feelings about my impending — come on don't mess about, say the word — death are not what I would have expected. At various points in my life, I have been terrified of dying — the absolute end of consciousness, black eternity that I won't even be able to experience. Twice during my climbing career I have come too close for comfort to oblivion: faced with a boulder/mud slide avalanche on the Trango couloir, and being swept into the icy torrent on Rangrik Rang. On neither

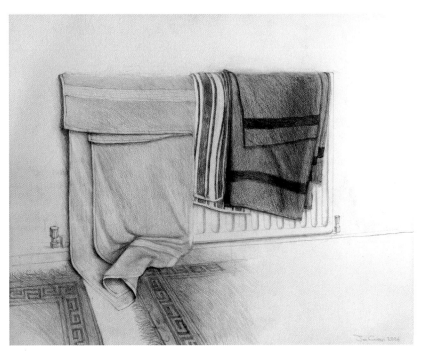

> *Towels on a radiator.*

< *Corner cabinet and decanters.*

occasion did I face my demise with anything other than panic and foul language. Now that it is inevitable (or rather that I acknowledge that it is), my main feeling is that I have got to finish all the projects I have in mind. I hope that when it arrives it won't be too painful, and that I will be able to do whatever it involves with some dignity. It only happens once, and you don't get a second chance to do it again. However, I might get run over by a bus tomorrow, so there's not a great deal to do by way of preparation.

If ever anyone taught me how to cope it was Charlie Clarke's wife, Ruth. She had been diagnosed with breast cancer and lived with it for five years — her incorrigible humour lasting to the very end. She died in 2009, mourned by hundreds of friends. Her funeral at Golders Green Crematorium was both the funniest and saddest I have ever attended.

I realise this chapter is getting morbid and I fear there is worse to come. So I will leave it here, and try to be a little more cheerful on the next page.

< *Towels on a radiator II.*

Chapter forty two: A Broken Heart and a New Knee

After I hit my unwelcome 60th birthday, I gradually realised that a lifetime of climbing and walking had almost completely wrecked my knees. Before the last arthroscopy the specialist had amazed me when I walked into the consulting room. "No cartilage or rear cruciate ligament in your right knee," he opined before I had even sat down. X-rays confirmed this diagnosis later. Despite the operation, after only a couple of years it was worse than ever, with bone grating on bone. The surgeon at the Northern General asked me what I hoped to gain? Being able to walk without pain was my main wish. He thought that was quite feasible, but warned that climbing was probably not on (though Doug Scott, for example, has had both knees done and still climbs).

I had never imagined that I would stop climbing, or that if I did, it would be a horrible wrench. In fact, faced with the inevitable, it wasn't as bad as I feared. I had loved the feeling of moving over rock when I was fit and climbing well (yes, it did happen occasionally). But I couldn't get my head round struggling on the easy routes that I used to solo. Better to make a clean break than make a fool of myself. I was so used to comparing myself with climbers like Joe Brown, Chris Bonington and Martin Boysen that I tended to forget that half a century of climbing wasn't a bad score. Joe actually encouraged me in his own way. I was chatting to him and Val over a cup of tea in their kitchen. Joe, who was approaching 80, said he hardly climbed at all these days, and his body was completely knackered. I said that I wished I had climbed several great classics when I had been capable of doing so. *Vector*, *White Slab* and *Centurion* on Ben Nevis probably topped the list. "That's bollocks," said Joe. "Whenever you stop, there will always be a list of routes you wish you'd done. But if you had, you'd just think of another list." Irrefutable logic from Joe, which helped me accept the truth that a huge part of my life was over.

I wish I could say the same about Sue. She met someone else. Again. But it was serious. If I had been upset in 1998, I was absolutely devastated this time. I am ashamed to say that, in my depression, I found myself thinking very black thoughts indeed. Pam Beech took me to a doctor and Becky came over from Cheshire and drove me back to stay with her until I felt a bit better. I was smoking again (after a 17 year lay-off) and physically ached with sadness that never seemed to go away. I honestly don't know how I got through those months. There didn't seem to be anything worth living for, but out of habit I carried on painting.

By now I was renting a studio in the middle of Sheffield at an artists' co-op called BLOC. It was the best thing I had done for ages. Just getting out of the house was a step in the right direction

^ *Steve, childhood friend and longest serving climbing partner.*

and, as if I was trying to make up for lost time, I had exhibitions almost annually — two in the Alpine Club and three in Kendal. Until the financial crisis in 2009, every exhibition was a financial success (by which I mean I didn't actually lose money by the time all the overheads were taken care of).

Over the years I had stayed erratically in touch with my oldest friend, Steve Durkin. He had moved back to Tunbridge Wells to be near his beloved sandstone outcrops. Steve became something of a local guru and did a huge amount of research into both the history of sandstone climbing and the early exploration of many of the minor outcrops, very reminiscent of our early days. He was known to the Harrison's fraternity as Buzzard and had several first ascents named after him. The best was called *One Flew Over the Buzzard's Nest*. He was a close friend of Sarah Cullen, who runs climbing courses for adults. I had got to know her when she was based for a few months in Leek in Staffordshire, and we climbed every week at the Roaches. Sarah was pregnant with her first child, but still climbed beautifully. She moved back to live in Groombridge and, when her marriage failed, Steve became a wise mentor to her, and almost a surrogate grandfather to her girls, Emily and Charlotte, who doted on him.

In an attempt to broaden my circle of friends, but also for painter's reasons, I started visiting Harrison's again, staying either with Steve or Sarah, and visiting the long-lost scenes of my youth. But now I was entranced by the appearance of the rocks themselves — I couldn't believe that when I was at Ealing School of Art I didn't see their visual potential, which now seemed quite wonderful. I was torn between wondering how I could have ignored them for so long, and delighted that, 50-odd years later, I had found them again. Now the paintings had moved on. From doing smallish paintings of very large mountains, I was producing ever-larger paintings of relatively small outcrops. I was hooked on the typical sandstone formations and textures, particularly the ubiquitous wind-eroded pockets that appear all over the rocks, following the strata of bedding planes.

I was delighted when flicking through a book of Cézanne's paintings I found one of rocks at Fontainebleau. These rocks, as I have explained, are part of the same formation as the sandstone of the Weald, and I felt that if they were good enough for my childhood hero, they were good enough for me.

When the date of the knee 'op' was fixed, I was told I would be in hospital for about five days. I was also told not to take any blood thinning medicines like aspirin for a couple of days before the operation, which I realised to my increasing trepidation, would be carried out with just an epidural injection in my spine. A screen across my legs discreetly covered the view, but, oh, the sounds! It was like being in a breaker's yard or a building site. What was curious was that being completely numb from the waist down, all the hammering and drilling reverberated through my skull and, in my slightly drowsy state, I kept trying to see who was banging on my head.

Eventually the surgeon appeared from behind the screen and told me they were finishing off: "Don't do what builders do, and bugger off for a fortnight." Back on the ward I had a button to press to give myself a shot of morphine whenever the pain got too bad, but after a day or so it was just a dull ache. On the second day I started to feel cold and asked the nurse for an extra blanket. I got colder and colder, then I began to panic and passed out. I was dimly aware of being wheeled out of the ward, then, drifting in and out of consciousness, I seemed to be having a scan. But for the next 48 hours I was more or less out of it.

What had happened, I found out much later, was that I had developed pulmonary embolisms on my lungs — blood clots that, if they had reached my heart, could have killed me. Gemma and Becky were kept in the dark about my condition and Becky in particular was incensed. As she is a lawyer and at the time worked for the Law Society, she sent a very stroppy letter to the hospital, which obviously hit the spot. But even so, information was hard to come by and I thought the hospital's communication skills were quite woeful. It wasn't until weeks later that, while undergoing physiotherapy at the Hallamshire Hospital, a physio who had seen me at the Northern General let slip that I had had, not just had one or two clots, but several small ones on each lung.

Instead of five days, I was stuck in the Northern General for almost a month. During this time I had very little physiotherapy and consequently found walking desperate, even with crutches. What rubbed salt into the wound (!) was a report in the press which found post-operative blood clotting was the biggest avoidable cause of unnecessary deaths in NHS hospitals.

Once again I was seriously depressed. With the cancer, and now the knee, I seemed to have gone from quite active middle-age to being an old man in only a couple of years. What saved me were my GP, Dr Nikki Hall, and the Hallamshire Tennis Club, which has a gym that I have been going to for nearly 10 years. Dr Hall never stopped encouraging me and, at the time, she went to the same gym herself. Slowly I managed to increase the movement in my knee until the day when I managed a whole revolution on the exercise bike. I had spent hours painfully nudging my knee, a degree at a time until one day it actually turned full circle to a whoop of delight from me and puzzled looks from fellow gym

326

members. Sue Evans, who types these words, also goes to the gym and has become my dominatrix (not really), encouraging me when my natural laziness threatens to turn me into a jelly. I slowly realised that when the surgeon told me that he would get me walking again, we probably didn't have quite the same idea of what that meant. I thought that maybe the Pennine Way was asking a bit much, but that an ordinary seven or eight miles in Derbyshire would be fine. I now realise that his idea was probably going to the shop and back.

Though the knee is now painless, my hips ache after only a few minutes, and I am also conscious that my left knee will need surgery if I do too much. What is infuriating is that I can walk for short distances on the flat, and even uphill. But on rough ground, and in particular going downhill, I am absolutely pathetic and flounder around like a — well, like a man with a plastic kneecap.

Once again I found some solace in painting. Gemma gave me a set of watercolours for Christmas 2005, a medium I hadn't used since schooldays. It took me about six months before I summoned up the courage to take the plunge, for watercolour is perhaps the most demanding medium of all. To my delight, I took to it like a duck (no, don't say it — not remotely funny). Over the last four or five years I have produced about 30 large watercolours of sandstone rock formations which Sarah, down in Groombridge, has publicised, and occasionally sold for me, as well as many other mountain landscapes.

I certainly felt that the sandstone paintings were a step in the right direction for me. In fact, I was becoming a bit obsessed with sandstone and in the autumn of 2006 I went with Terry Gifford on a little painting expedition to Hoy. Thanks to the amazing generosity of Jack and Dorothy Rendall, we stayed (for nothing) in their holiday cottage, which commanded a magnificent view of the cliffs of Rackwick Bay.

While Terry went for walks to the Old Man, Rora Head and St John's Head, I could sit in warmth and comfort, studying the ever-changing panorama as sun, wind and rain played on the rich red sandstone ramparts in front of me. Gemma's watercolours came into their own here, and I spent the best part of three days doing study after study. Monet's great paintings of the façade of Rouen Cathedral were never far from my mind. As usual, Terry and I were relaxed and happy in each other's company, and in the evenings we joined Jack and Dorothy for a wee dram. Terry was entranced with the whole history and culture of Hoy, so much so that I feared a poem was imminent.

On the way home, Terry gave a lecture in Elgin and afterwards, on a wet and windy night, we bivouacked on a steep forestry track somewhere not very near anywhere else. I curled up in my Gore-Tex sleeping bag and Thermarest mat. It rained all night and I woke up having slid down the track in the mud: "I think, Terry, that I really am getting a bit long in the tooth for this sort of thing."

The result of this trip was several big watercolours and two or three very big oil paintings — one double canvas is of the cliffs of Rackwick, glowing an unearthly red in the setting sun, with the grassy banks at the top of the cliffs a luminous green. It took longer to paint than anything I had done before. It is one of my favourites and, probably because of its size, it has never sold, so it hangs in my old studio at home, and every so often I wonder whether it is finished or not.

Despite my lingering heartache for Sue, I felt that, at last, I was emerging from the darkest shadows of my life. I tried to tell myself how lucky I was: loads of really good friends, two wonderful children (adults actually), the time to do whatever I wanted (well, not exactly, but quite a lot). I owned my own home and I was financially secure. All I wanted was a partner, but if that was asking too much I should be more that happy with what I have got, which is a lot more than many other people my age. But I was still lonely.

Chapter forty three: The Loss of an Old Friend

In March 2009, as I have already written, Steve and I celebrated our 50th anniversary by trespassing, with Sarah Cullen, at Chiddlinglye Wood Rocks. After we had done (or, in my case, not done) our climb we adjourned to the nearby hermit's retreat, Cave Adullam, to drink champagne and eat smoked salmon. A couple of months later Steve came up to Sheffield and we went to Windgather Rocks where Steve led a simple V Diff — the first time he had led me up anything for years. This was to be our last climb together, and probably my last climb with anyone.

With us that day was Liz Sharples, the ex-wife of the long-standing Peak activist, climber and photographer, Keith Sharples. Liz is a Principal Lecturer at Sheffield's Hallam University and has two girls: Kathy, who has just qualified as a doctor, and Vicky who is at Salford University studying drama and, I confidently predict, will become a famous actor one day. I hope I am still around to see her success. Though Liz probably doesn't realise it, her friendship has brought a degree of stability into my life. Liz and

^ *Liz Sharples.*

I went walking in Derbyshire when I was still able to keep up with her, and now we go to the cinema regularly, we have meals at our respective homes and see each other every week.

In the winter, Steve came up to Derbyshire for a Sandstone Club dinner. I was invited and took Liz. As soon as I saw him, I realised something was very wrong. He was short of breath and there was something about his eyes that made me fear the worst.

In March, he admitted that he was not at all well. I was going to attend a dinner organised by Sarah at the High Rocks Hotel to celebrate the fact that at last the British Mountaineering Council had bought Harrison's Rocks. As I drove round the M25 towards the Dartford Crossing, Sarah left a message on my mobile telling me to visit Steve on my way to see her. He was in the Kent and Sussex Hospital in Tunbridge Wells. He looked terribly ill and was in a ward with what were all too obviously terminally ill cancer patients. We made small talk and Steve said that he was only in for some tests and still hoped to go to the dinner. I doubted that he would. The dinner featured many of the great and the good of sandstone climbing, but Steve was too ill to attend. I was supposed to make an after-dinner speech, which I did with a heavy heart.

Three weeks later I drove to Tunbridge Wells again. Steve had been discharged from hospital and diagnosed with advanced lung cancer. He had not long to live. Robin Devenish came down from Oxford and the three of us on a damp, misty day drove round some of the outcrops: High Rocks, Bowles, Bull's Hollow and Eridge. It would be the last time Steve would see the rocks that had meant so much to him for over 50 years.

Before the seriousness of his condition had fully dawned on him, Steve had a typically eccentric ambition to make the first ascent of *Dark Chimney* (just about the easiest route at Harrison's) using bottled oxygen. Sadly, he could never put his plan into action. It remains a tantalising first for anyone using oxygen with a mad desire to achieve the barmiest climb since the Monty Python team made the first ascent of the Uxbridge Road.

Steve was half-convinced that his illness was caused by hill-walking in Snowdonia the day after the Chernobyl disaster in1986, when an easterly wind blew a radioactive cloud across from Russia. He claimed that his hair had started to fall out at the same time. Reluctantly, he also admitted that a lifetime of smoking 30 a day might also have been a contributory factor.

Steve's sister Caroline came to stay and warned me that his specialist had given him only weeks, not months, to live. I went back to Sheffield promising to return as soon as I could. One of the last things Steve said to me was that at least it sorted out what to do with his retirement.

A couple of weeks later, I once again drove round the M25 and down to Tunbridge Wells to stay with Sarah and her partner Chris Gibson. Steve was back in hospital and Sarah had visited him that day, bringing a book for him. Steve said he didn't think he would have the time to read it, and then thanked Sarah for being such a good friend. She warned me that she thought he wouldn't last more than a day or two.

In the morning when I got to hospital Steve had sunk into a coma. Caroline, her husband, Edmund, his nephew and nieces, Robin Devenish and Maureen, his wife, and Sarah, as well as several other close friends, sat with him all day as he slowly faded away. He died peacefully at eight that evening.

At his funeral I was almost too overcome to speak. My earliest memory of him was in the back garden of 27 Rathgar Avenue when I climbed our apple tree. We must have been about 10 years old. I was hanging upside down from the lowest branches when Steve shot me, in the backside, with an air pistol, at point blank range. Somehow our friendship survived for almost 60 years. Steve could always make me laugh. One of the best stories he told me recently was of a balloon flight with Sarah and two or three middle-aged ladies. The pilot was under supervision and at first tried to land them in a field with electricity pylons. He then aimed for a clearing surrounded by trees. His supervisor told everyone to brace themselves for a crash landing. Steve said that, as they crouched down in the basket, an incredibly posh Home Counties voice said: "You are going to kill us all, fuckwit!" It got a laugh from the packed crematorium, but most of us were in tears all through the service.

Steve's wake was held in the High Rocks Hotel where only weeks before, we had celebrated the purchase of Harrison's Rocks. It was a beautiful spring evening and, as the mourners dwindled, several of us sat outside. Someone asked me, rather bluntly, whether it was true that I had cancer too. In my cups, I replied pompously: "Only when it suits me."

Since Steve's death most, if not all, of his friends discovered things about his life they had never suspected, including each other. He had a really funny and original ability to write poetry, a deep interest in philosophy and religion (he was the only person I have ever known who would invite a Jehovah's Witness in to argue with them), an extraordinary wide circle of friends who never knew about the existence of the others, an ability to write about his often solo travels and, above all, a loyalty to his childhood friends that was unswerving. I couldn't believe how upset I was by his death, and how much I still miss him.

< Steve and Sarah under the Isolated Buttress, Harrison's Rocks (painting).

331

Chapter forty four: Two Old Loves Revisited: a Woman and a Country

As must be obvious from these pages, I am still a terrible old Luddite and, though I can just about send emails with one finger typing, Facebook, Skyping and Tweeting all make my brain hurt. So it was rather uncharacteristic of me to get Gordon Stainforth, photographer and author, to set up a website for me. Julian Cooper told me that you had to have one for your work to be taken seriously, but you shouldn't expect to sell anything. He was quite right. But what he didn't tell me was that all kinds of people from my past would contact me. To hear from them has been a delightful surprise. Ex-students from Rotherham and Bristol have emailed me and I remain amazed that they have remembered me. So far nobody has been abusive, but I suppose there will be a first time. (This is not an invitation.)

Perhaps the best and most successful reunion was with my old college friend Adrian Mallett, who I bumped into at the Haywood Gallery. We now see each other every few months and spend most of the time moaning about old age, or reminiscing about the Neasden railway yards. Now retired, Adrian is painting again and, after half a century, unspoken rivalry has resumed. To my consternation, I still envy his drawing skills which are, if anything, stronger than ever.

So in the years from 2005 when I first knew I had a cancer, until the end of 2010, my life had centred around painting, going to the studio and seeing what, sadly has become a dwindling collection of friends. The snag is, the older we all get, the harder it is to get up off your arse and go and see them. But we all do our best to maintain contact.

The only friend who had disappeared off the radar completely was Trish, who I hadn't seen or heard from since 1988. I often wondered where she was and how her life had turned out. Then, in early November 2009, right out of the blue Trish sent me an email. She was living in Devon, had two teenage children, worked as a self-employed interior designer and had split from her husband. We started emailing regularly (I never thought I would write those words) and she sounded exactly the same as I remembered her.

In some trepidation, I arranged to see her in her farmhouse near Tiverton. As soon as we met I knew that my worries were unfounded. She was the same old Trish I used to know — funny, intelligent and just as beautiful as I remembered. In fact, though she was in her mid-50s, she didn't seem to have aged at all. (Could there be a portrait in the attic?) The friendship had survived over 37 years and hadn't suffered at all, though I was aware that once you take sex — the elephant in the room — out of the equation, friendship is a lot easier. (The elephant has now gone off and taken his trunk with him.)

^ *Trish.*

I stayed for a couple of nights, as Trish had to work one day. Alone in her farmhouse with just her dog for company, I wrote most of the first chapter of this book. In the evenings we talked, inevitably, about the old days. What I still find quite extraordinary is that after so many years, we both had exactly the same memories. Even now, a year later, there seems to be very little that only one of us remembers, and that includes a lot of embarrassing things — the infamous zip-in-the-loons, for example. The real difference, as Trish quickly observed, was that now we were both much more prepared to talk. I suppose that when our friendship was based around a student-lecturer relationship, there must have been areas that probably I, and maybe she as well, were reluctant to explore.

I drove back to Sheffield, delighted that we had got on so well, and visited her again in early 2010. This time I found her in a much less happy mood as a romance had gone wrong. She told me a lot about her marriage, and I realised that she had had a very difficult few years. There wasn't much I could do except listen and try to be a good friend. Steve's condition at this time didn't make this any easier.

When I got home I found an email from my old friend Harish Kapadia in Mumbai, asking me if I would be interested in attending a Mountain Literature Festival in Mussoorie in the foothills of the Indian Himalaya in October. The festival was being organised by a man called Stephen Alter, and Harish had very kindly recommended me.

Initially, I had very mixed feelings. I would love to go, but the thought of a long-haul flight to Delhi on my own made me feel stressed, even though it was six months away. Impulsively I rang Trish: "If I pay for your flight, would you like to come to India and be my carer?" To my delight Trish said yes immediately, and we also planned a 10-day holiday in Rajasthan, a place I had long wanted to visit, and get new material for painting.

By now I was in danger of being labelled exclusively as a mountain painter, which I didn't mind, but it implied that I couldn't do anything else. Trish wanted to get source inspiration for her interior design business, and so in the end we planned to be away for three weeks. Her daughter Alice had just started at the

University of WoE (West of England) and her son Tom would stay with his father. Alice's boyfriend would look after her old dog.

As the date of departure loomed, I began to get the same old nerves that I had before expeditions. This, I kept telling myself, is quite ridiculous. You are going for what it is just a glorified holiday with an old friend with whom you get on brilliantly. Stop fretting and turning into a male version of your mother.

Of course, once we took off and had our first G&T, my worries started to evaporate. But nature abhors a vacuum and the next thing to worry about was my contribution to the conference. All the guests had been invited to speak for 20 minutes maximum, and say or read something they had never done before. The keynote speaker was to be the renowned American zoologist and naturalist George Schaller. I looked forward to meeting him.

From Delhi we took an internal flight to Dehra Dun and were met by a driver for a three-hour drive ending with an ascent up never ending zigzags to the town of Mussoorie. Here I met old friends Harish and his wife Geeta, and Bernadette MacDonald from Banff, Canada, as well as Stephen Alter who proved to be a born organiser as well as a thoroughly good man. George Schaller himself was a tall, rangy man with granite features and piercing eyes. He was, I thought, probably more at ease with animals than people, and clearly didn't enjoy small talk. Trish was wonderful with him and, to my surprise, the two hit it off. A Chinese lady who hung on his every word accompanied George. Trish, who often told me she took people as they came, and was unimpressed by reputations, probably came as a breath of fresh air to George.

The festival ran smoothly, but I knew from experience at Kendal that behind the scenes there would be a never-ending series of problems to be solved, and crises to be averted. Rather unsurprisingly, I thought, most of the speakers stuck to fairly predictable slide shows. On the first day there was a huge attendance, for the conference was held at the Mussoorie International School, and the sixth formers made up a fair proportion of the audience. George Schaller gave a brilliant presentation about saving the tiger in the Himalayan foothills, and when the applause died down, I, as nervous as I have ever been, gave my talk, 'Why did I climb when I got so scared?' The title was the best bit of the talk and I did it without slides. I don't know quite what the audience thought, for very few had English as a first language, but at least I stuck to the 20-minute brief.

I realised early on that Trish was an inspired choice of companion. She was extrovert and natural, and she befriended everyone at the conference. More importantly, she took almost all the pressure off me.

334

Chapter forty four: Two Old Loves Revisited: a Woman and a Country

On the last day I gave a short slide-talk about my painting, which was back on familiar territory and in front of a much smaller audience. This was very well-received and in the afternoon we left Mussoorie for the long drive to Chandigarh and a flight to Mumbai to give a lecture to the Himalayan Club. The journey was notable only because our driver seemed determined to kill us all, 'us' being George, Trish and me. The flight was notable only because we shared it with the Dalai Llama.

Trish and I were billeted at the Bombay Yacht Club, an imposing building only yards from the sea front, near the great arch, the Gateway of India, and the Taj Hotel, which was badly damaged in the terrorist attack of 2008. In its dark corridors, which hadn't changed since the days of the Raj, we were half appalled, half amused at a pile of cat shit on the ornate tiled floor outside Trish's room. Feral cats occupied the bottom of the lift shaft and, despite the obvious health hazard, were allowed to remain. Our bedrooms were about the size of tennis courts and, as so often happens in India, you can feel like royalty one minute, and utterly appalled and guilty at the desperate poverty the next.

Before the lecture the next day I was delighted to meet two old friends from the Rangrik Rang expedition, Vijay Kothari and Divyesh Muni. Both seemed unchanged since 1994. After the lecture many of us gathered for drinks at the Yacht Club, and at the end of the evening we said our goodbyes to Harish and Geeta, knowing that we would meet again — in India? In England? Who knows?

The next 10 days were pure enjoyment. We both loved Udaipur, the city with palaces apparently floating on Lake Pichola. Visually it was everything I could have wished. If there was a snag, it was that I had forgotten how it is almost impossible to do anything like sitting down to paint a watercolour without half the population of Rajasthan gathering round to watch. Reluctantly, I realised that, once again, photography would have to be my main source of information.

The 10 days passed all too quickly. I had also forgotten just how much I loved India. Like my friendship with Trish, my feelings for India hadn't changed at all. I enjoyed being an ordinary tourist, and realised that this was my first proper holiday since... well, I can't actually remember when. We visited (and stayed in) a wonderful palace in Deogarh and stayed three days in Jaipur before visiting Agra and the Taj Mahal on the way back to Delhi.

Flying home on a half empty plane, I realised that I had actually been happy for three solid weeks. Steve's death was still fresh in my mind, but the grief was being replaced by good memories. And I could go for almost a day at a time without thinking about Sue, and when I did, it was without that alarming blow to the sola plexus that I had almost grown used to.

Leaving Trish at Heathrow (this time with no ghastly bits of bad news to contend with), I spent a couple of days with Mac in Kensington before going home. We went to see Julian Cooper's latest exhibition and, as usual, I was half impressed, half jealous of his wonderful new paintings of the quarries at Carrara. I resolved that when I finished this book, I would spend the next year in the studio, immersed in the buildings, lakes and fortifications of the cities of Rajasthan. This time is now approaching. To my relief, and probably yours as well, the end is only a couple of pages away.

Afterword
Putting All My Egos in One Basket
(Typo from Sue Evans)

It has taken me just over a year to write the first draft of this book. After about six months, someone asked me how I was going to finish it, and I realised I hadn't given it any thought at all. In a book I have just read, written by Martin Gayford, the author describes the interminable time he spent sitting for his portrait by Lucian Freud. The writer compares finishing a book with finishing a painting. He makes the point that whereas a finished painting can only be judged by the last brushstrokes that

^ *Self-portrait with daffodils.*

the artist has decided to leave, the final words of a book may not be quite so important, as the reader still has the rest of the book to digest. He points out that many famous writers, including Dickens, didn't always have great endings.

I'm not sure that I totally agree with that. Sometimes the very first marks a painter makes on a canvas are still visible at the end, and the whole process of making the painting is revealed. By contrast, a detective story needs the final cunning twist of plot and dénouement to make the rest of the book meaningful.

As this is neither a painting, or a detective story, I don't quite

337

30/10/07

Self Portrait after radiotherapy   Ji Curan

^ *Self-portrait after radiotherapy.*

know how important the end should be. But I would like to be able to wrap it up neatly. The best way, of course, would be my death on the last page and the book would finish in mid ………………………….. False alarm! As I don't think I am going to die in the imminent future, and topping myself for the sake of a good ending seems an unnecessary embellishment, maybe I should settle for something a little more prosaic.

I hope that, despite the inevitable sadnesses, the reader will think, as I do, that, in the main, I have lived a challenging and fulfilling life. It is not over yet, and I still have plans and projects for the future. I have, at times, through low cunning, made myself very lucky indeed, though I am still aware that I have been extremely selfish in putting painting, making films and having adventures ahead of nurturing relationships and maintaining family responsibilities. If I had my time again, would I change anything? The answer is probably no. Even the depressive episodes have been balanced by periods of enormous happiness and elation. There are some regrets — pretty obvious ones that I have described in detail, and need no further mention.

When I finished my last book, *The Middle-Aged Mountaineer*, I wrote that, at last, I was beginning to accept life as it is, not as I would like it to be. This has been a hard lesson to learn and, 10 years later, one that I am still trying to practise, sometimes failing completely. The next, almost impossible, stage is to try not to even want. I really do have everything I need: my friends, my house, my painting. Why should I want anything more? If I ever achieve that state of mind, I suppose I will be well on the way to being a Buddhist, or a saint. But, it is something that I do want to achieve — oh bugger! See what I mean?

One question I will never know the answer to is, if I had put all

338

Afterword
Putting All My Egos in One Basket (Typo from Sue Evans)

my egos (sic) in one basket, as a painter, or filmmaker, or writer, would I have achieved more? I can't help feeling that I am a jack-of-all-trades and master of none. Mountains, and the people who climb them, have provided me with a high proportion of my creative input, and it has manifested itself in different ways at different times. But if there is one activity that has underpinned all these activities, it is drawing. It was the basis of all my teaching, and it is still the way I think through paintings, films and, in some strange way, even writing. To me, drawing is understanding, and understanding is the basis for all creative disciplines. Drawing a steam engine in my grandmother's sitting room in Stevenage is just about my earliest memory. As long as I have the energy to do it, drawing will, I hope, keep me going right to the end.

> Self-portrait after radiotherapy.

^ *The Cioch, Burbage Quarries (pencil drawing).*

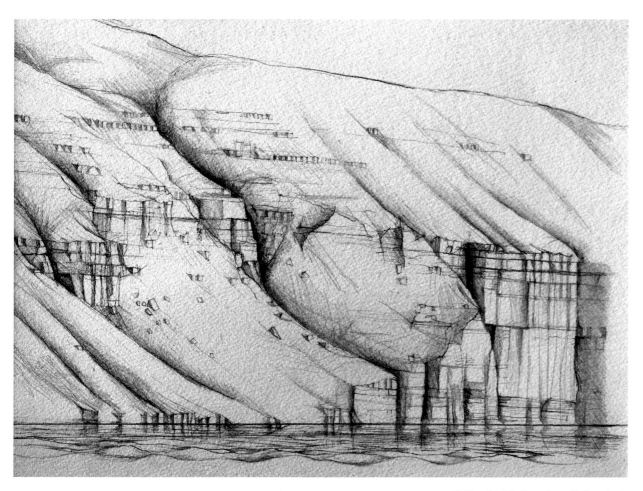

^ *Rackwick Bay (pencil drawing).*

The Paintings
An Appraisal by Julie Summers

J im has described himself on more than one occasion as a jack of all trades but master of none. I am going to argue that in the realm of painting, at least, Jim is a considerable master of his art. Uncharacteristically he never jokes about his painting except when he laughs about the problems of exhibiting or storing the very largest ones. Since 2001 Jim has been focusing on rocks and landscape, with ever-increasing interest in the essence and the inherent monumentality of natural forms.

His artistic career follows an interesting path of discovery with a 30 year break in the middle which, one might be forgiven for thinking, would have proved a setback. Very far from it as we shall see. Jim's art school career was of its time. At the end of the 1950s and the beginning of the 1960s a lot of art was experimental and there were some big hitters around on the London art scene, which he particularly noticed during the second half of his time at college. Ron Kitaj (1932-2007), the gifted American who had wowed the world with his big, bold figurative paintings was teaching at Ealing and influenced a generation of British artists. Kitaj belonged to a group he named the School of London, which included Francis Bacon, whose early work Jim also admired, and Lucian Freud. Another American, Edward Hopper (1889-1967),

(fig i) **Still Life** *(1960) oil on canvas.*

whose use of shape and light has been a major influence on Jim's more recent work. But the foremost inspiration was Cézanne and an early Still Life in oil (fig i) points towards the influence of the great French painter.

More than anything else Jim has taken his palette from Cézanne and in recent works, most especially the monumental paintings of Stanage and Harrison's Rocks, the use of colour is, to my mind, reminiscent of Cézanne's series of paintings of Mont St Victoire, while a painting in the National Gallery entitled Hillside in Provence, where Cezanne depicts a quarry in the Provence landscape, provides an even stronger link to Jim's subject matter. Early works are difficult to define and easy to dismiss but, as with all artists, the roots of Jim's later work can be traced in the shapes and composition of his early paintings as well as in the palette. Two early paintings strike me as confident indicators of what was to come. The first is a riverside scene (fig ii) with Tower Bridge in the background, which is a strong composition. The second, painted in 1962-3, is of Cenotaph Corner on Dinas y Gromlech (fig iii). It is a large painting in oil on board which was bought by a collector in Bury St Edmunds. Jim had not seen the painting until recently and

(fig ii) **Tower Bridge with cranes and barges** *(1961) oil on board.*

(fig iii) **Dinas y Gromlech in the rain** *(1962) oil on board.*

was surprised how closely it related to his work since 2001.

A series of paintings which have not survived the passage of time are a number of abstract works heavily influenced by the artist Bernard Cohen. 'I'm not sure I particularly liked the paintings. I might even describe them as pretentious, but when I reflect on how strongly Bernard influenced me then I appreciate what an important part they played in my artistic development. Bernard made me understand that painting wasn't just about daubing paint onto canvas. It was much more intellectual and interesting than that.'

In 1972 Jim drew some cardboard boxes (see page 113). He described it as a pivotal work — a crux perhaps. He wanted to see if he could make something boring and everyday have a sense of the monumental. It worked and it convinced him that if he could imbue vernacular objects with interest then he would have the confidence to delve into the essence of a subject. It was a step up from the paintings of the 1960s where, in retrospect, he can see that he was learning about handling paint, using thin washes and developing his vocabulary whilst focusing on abstract forms. 'Those drawings, and the ones I did of the curtains, were a major breakthrough and did something to my brain that has never gone away.'

Such was the leap made in the cardboard box drawings that he instantly gave up painting for 30 years. Or at least, that is how it would seem from the bald details of a curriculum vitae. He had begun to develop an interest for and a talent in filmmaking and for the next three decades he concentrated on a new art. Painting went by the board but Jim continued to draw, photograph, write and travel. The majestic landscapes of the Himalaya and Karakoram, where he spent weeks and months over a dozen expeditions, were absorbed into his subconscious and his narrative. When he finally returned to the easel in 2001 it was these mountains that provided him with the first, rich source of material.

Why the return? Jim had become frustrated by the fact that filmmaking was a labour intensive but slow process. It could take a year between filming and seeing the project completed. He wanted to find something more direct and he began to realise that a return to painting was what he wanted. At first he turned to the Karakoram, drawing on photographs and memories. This series of paintings — of Storm Clouds on K2 and Gasherbrum IV (figs iv, xviii) — are amongst some of the most popular in his oeuvre. I think part of their appeal is the fact that they are inextricably linked with the powerful stories that shaped his life on K2 in 1986. He took the photographs of Gasherbrum IV and Masherbrum, on which paintings are based, when he was walking out of Base Camp

(fig iv) **Storm Clouds on K2** *(2003) oil on canvas.*

alone without Al Rouse. As paintings they are bold and strong but the mountains dominate. He does not own them visually. This was still to come.

In October 2004 he made a fifth visit to Hoy with Terry Gifford. Previous visits had been for filming and climbing. This trip was purely for painting. Jim completed 15 watercolours in just four days, a prodigious output, and gathered material for his first monumental oil of Rackwick Bay. He said: 'I barely left the bay on the west side of the island. There was so much material there. Terry walked over the headland to see the Old Man but I was just completely absorbed in the rocks and shapes and moods and light in front of me.'

A visit a year earlier to the Verdon Gorge had yielded a powerful series of paintings which Jim, slightly tongue in cheek, says are his reply to David Hockney's Grand Canyon series (figs v, xxxvii, xxxviii). They are strong and well-structured but there he was an observer. On Hoy he was an interpreter. The Hoy series, for me, marks the start of Jim's strongest period to date. Here he is beginning to master the rocks and discover the monumentality that lies within. The Cliffs at Rackwick Bay (fig xxxv) are solid but not heavy. They have a light, almost musical rhythm from left to right. It is also an intensely sensual painting. The evening light, reflected in the warm hues of the rocks contrasts with the gentle emerald green slopes that meander gently but inexorably downwards. The sensuous curves meeting the erect vertical faces in a sharp edge is satisfyingly abrupt. Strong horizontal strata cut across the rocks

(fig v) **Verdon Gorge** *(2006) oil on canvas.*

345

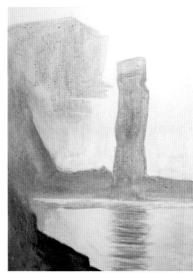

and the painting and it is only the thin strip of blue at the base which reminds the viewer that this is a seascape after all.

Another painting from the Hoy series is a ghostly depiction of the Old Man of Hoy (fig vi). Painted from an elevated perspective Jim has captured the mysticism of the rock in the misty morning light on Hoy. As The Cliffs at Rackwick Bay are bold and dramatic, so the Old Man of Hoy is mysterious and wistful.

At about this time Jim had begun visiting Terry Gifford in Spain. The landscape around Sella on the Costa Blanca confused him initially. He did not know how to interpret it, or how to find a visual language in which to engage with it. But on the third visit in

(fig vi **Misty Hoy** *(2005) oil on canvas.*

(fig vii) **Sella – Terraces** *(2007) oil on canvas.*

2006 he made a series of watercolours on the spot, revelling in the linear structure of the landscape. The terraces, made a thousand years ago by farm workers, reminded him of contour maps (figs vii, et al). He liked that illusion and it appealed to him to think that contour maps had been drawn in the landscape hundreds of years before the Ministry of Defence began cataloguing Britain's south coast in 1791. The paintings that resulted from this exploration into the landscape are more stylised than his other work, but the palette is still Cézannesque and the linearity has a horizontal rhythm in the same way as The Cliffs at Rackwick Bay.

In 2005 Jim set off to explore two areas of rocks closer to home. The first was Harrison's Rocks in East Sussex where he

347

had started climbing in the early 1960s. 'It seems strange to me now that I didn't see the landscape where I was climbing as a student. I never saw it as something to paint and draw. Painting was what I did in the week at Ealing. Climbing was what I did at weekends with my friends. The two worlds were unconnected and had nothing in common. Now, when I am there, I can barely move for seeing a scene or a sketch or a subject.' The second area he began to focus on was his local

(fig viii) **Quarry Burbage South** *(2009) pencil drawing.*

(fig ix **Quarry Burbage South I** *(2009) oil on canvas*

Derbyshire. A collection of abandoned millstones from a hundred years ago lie forgotten below the rocks at Stanage, where climbers drop their gear, while Burbage Quarries near Hathersage provided a change to study rocks opened up by blasting. These areas began

to intrigue him and if he had got into his stride in Spain he was into a different gear at Harrison's and in Derbyshire. This was where he began to look at something that is not inherently large but to see the monumental in it.

Both these series have majesty and authority which demonstrate confidence and artistic maturity. Here, in these works, is a lifetime's experience of art. Five decades of knowledge and understanding of the composition and palette, of looking at great artists of the past and absorbing their influence rather than following it. It also encompasses years of being intimately close to rock. Jim stopped being an observer, stopped even being an interpreter. These works convey the character and the being of the stone. Jim moved away from the figurative depiction of the landscape towards the abstract. 'When I painted the oils from the drawings I did of the quarry at Burbage (figs viii, ix, x) I wondered what it would be like to put a dark surround behind the rocks. Would it bring the central composition forward? It wasn't a complete whimsy to remove the natural background. I really wanted to see what would happen.' The result is a monumental and powerful abstraction. The eye is drawn to the detail but the overall sense is of a huge and powerful

(fig x) **Quarry Burbage South II** *(2009) oil on canvas*

349

(fig xi) **Between a tree and a hard place, High Rocks** *(2007) oil on canvas.*

force. As I have written before, Jim Curran really *gets* stone. He understands all its properties and characteristics and most importantly, he can convey that in a picture with grandeur.

I asked him whether he paints from memory or from photographs. He explained that it is a mixture. 'I use photographs to show dimensions and light effects but they are, after all, only two dimensional representations. And I only ever use my own photographs. I couldn't paint a picture from someone else's images. If I don't feel it in my bones I don't like doing it. I like to look for the detail: at Stanage it is the water-worn marks and the manufactured stones which will eventually be eroded to become part of the landscape from where they once came. At Burbage it is the chiselled and blast-scars made by the quarry men.'

The sandstones of Harrison's provide an equally rich source (figs xi, et al). 'I like playing with illusions with the rocks. Something that is very solid, like a lump of rock, you can get inside with your imagination and that's what I'm trying to do. I don't just want to represent the surface. I want to convey the stoniness and the power of the rocks.'

So this Jack of All Trades has indisputably mastered the art of painting stone and rock. He might protest that his influences are the great figurative painters of the 20th century but I think that like his hero, Cézanne, Jim has succeeded in finding the abstract in the everyday, the monumental in the landscape. His best work may be yet to come but the Derbyshire and Harrison's series are a magnificent testament to his abilities as a painter.

Julie Summers
Oxford, July 2011

(fig xii) **Stanage Millstones** *(2009) watercolour*

(fig xiii) **Paradise Lost, Cheddar** *(1972) oil on canvas.*

(fig xiv) **Chogalisa** *(2002) oil on canvas*

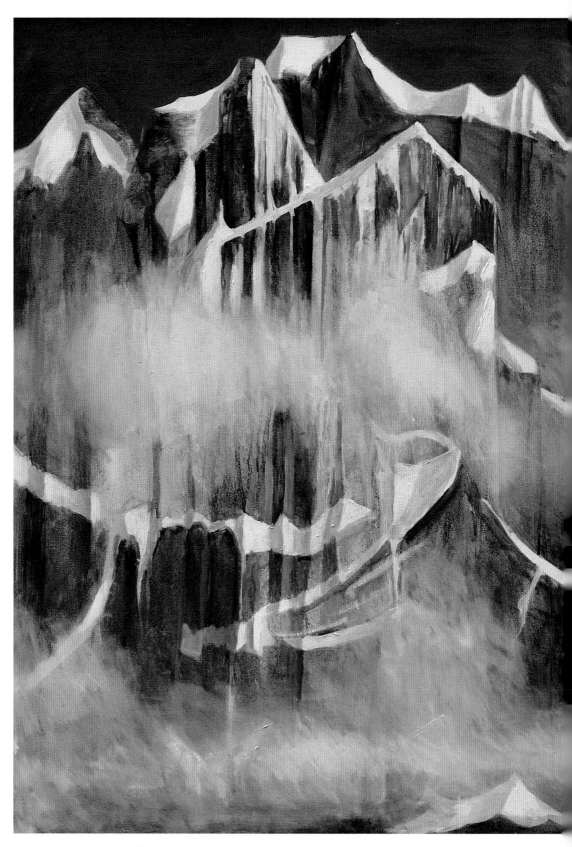

(fig xv) **Trango Towers** *(2003) oil on canvas.*

355

(fig xvi) **Everest from the Rongbuk Glacier** *oil on canvas.*

(fig xvii) **Trango Tower.**

356

(fig xviii) **Gasherbrum IV** *(2003) oil on canvas.*

(fig xiv) **Gasherbrum IV** *(2007) watercolour.*

357

(fig xx) **Mount Kenya** *watercolour.*

(fig xxi) **Mount Kenya** *oil on canvas.*

359

(fig xxii) **K2 West Face** *watercolour*

(fig xxiii) **Looking into Tibet from Rangrik Rang** *watercolour.*

(fig xxiv) **Ice cliff – Kongur** *watercolour.*

361

(fig xxv) **View from Kongur** *oil on canvas*

(fig xxvi) **Karakol Lakes – Kongur.**

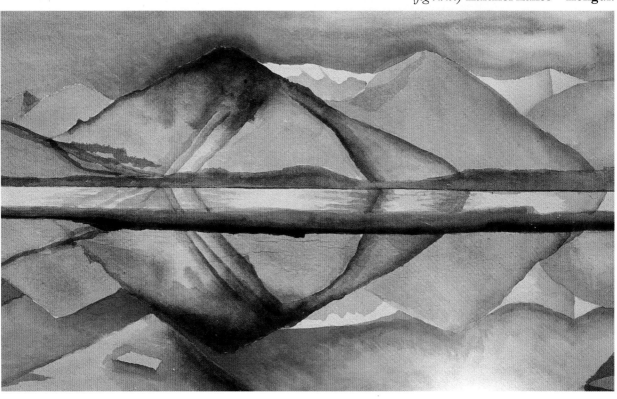

(fig xxvii) **Gasherbrum IV** *watercolour.*

(fig xxviii) **Masherbrum** *watercolour.*

(fig xxix) **Old Man of Hoy and St John's Head** *(2007).*

(fig xxx) **Sunset – Old Man of Hoy** *(2007).*

(fig xxxi) **Yesnaby Cliffs, Orkney** *(watercolour).*

(fig xxxii) **Rackwick Bay, Twilight** *(2007) oil on canvas.*

(fig xxxiii) **Rackwick Bay** *(2007) watercolour.*

(fig xxxiv) **Rora Head** *(2007) watercolour.*

365

(fig xxxv) **The Cliffs at Rackwick Bay** *oil on canvas.*

(fig xxxvi) **Old Man of Hoy** *oil on canvas.*

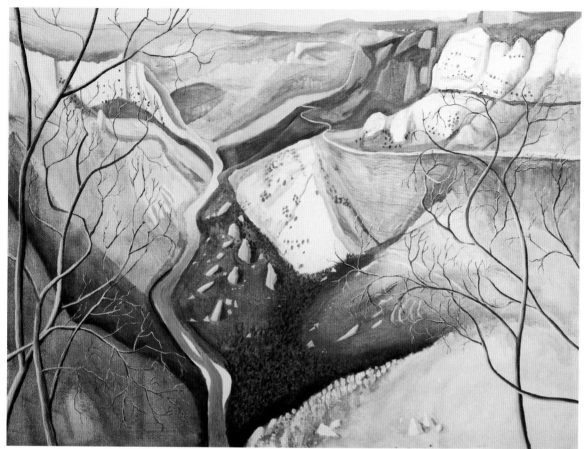

(fig xxxvii) **Verdon Gorge** *oil on canvas.*

(fig xxxviii) **Verdon Gorge** *watercolour.*

(fig xxxix) **Triptych – Sella Panorama** *oil on canvas*

(fig xl) **Sella Panorama** *4 watercolours*

371

(fig xli) **Sella Study I** *watercolour.*

(fig xlii) **Sella Study II** *watercolour.*

(fig xliii) **Sella Study III** *watercolour.*

(fig xliv) **Sella Study IV** *watercolour.*

(fig xlv) **Terry and Gill's Patio – Sella.**

(fig xlvi) **Sossblitz, Harrison's Rocks** *watercolour.*

(fig xlvii) **Isolated Buttress, Harrison's Rocks** *watercolour.*

(fig xlviii) **Tree Roots at Harrison's Rocks** *(2007) oil on canvas.*

(fig xlix) **Triptych – High Rocks** *(2008) oil on canvas.*

(fig l) **Bowles Rocks** *(2007) watercolour study.*

(fig li) **Windgather Rocks I** *(2009) watercolour.*

(fig lii) **Windgather Rocks II** *(2009) watercolour.*

(fig liii) **Stanage Millstones I** *(2009) watercolour.*

(fig liv) **Stanage Millstones II** *(2009) oil on canvas.*

(fig lv) **Stanage Millstones III** *(2009) watercolour.*

(fig lvi) **Stanage Millstones IV** *(2009) oil on canvas.*

(fig lvii) **Millstones I** *oil on canvas.*

(fig lviii) **Millstones II** *oil on canvas.*

Thanks

My thanks must go to all those who now own many of the paintings and drawings in this book. They are, in no particular order Dr Stephen Oliver, Phillip and Heather Curran, Julie Sumners, Allen Jewhurst, Jim Lowther, David and Carol Hayward, Anna Lawford, Peter Mallalieu, Ian McNaught Davis, Jim Fotheringham, Paul and Kate Hodgkin, Bob and Rebecca Hetherington, Chris Bonington, Annabelle Rennison, Tony and Tina Iveson, Sue Coonan, Geoff Birtles, Ian Smith, Adrian Mallet, Hilary Nunn, Stuart and Gemma Driver, Terry and Gill Gifford, Michael Richardson, Julian and Linda Cooper, Helen Young.

Photo Credits

Frontispiece		Ian Smith
42		Mike Watkins
48		Mike Watkins
59		Mike Watkins
70		Mike Watkins
71	Lower Right	Mike Watkins
78	Lower Right	Mike Watkins
87		John Cann
104	Bottom Left	Trish Mohan
119		Tony Riley
130		Tony Riley
137		Ian Smith
139		Martin Boysen
141		Geoff Tier
157		Dave Potts
161		Ian Smith
168		Tony Riley
181	Bottom Left	Terry Tullis
188	Top Left	Ian Smith
191	Top & Bottom	Ian Smith
194		Geoff Tier
219		John Warburton
241		Gerry Wilson
255		Chris Bonington
260		Ian McNaught Davis
263		Ian McNaught Davis
264	Top & Bottom	Ian McNaught Davis
273		Ian McNaught Davis
285	Bottom Left	Ian McNaught Davis
293		Chris Bonington
297	Both	John Whittle
299		Gavin Crowther
303		John Porter

Index

Afghanistan 144, 145-8
Agden Rocher 101
Aiguille du Géant 80
Aiguille de l'M 80
Aiguille du Midi 81
Aiguille du Peigne 81-2;
Lépiney Crack 81
Aiguille des Pélerins 82
Aiguille Verte 79
Allain, Pierre 80
Allport, Derek 105, 132
Alter, Stephen 333, 334
Altrincham All Stars 173
Alvarez, Al 228, 312
Annapurna South Face 138, 188
Anthoine, Jackie 135, 158,
160, 185, 282
Anthoine, Mo 123;
on Trango 135-6, 138, 140, 144; on Ogre149;
165, 185, 192, 207, 210-11; on Everest NE
Ridge 212; 213-14, 223, 282, 283-4
Aonach Eagach 282
Arkless, Brede 158
art school teaching systems 49-50,
61, 102-3, 107
Ascott, Roy 61, 74
Astill, Chris 164
Aston, Nev 108, 111,
120, 155, 156, 157, 182, 184
Atacama Desert 243
Auerbach, Frank 38, 66
Avon Gorge 107, 173, 219;
Lich Gates 219; Pink Wall Direct 219
Ayres, Gillian 66

Bacon, Francis 38, 342
Badile 83
Bakhor Das 158
Balderston, Martin 300, 301,
302-3, 304
Baltoro Glacier 80
Bancroft, Steve 192
Banks, Mike 295, 310
Banwell 118, 120
Barber, Henry 167
Barker, Bill 214
Barnaj 144-54, 193 223
Barnicott, Martin 131
Barrard, Liliane and Maurice 201
Barry, John 227
Bates, Bob 316
Bauer, Willi 204-5, 207-8
Beatles, the 58, 95-6, 136
Beech, Bill 103-4, 107,
108, 115, 117, 125, 128, 130
Beech, Pam 104, 107,
117, 266, 311, 317, 324
Ben Nevis 64, 324;
The Bat 127, 161-2; Carn Mor Dearg Arête
64; Castle Ridge 64; Tower Ridge 282
Beney, Paul 82
Berry, Steve 266
Birch, Dr 156, 175
Birtles, Geoff 107, 192,
198, 208, 209, 225, 229, 253, 257, 266
Birtles, Jackie 107
Bishop, Cherry 84, 88
Blackshaw, Alan 41

Blake, Peter 73, 74, 108
Blatière 79
Boardman, Dorothy 227
Boardman, Peter 36, 140,
175, 178-9, 180, 184-5, 201, 206, 249, 276
Boardman Tasker Award for
Mountain Literature 223, 227
Bochlwyd Buttress 55
Bolland, Dr 168
bolts 79, 287-8
Bonatti, Walter 312
Bonington, Chris 30, 59, 82,
118, 129, 136, 140; on Ogre 149; K2 (1978)
157; 163, 167; on Kongur 173, 175-6, 178-
9; 181, 198, 206, 210, 227, 228, 231, 232;
on Elbrus 234, 236, 237, 239-40, 242; on
Rangrik Rang 249, 250, 251, 252, 254, 255,
259; on Sepu Kangri 276-7, 289-92, 294,
302, 304; on Paine 278-9; 295; his biography
309; 324
Bonington Daniel and Rupert 259, 309
Bonington, Wendy 206, 235
Bosherton 167, 169, 184
Bosigran: Desolation Row and
Thin Wall Special 191; Doorpost 281-2
Boysen, Maggie 140
Boysen, Martin 135, 136,
137-8, 140-1, 143-4, 167,
173, 190, 225, 324
Bozik, Peter 204-5
Brasher, Chris 129
Bretton Hall International Festival of
Mountaineering Literature 232, 311-12
Brewster, Barry 59-60
Brice, Russell 211, 213
Bristol Poly Faculty of Art and
Design 107-9,
135, 155-7, 209, 217-19, 223, 227, 232-3
Brit Art 218
Broad Peak 203, 208
Brooker, Bill 58, 66, 73, 74
Brown, Joe 41, 46,
76, 82, 123, 129; on Trango Tower135, 136,
138-9, 140-1, 149; his myth136-7; 167, 169,
188, 190, 192; on Everest NE Ridge211-12;
214, 220, 225, 317, 324
Brown, Val 138, 324
Buhl, Hermann 67, 208
Burbage 104, 348-9
Burke, Mick 138
Burke, Phil 187-8
Burn, Bob 118, 120, 123, 127, 173
Burn Pat 118, 173

Callaghan, Barry 127, 132
cameras 212, 281, 289
Campbell, Donald 180
Cann, John 86
Carn Gowla: Mercury 191
Carnmore Crag: Fionn Buttress 312
Carrington, Rab 161-3, 167, 192
Carter-Ruck, Peter 226
Casarotto, Renato 201
Casey, Mrs 85
Caucasus 236-42
Cavinder, Jane 114-15
Cenotaph Corner 125
Cerro Torre 80, 139, 278-81

Cézanne, Paul 52, 56, 325, 343
Chadwick, Helen 114
Chameleon Films 138, 154,
160, 183-4, 232, 249, 277
Chamonix 79-80, 165, 210
Chamonix Aiguilles 79
Changabang West Face 36, 140
Chase, Brian 82-3
Chatyn-Tau 238-9
Cheddar Gorge: Coronation Street 118,
121-3, 124, 170; High Rock121; Paradise
Lost117; Sceptre121; Sunset Buttress117
Chiddinglye Wood Rocks 42, 44,
46, 49, 329
Choktoi Peak 157-8
Clarke, Annie 215-16, 246, 300
Clarke, Charles 227, 250;
Sepu Kangri 276, 289, 292-4, 302-4, 317
Clarke, Hugo 215-17, 246, 300
Clarke, Ruth 276, 317, 323
Climber and Hillwalker 225, 226-30
Clogwyn Du'r Arddu 137, 190
Clogwyn y Grochan 130
Cohen, Bernard 58-9, 62,
66, 73, 75, 96, 107, 344
Cohen, Harold 58, 73
Coldstream, William 58, 66
Compton, Denis 21
Contractor, Muslim 249, 253, 255
Coonan, Sue 266, 300,
304-6, 308, 313-15, 316, 317, 320, 324, 328
Cooper, Julian 311, 332, 336
Cooper, Linda 311
Craig Gogarth: A Dream of White Horses
190, 281-2; Mousetrap 173
Cratcliffe Tor 198
Crew, Pete 136, 190
Crisp, Quintin 51
Crowhurst, Donald 180
Crowther, Gavin 297-8
Cubitt, Greig 301
Cullen, Sarah 46, 325, 327, 329
Cunningham, Mr 89, 90
Curran, Alison 13, 86;
marries JC 87-8; birth and death of Zoe
90-1; 92, 93, 94, 95, 99, 101, 104; birth of
Gemma 105; 109, 110; birth of Becky 110-
11; 112-13; marriage break up 114-15, 117;
142, 186, 209, 226
Curran, Becky 74, 110-11,
142, 144, 173, 180, 187, 210, 271,
277, 307, 310, 312-13, 317, 320, 324, 326
Curran, Gemma 13, 105,
110-11, 127, 142, 144, 173,
180, 187, 206, 210, 224, 271,
277, 300, 307, 317, 320, 326, 327
Curran, Heather 271-2, 316, 317
Curran, Jim art, childhood love of 24, 25
audience control ability 23, 85
bike ride length of Britain 290, 310
birth and early childhood 13-20
birth of Becky 110-11
birth of Gemma 105
birth and death of Zoe 90-1
Bristol Poly Faculty of Art and Design,
teaching at 107-9, 155-7, 209, 217-19, 223,
227, 232-3
calling it a day on expeditions 257-8, 304

cricket, love of   21, 23, 31-2, 60, 253
death of father   93-4
death of mother   171-2, 182
depression   62, 110,
    181-2, 183, 308-9, 324, 326
discovers the guitar   39-40
drawing   19, 32,
    111, 281-2, 310, 321, 339, 344
Ealing Art School   38, 49-53,
    57, 58-9, 61-2, 66-7, 73-5, 76-7
early retirement   233
easily influenced artistically   66, 74
editing film   128, 132, 306, 307, 344
film course at Sheffield   125, 127-32
first ascent Ealing Tech direct   75-6
first ascent Palomani Tranca   193
first climb at Chiddinglye
Wood Rocks   42, 44
first experience of snow and ice   64
first independently
attested embryonic erection   18
first love   35-7
first marriage breaks down   114-15
first teaching job at
St Ignatius School, Moss Side   88-9, 90-1
hash, cautionary tale about   153-4
Inca stonework underwhelming   195
Kendal Mountain Film Festival   171-2,
    223, 306
knee problems   318-19, 324, 325-7
Manchester art teachers'
diploma course student   84-8
mountains, passion discovered for   25, 41
Nether Edge, buys house in   186
painting   32, 96,
    105-7, 111, 118, 219, 310-11,
    316, 317, 324-5, 327-8, 332, 342-51
prostate cancer diagnosed   94,
    319-20, 321, 326
the Proust of West Ealing   11
Rotherham School of Art,
teaching at   95, 99-101,
    103, 105
schooldays   21-2, 29-33, 34-5, 38-9
second marriage breaks down   182
Sheffield, move to   99-101
sues for libel   226-30
upstaged by dog   64-6
wedding (first), shotgun   87-8
wedding and honeymoon
(second), non-textbook   163-6
Young Contemporaries exhibitor (1963)
    74-5

BOOKS
High Achiever:the Life and Climbs of
Chris Bonington   306, 308, 309, 310
K2: the Story of the Savage Mountain
    231, 308
K2: Triumph and Tragedy   206-8, 231,
307-8
The Middle-Aged Mountaineer   308, 338
Suspended Sentences from the
Life of a Climbing Cameraman   308
Trango, the Nameless Tower   307

EXPEDITIONS
Barnaj   144-54, 193, 223
Chile   243-8

Choktoi Glacier   157-60
Elbrus   235-42
Everest NE Ridge   211-13, 214, 231
K2   198-209, 231
Kilimanjaro and Mount Kenya   259-61,
    262-5
Kongur   173, 175-9, 276
Patagonia   278-81
Peru   193-7
Rangrik Rang (Kinnaur)   249-58,
    277, 322, 335
Sepu Kangri   276-7, 289-94, 300-4
Trango Tower   136, 137-41,
    193, 231, 258, 322
Yosemite and Red Rock Canyon   283-8
Zanskar trek leader   266-71

FILMS
Barnaj   154
The Bat   161-3, 171-2, 173
Everest 40th anniversary of first ascent
    232
A Great Effort   36-7, 60, 129-32, 160
K2   200-1, 208
Kongur   183-4, 176
Rangrik Rang   254, 277
Rock of Gibraltar (Gibraltar tv)   318
Rock Queen   295-8
Sepu Kangri   289-90,
    301, 302, 307, 309
Tracks (BBC2)   281-2
Trango   143-4

Curran, Ellie (JC's mother)   13, 14-15,
    16, 18, 20, 22, 26, 33, 34, 35, 36,
    39-40, 60, 62, 87, 92-3, 124, 142, 171-2,
    182, 185, 315
Curran, Laraine   130-1, 142,
    144, 163-6, 167, 222
Curran, Phil   21-2, 24,
    32, 35, 36, 60, 92, 93, 97, 132,
    171, 172, 185, 271-2, 316, 317
Curran, Sam (JC's father)   13-14,
    15, 22, 25, 35, 38-9, 48, 57, 62,
    87, 92-4, 315
Curran, Truda   15, 22, 24
Curry, Dennis   108, 111, 155
Cuthbertson, Cubby   297-8
Cwm Silyn: Crucible   222;
    Great Slab 222; Ogof Direct 191

Dalai Lama   335
Dark, Bill   187-8
Davies, Claude   317
Davies, Laing and Dick crammers   39,
    46, 48
Davis, Penny   34, 35
Dawes, Johnny   190, 225, 252
Dearman, Bob   131
death in mountains   59-60, 140, 185, 322
Decamp, Erik   297, 298, 318
Desio, Ardito   25
Destivelle, Catherine   137, 295-8,
    312, 318
Devenish, Robin   22, 40-1,
    44, 59, 68-73, 80, 82-3, 92. 94, 316, 330
Devil's Kitchen   130

Diemberger, Kurt   202, 203,
    204-5, 206, 207-8, 312
Dinas y Gromlech   62, 76, 343
Dinas Mot   222
Dolomites   78-9
Donini, Jim   158
Drakensberg Mountains   273
Dru   79
Duchamps, Marcel   218
Dunagiri   36
Dunderdale, Mr & Mrs   84, 85
Durkin, Steve   22, 40-2,
    55, 59, 60, 76, 94, 121, 124-5, 131,
    185, 316, 325, 329-31, 335
Dyer, John   105

Ealing Art School   49-53,
    57, 58, 61-2, 66-7, 73-5, 76-7
Edwards, J. Menlove   52;
    'A Great Effort' 128-30, 131; 132, 169
Eel Pie Island   57
Ehrenzweig, Anton   67
Elbrus, Mount   239, 240-2
El Capitan   288
Elizabeth, HRH the
Queen Mother, a follower of JC   52
Else, Richard   231, 235, 236, 238, 240
English, Michael   61
Estcourt, Carolyn   157
Estcourt, Nick   157, 173, 179, 185, 226
Evans, Al   171
Evans, Sue   307, 327, 337
Everest, Mount: 1924 Mallory and Irvine
26; 1953 first ascent 175; 1975 SW Face
expedition 36, 138, 161; 1980-1 West Ridge
175; 1982 NE Ridge 184-5, 211, 213; 1988
NE Ridge 211-13, 214, 231; 1993 1st
English woman ascent 232; 1996 201

Fanshawe, Andy   229
Fawcett, Ron   225
February, Ed   275
Feiler, Paul   109
FitzRoy, Mount   80, 139, 278, 281
Flammes, de Pierre   79
Fontainebleau   221, 222, 325
Ford, Richard   99-100
Fotheringham, Jim   167, 235,
    236, 237, 239, 241, 249, 254, 255,
    276, 292, 301, 302, 310, 317-18
Fotheringham, Marcia   310, 317
Frankenthaler, Helen   66
French, Bruce & Elaine   282
Freud, Lucian   38, 337, 342
Frost, Terry   58

Gabbani, Jill   105
Gavarnie, Cirque de   69-70, 71
Geddes, Stuart   217
Gibraltar, Rock of   317-18
Gifford, Gill see Round, Gill
Gifford, Terry   310, 311-12,
    320, 327-8, 345, 346
Gilkey, Art   201, 231
Gimmer Crag: Kipling Groove 191; 281-2
Gleadall, Pam   266
Gosbach, Vochka   237, 239-40
Grandes Jorasses   80, 82, 165

Gray, Dennis 227
Grépon 82-3; Knubel Crack 83
Gross Fürkahorn 221
Gytrack, no show 42, 44, 46

Half Dome: Snake Dyke 286-8
Hall, Brian 161-3, 171, 200, 306
Hall, Dr Nikki 326
Ham, Phil 171
Hamdy, Prof. 319, 321
Harding, Warren 283
Hargreaves, Alison 180, 270
Harold, Father (JC's uncle) 23-4, 67
Harris, Al 181-2
Harris, Vivien 46
Harrison's Rocks 41, 44, 46, 53-4, 60, 62, 75, 83, 181, 203, 221, 260-1, 325, 329, 330, 331, 347-51; The Niblick 83; Stupid Effort 138; Unclimbed Wall 83; West Wall 83
Haston, Dougal 161
Haszko, Richard 187-8, 192
Hawkins, Liz 56-7, 59, 73
Heaton-Cooper, William 311
Hedin, Sven 173
Hegarty, Fran 128, 130-1
Hendrix, Jimi 61
Herrligkoffer, Kar l25
Hetherington, Bob 310, 312-13, 317
Hetherington, Patrick, Sophie and Theo 313, 317
Heywood, Paul 127
High 225, 227
Hilton, Roger 109
Himalayan Kingdoms 266
Hirst, Derek 58, 66
Hockney, David 52, 62, 73, 74, 103, 118, 345
Hodgkin, Howard 66, 73
Hopper, Edward 342-3
Hopwell, Ruth 91
Horniblow, Dr Philip 211, 212, 213
Houston, Dr Charles 201, 231-2, 312, 316
Howard, Ken 51-3, 58
Howell, Ian 262
Howells, Malcolm 136, 138, 139, 140, 157, 173
Hoy 327, 345; Old Man of 189, 295-8, 346
Hunt, John 175
Hupfauer, Sigi 231
Hutton, Len 21, 32, 52, 137

Imitzer, Alfred 204-5
Inca Trail 193, 195-7
Ingle, Bas 190
Innes, John 29, 32, 38
Innocent, Carole 181
Inshaw, Dave 109
installation art 218-19
Iran 144, 145
Irvine, Andrew 26, 41, 180
Iveson, Tony 223, 248, 259, 282
Ivy Sepulchre 124

Jagger, Mick fails to run over JC 57
Jewhurst, Allen 138, 142, 143, 154, 232

Jordan, Rodrigo 278

K2: (1953) 201, 231; (1986) 149, 188, 198-205, 344-5; (2008) 201
Kapadia, Harish 248, 249-58, 333, 334, 335
Kapadia, Geeta 250, 253, 334, 335
Kashgar 176-7
'Kaz' Kaspczyk 39-40
Kemp, Dennis 207
Kendal Mountain Film Festival 171-2, 203, 223, 232, 276, 306, 316
Kennedy assasination 62
Kennedy, Senator Edward 160
Kennedy, Michael 158
Kershaw, Phil 219, 295
Kilimanjaro 259-61
King, John 281
King, Neville 91
King, Simon 281
Kinnaur see Rangrik Rang
Kishtwar 144, 150
Kitaj, Ron 58, 342
Kongur 173, 175-9, 276, 309
Kothari, Vijay 249, 250-1, 335
Kukuczka, Jerzy 201

Lane, Cass 187-8, 189-90, 197, 207
Lanyon, Peter 109
Las Vegas 283
Latok 1 158
le Feuvre, Dick 217
Leh 269-70
Lhasa 212, 289
liaison officers, inadequacies of 150
Licancabur 243-6
Lister, Chris 138, 142, 143, 154, 183, 294, 295, 297, 298, 300, 309
Little, Graham 249, 254, 255, 301, 304
Littlejohn, Pat 169
Llanberis 64, 130
Lliwedd 94, 130, 131, 263; Central Gully 131; Central Gully Direct 130; The Sword 131
Longland, Jack 214
Louis, Morris 66
Lowe, George 158
Lowe, Jeff 158, 160
Lowther, Jim 249, 253, 254, 255, 276, 301
Lumley, Joanna, mystery phone call 128
Lyons, Nick 297

MacDonald, Bernadette 334
McHardy, Richard 190
McIntyre, Alex 226
Macleod, Angus (JC's uncle) 25
Macleod, Chris (JC's cousin) 24-5, 172
Macleod, Jean (JC's cousin) 24-5
Macleod, Sheila (JC's cousin) 24-5
McNaught Davis, Ian 81, 135, 154, 167, 190, 219-22, 228; Chile 243-5, 247-8; Africa 259-65; 271, 272-3, 274-5; Patagonia 278-81; Yosemite and Red Rock Canyon 283-8; 336
McNaught Davis, Loreto 221, 243, 278
McNaught Davis, Simon 286, 287

McNeish, Cameron 240, 242
Mallett, Adrian 52, 56, 61-2, 66, 67, 73, 75-6, 77, 332
Mallory, George 26, 41-2, 180
Manchester 77, 84-7
Manirang 257-8
Maraini, Fosco 139, 173
Maskrey, Andy 193
Matterhorn disaster 180
Mercury, Freddie 61
Messner, Reinhold 295
Metzer, Gustav 61
Mewsford Point 167
Michelangelo 56
Midi 79
Minks, Pete 153, 154
Mistri, Kaivan 249
Moffatt, Jerry 137
Mohan, Trish 124-6, 332-6
Monet, Claude 52, 57, 327
Mont Blanc 79, 82, 210
Moon, Ben 137
Morandi, Giorgio 57, 66
Mount Kenya 262-5
Mountain Club of South Africa 272-5
Muir, Scott 301, 304
Mummery, Alfred 231
Muni, Divyesh 249, 253, 258, 335
Murison, Neil 108, 111, 155, 156, 182, 184, 217, 232, 316
Murray, Bill 228
Mussoorie Mountain Literature Festival 33, 334-5

Nally, Brian 59
Nanga Parbat 67, 231
Noland, Kenneth 66
Noyce, Wilfrid 25, 137
Nunn, Hilary 130, 184, 187, 272
Nunn, Paul 117, 120, 125, 127, 130, 140; on Barnaj 144, 151, 152; The Bat 161, 163; 167, 169, 179, 184, 187, 190-2, 208, 210, 222, 228; on Rangrik Rang 249, 252-3, 254, 255, 257-8; 266, 271-2, 275, 276, 277, 295

Oakley, Chris 82
O'Brien, Mary (aka Dusty Springfield) 20, 34
Ockendon, Miss 49, 74
Ogre 149
Old Spice Girls 266, 310, 316, 317
Oliver, Dr Raymond 27-8, 76
Oliver, Stephen 27-9, 76, 316
Ono, Yoko 13
O'Sullivan, Pete 120-3
Oswald, Dennis and Dorothy 26-7
Oswald, Mick 53

Paine, Towers of 80, 139, 278-9
Palmowska, Krystyna 207
Palomani Tranca 193
Parinacota 243
Pascoe, Ernest 109, 157
Patagonia 278-91
Patey, Tom 82
Payne, Maurice 62
Paragot, Robert 190

Peak District   99, 101, 173
Pearce, Dave   173
Pearson, Keith   75-6
Pennington, Alan   201
Pensford   120
Perdu, Mont   70
Perrin, Brian   58, 62, 77
Perrin, Jim   167, 169-71, 188, 189, 225-30
Pertemba Sherpa   36
Piana, Paul   312
Piasecki, Przemyslaw   204-5
Pik Schurovsky   240
Pink Floyd   61
Piotrowski, Tadeusz   201
Plan des Aiguilles   81
Pop Art   74
Porter, John   171, 200, 208, 276, 292, 301, 306
Potts, Dave   135, 157, 160
Presley, Elvis   13, 34, 40
Price, Dave   61, 66, 73, 76-7
Proctor, Tom   107
Punta Arenas   278
Pyrenees   68-72

Ramsey, Hilary   175, 187, 198, 202
Rangrik Rang   249-58, 277, 322, 335
Rawson-Tetley, Chris   107
Reading Climbing Club   144
Red Rock Canyon: Tunnel Vision   283-5
Redman, Anne   158
Rendall, Dorothy & Jack   327
Renshaw, Dick   36
Requin: Mayer-Dibona route   80-1
Reynolds, Barry   297
Richardson, Mike   192, 222-3, 282, 308
Right Angle (Gurnard's Head)   27
Riley, Tony   127; A Great Effort 130, 131-2; Trango Tower 135-6, 138, 139, 149; 140; Barnaj 144, 151, 153; The Bat 161-3; 164
risk, the element of   179-80, 185
Rivers, Larry   74
Roaches: The Sloth   198
Robbins, Royal   283
Robertson, Rhory   226, 228, 229
Rochefort Ridge   80
Rodin, Auguste   56
Roland, Brèche de   70
Roper, Ian   171
Roper, Steve   288
Rotherham School of Art   95, 99-101, 103
Round, Gill   310, 320
Rouse, Al   140, 161, 165, 167; on Kongur 175-6, 178-9, 276; 180, 181, 184-5, 187-8; on K2 198-202, 203-5, 206, 207, 209, 258, 345
Rowell, Galen   139
Rowland, Clive   149, 190
Russell, Count Henry   69
Rutkiewicz, Wanda   201

Saunders, Mr   85
Saunders, Victor   301, 304, 318
Schaller, George   334

Scott, Doug   149, 161, 164, 167, 312, 324
Scott, William   58
Sella, Vittorio   118
Sepu Kangri   276-7, 289-94, 300-4
Sharples, Liz   329
Sheffield, as a great place to get out of   99-100
Shimla   252
Shipton, Eric   137, 173, 176
Shkelda   238, 239
Shorncliffe   223
Sickert, Walter   52
Simmond, Maurice   79
Simpson, Joe   192, 228
Skye: Crack of Doom   59
Smith, Geoff   152
Smith, Ian   187-8
Smith, Richard   66, 73, 105
Smith, Robin   161
Smolich, John   201
Snowdon, Lord   73, 74
Snowdon, Mount   55
Spear, Roger Ruskin   61
Sperry, Duncan   249, 276
Stac Polly   281
Stainforth, Gordon   332
St Ann's Convent   16, 18
St Benedict's School, Ealing   21, 29, 60, 269
St Ignatius School, Moss Side   88-9, 90-1
St Kilda   210, 291
Stanage Edge   87, 99, 127, 281, 350
Startup, Peter   58
Stella, Frank   66
Stephens, Rebecca   232
Stockam, Alf   109
Stokes, Brummie   211, 212-13
Stokes, Mark   232
Stoney Middleton   107
Strapcans, Arnis   175
Suilven   281-2
Summers, Julie   97, 342-51
Sutton, Geoff   137
Swain, Rob   108, 111
Swinging Sixties   74

Table Mountain   274-5
Tasker, Joe   36, 140, 167, 175-6, 178-9, 180, 184-5, 201, 206, 226, 276
Taylor, Harry   213
Telluride Mountain Film Festival   144
Thatcher, Dennis   181
Thornton, Mag   313-15, 320
Tier, Barbara   193, 195, 272
Tier, Geoff   144, 145, 148, 150, 152, 154, 192, 193, 195, 271-2, 275, 277
Toogood, Bob   144, 148, 150
Townshend, Pete   57, 61
Trango Tower   127, 135-41, 193, 231, 258, 281, 322
Trevedra Farm   187, 189
Tryfan   55, 80
Tsini   292-3, 303-4

Tullis, Julie   202-5, 206, 207
Tullis, Terry   203, 207

UIAA   272, 275
Unsworth, Walt   228, 230
Uppingham School   10, 14, 15, 26
Ushba   237, 239-40

Vajolet Towers   78-9
Vasko, Sasha   236-7, 239
Venables, Stephen   223, 228, 229-30, 248
Vezzulli, Luciana   35-7, 46
Victoria, Queen   180
Vignemale   68-9;
Petit Vignemale   69
Voyage Out   169-71, 226

Walker, Derek   189, 278-9
Walker, Steve   32
Wall, Brian   58
Wall, Ian   171
Warburton, John   219
Ward, Michael   173, 175
Watkins, Mike   40, 44, 46, 59, 64, 68-72, 80, 82, 94
Weiser, Hannes   204
Wells, Simon   232, 267
Wharncliffe Edge   101
Whillance, Pete   210
Whillans, Don   46, 59, 129, 136, 167, 188-90, 197, 225; Paine 278-9; 318
White, Caroline   134, 155, 156, 185
Whittle, John   297-8
Whybrow, Barry   157
Wilfred, Father (JC's uncle)   23, 24, 88, 93, 172
Wilkinson, Dave   165-6
Williamson, Mr   41-2
Wilson, David   177-8
Wilson, Gerry   235, 236, 239, 241, 242
Wilson, Ken   161
Wilson, Louise   235, 236, 239, 241-2
Wilson, Maurice   180
Wilson, Natasha   178
Windgather Rocks   329
Wintringham, Marion   158
Wolf, 'Mrufka'   202, 204, 205, 206, 208
Wood, Ronnie   61
Wröz, Wojciech   204-5
Wye Valley   223, 248

Yardley Mills, Juliet   66
Yates, John   151-2, 153-4
Yosemite   283, 286-8
Young Contemporaries exhibition (1963)   74-5
Younghusband, Sir Francis   173

Zinal Rothorn   221